The Wye Tour
and its Artists

The Wye Tour
and its Artists

by

Julian Mitchell

Logaston Press

LOGASTON PRESS
Little Logaston Woonton Almeley
Herefordshire HR3 6QH
logastonpress.co.uk

Published in association with Chepstow Museum, Monmouthshire Museums Service 2010

ISBN 978 1906663 32 2

Typeset in Garamond by Logaston Press
and printed and bound in Poland
www.polskabook.pl

Front cover: Detail from Catalogue no. 51
Rear cover: Catalogue no. 66

Contents

This book accompanies, and will be a legacy from, the special exhibition 'The Wye Tour and its Artists' staged at Chepstow Museum, May 1st – September 5th 2010, itself the culmination of a *Cyfoeth Cymru Gyfan – Sharing Treasures* project.

Partneriaeth
national museum wales
amgueddfa cymru
Noddir gan Llywodraeth Cynulliad Cymru
Sponsored by Welsh Assembly Government
Partnership

monmouthshire
sir fynwy

Llywodraeth Cynulliad Cymru
Welsh Assembly Government

Preface & Acknowledgements

This book has grown out of what was originally intended as a relatively simple introduction to the catalogue of the 2010 Chepstow exhibition THE WYE TOUR AND ITS ARTISTS. It became clear during the writing, however, that the art needed its historical context, and so the history of the Tour and the catalogue of the exhibition have become one.

There are a very great number of manuscript and published diaries of the Tour, and I do not claim to have read anything like all of them. In fact I have depended very heavily on the research of Anne Rainsbury, who is responsible for the book in more ways than one. It was her idea to have a Wye Tour exhibition, her idea that I should curate it, her idea that I should write the catalogue which has turned into this book. Though all the faults in it are my own, any praise should be as much hers as mine. In turning Chepstow Museum from a minor to a major local museum, and showing a dedication to the history of the area which is second to none, she has been an inspiration.

The exhibition has been made possible through a grant from the *Cyfoeth Cymru Gyfan – Sharing Treasures* scheme which is funded by the Welsh Assembly Government and administered by CyMAL: Museums Archives and Libraries Wales. The scheme enables local museums in Wales to build partnerships with Amgueddfa Cymru – National Museum Wales and with their expertise, advice and support to upgrade facilities, enabling the museum to borrow and display objects from the national collections, giving the museum and its community access to the nation's great treasures.

At Amgueddfa Cymru – National Museum Wales, Beth Macintyre and Charlotte Topsfield together with the Angela Gaffney, Bryony Dawkes, Clare Smith, Bob Child and Charlie Upton have been specially helpful, but many others have given advice and help. The major collection at the National Library of Wales has also been heavily drawn on and thanks are due to Jaimie Thomas and Emyr Evans. Andrew Helme and Sue Miles at Monmouth Museum, Robin Hawkins at Newport Museum & Art Gallery, Catherine Willson at Hereford Museum & Art Gallery, Rhys Griffith and Elizabeth Bowerman at Herefordshire Archive Service, and Carolyn Noall and Katrina Coopey at Cardiff Central Library all gave strong local support. Further afield, I am most grateful for the time and trouble taken by Helen Daniels at the Victoria Gallery, Bath; Victoria Osborne at Birmingham City Art Gallery; Anita Foster at Auckland palace, Bishop Auckland; Harriet Bridgeman at the Bridgeman Art Library; Felicity Myrone, Barbara O'Connor and Laura Fielder at The British Library; Angela Roche, Marta Cacho Casal, Janice Reading and Agata Rutkowska at the British Museum; Joan Williams at Durham Cathedral Library; Marit Gruijs, Thyrza Smith and Emma Darbyshire at the Fitzwilliam Museum, Cambridge; Melva Croall at Manchester

City Art Gallery; Heather Birchall, David Morris, Gillian Smithson and Hannah Brookfield at The Whitworth Art Gallery, The University of Manchester; Giorgia Bottinelli and Fiona Ford at Norwich Castle Museum & Art Gallery; Colin Harrison and Karine Sauvignon at the Ashmolean Museum, Oxford; Ian Warrall, Christine Kurpiel and Catherine Clement at Tate Britain; Stephen Calloway, Sarah Gage, Rebecca Wallace and Roxanne Peters at the Victoria and Albert Museum; and Jo Digger and Cheryl Jones at the New Art Gallery, Walsall; Jennifer Rennie at Haworth Gallery, Accrington; Kirsty Archibald at Bolton Museum and Archive Service; Alex Miller at Wigan Archives Service; Dr Stephanie Buck at the Courtauld Gallery; Lesley-Ann Kerr and staff at CyMAL Museums Archives and Libraries Wales; Pete Goodridge at Artworks. Many other people have contributed to this Sharing Treasures project in many ways – thanks to all of them, and last but not least all the staff of Chepstow Museum, Monmouthshire Museums Service.

Among many individuals I have to thank particularly Jonathan Badham, Patrick Conner, Malcolm Dyer, Jane Garnett, Luke Herrmann, Rosie Humphries, Keith Kissack, Lowell Libson, Rosalind Lowe, Guy Peppiatt, Michael and Ann Robinson, Jim Simpson, Susan Sloman, Bethea Smith, Andrew Wilton and Andrew Wyld. As will be clear, I have borrowed extensively from the researches of John Evans, Charles Lane, Liz Pitman, Anne Rainsbury and Elisabeth Whittle, to whose generosity I am much beholden. Extra special thanks go to Ned Heywood for his photographical help and to Richard Rowson.

I am grateful to all the institutions for granting permission to reproduce images of the pictures they have so generously loaned for the exhibition.

In order to avoid a blizzard of endnotes, books and manuscripts are noted only when they are first cited, unless there are different editions, as there are of the many guide-books of Charles Heath, Mark Willett and T.D. Fosbroke.

Abbreviations

BM	The British Museum
BL	The British Library
Fitzwilliam Museum, Cambridge	Lent by the Syndics of the Fitzwilliam Museum, Cambridge
Hereford Museum & Art Gallery	Hereford Museum & Art Gallery, Herefordshire Heritage Services
NLW	Llyfrgell Genedlaethol Cymru / The National Library of Wales
NMW	Amgueddfa Cymru – National Museum Wales
NPG	The National Portrait Gallery, London
RA	The Royal Academy
V&A	The Victoria and Albert Museum
Whitworth Art Gallery	The Whitworth Art Gallery, The University of Manchester

Introduction

Start hence with us, and trace, with raptur'd eye,
The wild meanderings of the beauteous Wye.
Robert Bloomfield, *The Banks of Wye*, 1811, ll 17-18

Its banks are a succession of nameless wonders!
Thomas Gray to Thomas Wharton, August 24th 1770.[1]

The Wye

The rivers Wye and Severn rise about two miles from each other on the flanks of Plynlimon in central Wales. The Severn heads immediately north towards Shrewsbury while the Wye runs due south-east to Hay, Hereford and Ross, then through a series of gorges to Monmouth and Chepstow where it and the Severn finally meet in the Bristol Channel. In the centuries before the railways came to change the whole nature of transport and travel, the Wye was deep enough, at least after rain, to be a main trade route from Chepstow as far as Hay, and even higher on flood water. But sea-going vessels, though they could get as far up-river as Llandogo on spring tides, usually transferred their cargo to barges or trows with flatter bottoms and of smaller draught at Brockweir, some seven miles from the river mouth. This included ore from Cornwall for the copper works at Redbrook. Most of the coal consumed in Hereford and its neighbourhood came from the Forest of Dean and was brought up from Lydbrook after a swell in the river. Various other heavy articles, such as grocery, wines, spirituous liquors &c., were similarly conveyed at a much easier rate than by land carriage.[2] On the return journey, they brought down oak bark, timber, grain and cider, and the products of the many riverside industries.

The barges had a square-rigged sail to take advantage, when they could, of the wind which, because of the narrowness of the gorges, blew either straight up or straight down the river. Otherwise the barges were literally manhandled, as the rapidity of the river sometimes forced them to make sudden stops, something with which horses could not cope.[3] Teams of men called bow-hauliers, who wore harnesses (like horses) attached to a rope quite high up the mast (to avoid bushes along the bank and to make steering easier) heaved them up and down. It was heavy labour, though the captain had a relatively easy though responsible life on board, navigating past the many rocks and shallows. A laden barge, said Charles Heath in his guide to *Monmouth* (1804), required the proportion of 15 men to 25 tons to haul it up. 'In passing the different wears [weirs], they are then obliged to fall, with all their force, flat on the ground, which is done by the shout of *yo, ho !* in which position they continue for a short space, when on another shout being given, they rise up, and securing their step, fall down a second time, and so on, till they gain a more peaceful and greater depth of water.'[4] Packhorses followed the course of the river up and down, but it was only after a proper towpath was constructed following the Rivers Wye and Lugg Navigation Act of 1809, that horses could be used for towing. Hence, according to Thomas Fosbroke, the philoprogenitive and usually penniless guide-book writer and cleric of the Wyeside parishes of Walford and Ruardean, 'the square shoulder, the fierce eye, and the athletic figure of the Celt will frequently appear in the Bargeman'.[5]

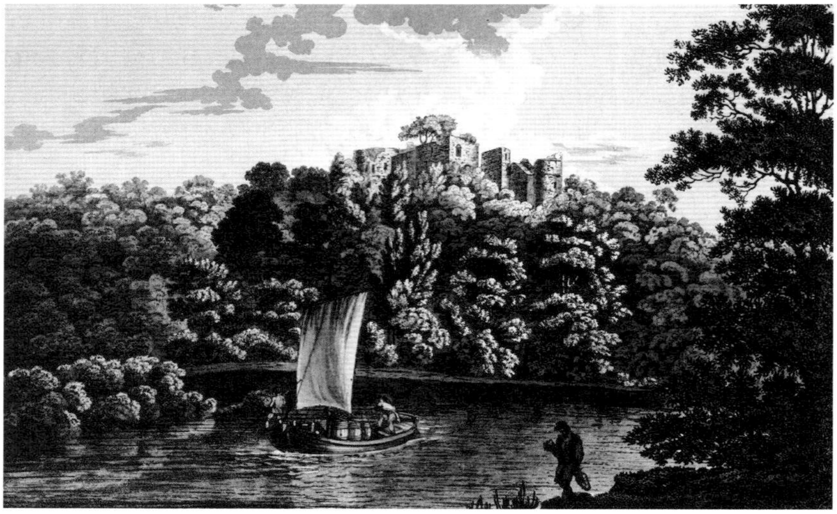

View of Gotheridge Castle on the River Wye, by John Gardnor, 1792 . Note the barge carrying barrels of cider (© The British Library Board, Maps K Top vol 15, 108b)

The Wye was also a great source of salmon (though people complained, as they still do, that they were growing scarce because of poachers), and there was regular conflict between netsmen, who wanted weirs in which to catch their fish, and bargemen, who had to negotiate them.[6] The fishermen poked at the salmon with long poles to dislodge them from their lies and drive them into the nets.[7] They did this from coracles, very small and fragile craft which could be taken out of the water and carried on the fishermen's backs to their cottages, where they sometimes served as cradles for children. It made them look like tortoises, said the Duke of Rutland, and they reminded him of what he'd read of American Indians in their canoes. The poet Samuel Rogers described how they worked: 'The coracles go down the river two at a time, one on each side, drawing the net along to sweep the river. These pairs succeed each other every ten minutes.'[8] But the Wye has always been a dangerous river and the

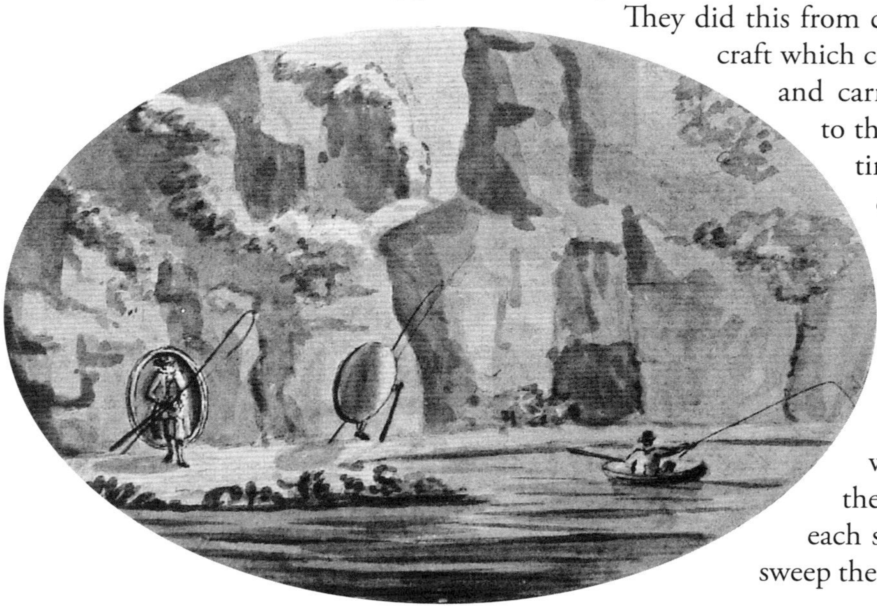

Coracle Fishermen at Coldwell Rocks. From journal of a tour down the Wye by Anne Cooper 1786. (© Chepstow Museum)

coracles frequently upset; many fishermen were drowned. The current was particularly strong at New Weir at Symonds Yat, the last working weir left on the river by the 1750s. It was five and a half miles downstream from Ross-on-Wye as the crow flew, but fifteen and a half by water. It belonged to the Duke of Kent and it was his son-in-law, John Egerton, rector of Ross, who introduced pleasure-boats to what had been a purely commercial river in the late 1740s or early 1750s – thus beginning, quite by accident, what may well have been the first package tour in Britain.

Early Travel and its Vicissitudes

'We travel for various purposes', wrote William Gilpin in his *Observations on the River Wye and several parts of South Wales, etc., relative chiefly to Picturesque Beauty; made in the summer of the year 1770* (1783),[9] '– to explore the culture of soils, to view the curiosities of art, to survey the beauties of nature, and to learn the manners of men, their different politics and modes of life'. He was an aesthete and his use of the word 'travel' shows that he thought of the world as a place to explore for its own sake rather than, like most of his fellow-countrymen, to conquer, exploit and trade in. Travel in this sense has a very long history, beginning, it could be said, with Odysseus, the first recorded man with good reason to want to sue his travel agents, the highly unreliable Olympian gods. In the middle ages the roads and often rivers of Europe were as busy as war and plague allowed with pilgrims going to and from Rome and Compostela and, nearer home, Canterbury, Walsingham, Durham and St David's. But as we know from Chaucer and others, though religion was a powerful excuse for travel, an even more powerful urge was the desire to see what the rest of the world, including distant parts of one's own country, was like, and who lived there. In Britain in the sixteenth and seventeenth centuries John Leland and Thomas Churchyard, William Camden and William Harrison, all travelled round Britain and published descriptions of it in prose and verse. In the late seventeenth and early eighteenth centuries Celia Fiennes, who deplored 'the evil itch of overvaluing foreign parts', visited every county in England, showing how a woman of the upper classes could be quite as good at poking her nose into things as a man. Her given reason for travel was more practical than Gilpin's, being 'to regain health by variety and change of air and exercise'. As well as visiting grand country houses, she took a keen interest in the commerce of the towns she passed through.[10] Daniel Defoe in 1726 placed similar emphasis on 'economic' tourism.[11]

By then only a few prints of British scenes had been published, but they included the first views drawn by the brothers Samuel and Nathaniel Buck. Over the next two decades the Bucks were to publish more than four hundred engravings of castles, churches and abbeys (see overleaf). It was the first opportunity most people had to grasp the extent and grandeur of Britain's architectural remains. Having seen these pictures, they began to want to see the places themselves, and among the earliest travel diarists was Jeremiah Milles, who went from London to Holyhead in July 1742.[12] But the word 'travel' was not derived from 'travail' without good reason, and there were still some very basic requirements before a tourist industry could begin – decent roads, comfortable carriages in which to travel them, and at least passable inns in which to stay.

For many years there had been public coaches and livery stables such as the one in Cambridge run by a man called Hobson, the point of whose famous 'choice' was that there was none; you took the horse he allotted you or you didn't get one at all. The introduction of arab bloodstock in the middle of the seventeenth century had led to an improvement in the physique of native horses and so to greater speed – perhaps to as much as 6-7 miles per hour.[13] Even so the roads were mostly terrible,

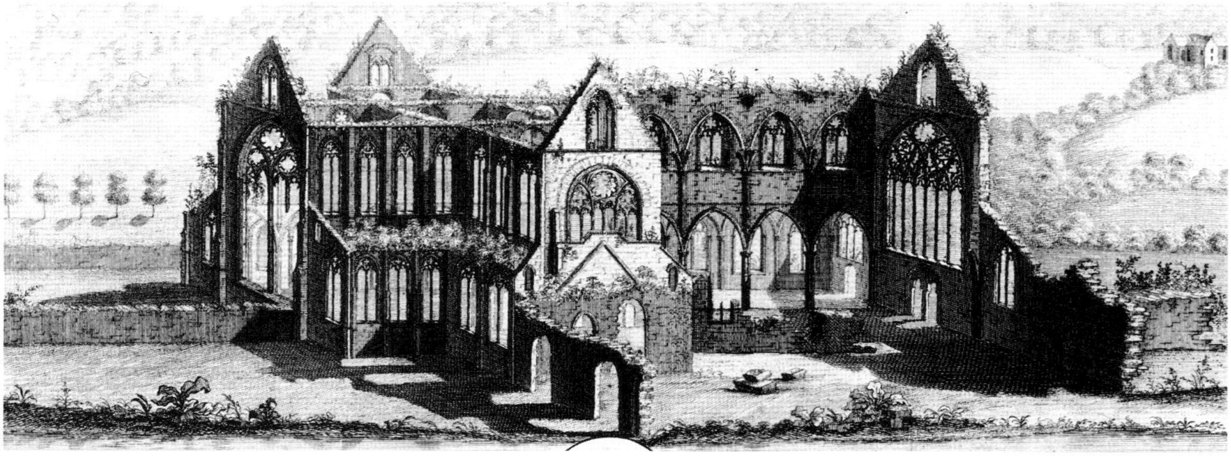

Tintern Abbey, The North east View drawn and engraved by Samuel and Nathaniel Buck, 1732. (Chepstow Museum)

and even though the first turnpike trust for Monmouthshire was formed in 1755, and the first Act passed in 1758, it was still some years before there was any real improvement – though the tolls did at least keep the drovers and their cattle and sheep off the main roads.[14] Earlier, Mr Mountain's stage wagon, with seats along the sides, left Monmouth at 2 o'clock on a Monday morning and didn't get to London till the Saturday evening, and Heath said to take the trip 'imposed a species of *terror* on the mind of the traveller.' The first stage coach from London reached Monmouth in November 1763; it had taken three days, which was an improvement, but it was soon given up for lack of passengers. Post chaises could be hired from the King's Head.[15] There were few private carriages; the first person to visit Monmouth in one was Capel Hanbury of Pontypool, and the 21 miles took nine hours. The carriage was accompanied by labourers to open gates, pull down hedges and make new ways. It took five hours to do the eleven miles to Usk, as the public roads were in a state of scarcely believable barbarism.[16] Even if you had your own carriage, there were frequent breakdowns from lamed horses, broken wheels and deep mud. According to Arthur Young the main roads were 'mere rocky lanes, full of hugeous stones as big as one's horse, and abominable holes.'[17] Gilpin, travelling up the Usk valley from Abergavenny, found 'many little foaming rills crossing the road (some of them large enough to make bridges necessary).' An indignant traveller to Ross from Monmouth in 1804 reported 'roads scarcely passable for unpardonable neglect or dishonesty ... The commissioners of the turnpikes we understand are both at Monmouth & Hereford at present very justly under an indictment.'[18]

Francis Grose, in 1775, travelled in constant fear of accident, and with reason. At Monmouth the stage coach had been overturned ten times that summer as it was too high and overloaded. He wanted the Government to pass a law against the avarice of the owners of such vehicles.[19] The roughness of the road to Symonds Yat appalled him, 'every step seeming to threaten Immediate Death. Nevertheless, the Horses of this Country Pick out the way with great safety to the Rider'. Going from Clearwell to Bigsweir, the road was 'Narrow Steep & Rocky & full of Rolling stones, in a word such as can only be passed with Fear & Trembling'. When he arrived at Bigsweir safe and 'with Limbs Unbroken' he called it 'a wonderous Token of Heavens Kind Care'. Then, on his way from Newport to Caerphilly, his post-chaise got stuck in the mud, and he had to get out and help push.[20] Anxiety was understandable. In 1698 the heir to the first Duke of Beaufort was coming down the hill towards Troy House outside Monmouth when his horses bolted. He jumped out of the coach before it overturned, injuring himself so badly he died soon afterwards.[21] Heath records how a Mr Perkins of Pilstone, returning with his wife from Trellech one summer evening, had a similar accident. The horses of his carriage took fright, and Perkins got entangled in the harness 'by which means his body was dragged with great violence for some distance, and rendered a spectacle too shocking for description.' Mrs Perkins, unable to help, stayed in the carriage which the horses then took safe home.[22] In 1808, even before they'd got to Wales, Millicent Bant and Lady Wilson had a scare caused by inebriated drivers 'who were incapable of governing the Horses, which ran away at a great speed down a steep Hill; fortunately, there were no obstructions, but the Banks on either side the road were very steep and we were repeatedly dashed with great violence against them. At one time the Roof of the coach was within three feet of the Ground. Thank God!, the carriage righted, the front horse having got entangled in the Traces, and one of the front Wheels coming in contact with a foot Bridge at a Cottage Door, the further progress of the coach was stopt, and we luckily escaped injury, sustaining only a violent fright at the peril to which we had been exposed. (29th May 1808)'.[23] As late as 1833 Catherine Sinclair, tongue in cheek, reported the way into Ross was so steep that 'one or two wagoners [*sic*] were said to have been annually killed there for some years past, while leading their loaded carts down the hill'.[24]

Roads did eventually improve, thanks to the turnpike trusts, and with the invention of steel coach-springs travel became possible and even comfortable,[25] though not always. The weather had its part to play, and even a duke, travelling in his curricle with the hood up, found himself sitting in pools of water as he went from Gloucester to Ross. But the inns were often filthy and flea-ridden, especially in the remoter parts, and the sheets unreliable. Someone wrote a note in a British Library copy of Henry Penruddocke Wyndham's *A Gentleman's Tour Through Monmouthshire and Wales in the Months of June and July 1774*: 'Carry your own sheets if you have any convenience for that purpose, as the sheets in all the Inns in Wales are too little for the Beds, so that they slip aside and you very soon find yourself between the Blankets.'[26] After Henry Wigstead went round Wales with Thomas Rowlandson as late as 1796 he wrote: 'The bad accommodation at most of the receptacles for the traveller, and the insolence and inattention of their proprietors, joined to the filthiness of their attendants, [cannot] be sufficiently censured. No possible excuse can be made for the dirtiness, everywhere predominant. Water is everywhere in abundance, but the rooted laziness of the commonalty will never suffer proper use to be made of it.'[27] Clearly by the end of the eighteenth century a London gentleman thought travel should no longer be an adventure so much as a properly regulated leisure activity; and was often disappointed.

Piercefield in the History of Landscape Gardening

By then the English and Scottish economies (though as Wigstead complained, much less so the rural Welsh) had been rapidly expanding for more than a hundred years, and the middle classes with them. Among the most leisured of the latter, the keenest travellers were the clergy, many of whom were the younger sons of the gentry and aristocracy, educated at Oxford and Cambridge. Bishop Richard Pococke (1704-1765), for instance, had been to Egypt, Jerusalem and Greece as well as most of the rest of Europe and the British Isles, before arriving at Piercefield on the Wye above Chepstow in 1756. (He travelled with two servants and a packhorse.) His judgement that it was 'one of the most beautiful places I ever saw' had, therefore, all the authority of a seasoned aesthete.[28]

Piercefield was a prime example of the landscape gardening that had become fashionable among Georgian land-owners, indeed had become a craze as obsessive, and often as ruinous, as gambling. It certainly contributed to the ruin of Valentine Morris, a gambler from his youth, who inherited the estate along with a fortune from sugar plantations in Antigua (worked, of course, by slaves) in 1743. As soon as he was of age he began spending his money refashioning his property. The park – mostly what is now the racecourse – was in the classical landscaping style, like Stowe, Painshill, Hagley or Stourhead, but his walks had a new and, apart from some examples in Scotland, original idea. They were designed to show off the natural landscape rather than an artificial one. He threaded paths through the woods on the high cliffs above the Wye, and cut strategically placed views down to the river, across to the Llancaut peninsula, and to Chepstow Castle. Some of these had a built element, as at the Giant's Cave or the Alcove. The originality of this landscaping brought tourists such as Pococke to Piercefield before it was even finished, a visit there already obligatory. The poet, playwright and publisher Robert Dodsley came in 1759, and writing to William Shenstone, who had made his own garden at the Leasowes, Halesowen, called it great and sublime. Not nearly so aesthetic was an anonymous lady, 'a poor prattling insignificant being', she claimed, not altogether unconvincingly, who came the following year and also described it to Shenstone. More a tripper than tourist, she came with a 'wild and whimsical' party from Bristol. They were all quickly 'fatigued', there was so much to see, but they perked up after cake and wine at the house, after which one of Morris's servants took them to some special viewing spots. They were amazed by the height of the cliffs from which the cattle at Lancaut looked so small that one of the group – it seems the appropriate if anachronistic word – took them for hens.[29] Young, himself the son of a clergyman, came in 1767. Though usually most interested in 'the culture of soils' and the price of turnips, he was a sophisticated traveller who always stopped to look at country houses as well as their estates, and launched into a long description of what was now 'a famous place', deploying the full new critical vocabulary invented to comment on and criticize the new art-form. It was 'wonderfully romantic', had situations 'full of the terrible sublime', views 'bewitching' and 'delicious beyond all imagination' which 'the united talents of a C*laud*, and a *Poussin*, would scarcely be able to sketch'. Altogether he thought it a landscape 'as truly picturesque as any in the world', though – like every tourist always – he thought it could be improved, in this case with a cascade.

The Picturesque

Landscape gardeners were usually (though not always, and certainly not Valentine Morris) trying to imitate in their three-dimensional grounds the two-dimensional ones they'd seen in neo-classical pictures of the previous century, particularly those by Claude Lorrain, Salvator Rosa or Nicolas Poussin. For picturesque theorists like Dr John Brown, an early writer on the Lake District, those three painters represented Beauty, Horror and Immensity.[30] It would be interesting to know how many people would have seen actual examples of their work. There were no exhibition galleries in Britain so early,[31] though it is true that there were many paintings by these artists in country-houses, and as visiting was well-established, they served to some degree the same purpose, sometimes even providing catalogues of the art on display. But visitors were confined to 'those who might call themselves gentlemen', which did not necessarily include artists.[32] If they could neither afford to go to Rome, nor find a patron to send them, they had only prints to go by, and those not all of the highest quality. It was only in the late 1770s that Claude's *Liber Veritatis*, drawings made by the artist as a record of his own work, began slowly to be available in Britain through the etchings of Richard Earlom with tone added in mezzotint. (The *Liber Veritatis* had been owned by the Dukes of Devonshire since the 1720s, but few had seen it.)[33] Its influence was immediate; Paul Sandby saw Earlom's prints before they were published, and leaned on them heavily for his first book of Welsh aquatints of 1775. It was Claude's method of composition which was particularly influential. Today, with our digital cameras and universal visual language, we all know about framing without having to think about it, but then it was still a matter of debate.[34] Many tourists carried 'Claude glasses', convex dark mirrors which minimized and framed the view for the amateur artist, though professionals used them too – Gainsborough can be seen using one in a well-known self-portrait. Being mirrors, they got the view back to front, but they gave depth and contrast which would have been flattened out in bright sunlight. 'The effect was like having a series of transparencies one in front of another, highlighting the different picture planes and making it easier to fill in the perspective and know what to define.'[35] But Claude's formula of trees on one side and ruins on the other quickly became a cliché of landscape painting which to some extent it remains to this day.

What made one view in nature more 'picturesque' than another? People couldn't agree, and by the time of J.M.W. Turner's *Liber Studiorum* (1807), a survey of landscape styles and types paying homage to the *Liber Veritatis*, argument about it had been going on for more than fifty years. All most people meant by 'picturesque' was, as Gilpin himself put it, 'that peculiar kind of beauty, which is agreeable in a picture'. But everyone felt entitled to his own opinion on that, and on how a partic-

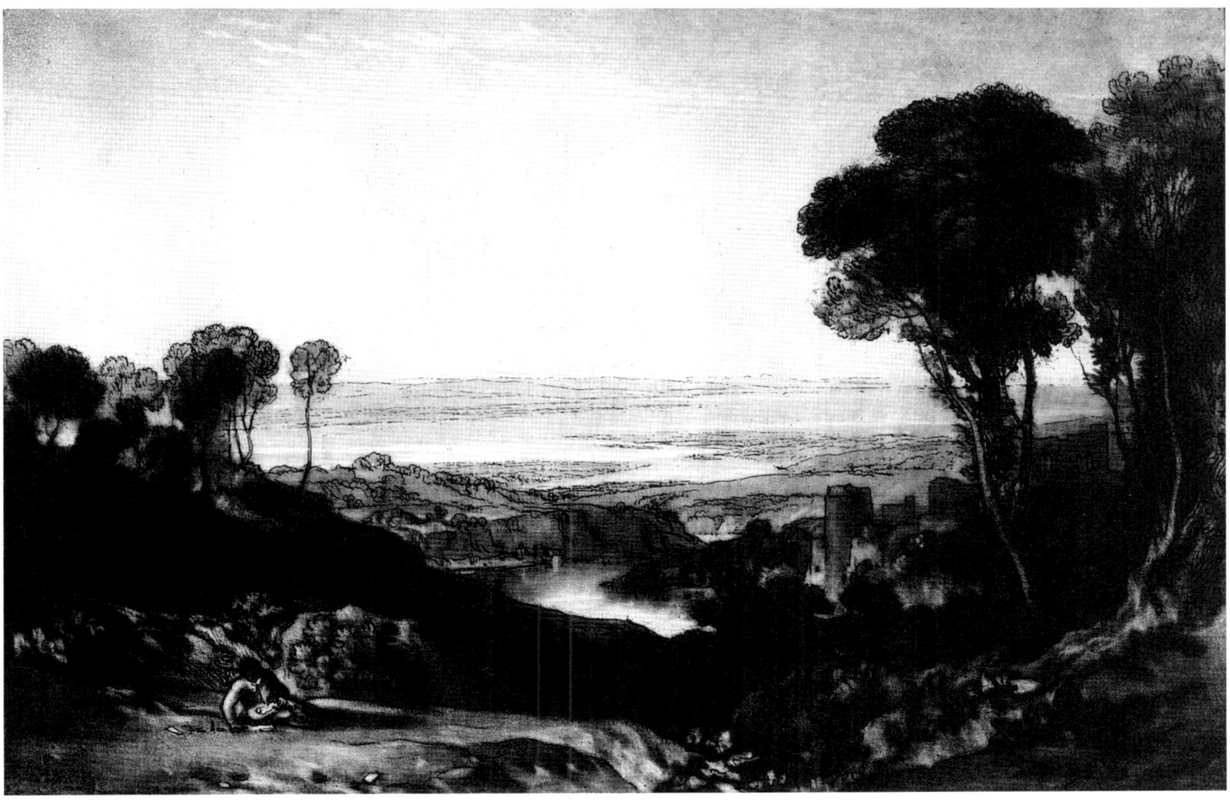

The Severn and Wye, from Liber Studiorum, *drawn, etched and engraved by J.M.W. Turner and published by him June 1811. (Chepstow Museum)*

ular view could be 'improved', and what emotions could (or should) be aroused by it. As a result the 'picturesque' was a shifting concept, supposed to be distinct from but in fact frequently confused with such other equally vague concepts as 'romantic' or 'beautiful', and things which were considered picturesque in 1750 were often no longer thought so by 1800, and vice-versa. As taste changed, the words to describe it remained confusingly the same.

Early in the debate, and very influential, was Edmund Burke's *A Philosophical Enquiry into the Sublime and Beautiful* (1757), written when he was still in his twenties. According to him the sublime invoked thrilling feelings of terror. It included such 'horrors' as Alpine precipices and cataracts, or the Lover's Leap at Piercefield, down which Valentine Morris nearly fell. Defoe had called the relatively low ridge between Twm Barlwm and Blorenge in Monmouthshire 'these horrid mountains', which is bewildering to us now, but 'horror' and 'horrid' derive from the Latin word for 'to bristle', and it was quite easy in the eighteenth century to make people's hair stand on end. In Jane Austen's *Northanger Abbey* (written 1798-99 but not published till 1818), Henry Tilney tells Catherine Morland that he had read Mrs Radcliffe's *The Mysteries of Udolpho* (1794) in two days 'My hair standing on end the whole time.' Horrifying places could be enjoyed, but at a distance, perhaps with guard-rails, rather as we may today watch horror films at home on DVD, scaring ourselves while knowing we're perfectly safe on our sofas. As Sir Thomas Whately said in his *Observations on Modern Gardening* (1770), another very influential work: 'The terrors of a scene in nature are like those of a dramatic representation; they give an alarm; but the sensations are agreeable, so long as they are kept to such as are allied only to terror, unmixed with any that are horrible and disgusting.'[36] For Burke the beautiful invoked more genial social impulses, including sexual ones; it was more feminine, less exciting, leading sometimes to the very eighteenth century concept of 'pleasing' or 'delightful' melancholy.[37] Key texts on picturesque theory were published in 1794 by two Herefordshire neighbours, William Payne Knight (who owned 300 Claude drawings) and Sir Uvedale Price. But the work which brought the word 'picturesque' into general if imprecise use was Gilpin's *Observations.* It was this book which intrigued the new travellers and had a major influence on the process by which they were turned into tourists.

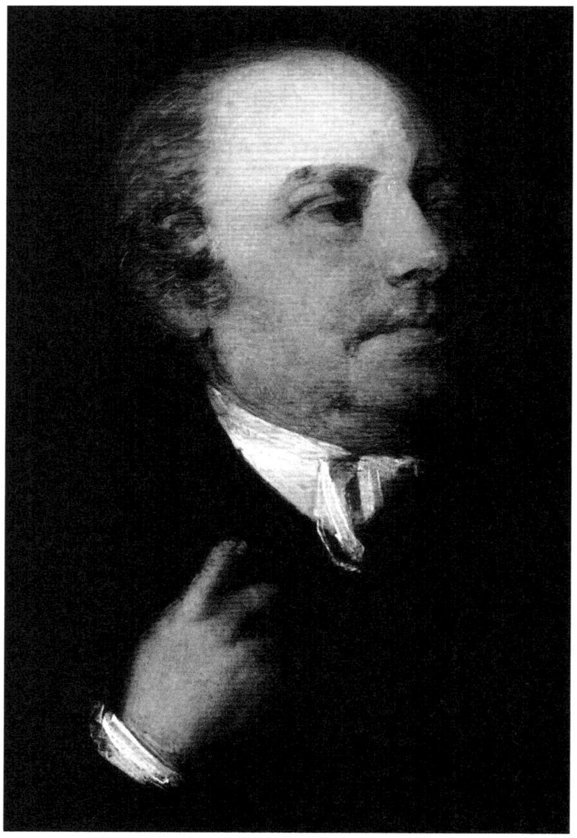

William Gilpin by Henry Walton (detail).
(© NPG, London)

William Gilpin

Gilpin's first book had been a *Dialogue on Stow Gardens* (1748), in which he discussed at some length the nature of views and first defined the picturesque as whatever would make a suitable picture. He went on to elaborate this (what seems at first simple) idea: a picturesque ruin, for example, should be ragged and rough, not smooth and neat; variety was all-important; and Stow was praised for representing a turning back to nature after the formal gardens of the seventeenth century, which for many English people had repugnant associations with Louis XIV and tyranny. His second book was an *Essay on Prints* (1767) in which his object was to put their collection 'on a more rational footing', and putting ideas about the picturesque 'on a more rational footing' was the main object of the many books which followed. He was a schoolmaster as well as an aesthete, and though he was a very liberal one for his day – he avoided corporal punishment if possible – he liked to lay down rules for his pupils to copy. He was a neighbour of Whately, who in fact designed his garden for him, and they must have discussed the notion of the picturesque together. (Whately called it 'a denomination in general expressive of excellence, but which, by being too indiscriminately applied, may sometimes be productive of errors', which is not exactly helpful, though one sees what he means.) It was in *Observations* that Gilpin added a crucial new reason for travelling: '[to examine] the face of a country *by the rules of picturesque beauty*'. Instead of judging a picture by its truth to nature, the traveller was to judge nature by whether or not it was true to Gilpin's idea of what made a good landscape painting. In a series of further *Observations* and *Remarks* over the next ten years, Scotland, the Lake District, the New Forest and other places were sometimes praised but more often taken to task for failing to resemble the paintings he liked. Like Nicholas Pevsner two hundred years later, who brought a specialised architectural historian's approach to the buildings of England, often leaving the reader frustrated by terse technical descriptions and the exclusion of almost everything of historical and social interest, Gilpin criticized views – often ones he might, for other reasons, enjoy – as 'correctly' or 'incorrectly' picturesque as though that was all that mattered about them. 'I am so attached to my picturesque rules', he confessed to William Mason, 'that if nature goes wrong, I cannot help putting her right.'

Goodrich Castle, seen from the river, was, he considered, one of the grandest views on the Wye, one which 'I should not scruple to call *correctly picturesque*; which is seldom the character of a purely natural scene'. He didn't, as a clergyman, want to be seeming to criticize God, so he had to explain why nature so often failed to come up to his standards; nature is on 'a *vast scale*', and we can only see a part of the grand design, while the human artist is confined to 'a *span*', so 'the complex scenes of nature are generally those which the artist finds most refractory to his rules of composition.' The reach of the river below Goodrich, for instance, included a view of Ruardean church, 'a noble piece of natural perspective' and 'a scene of great grandeur' – until, that is, by the passage of the boat, the church spire came directly in front, whereupon the grandeur of the landscape was gone. No artist, presumably, would be so obvious as to put the spire in the middle of his picture. Criticized for his narrow perspective, by Horace Walpole among others, Gilpin defended himself by saying in one of his *Three Essays* (1792) that his picturesque rules did not apply to all beauty, just to that 'suited to the pencil'. He was concerned, that is, only with pictures and how they should not be imitations of nature, but formal constructions based upon it. In fact, as he himself said, artists have always felt free to alter nature in the interests of picture-making; they are all 'mannerists', each with his own way of portraying nature. As the painter John Varley said later 'nature needs cooking' ; the artist 'surmounts' obstacles, by the omission or concealment of those objects which in nature are inconsistent with the general sentiment ... [and] he can obscure those objects which cannot, though unpleasant to the eye in a view, be dispensed with, and increase the effect of those on which the subject principally depends.'[38] As Whately observed, it was the job of the landscape painter to select from what nature had to offer. So much is common sense, but that, perhaps, is something art theorists have never had too much of. The Reverend Michael Tyson said 'a book only of Picturesque Beauty is to me as palling as a Dinner made of Plumb-cake, Trifle, and Caraway Comfits' – though he would 'rather have Gilpin's Plumb-cake than Pennant's hard dumplings'.[39]

Gilpin set out on his journey to the Wye from London, and showed his critical teeth at once, dismissing the Thames for failing to 'exhibit those ample sweeps, in which the beauty of a river so much consists.' He didn't think much of the Cotswolds, either; stone walls were 'the most offensive separation of property'. (Coleridge agreed: on his own way to the Wye in 1794 in his *Perspiration : A Travelling Eclogue*, all twelve lines of it, he wrote of 'Where scorching to th' unwary Traveller's touch / The stone-fence flings it's narrow / Slip of Shade'.[40] It must have been an unusually warm July.) However the road from Gloucester to Ross got Gilpin's approval as it led 'through a country, woody, rough, hilly, and picturesque', and the Wye had 'a succession of the most picturesque scenes'. He praised its lofty banks and mazy course which freed it from the 'formality of lines'. Then he laid down his rules. 'The most perfect river-views ... are composed of four grand parts; the *area*, which is the river itself; the *two side-screens*, which are the opposite banks, and mark the perspective; and the *front-screen*, which points out the winding of the river.' The Wye views were '*exceedingly varied*' by 'the contrast of the screens' and by 'the *folding of the side-screens over each other*; and hiding more or less the front'. Then there were the '*ornaments*' which he defined as '*ground – wood – rocks –* and *buildings*'. Here he was quoting directly from his neighbour Whately's *Observations on Modern Gardening*, which he would have read before taking his tour. Whately is much more precise than Gilpin and lays down detailed rules for the correct arrangement of these 'ornaments', using New Weir, Tintern Abbey and Piercefield as examples of how his theories could work in practice. Like him, Gilpin liked variety, praising the contrast of steepness and flatness of the Wye's ground, its brokenness and colour. The woods, however, possessed 'little beauty and less grandeur' and were only acceptable 'for a *general effect*', and there weren't enough large trees on the edge of the water. (He acknowledged that they would have got in the way of the bow-hauliers.) But he very much liked the smoke rising from charcoal burning which 'spreading its thin veil over a part of [the hills], beautifully breaks their lines, and unites them with the sky.' Again it was variety which pleased

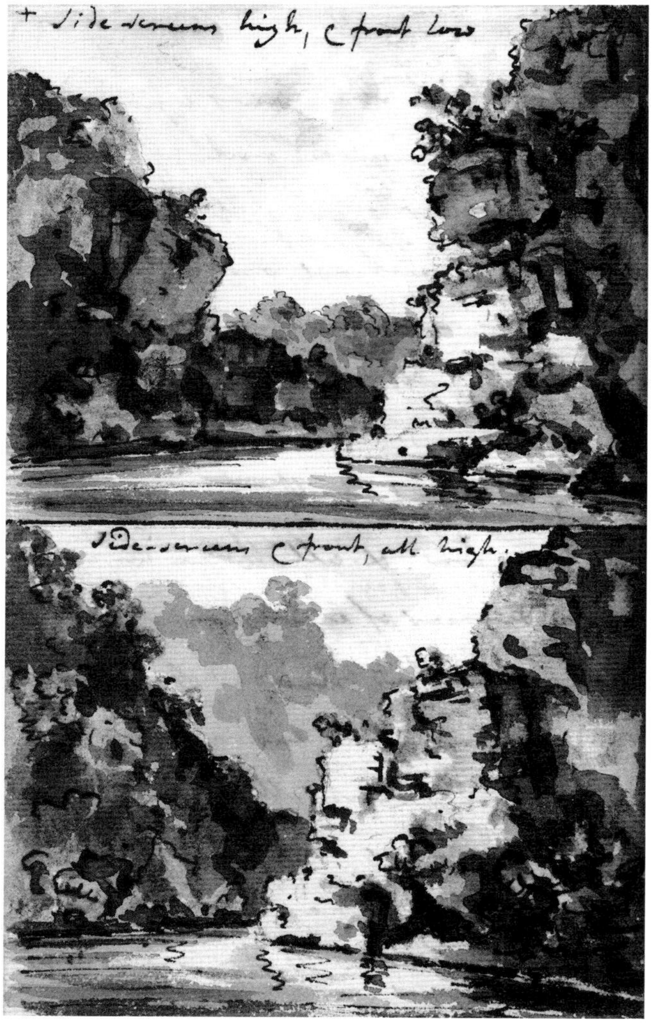

William Gilpin – Sidescreens, from his 1770 journal. (By permission of Lyfrgell Genedlaethol Cymru/ NLW)

him about the Wye's rocks and buildings. The latter were more useful 'in *artificial*, than in *natural* landscape'. In a picture 'we want the castle, or the abbey, to give consequence to the scene.'

Gilpin's rules are neatly satirised in the same chapter of *Northanger Abbey* as that in which Henry Tilney boasts of his hair standing on end. As they look at a view, he gives Catherine Morland a lecture on the picturesque:

> He talked of fore-grounds, distances, and second distances – side-screens and perspectives – lights and shades; – and Catherine was so hopeful a scholar that when they gained the top of Beechen Cliff, she voluntarily rejected the whole city of Bath, as unworthy to make part of a landscape.

Jane Austen obviously thought Gilpin's rules too simplistic and didactic, which is why, no doubt, they never caught on with any but the most amateur artists, those who felt the need for a schoolmaster's hand to guide their pencil or brush. But for non-artists, for tourists for whom the aesthetics of landscape were a new and unknown science, and who needed help first to look in the right direction, then to know how and what to feel, and finally to talk with authority about the beauty of sheep, the picturesqueness of goats, the sublimity of bulls, and the disagreeable glare of white houses, they were a godsend. Like Catherine Morland they could grasp the principles in five minutes, and apply them at once, confident they were in the vanguard of contemporary thought, and they often carefully copied what Gilpin had written into their diaries, as though his feelings were their own. In this they were just like modern tourists, perhaps all tourists at all times. If we know in advance, from a particular drawing or water-colour or photograph, what something looks like, the Taj Mahal, say, or Sydney Opera House, or the Colosseum, that image is the one we feel we must see. Whately made the point: 'we are delighted to see those objects in the reality, which we are used to admire in the representation; and we improve upon their intrinsic merit, by recollecting their effects in the picture.' It is the rare tourist who wants to get his own angle on a famous beauty spot.

In Gilpin's case, though, it was his written descriptions not his illustrations which brought the tourists to the Wye. The illustrations were derided by boatmen and aesthetes alike, and they baffled tourists because they simply didn't look like the sights depicted. But then Gilpin didn't mean them to. They were supposed to be examples of 'correctly picturesque' idealisations based on real views, not literal copies of them. This was, though, too complicated for people with

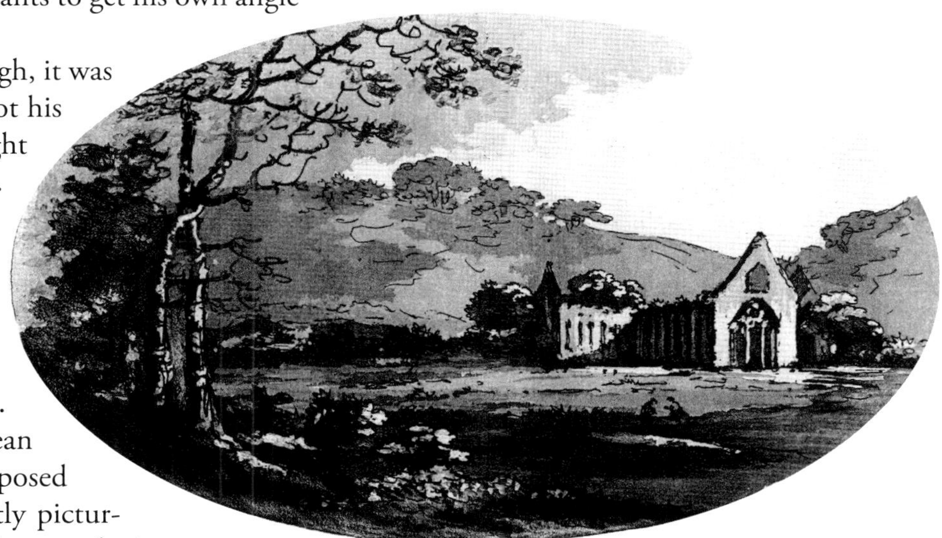

Tintern Abbey, engraving from William Gilpin's Observations on the River Wye *(1783)*

the *Observations* in their hand, and the quite different views in front of their eyes. Even Tyson, who thought Gilpin had 'the absolute command of Light and Shade', and said they were 'gems in the Collection of a Landscape Painter', confessed that 'a Topographer or Antiquary, would throw them away as dirty pebbles.' Tyson had himself visited Tintern by water from Chepstow, and he recalled 'enough of the places to remember the Drawings have very little resemblance – indeed they do not even agree with his own descriptions.' (People before the invention of the camera may have had better visual recall than we do today, but their conception of what was or was not a true representation was much more personal.) The failure of the illustrations did not prevent Gilpin's book being reprinted five times by the end of the century, since it served as the main ordinary guide to the sights as well as to their picturesqueness till Heath began to publish more detailed guides, with long historical references, from 1791.[41]

Towards the end of the century people were getting bored with the picturesque – and with Gilpin. A critic is almost always dealing with the past, he rarely understands what is happening in his own time, and Gilpin had had a typical upper-class classical education, finishing at Oxford. The landscapes he admired were primarily literary in inspiration, based on Greek and Roman pastoral poetry, with little or no relation to British life. All a modern painter could hope to do was find new variations on the established formulae, which is what Richard Wilson tried to do.[42] But the new middle-class British travellers were not always so well educated, and did not like having the classics imposed on them – all those superior nymphs and shepherds with difficult names in the foreground, with temples stuck on the tops of hills behind. They were nothing like the farm-workers or parish churches of the landscape they knew. Significantly, in the first edition of his book, Gilpin left all his classical quotations in the original language, assuming his readers would have no difficulty with them, but when the second edition came out in 1789, there was a prefatory note translating them into English. The new travellers might not have known much about art, they might (some of them) have needed a schoolmaster to tell them what was what about the picturesque, but they were confident enough about their country and its growing empire and wealth to be proud of it. There came a growing desire for British rather than baroque Italian landscapes. Idealisation, though, remained. Paul and Thomas Sandby's landscapes of British rural life were painted by men who spent much of their life in government service. They presented Britain as a place of peace and prosperity at a time when industrialisation was beginning to threaten the whole fantasy of a rural paradise, and frequent bad harvests were creating periods of extreme poverty.[43] One should not, therefore, exaggerate the change; many painters continued to put implausibly clean and happy peasants into their landscapes, the Wye's own Joshua Cristall among them, and J.M.W. Turner remained haunted by Claude his whole life. But as time went by Gilpin's classically-derived rules seemed increasingly arbitrary and vague; in fact mockery of him began quite early. Hannah More, coming down the Wye in August 1789 with William Wilberforce and his sister Sarah, the *Observations* in hand, complained to Horace Walpole of 'all the cant of connoisseurship'; Gilpin, she said, aimed to subdue her imagination 'which had been not a little disordered with this enchanting scenery'.[44] A bored poet wrote: 'Renounce all Gilpin's jargon, said or sung / And talk of Nature's works in Nature's tongue'. George Cumberland, who quoted this, had travelled in Wales since the 1780s, and thought Gilpin had 'made a chaos of art'.[45] Later there was William Combe's very popular parody of Gilpin, *The Tour of Dr Syntax in Search of the Picturesque* (1809), about a clergyman and schoolmaster, who, Don Quixote-like, sets off on an old horse called Grizzle with the intention of 'picturesquing it everywhere' and writing

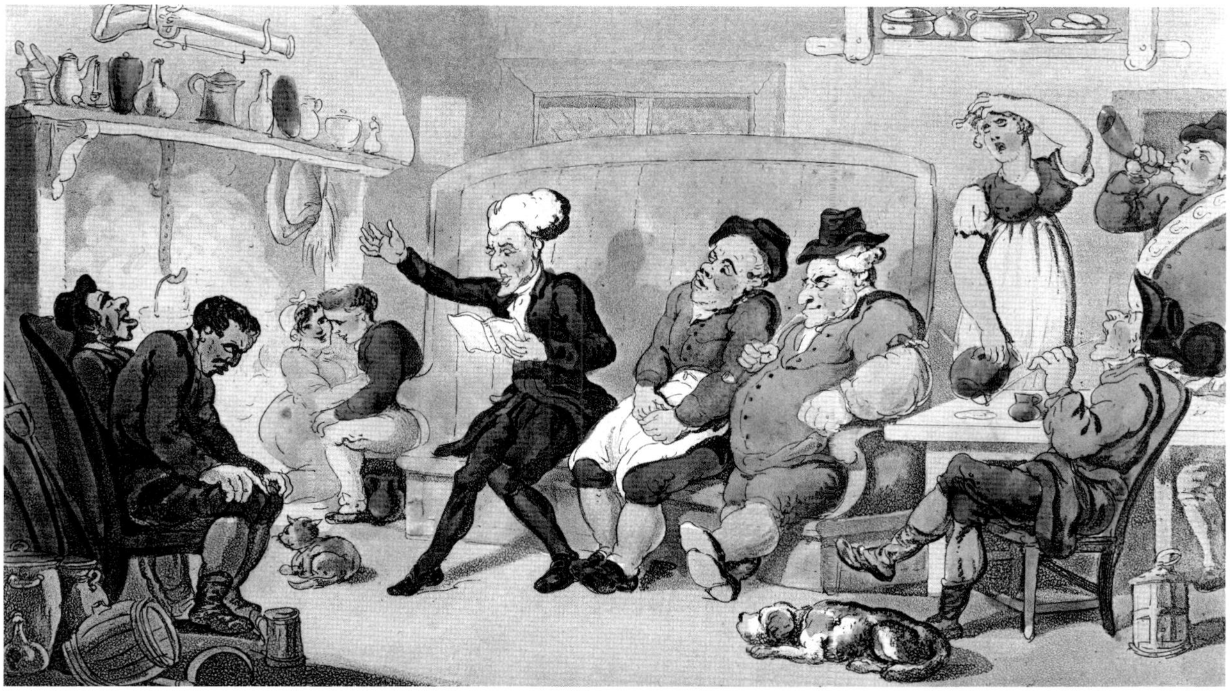

Thomas Rowlandson, 'Dr Syntax reading His Tour' from The Tour of Doctor Syntax in Search of the Picturesque, *1809*

a *Tour*, only to be told by a publisher that he can get *Tours* any day from Grub Street writers who never leave London. *Dr Syntax* was written to accompany Rowlandson's very funny but quite unkind illustrations. Soon there was a market for Syntax china figures, hats, wigs and coats – early examples of home-made tourist tat. The poem was so popular that it was translated, and two new *Tours* were published in 1820 and 1821. The demand for mockery was such that by 1826 the first Dr Syntax *Tour* was in its ninth edition, and Gilpin had been dead for 22 years.

Gilpin had grown up in an artistic family in a castle in Cumberland and was obsessed, even as a child, by pictures, always carrying a sketch-book with him. He knew many artists, and his brother and nephew were both artists themselves. But his classical background – and perhaps too his love of Dutch painting – seems to have made him suspicious of the possible worth of British art and artists. And though he knew much about the latest developments in printing technique and wanted Paul Sandby to show him the secret of making aquatints, which reproduced the quality of watercolours far more effectively than engravings (Sandby, though a family friend, refused), he seems to have been slow to see, if he ever saw it at all, the effect of the arrival of commercial watercolours on British artistic practice in the second half of the eighteenth century. Before then artists had to make their own watercolours from raw materials, but now they began to be marketed in cakes, ready-mixed with gum arabic and honey or glycerine. John Middleton was advertising such in 1775, with camel-hair brushes at a penny and blacklead pencils at sixpence each,[46] and Reeves was supplying them by about 1780.[47] Artists, particularly landscape artists, soon saw their usefulness; they were cheap and easy to carry about; amateurs could produce respectable results with them, and professionals superb ones. The latter soon began mixing them with almost anything to hand to create a wide range of effects, opaque and translucent. Sandby, for instance, once added burned crust to create 'an excellent warm black colour', and the technical description of some of his 'watercolours' involves pen, ink, pastel and body colour as well as watercolours themselves.[48] (Body colour, now more commonly known as gouache, was created by mixing colour pigment and opaque white with a binding agent – distemper, gum arabic or fish glue – to create an effect like oil paint). Though artists used watercolour at first mainly to 'stain' their pen or pencil drawings – that is, they added the colour after the drawing was finished – they soon began to paint with them directly on the paper, till in the hands of J.M.W. Turner and Thomas Girtin 'watercolour' involved complex rubbing out and sponging and scratching to create, by the turn of the century, a major medium of artistic expression. This was accompanied by a shift from the more or less accurate illustration of a scene to an emphasis on the emotional response of the artist to it. A.D. Fraser Jenkins put it very well: Girtin and Turner 'make the treatment of the whole work more important than the impact of the main subject. The landscape is no longer a "view", although a building or a waterfall in it is still often spectacular. In fact, it is the emotional "spectacle" that the picture is now about, and everything is directed to this one end.'[49] Artists painting in watercolour did not feel hampered by the example of Old Masters, as were those painting in oil.[50]

The art world is always fiercely competitive, and the earlier painters soon became sneered at as 'mere topographers', though the demand for descriptive images of places continued alongside the appreciation of an artist's feeling in front of them. Indeed the proliferation of books of prints of houses and castles and abbeys, usually with accompanying text, has never ceased. Though the prints today are usually of photographs, 'artistic' or otherwise, there is still a market for topography, 'mere' or not. But watercolour painting from 1770 to 1850 remains one of the highest achievements of British art, a unique contribution to that of Europe. Though artists in other countries used the medium, nowhere else did it gain such high status, with its own professional societies and exhibitions. It helped make possible a change in attitude to the subjects of painting similar to that to the subjects of poetry, heralded by Wordsworth's manifesto in the second edition of *Lyrical Ballads* (1800) against the conventional (and extremely tired) 'poetic diction' of the day. Just as he was in revolt against the latinate language which had dominated English poetry since Milton, so the watercolourists, though less consciously political for the most part, but still looking with new eyes, preferred to paint real British subjects rather than scenes from an idealised or imaginary Italy or Greece. The French Revolution and subsequent war helped to strengthen this focus on their own country. The classical temple gave way to a ruined medieval castle, or an abbey plundered by Henry VIII. These buildings came with a completely different set of attached values. Instead of suggesting a prelapsarian innocent world, they reminded the viewer of the often brutal history of his own country, of tyranny overthrown, and a corrupt catholic church replaced by the godly protestant Church of England. Thus the proper response to a Michael 'Angelo' Rooker of Chepstow Castle was very different from that to a scene by Claude, even if Rooker may have borrowed the useful framing tree, and sometimes a Claudean light. Chepstow and the Wye Valley were one of the first places artists went in search of their new subjects – for which, however irritating he may sometimes be, we must be grateful to William Gilpin.

The Wye Tour

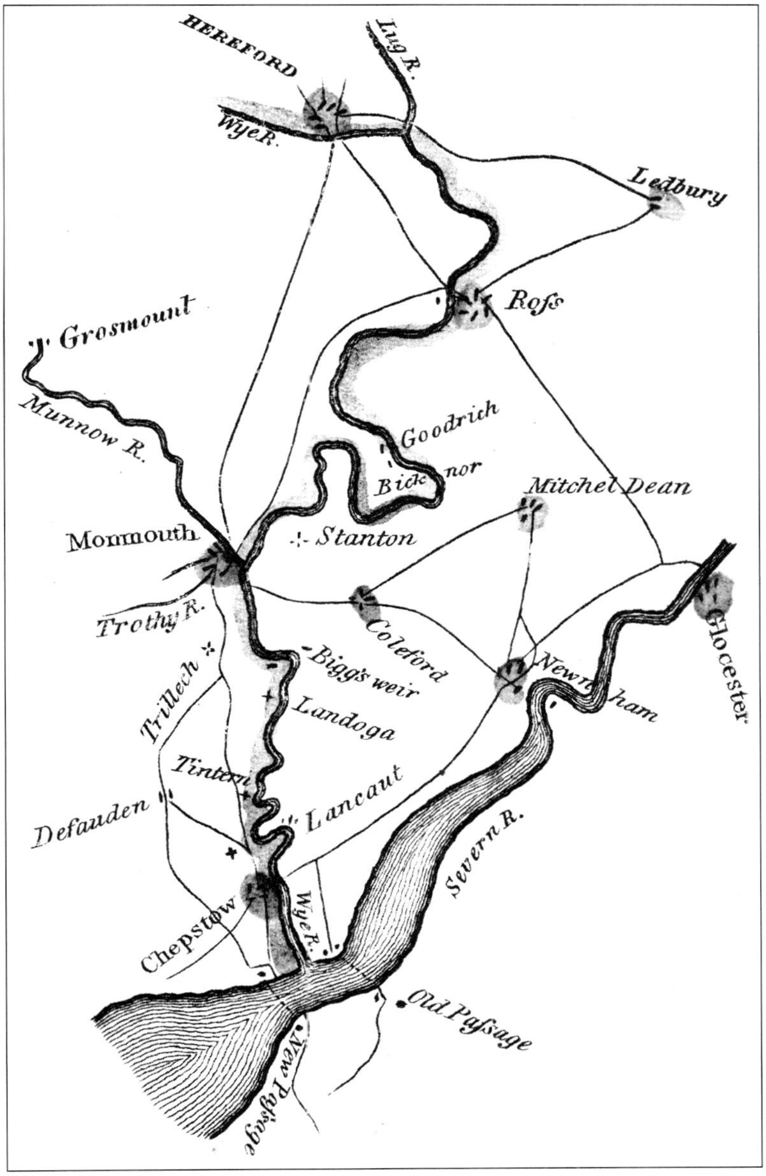

Map of the lower Wye from Mark Willett's An Excursion from the Source of the Wye, *(1810)*

Beginnings

Charles Heath, the Monmouth printer and publisher of four decades of local guide-books, did not know the Reverend John Egerton (1722-1787), the founder of the Wye Tour, personally, and did not mention him in early editions of *The Excursion down the Wye from Ross to Monmouth*, waiting till 1803 to give his account of its invention. Two years before that, Thomas Martyn had had as his steersman George Evans, the oldest waterman on the river and known as the Commodore because he had been one of the first 'captains' of Egerton's pleasure-boat. Evans spoke of the rector's 'excellent worth, amiable manner, and unbounded charity ... in a strain that appeared evidently to come from the heart.'[51] In the 1815 edition of *The Excursion* Heath, who continually brought his guides up to date as he republished them, and may have thought it wise to wait till Evans was dead, had a flowery footnote on page 2: 'It may not be uninteresting, to many inhabitants of Ross, the being told, that Mr **EDWARD FLOYD**, of that town, had the management of the vessel; with Mr **GEORGE POLLARD** and Mr **GEORGE EVANS** for his assist-

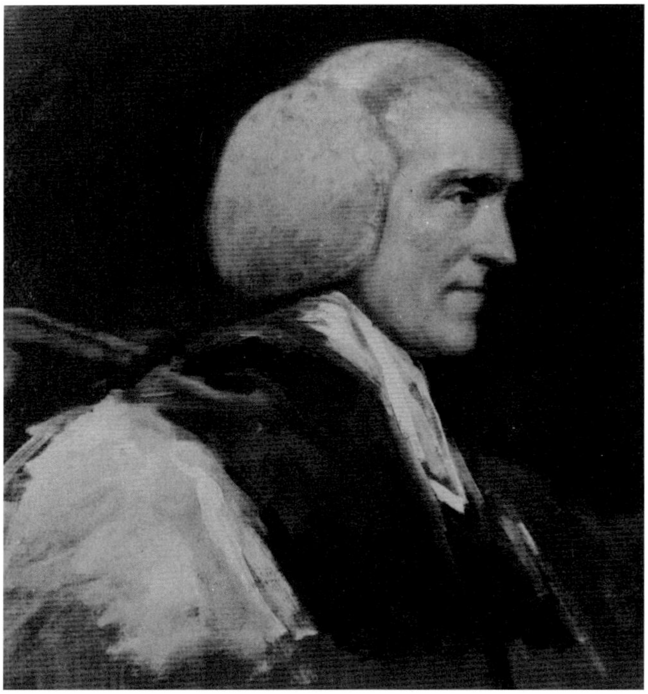

The Rev. John Egerton as Bishop of Durham, by an unknown artist (detail). (© Durham Cathedral)

ants; – whose duty, to use the language of my informant, the late Mr John Taynton, principally consisted in taking copious libations of fine cider, -- to which, he further observed, "they did not manifest any very violent objection".' The tradition endured.

Egerton was a man of fortune, in both senses. Not only the son-in-law of the Duke of Kent, he was the grandson of two earls, Portland and Bridgewater (his sons inherited the latter title, though he himself missed out) and his father was Bishop of Hereford. After Eton he went to Oxford, where he graduated Bachelor of Civil Law in May 1746. The previous December 22nd, still only 24, he had been deaconed, and the very next day, the eighteenth century Church of England having no objection to nepotism, his father made him rector of Ross-on-Wye, with the excellent salary of £600 pa. As if that was an insufficiently good Christmas present, the bishop made up for it ten days later by making him a Canon of Hereford. So when Egerton married his cousin Lady Anne Sophia de Grey in 1748, they were a very wealthy and well-connected young couple who could afford to entertain a great deal. Heath makes it sound as though they made tourism an important part of the local economy: 'the sociability of [Egerton's] disposition attracting a large circle of friends to his mansion – the town was continually enlivened by parties of his relatives or acquaintance, which conferred a great advantage on the trading part of his parishioners.' In order to entertain these visitors, Egerton had 'a commodious Pleasure Boat' built and 'whenever any of his friends visited him in the summer an excursion down the Wye formed always a part of their amusement.' There is one gloss on this version which may be no more than malicious gossip, but perhaps not. It was told to the modern Monmouth historian Keith Kissack when he was writing *The River Wye* (1978). In this variant Egerton was much less social than his wife and found their many guests a nuisance, so he had the boat built to get them out of the house. Whether the more tiresome guests were encouraged to go as far as Monmouth and spend the night – and the more tiresome still to Chepstow, which meant two nights away – was not, alas, part of the story.

The boat, in any case, was built, and the idea of taking trips downstream from Ross to see the local sights soon caught on. There was first Wilton, still within sight of Ross, with its bridge – in those days the last one till Monmouth – and its ruinous castle. (Kerne Bridge was not built, and main road from Ross to Monmouth changed, till 1828). A few miles down river was the much more imposing castle on a crag at Goodrich, below which the road crossed the river over a 'rope' – a ferry on which a rope was used to haul the boat across the river. (Thomas Martyn noted at the Huntsham ferry the posts on either side of the river which had pulleys to raise the rope when a barge wanted to pass.) For the Egertons' first guests the castle may have been as far as they went. If they were staying at Ross, the boatmen had to get them back against the flow of the river – though the passengers could always ease their labour by walking the three or four miles home. But they may have gone on to Symonds Yat, getting out of the boat to toil up the cliff for the view of the great loop the river makes at Huntsham, then walking down to New Weir, where they could admire barges being taken through the lock and enjoy the clamour of the forge before heading home, perhaps in a chaise sent to collect them.

Preparing for Tourists

For the Tour to become more than a rich man's entertainment, to become a two-day journey to Chepstow, there had to be good enough inns for self-respecting travellers at Ross, at the stopover at Monmouth, and at Chepstow itself. Furthermore, some of the ruins needed to be tidied up. Tintern, for instance, was a largely industrial village in the 1750s, and visitors to the abbey were few. The modern road had not been built, and the only approaches from Chepstow were down a very steep and stony track from St Arvans via Porthcasseg to the abbey, or the equally steep road down the Angidy valley to the iron works. It was easier to reach by water. Grose wrote in 1775 that parties were coming from Bath and Bristol, showing that the lower Wye tour from Chepstow to Tintern and back was flourishing some time before the two-day tour from Ross. When visitors did arrive they were likely to be shocked. Though the abbey's remoteness had protected it somewhat from the usual depredations of stone-robbers, the church was used as a fives court and the head of Sir William Herbert had been removed from his tomb by a local barge-builder called William Sparks who 'went into the Abbey with a ship-builders adze, and, with savage fury and indecency, not only severed the head from the body, but also broke the face, legs and other parts', taking the head to serve as a backstop for quoits. When the Duke of Beaufort, whose family had acquired the abbey after the dissolution of the monasteries, and who counted Sir William among his ancestors, heard about this, a warrant was issued for Sparks's arrest, but he had wisely left the area. The floor, meanwhile, was covered with bits of collapsed choir screen, and the duke decided in the late 1750s to clean the whole place up. Mr Knowles of Chepstow, from whose son Heath got the story, was in charge of the work under the duke's steward, Mr Harding. 'At that time, the interior was choaked [*sic*] up with rubbish, several feet above the present surface, and overspread with ashlings, alders, and other trees, the growth of such situations, to a very considerable height.' Some of the rubbish was thrown into the river, and 'what was useful they spread over the adjoining ground', whatever that may mean.[52] A hundred men were employed on the work, supplementing their wages by selling medieval tiles and bits of sculpture, including the brass hand from someone's tomb, to early tourists. The duke replaced the broken floor with smooth grass, and put doors with locks on the entrance to keep out the squatters who lived in the uncleared ruins of the monastery between the abbey church and the river. Everything he did, though, managed to annoy someone. Romantic tourists considered he had done too much. They preferred their ruins as ruinous as possible; they wanted plenty of lichen and moss and ivy; they thought he should have left things as they were; the smooth grass gave quite the wrong impression. Visiting in 1781, the honourable John Byng, the future Lord Torrington (for a fortnight), thought the duke should have planted a few cypresses and installed a harpist to twang away as people were having their picnics. Ten years later E.D. Clarke wanted signs to help him understand what he was seeing. Others complained that the duke should have tidied away the poverty-stricken squatters as well as the broken sculptures. They had to fight their way through beggars to get to the west door, something that prevented a proper melancholy contemplation of the past.

Local reality, and local people, often get in the way of tourist fantasies. In Monmouth and other towns, wrote George Walpoole, in *The New British Traveller* (1784), 'those who have had a genteel education are as polite and as affable as any in the neighbouring counties; but the lowland husbandmen, and others engaged in rural employments, are for the most part very rustic in their manners, and far from being acquainted with the principles of hospitality.' Heath records a visiting clergyman, used to a sophisticated London congregation, giving a 'very polished discourse' to the people of Welsh Newton, which clearly baffled them. The preacher sniffily said it would be difficult to find a language they would understand.

In the middle of the eighteenth century Britain was still a largely rural and agricultural society, but over the next hundred years, with the industrial revolution, a huge shift took place. Not only did the population vastly increase, by 1850 the majority of it lived in towns. It was a period, therefore, of extraordinary social disruption. There were also the regular natural hazards brought on by the British climate. There were severely bad harvests in 1789, 1795, 1800, 1809-11 and 1817, and 1792 was a very bad year for sheep and potatoes. There was grave scarcity in 1799 and by 1801 the price of wheat had leapt from 7 shillings a bushel (35p) in 1795 to 19 shillings and threepence (92p). The end of the Napoleonic wars in 1815 led to an extreme economic depression, and the old Poor Law, which was applied by each parish according to its own lights, some more generous than others, was unable to cope with the soaring demand for relief. (A new Poor Law was enacted in 1834.)[53] The poor were, therefore, often hungry, a fact which casts a not altogether flattering light on Gilpin and his famous or infamous dilemma: 'In a moral view, the industrious mechanic is a more pleasing object than the loitering peasant. But in the picturesque light, it is otherwise. The arts of industry are rejected; and even idleness, if I may so speak, adds dignity to a character. Thus the lazy cowherd resting on his pole; or the peasant lolling on a rock, may be allowed in the grandest scenes; while the laborious mechanic, with his implements of labour, would be repulsed' – though he did make allowances for working fishermen.[54] Few tourists were able to take such a detached view. From their regular complaints, it seems they wanted their peasants loitering, lazy and lolling – as in a Claude or Poussin, in fact, posing classically under trees or gently herding sheep under a blue sky. The reality of beggars at Tintern and Symonds Yat was as upsetting to them as it is for modern tourists at the pyramids or the Taj Mahal.

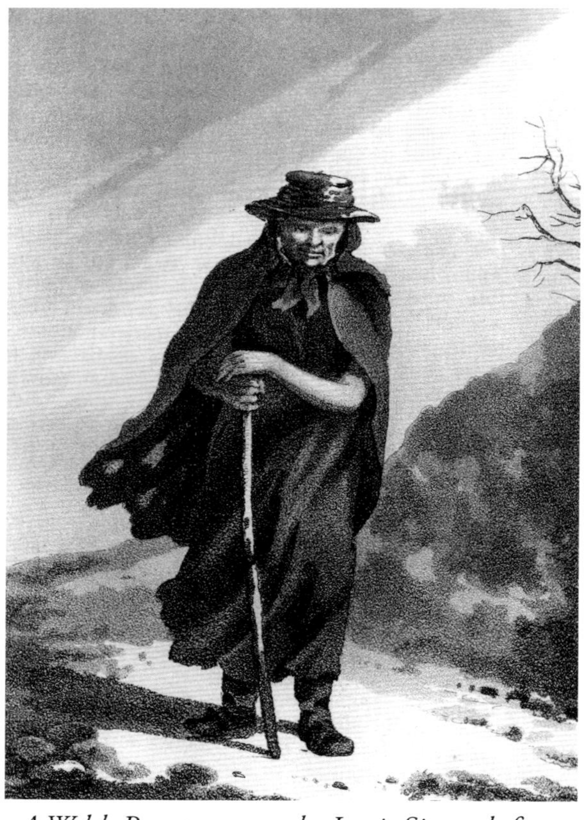

A Welsh Beggarwoman by Louis Simond, from Journal of a Tour and Residence in Great Britain during the years 1810 and 1811, *second edition, 1817*

England or Wales?

For English tourists, Wales was almost as foreign a country as Egypt, and most were unclear whether Monmouthshire was in Wales or England. Walpoole said it was 'reckoned an English county ... because the judges began to keep the assizes here in the Oxford circuit under Chas II. But its inhabitants still resemble the Welch more than the English, especially in the interior parts. In many places both languages are spoken, but still with the British accent; for it requires many years to discern the purity of speech among people who live at such a distance from the capital.' Stebbings Shaw (yet another clergyman) said Monmouthshire was 'formerly a Welch, but [is] now an English county',[55] and Charles Dibdin, in 1801, was told by a Monmouth waiter (with a strong accent) that 'It is Waales, but it is not Welch Waales'.[56] De Loutherbourg was quite certain it was English, 'the Welsh boundary in this quarter being removed from the Wye to the Romney'. When they wished to patronise, though, English visitors were sure it was Welsh. Mark Willett, born and brought up in Monmouthshire, was indignant at

> the uncharitable allusions, and illiberal stigmas cast upon the good people of Wales, by their English neighbours, who deign to sojourn amongst them in the summer season, charging them with the most *heinous* crimes of superstition, and a belief of fairy and goblin tales ... The relation of legendary tales by the peasantry, after the toil of the day is past, is a relief to the mind, and a soother of their cares, and further, inculcates in the unlettered a sublimity of thought.

He would rather, he went on defiantly, 'sit down in a cottage, listening to an old wife's tale, than be introduced to the most fashionable card party in the dominion of England, or town of Berwick upon Tweed.'[57]

Early Days of the Tour

How many people made what became the full Tour in the early days we do not know, but there does not seem to have been anything like a regular tourist trade. Egerton is said to have liked Ross more than anywhere else his very successful ecclesiastical career took him, and to have lived there for nearly thirty years. Though appointed Dean of Hereford in 1749, and Bishop of Bangor in 1756, he kept the living of Ross *in commendam*. Later, though said to have been reluctant to accept further promotion, he was elevated first to Lichfield and Coventry (with a canonry of St Paul's) in 1768, and then, in 1771, to Durham. During his absence in the north his pleasure boat, said Heath, 'was moored on the bank of that river which it was first destined to navigate – and the ship's crew committed to that destiny – the element of Fortune – which we are all, more or less, forced to weather.' He meant they were unemployed; but let's not forget those copious libations of fine cider.

The water tour from Ross was not the only way of seeing the Wye valley; many people walked or rode, both up and down the river, and most, at least in the early days, saw only the lower quarter of it. When Joseph Banks visited Piercefield in 1767, he did so from Chepstow, and Young, the same year, also went by road, though he said the water route (from Chepstow, that is) was 'a pleasant scheme enough'. The idea that John Wesley might take two days out of his intense preaching schedule to drift down the Wye and admire ruined castles and abbeys is unthinkable, but, perhaps surprisingly, he did take 'a walk through Mr Morris's woods', also from Chepstow, in August 1769, and thought there was 'scarce anything like them in the kingdom'. But though he obviously very much enjoyed what Morris had done, he disapproved of aestheticism and brooded on what would happen to Piercefield at Judgement Day: 'And must all these be burned up? What will become of us, if we set our hearts upon them?'[58] Probably that same year Whately, a leading figure in the government as well as a landscape aesthete, both activities which might have brought him Wesley's disapproval, seems to have found time to make the actual tour. Gilpin himself took it a month or two after his friend the poet Thomas Gray in 1770. Gray had made many tours through England and Scotland and had, like Gilpin, read his Whately in advance. He described the Wye's banks as 'a succession of nameless wonders' and later read Gilpin's notes on his trip and encouraged him to publish them. But Heath states that for some years after Gilpin's visit 'a single boat was sufficient to convey the company down the Wye'. Henry Penruddocke Wyndham, in the summer of 1774, was another who confined himself to visiting Tintern from Chepstow, advising that 'the water passage ought in every respect to be preferred' to the very indifferent road because of the beauty of the scenery. (P.J. de Loutherbourg praised this route as late as 1805).[59] However by 1787, Torrington said, there were at least two boats available at Ross, and in September 1803 Joseph Farington counted five pleasure boats 'laying ready for passengers'. Heath said there were eight, and more were sometimes required to meet the demand.

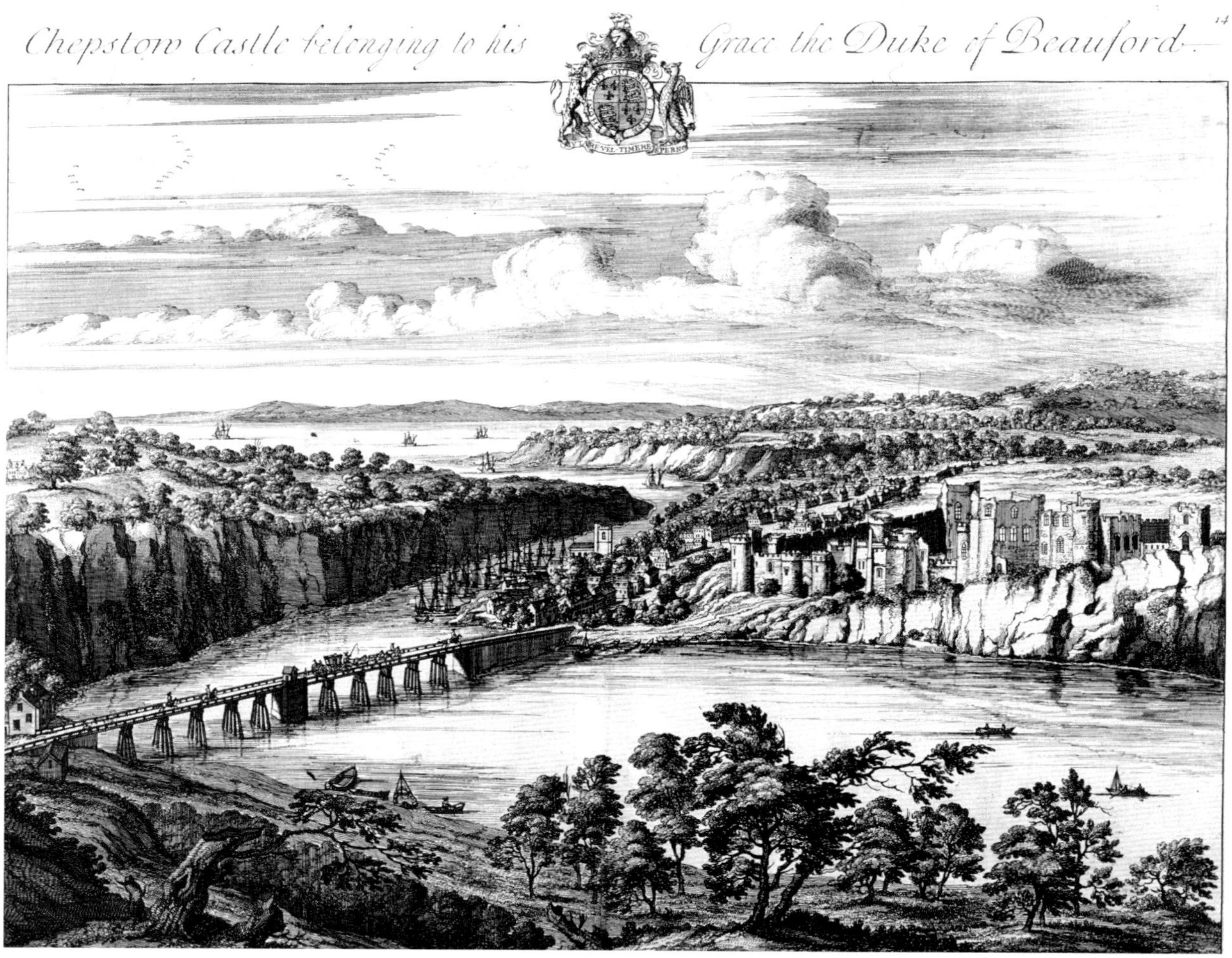

Chepstow, drawn and engraved by Johannes Kip, n.d. (Chepstow Museum)

Pictures of the Wye

This great increase had been created partly by the increase in images of the sights. The earliest image of the Wye valley is probably the oil painting of a panorama of Monmouth painted in the 1670s by Hendrik Danckerts for the first Duke of Beaufort when he was still only Marquis of Worcester. It shows the old Troy House, replaced in the early 1680s, and is a genuine landscape painting, with hills, river and town redeployed for artistic purposes. It is now in Monmouth Museum. At Badminton there are other early oils, including a view of Tintern attributed to Michael Dahl. There are also paintings of Chepstow, Troy House and Monmouth, all attributed to Thomas Smith, though these pictures do not all seem to be by the same hand, or to be of anything like the same date.[60] These are essentially social records, asserting the duke's pride in ownership of the scenes depicted – his carriage, for instance, seen passing down the double avenue at Troy, can also be seen also crossing Chepstow Bridge in Kip's print published in Sir Robert Atkyns's *Gloucestershire* (1712) – the first public as opposed to private picture of the Wye. After the Beaufort pictures come the Buck prints of the 1730s.[61]

In Wyndham's first edition of his *Tour* (1775) he said he didn't 'meet with a single party of pleasure, during his six weeks journey through Wales', and he had been hampered by 'the little intelligence he could learn from former publications, and the trifling assistance he could obtain from the natives'. But in his second edition (1781), intended for 'the general traveller', he says he has omitted engravings of Chepstow, Tintern and other places 'because they have been so frequently published, and are too well known to be again repeated'. As well as the reissued Bucks, there were two prints of Tintern by Richard Godfrey in *The Antiquarian Repository* of 1773, but Wyndham was probably thinking of Grose's *The Antiquities of England and Wales* (1772-1776), the second volume of which included one engraving of Chepstow (from a 1762 drawing by John Inigo Richards) and two of Tintern (with Monmouthshire classified as part of England). All three were taken from what became standard viewpoints. Monnow Bridge, drawn by Grose himself on his visit in 1775, was added in Vol I of the Supplement (1777), with a note that 'as a picturesque object [it has] long been noticed by the connoisseurs'. He also lists the 'ANTIQUITIES in this COUNTY worthy NOTICE', which shows the audience he was hoping to reach.[62] His plates and text did not meet universal acclaim. 'A mere picture book' snorted the Revd William Cole, 'in which to seek 'old women's tales and vulgar traditions'. But Grose kept going, producing a thousand plates over the years with accompanying descriptions, and adding Scotland and Ireland to England and Wales.

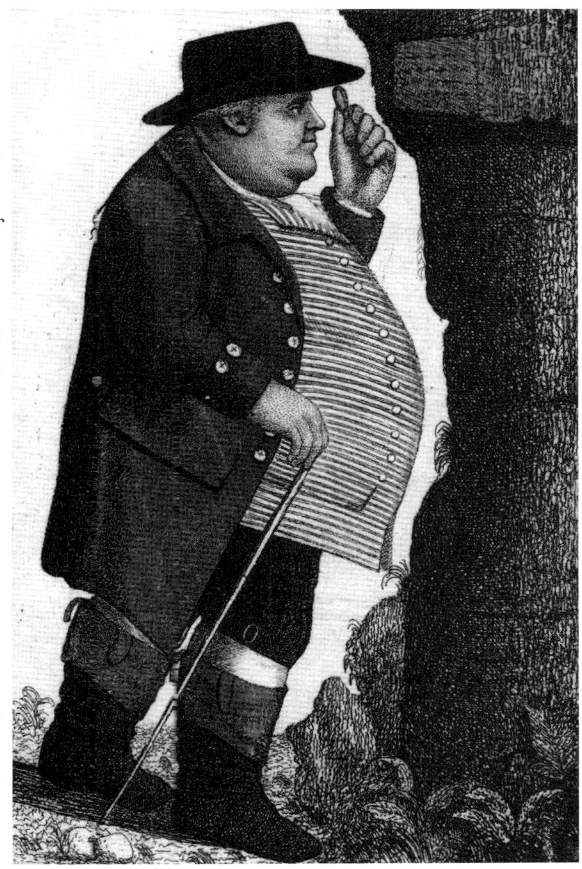

Francis Grose by John Kay (© NPG, London)

His plates cost sixpence each. Paul Sandby's *XII Views in Aquatinta from Drawings Taken on the Spot in South Wales* appeared in 1775, with Chepstow Castle as the very first plate (catalogue no 85). Sandby had provided Grose with some of his views – the antiquarian print-making world was quite small – but his superior artistry was recognized and the Chepstow aquatint at once copied, though the copies are always inferior to the original. His *Virtuosi's Museum* (1778-1781), much approved by the aesthetes, had 108 engravings at a shilling each, among them three more of Chepstow, different from the aquatint of the castle, one of which is catalogue no. 86. Thomas Hearne and William Byrne began their *Antiquities of Great Britain* in 1776. It also had the aesthetes' approval, but published only 52 engravings in eight years at three shillings each. By the time Gilpin's *Observations* appeared in 1784, people had many views of the main Wye sights to compare to his bafflingly 'picturesque' ones.

Soon artists were specialising in Wye scenes: Edward Dayes published a series of beautiful prints of the river between 1792 and 1802, and Samuel Ireland produced *Picturesque Views on the River Wye*, describing the Wye from its source to the sea, with his own illustrations, in 1797. They were followed by T.H. and A.V.C. Fielding (1802), W.H. Bartlett (1835), David Cox in Thomas Roscoe's *Wanderings and Excursions in South Wales* (though others contributed too) (nd, but after 1839)[63] and T.H. Fielding on his own in 1841. There was, however, no very early guide-book to the Wye as such, though there were general guides like Walpoole's *New British Traveller* and 'A Gentleman's' *Pocket Vade-Mecum Through Monmouthshire and a Part of South Wales*, both of 1784. Tourists were probably still few at that stage, though travel diaries of people coming to Monmouthshire begin to be written from the mid-1770s.[64] There were, too, some early oil paintings of Chepstow by John Inigo Richards (exhibited 1765) – he also contributed views to Grose's *Antiquities* – and Mary Gardner. Professionals as serious as Francis Towne (1777) and in the 1780s, Hearne, John Webber, William Day and Michael 'Angelo' Rooker, all came to paint scenes of the Tour, as did many amateurs, such as Joshua Gosselin (who drew Chepstow and Monmouth in 1784, but may have come to the area earlier).

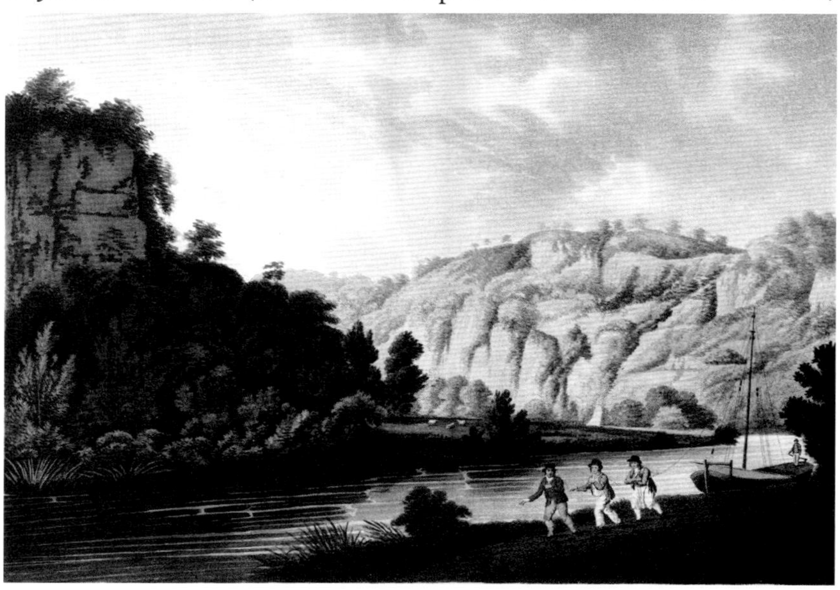

The Doward, engraving by Edward Dayes (1800). (Monmouth Museum)

It was rare for any artist actually to hire a boat and go down the river like a tourist, though Farington and Hoppner did so together in 1803. So long as it was not raining, a boat trip was an ideal way of seeing passing scenery. It was smooth, unlike even the best of modern carriages, and it was slow enough for a passenger to have plenty of time to gaze about. The scenery, said Catherine Sinclair, was like a series of moving theatre sets, 'as if some skilful scene-shifter were perpetually drawing his invisible wires'. But it still passed too quickly for an artist to make a drawing. Besides, the boatmen wanted to get to Monmouth before dark on the first day of the tour, and next morning they wanted to hurry their clients down to Tintern, in order not to miss the tide to carry them on to Chepstow, so lingering was not allowed, as Robert Bloomfield lamented:

> No loitering here, lone walks to steal,
> Welcome the early hunter's meal;
> For time and tide, stern couple, ran
> Their endless race and laugh'd at man ...

So his party got back in the boat and 'Hey for Chepstow', steer'd along.[65]

Artists needed time to set themselves up, even for making a pencil drawing. J.T. Barber, for instance, was clearly not on holiday. He locked himself in Tintern Abbey and 'employed several hours without interruption in sketching the interesting features of the ruin', from which he later created his frontispiece (catalogue no. 96).[66] The earlier artists, too, wanted to be as accurate as possible; they wanted their watercolours, even if they were worked up from pencil drawings when they got home, to be recognizably like the places portrayed – unlike Gilpin's much mocked plates. Wyndham, for instance, emphasized that the illustrations by Sebastian Hieronymus Grimm in his second edition were based on drawings 'taken on the spot' like Sandby's views of south Wales. Most artists, therefore, walked the Wye, as J.M.W. Turner did on his two visits in the 1790s, and would have spent much longer than the tourists' two days on the journey as they stopped to make their sketches. So, though their works may have served as advertisements for the tour, making people want to see the sights they drew, it was not from their custom that the Tour became a commercial success. What made it popular was the French Revolution, and the war with France that followed in 1793. 'Whether it be owing to the late unsettled state of affairs on the Continent, which rendered travelling, if not unsafe, at least disagreeable', wrote Heath in the Preface to *The Excursion*, '– or to that well-founded curiosity, which excites the Man of Observation to survey its attractions – certain it is that Monmouthshire has, in the course of the last four or five years, been honoured with a very large share of public Notice.' He goes on to acknowledge Gilpin, Whately, and 'the sensible and entertaining' Shaw as writers who helped make the area known. There is no question that he is right that the 'cutting off' of the continent vastly increased the demand for travel within Britain: G.W. Manby specifically cites the war as his reason for travelling in Wales. Guide books, such as Heath's own, began to be published and to go into their many editions and there was an outpouring of travel journals and poems. And more and more artists came, not just to record the sights, but using their paints to express what they felt about them. From being a backwater, the Wye had become a mainstream tourist destination, as it remains to this day. It was only with the arrival of the Hereford, Ross and Gloucester railway in 1855, with its speed, its protection from the weather, and its sheer convenience, that navigation above Monmouth[67] gradually ceased, and with it the two-day package tour by water.[68] It had lasted almost exactly a hundred years.

Gilpin's *Observations* was the first book with long descriptions of the Wye from Ross to Chepstow. He devoted 65 of his 152 pages to the river, the rest describing his trip up the Usk valley to west Wales and back. He was, of course, mainly concerned with the landscape and where it was and was not correctly picturesque, but he could not avoid some history and personal feeling, as when he recorded how moved he was by the poverty of the old woman who showed him her damp and slummy home in the ruins of Tintern Abbey. His reputation as an aesthete was such that many later writers (and diarists), as has been said, either copied his judgements about the scenery direct or paraphrased them, though as time passed, and he began to be mocked, people did occasionally dare to take issue with him on particular views. But though the *Observations* was carried by many tourists, who consulted it religiously about picturesqueness, it hardly served as a guide to the individual sights – Gilpin did not, for instance, actually visit Goodrich Castle – and the illustrations were wholly inadequate as mementoes of the tour. Yet for several years there was little else.

With the increase of tourism, however, came a corresponding increase in the writing of *Tours*, some more practical than others, some more aesthetic and opinionated. Grose's *Antiquities* (1772-6, with later supplements), though it had brief texts with historical information and occasional aesthetic comment with each plate, was in no sense a guide, being far too big for a tourist to carry about with him. But Wyndham intended his *Tour*, at least in its second edition (1777), for the general traveller, not just the reader at home, and gave asterisks to places with inns that could be relied on. Richard Joseph Sulivan, who travelled round England, Scotland and Wales in 1778, though he didn't publish his *Tour* till 1785, was one of the opinionated.[69] His book was in epistolary form, as many such books were – for instance, Penhouet (1797)[70] – and not only described a journey but added some often rather speculative history of the places visited as well as the inevitable critical comments on the landscape. As he was writing before *Observations* was published, Gilpin gets no mention, and Sulivan is probably the last to write about the Wye without invoking picturesque theory. Criticism of medieval monasticism is common in writers of *Tours*, but Sulivan is far and away the most splenetic, the sight of Tintern provoking a tirade against the times when 'superstition could so far have pervaded the minds of the people, as to draw from them the means of endowment of such expensive institutions'. He talks of 'pious imposition' and 'swarms of useless drones' (he meant monks) and 'the enormities and sensuality of the chosen of these foundations', which reminds us that the Gordon Riots against any toleration of 'Popery' took place in 1780. Shaw was much of Sulivan's mind, quoting William Mason on 'fell tyranny and ruthless superstition' though 'we now trace her footsteps with delight, and pleased to revere what once we should have hated.'

Many travellers came over the Severn to Chepstow, and were rowed up the Wye to Tintern and back, without exploring further. For them the first guide-book could be said to be the Reverend Edward Davies's *Chepstow, A Poem in Six Cantos* (1786). It cost one shilling, the profits going to charity. Davies was the pluralist vicar of Mathern and other local parishes in southern Monmouthshire, and a sound Protestant, who believed in good works rather than faith: 'All popish aid is useless in the grave, For nought but virtuous deeds can mortals save.' He was also a magistrate who vigorously promoted better roads, and was keen on everything to do with eating, drinking and defecating. Though no one would claim his poem a great one, it is often amusing and since he knew so many local people it has special value. He is particularly good on the castle, with its owl which 'quits at night her venerable house, To find for supper a fat Chepstow mouse'. A poet of the classical school, he calls the affectionate Mr and Mrs Williams who kept the castle Baucis and Philemon – 'Baucis loves Philemon, – Phil. his glass' – though he dwells rather too long on the castle lavatory, 'a small heathen temple' which hangs over the river. He covers everything later guide-books describe, and sometimes more: the life of the regicide Henry Marten imprisoned in the castle; the bridge with its loose planks which terrify animals as well as people ('Here oft the head-strong pig will start aside, Bounce through the rails, and plunge into the tide'); the busy docks; the view from Tutshill; the delicious local salmon and cider; and Tintern Abbey where he thinks the ivy is holding the ruin up:

> The tottering pile she clasps in her embrace,
> With a green mask conceals its furrowed face
> And keeps it standing on its time-worn base.

He describes the Tintern Ironworks 'where sooty Cyclops puffing, drink and sweat', the nightingales, Piercefield, Wyndcliff, Winter's Leap, and the town itself:

> He, who by land would enter Chepstow Town,
> Must quit his horse, and lead him gently down;
> The long descent so rugged is and steep,
> That even post-boys here, for safety, creep ...
> For if we careless walk the slippery street,
> Our prostrate bottoms will the pavement greet.

No other guide-book is at once so poetic and so down to earth.

In 1789 Shaw published his *A Tour to the West of England in 1788*. He was an obsessed antiquarian, whose passion for research may have contributed to his mental breakdown, madness and death at 40. He pays tribute to Gilpin, but he gives far more information about places; his description of Piercefield is one of the best there is. One of the seats, he says, 'may be called a front box of one of the compleatest theatres in the universe', and 'Here wants no painted canvas to express its scenery, nature's sweet landscape is quite enough.' Later writers found his *Tour* one of the most useful to pillage. But it was still not what we would today call a proper guide-book. Before Charles Heath set up his press in Monmouth in 1791 there was no guide to particular places either. George Gethin, the landlord of the Beaufort Arms at Tintern, had a manuscript of the history of the abbey which the author of the *Pocket Vade Mecum* was able to borrow, and which Heath later included in his own printed guides, but that was all. But Heath embarked almost at once on small *Descriptive Scenes* of Raglan, Tintern, Piercefield, and Chepstow (catalogue nos 97-99). The first of these was to Raglan, and he must have carefully tested the market before publication, for among the 45 listed subscribers were Dr Griffin of Hadnock and Thomas Hooper of Panygoitre, the patrons of the Monmouthshire historian David Williams (who also subscribed); Sir Richard Colt Hoare of Stourhead (two copies) and James Greene of Llansantfraed, who sponsored William Coxe, also a historian of the county; James Wathen; the Revd Luke Booker, a regular visitor to Monmouth; 12 other clergymen; and many local gentry on both sides of the river. *The Excursion* followed in 1795.[71] The *Descriptive Scenes* were mainly compilations from Young, Wyndham, Whatley, Shaw, Grose, Gilpin and others, but he quickly became a studious antiquarian, climbing a ladder, for instance, to examine the stained glass in Goodrich church. Though he wrote in 1803 that he had gathered everything that could be gathered about Tintern and had 'no hopes of adding to the value of any future edition', his guides got longer with each printing. He included notes on churches and their monuments; though he acknowledged people did not find these very interesting, he defended them by saying that 'in county histories, monumental remains have always obtained a distinguished rank'. He also described such local customs as wassailing, harvest suppers and Morris dancers, and included poems by himself and his friends. His style is often pompous, he fawns on the gentry, and in old age he grew garrulous, as Puckler-Muskau and John Britton found when they called on him shortly before he died, his daughters in the first case vainly trying to hush him. (When Britton met him, he had been drinking Welsh ale, and was so voluble and 'superabundantly good-natured' that rather than endure his company and talk – 'not conversation' – Britton invented an engagement at Tintern to avoid having to dine with him. For this he was punished by being caught in a thunderstorm and having to spend the night at Trellech, presumably at the Lion, with neither night-light nor bell, and where water poured through the roof and down the chimney.)[72] Heath's guides are, whatever his personal faults, far and away superior to anyone else's, and much plundered by later writers. His *Historical and Descriptive Accounts of the Ancient and Present State of the Town of Monmouth* (1804), for instance, is astonishingly detailed for the history of a small town, and still of great value to historians. In the early days he claimed he was publishing his guides more for 'the most enthusiastick love for antiquarian research' than money. 'It has engaged a large portion of time', he wrote in the Preface to the 1799 edition of the *Excursion*, 'which if devoted to even the printing of a spelling book, would better have rewarded my assiduity', but this was disingenuous, and he later modified the claim to 'pecuniary motives were but of secondary consideration.' He had to; by 1828 *The Excursion*, which described the trip for walkers or riders as well as boat passengers, was in its eighth edition, his account of *Tintern* in its eleventh. He had taken advantage of the fact that most previous books on the Wye were inconveniently large, or as he put it 'ill suited for companions on a tour' to produce ones of more convenient size: 'a book like this, which takes up little room, is far better adapted for the purpose.' It was also cheaper. He claimed not to revise his thoughts before transferring them to the composing-stick, but as the guides were so popular and continually reprinted, they were regularly rewritten. They were also frequently unpaginated and bound together in ways which baffle the modern bibliographer. His finest moment was when Lord Nelson and Lady Hamilton, with Sir William, came to buy guides from his shop, his account growing longer as the visit receded in time. He was twice mayor (1819-1820 and 1821-1822) and enjoyed being presented to such grand tourists as the Prince and Princess of Denmark, but he was not especially vain; his advertisements almost always simply call him 'Charles Heath, Printer'. His guides were, however, not illustrated, which gave an opportunity for others.

James Baker's *A Picturesque Guide Through Wales and the Marches* (2nd edition, 1795) was illustrated by himself. Dedicated to the Prince of Wales, and with a royal and lordly list of patrons, it goes into the history of places in some detail, often with an accompanying poem to point a historical moral. Gilpin is quoted at length, but Baker also says which the best inn was in Chepstow, and how much it cost to take a boat up the river to Tintern, so he intended a practical guide as well as a picturesque tour.

The first illustrated *History of Monmouthshire* was published in 1796. It was written by the well-known radical David Williams, who was invited to Paris after the French Revolution to advise on a new constitution. He arrived full of hope, soon to be disappointed by the raging political factionalism. He also disapproved strongly of the execution of Louis XVI, and was attacked by Robespierre. He was still regarded as a dangerous radical in England, however, and on his return found he had lost a well-paid assignment to complete David Hume's *History of England*. It seems likely that John Gardnor, the vicar of Battersea and a fellow radical, seeing him in need, got him the job of writing what turned out to be a rather bored text to accompany Gardnor's own often charming but eccentric aquatints. Williams had been shown round Piercefield by Valentine Morris himself, and disapproved of what later owners had done, but he had nothing to say about the Tour, and certainly did not mean his *History* to be a guide.

It was Samuel Ireland, who came down the Wye before the great floods of 1795 but did not publish his *Picturesque Views on the River Wye* till 1797, who first set out to give accurate views. He had already done the Thames, the Medway, and the Warwickshire Avon, and advertised his forthcoming two volumes on the Severn at the end of the one on the Wye (though it was not in fact published till 1824, long after his death in 1800). His tour began on Plynlimon, and he often stopped, got out of his boat, and walked to places not immediately on the river – the Kymin and Buckstone, for instance, at Monmouth, from which, like many other tourists, he also made an expedition to Raglan Castle. He must therefore have taken much more than the standard two days to make the passage from Ross to Chepstow. He was respectful to Gilpin in his Preface, explaining, fairly, that the much mocked illustrations were not meant to give 'exact representations' of the sights but to exhibit their 'general effect on the eye, when considered technically, and as picturesque forms by the learned and professed artist', but he built his own 'claim to public favour, on the fidelity with which he flatters himself he has delineated the scenery.' Fidelity might not be the first quality one would claim for his plates today, but they certainly give a far more accurate idea of places than Gilpin or Gardnor. His text is not long, but it includes as much historical information as aesthetic comment, and, unlike Gilpin, he visited all the sights.

He probably met James Wathen of Hereford on his journey as did some anonymous tourists in 1797:

> Stepping into a Booksellers Shop to make some local enquiries, we were by him referred for information to Mr Wathen, an ingenious Gentleman residing in Hereford, who has favoured the Public with some elegant specimens of his Pencil, particularly a Set of Drawings of the Cathedral, in its ruinous state ... though we had no other Passport to his acquaintance than that of the Bookseller he received us with much attention and politeness, shewed us his numerous collection of Drawings and accompanied us to our Inn in the Evening. In consequence of his recommendation we determined to return 7 miles on road to Kington to Foxley.

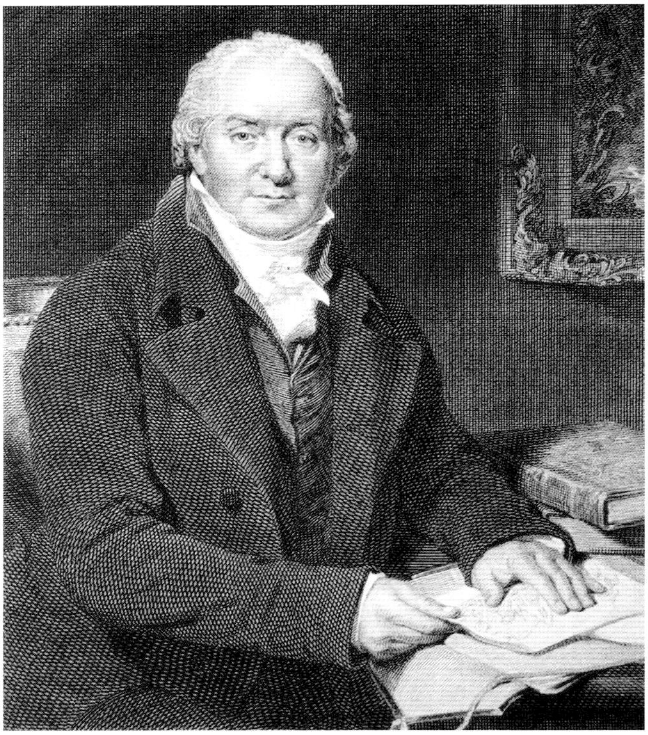

James Wathen by A.J. Oliver, engraved by T. Bragg. Wathen's hand rests on what looks like one of his own drawings. (BM Reserve Collection Class VII Period 4)

These tourists also went to Hampton Court before starting down the Wye. 'In forming our arrangements ... we were materially assisted by the friendly Offices of Mr Wathen who furnish'd us with a small chart of the course of the River and accompanied us a few miles on the way.'[73]

Wathen (1752-1828) was a Hereford glover known as Jemmy Sketch or the Sketcher, a vegetarian and teetotaller who could produce 20 drawings in one day. They were not, it must be said, of the highest quality as works of art, but they are often extremely valuable as topographical descriptions of lost scenes.[74] Though he wrote no guide-book, he not only provided people with maps of the river, but seems to have been the first guide to the sights who was not himself a boatman. In 1801 he inherited money and gave up gloving for picturesque tourism, walking up to 32 miles a day and outpacing his companions' horses. Barber met him at Monmouth in 1803, 'the benefit of whose local information and obliging assiduities has been felt by numerous tourists, as well as ourselves.' Later he travelled to India and China and published his *Journal* of the voyage.[75]

Richard Warner (1763-1857) was an extremely busy topographical writer in his youth, who published *A Walk Through Wales in August 1797* the year following and was thought by some to be very eccentric to go on foot. But his book was so successful that it had reached a fourth edition by 1801, by which time he had published a *Second Walk* in 1799. He was much influenced by Gilpin, whose curate he had been, though how he had time with all his walking and writing to fulfil his parish duties is unclear. At Hereford on his way south, he and his companion also came across 'our friend' James Wathen, who again provided a map and

> whose active attention and promptness to oblige are experienced and acknowledged by all who have the pleasure of his acquaintance. On him we depended for directions in our expedition down the Wye, and his usual kindness has been displayed in making out for us a minute delineation of the course of the river, its most picturesque points, and the objects of curiosity in the neighbourhood of its banks. Nor is this all: he has promised to meet us at Wilton-bridge, near Ross, on Wednesday morning, and to be our guide from thence to the beautiful scenery around Tintern Abbey.

Wathen also walked the first three miles from Hereford with them next day.

Warner's volumes were quite slim, and not illustrated. They would certainly have fitted into an eighteenth century gentleman's coat pocket. But most books, such as Ireland and Williams, were too big to carry, and one wouldn't want the aquatints to be damaged by exposure to water. *A Collection of Welsh Tours* (second edition 1797) had only five illustrations, but was truly pocket-size. The anonymous compiler claimed that 'Several of the most popular and interesting *Tours in Wales* having become scarce, the present Editor has been induced to compress various selections from them into one volume ...[and] has availed himself also of the most respectable histories.' This method of making guide-books by large-scale pilfering became increasingly common. *The Cambrian Directory* (second edition 1801) was more original, based on a tour taken by two friends and the author's dog Sylvio round Wales in 1798. It had no illustrations and was meant as 'a common *Itinerary*' and 'a convenient Pocket Companion', though it was a little larger than the *Collection of Welsh Tours*. Written by an anonymous 'Old Bachelor ... anxious that all minutiae should be properly attended to', it is the first guide-book which advises tourists what to avoid as well as where to go, and in this has a distinctly modern feel to it. He claims to direct the reader to 'the *best Inns*, and lay before him in one view, the *Distances*', and is eagle-eyed to spot laziness among the Wye boatmen. He has read Wyndham and Warner and pretends to be nervous of 'the anxiously expected publication' of William Coxe's *A History of Monmouthshire* (1801), Coxe being 'a Gentleman, highly classed in the literary world, for many celebrated productions'.

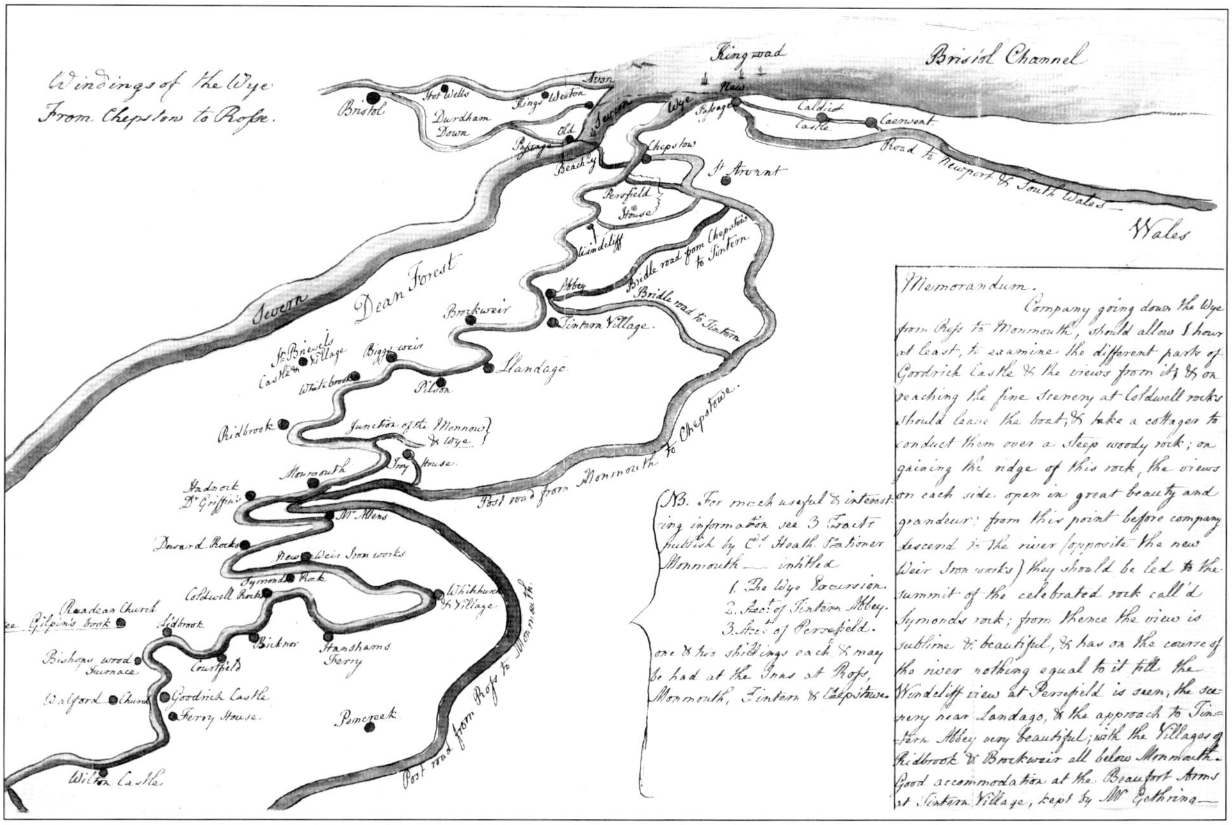

James Wathen, map of the Wye Tour, in A Tour through Monmouthshire and Glamorgan, *Anon, illustrated by Rose and Maria E Sotheby. (By permission of Lyfrgell Genedlaethol Cymru/ NLW)*

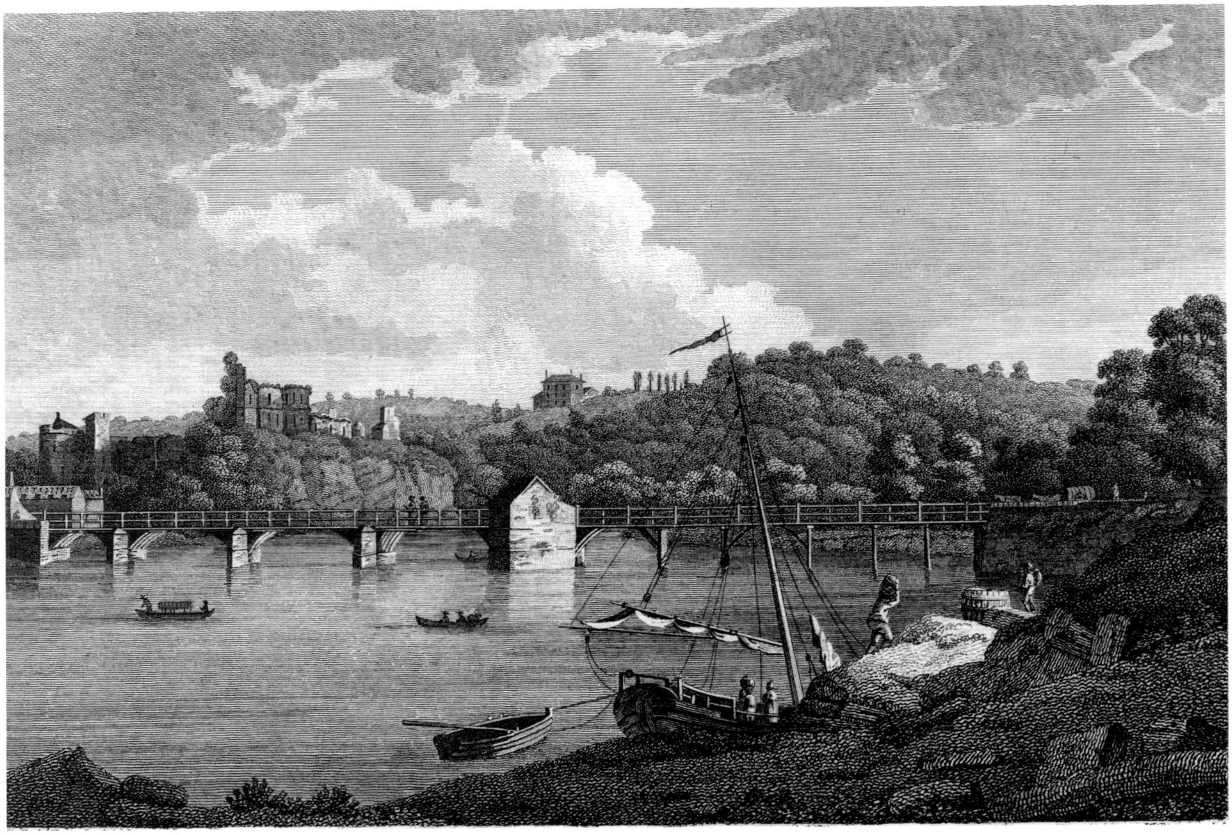

Chepstow by Sir Richard Colt Hoare, engraved by William Byrne, from William Coxe's An Historical Tour through Monmouthshire, *1801*

Coxe (1748-1828) was vicar of Bemerton just outside Salisbury, and indeed a much travelled and respected writer whom the artist and antiquarian Sir Richard Colt Hoare regarded as a mentor as well as a friend. He had begun as bear-leader to young noblemen on European tours, and gone on to publish two separate volumes on 'Swisserland', three on Poland, Russia, Sweden and Denmark, and lives of John Gay and Robert Walpole. His book was suggested and sponsored, and his Monmouthshire travels almost certainly paid for, by Colt Hoare, who accompanied him on much of his research (including the Wye Tour) and provided most of the illustrations. His *History* was intended in part as a response to the inadequacies of Williams.[76] Coxe and Colt Hoare would have seen themselves as following in the tradition of such earlier upper-class travellers as Wyndham and Thomas Pennant. But like their books, and those of Ireland and Williams, Coxe's volume was large – two fat volumes in fact. 'Few works have been so universally admired' said the *Gentleman's Magazine* in December 1802, 'but ... it is too bulky for the traveller, and from the costliness of the decorations, the price is too high for the common purchaser', so an octavo abridgement was published, by the same publisher, T. Cadell, and by 'a lady' who is thought to have been Coxe's wife or sister. It was called *A Picture of Monmouthshire*, though it had no illustrations. A further abridgement of the abridgement, called *A Description of the Town and Neighbourhood of Chepstow*, was published by the Chepstow printer Samuel Baldwyn Rogers in 1806, a metallurgist and inventor whose publishing was very much on the side.[77] This was the first book known to be printed in Chepstow.

While these abridgements were appearing, in clear response to tourist demand, a new *Tour Throughout South Wales and Monmouthshire* by J.T. Barber, FSA, appeared in 1803, dedicated to Richard Brinsley Sheridan, the playwright and politician, written in a rather high-flown style and illustrated by the author. Barber says in his 'Advertisement' at the beginning that he too is responding to demand: 'The usual plan of Tours only comprising a particular route ... a Tourist is obliged to encumber himself with several books, to enable him to gain all the information he requires. The Author ... has therefore selected from the best authorities an account of those few parts he had not an opportunity of visiting; in order that this Work may exhibit a general survey of Southern Cambria.' He doesn't care much for wilder Wales: 'the towns, for the most part, are miserably poor, and travelling accommodations very uncertain; the roads, too, are wretched beyond anything that a mere English traveller ever witnessed.' But – 'the chief beauties of South Wales are found in a compact route' and 'this part of the country may be explored in a close carriage, though the better mode of travelling is, certainly, on horse-back.' He thinks walking a mistake: 'a man enduring the fatigue of trudging day after day through miry roads' not being able to 'maintain an exhilaration of spirits congenial with the beauties that surround him.' This was a lofty sneer at Richard Warner. The beauties Barber is thinking of are frequently of the opposite sex. He does not do the Wye Tour as such, but covers all the main sights, going upstream on horseback.

John Britton had been publishing a county by county *Beauties of England and Wales* since 1801. The Monmouthshire volume, with the assistance of the Revd J. Evans, came out in 1810.[78] It is more of a gazetteer, hundred by hundred, with many illustrations, than a guide-book. Although openly derivative and quoting extensively from Coxe, it is more informative than any other county history up to that time, including, as it does, statistics about such matters as poor relief, a list of the main iron manufactories and details about bark-gathering. The Tour is not included as such, though all the sights within the county are exhaustively described.

By this time guidebooks were tumbling from the press, some from that of Mark Willett, who was born in Trellech and grew up at Tintern, and who established a printing business in Chepstow in 1808. His first guide was *An Excursion from the Source of the Wye* (1810), and made no pretence at originality: 'Gilpin, Grose, Coxe and other historic and descriptive writers, have been consulted.' The revised and enlarged second edition drew attention to its 'conveniently portable form' and urged artists to avoid the 'expense and risque of visiting foreign countries' when there was so much beautiful scenery at home – and where, he doesn't have to mention, there wasn't a war being fought. Under the title *The Strangers' Guide to the Banks of the Wye*, and with two more publishers, this went into five editions, the fourth (dedicated to Nathaniel Wells of Piercefield) claiming that 'three extraordinary large impressions' had already been sold. This was tailored to those taking an excursion on the steam packets from Bristol, which began to operate in October 1822, running daily in the summer and taking two and half hours to reach Chepstow.[79] Willett also wrote *The Stranger in Monmouthshire and South Wales* and *A Survey ... of the History of Monmouthshire*, which were bound together and published by Thomas Major to whom he sold his business in 1817.[80]

The other notable local writer was Thomas Dudley Fosbroke (previously Fosbrooke), vicar of Walford, near Ross, and Ruardean, and author of *The Wye Tour or Gilpin on the Wye* (1818), and *Ariconensia* (1821), which covered a smaller area, and was more archaeological. The former was sold

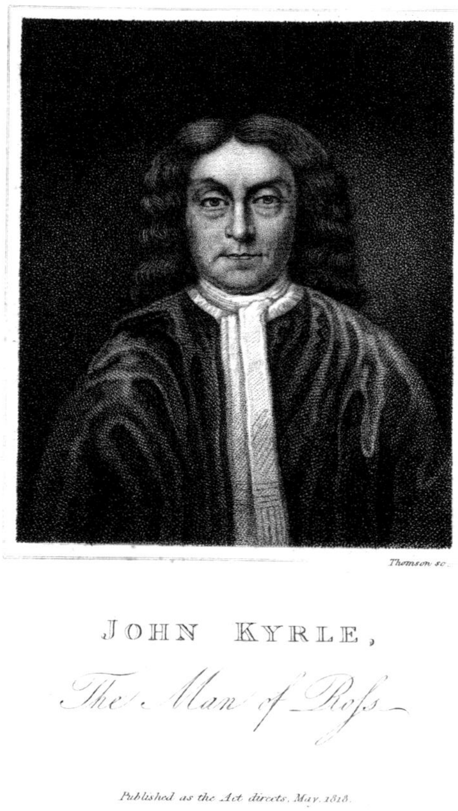

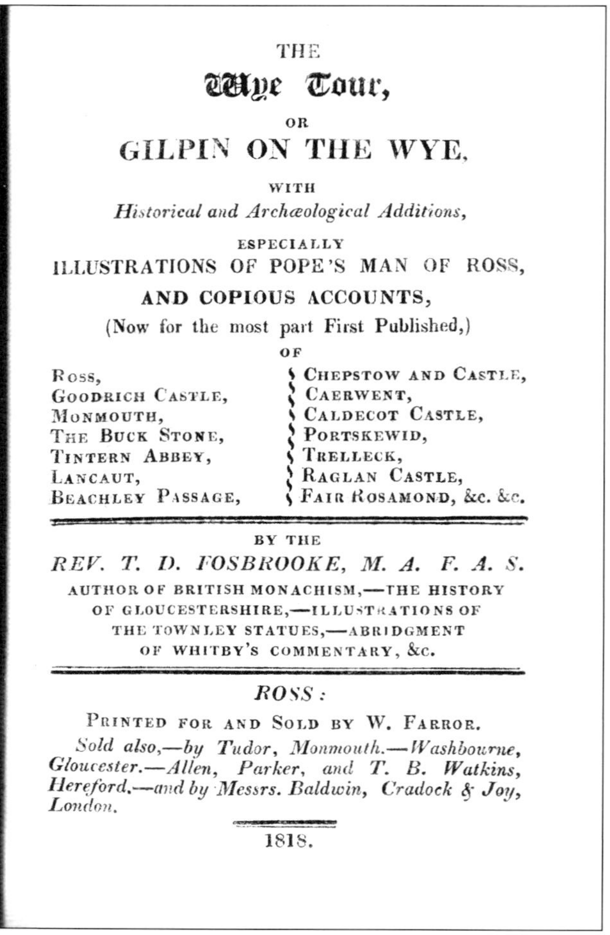
THE

Wye Tour,

OR

GILPIN ON THE WYE,

WITH

Historical and Archæological Additions,

ESPECIALLY

ILLUSTRATIONS OF POPE'S MAN OF ROSS,

AND COPIOUS ACCOUNTS,

(Now for the most part First Published,)

OF

Ross, Goodrich Castle, Monmouth, The Buck Stone, Tintern Abbey, Lancaut, Beachley Passage, Chepstow and Castle, Caerwent, Caldecot Castle, Portskewid, Trelleck, Raglan Castle, Fair Rosamond, &c. &c.

BY THE

REV. T. D. FOSBROOKE, M. A. F. A. S.

AUTHOR OF BRITISH MONACHISM,—THE HISTORY OF GLOUCESTERSHIRE,—ILLUSTRATIONS OF THE TOWNLEY STATUES,—ABRIDGMENT OF WHITBY'S COMMENTARY, &c.

ROSS:

PRINTED FOR AND SOLD BY W. FARROR.

Sold also,—by Tudor, Monmouth.—Washbourne, Gloucester.—Allen, Parker, and T. B. Watkins, Hereford.—and by Messrs. Baldwin, Cradock & Joy, London.

1818.

John Kyrle, engraving by Thomson after a 'Picture late in the possession of his Kinswoman Mrs Mary Flack', according to a slip inserted before the preface; and title page of Thomas Dudley Fosbroke, The Wye Tour or Gilpin on the Wye, *1818*

in Ross, Gloucester, Hereford, London and Monmouth – but in the last only by Owen Tudor, father of the artist Thomas, not by Heath. Rivalry was clearly at work, yet when Fosbroke said 'Cicerones on the spot supply catalogues and details', he must have meant they sold Heath's guides for there are none other so specific to particular places. He certainly quoted him as well as Gilpin and Coxe, though he added his own descriptions and was not afraid to criticize the former, now safely dead, for inaccuracy and for being commonplace about the landscape below New Weir. He also considered him wrong about Monmouth being neatly built; it was a jumble of houses in all styles. John Britton, to whom Fosbroke dedicated the first edition of *The Wye Tour*, invited Fosbroke to dine with him at Ross, but quickly regretted it. Like Heath, Fosbroke was garrulous, talking and talking till after midnight, and eventually staying the night. He was a rapid and prolific writer, Britton said, but his extracts from printed publications were so copious, and his own composition so blended and confused with them, they were of little use to him. The fourth edition (1834) of *The Wye Tour* was much altered, and the book now organized into three parts: the Picturesque for the tour; the Historical, to be read at the

Inn; and the source of the Wye, to be perused at leisure. By this time he had joined the aesthetes and written *The Tourist's Grammar*, but he was still first and foremost a guide. Of walks round Ross he listed only 'those within a distance, to which females would not object', and he said he himself used and recommended 'a well-known small yellow pocket glass, called a *Claude*' – that name again ! – 'which gives a sunrise view at full-day, without the obscuration of the morning mist'.[81] He was not describing the 'Claude glass' which helped frame the view, but one of the coloured glasses through which the view was supposed to look like it did at dawn or in moonlight or in his case at sunrise. To the modern eye these seem banal, but at the time they were thought exciting. The use of Claude's name for both types of glass shows how his influence went on and on.

From then till the end of the nineteenth century there were many guides to the Wye, and many published tours, most of which, like that of Daniel Carless Webb, were not 'endeavouring at the higher embellishments of literature', and added little or nothing to existing knowledge, repeating each other exactly as modern guides do.[82] Louisa Anne Twamley (1838) and Leigh Ritchie (1841) are examples of these, though Twamley is interesting in that she came from Birmingham; tourists were no longer confined to visitors from spa towns.[83] C.F. Cliffe said that by the 1850s, because of the railway, 'So many people make Gloucester … the starting point for the Wye Tour', that his guide does so too.[84] W.H. Thomas, a Tintern doctor, said that thanks to the railways, vast numbers now 'rusticate for a season amidst the recesses of Wales'. He was keen for naturalists and valetudinarians as well as ordinary travellers not just to make a day-trip to Tintern but to stay there for some time. In thirteen chapters he listed walks and rides, by moonlight as well as by day, taking the tourist as far as Caerleon and Raglan, with an appendix for the more adventurous to go as far as Abergavenny, Monmouth and Newport. But it was really a guide to the eastern half of the county, not to the water tour.[85]

Ross on Wye

The Wye was navigable from above Hereford, and one or two people took a boat from there down to Ross, but the landscape was declared tame by Gilpin, among others, and it was as rector of Ross, not Dean of Hereford, that Egerton invented the Tour. So it was there the Tour began.

According to the 1801 census Ross had 533 houses with 2,347 inhabitants, which made it smaller than Monmouth (677 houses, 3,345 inhabitants) but larger than Chepstow (348 and 2,080). The town 'stands high, and commands many delightful views', said the author of *A Tour of the River Wye* (published 1798) and 'the pleasure boats that are constantly employed between here and Chepstow give life and beauty to the town.'[86] There was no bridge across the Severn below Gloucester till the 1960s, so Ross lay on one of the main east-west routes into central Wales from England on what is now the A40. It was also on the north-south route through the Welsh marches, and nearby Roman remains suggest people must always have been passing through. Its three main streets met at The Market House, built in the reign of Charles II, and there were three large inns. According to Daniel Defoe, it was 'a good old town, famous for good Cyder, a great Manufacture of Iron Ware, and a good Trade on the River Wye; and nothing else as I remember, except it was a monstrous fat Woman, who they would have had me gone to see.' He declined, though 'they told me she was more than three Yards

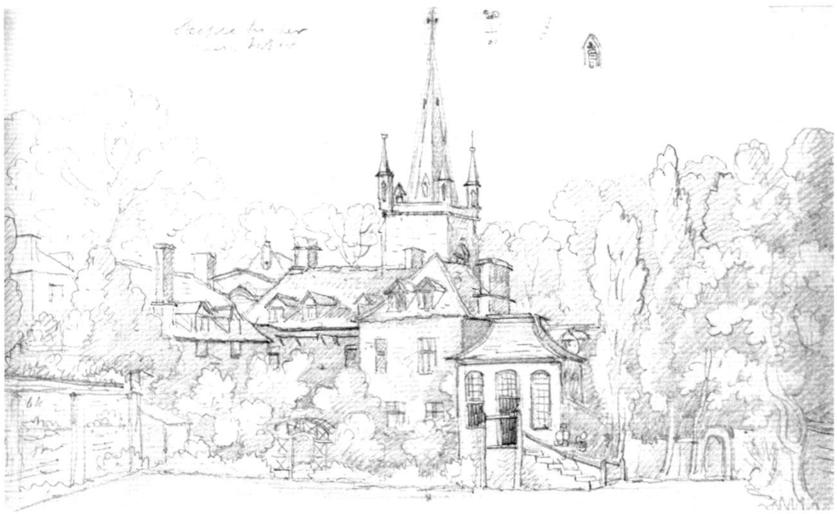

Ross Bowling Green by Sir Richard Colt Hoare. (Cardiff Central Library)

about her Wast [*sic*]; that when she sat down, she was oblig'd to have a small Stool plac'd before her, to rest her belly on, and the like'. Clearly Ross was already in the business of providing tourist attractions.

The man responsible for the less crude of these died the year before Defoe wrote. He was the local philanthropist John Kyrle (1637-1724), a comfortably off bachelor who planted trees along the river and created the Prospect in the churchyard, from which the visitor had a fine view over the Wye as it curved below the town on its way to Wilton Castle and bridge, with the Black Mountains in the distance. In 1775 Francis Grose wrote of how the river 'twists about its adjacent meadows in a beautiful manner', but complained that the rector had cut down the trees planted by Kyrle in the churchyard. All subsequent tourists agreed with him about this view; even Gilpin found it 'very amusing', though it failed, like so much else, his definition of 'picturesque'.

Kyrle's beneficence had been fulsomely praised by Alexander Pope in his *Epistle to Lord Bathurst* (1733) on *The Use of Riches*, lines of which every writer on Ross felt obliged to quote a few. Though he never met Kyrle and probably never came near Ross, in spite of local rumours, Pope used him as an example of the good citizen:

> Whose Causeway parts the vale with shady rows?
> Whose Seats the weary traveller repose?
> Who taught that heav'n directed Spire to rise?
> The 'Man of Ross', – each lisping babe replies.
> Behold the Market-place with poor o'erspread?
> The 'Man of Ross' divides the weekly bread.
> He feeds yon almshouse, neat, but void of state,
> Where age and want sit smiling at the gate:
> Him, portion'd maids, apprentic'd orphans bless'd,
> The young who labour, and the old who rest.'[87]

And so on and so on. It is not a particularly inspiring poem – where else, one might peevishly ask, could a spire be directed but upwards? – but as a piece of advertising it worked wonders for the tourist trade, and 'Spending a day at this pleasant town is like spending a day with the "Man of Ross" himself', wrote *The Penny Magazine* in 1836, 'for we are reminded of him every way we turn'.[88] His house in the High Street became the Kings Arms, where for a long time you could still see his portrait – 'though but a daub in colouring, [it] is valued for its extreme likeness', said Shaw – and where in

1791 Sophia Ward was shown the room where he had lain in state for six weeks.[89] The truth is, if Kyrle was everywhere in Ross it was because there was little else to see or talk about. The town did not acquire its deliberately picturesque fake medieval round tower and 'gothic' walls and the Royal Hotel till the 1830s, and the Market House, attractive to modern taste, was not to that of the time. (Samuel Ireland's comment in 1797 that it was in 'the worst style of saxon architecture' was exactly repeated in the 1801 edition of *The Cambrian Travellers Guide* and in Leigh's 1831 *Guide to Wales*.[90]) So it was Kyrle or almost nothing, and Heath, an early oral historian, published not only his pedigree and biography, Pope's lines (of course) and Dr Johnson's remarks on them, but many 'interesting particulars' and 'floating memoirs' received from such authorities as the town crier, as well as a great deal else. There was, it is true, the church, which, as can be seen from James Wathen's watercolour of 1797, literally towered over the town, whose houses ran down the hill from it towards the river (catalogue no.4). It had some fine monuments, naturally including Kyrle's, erected long after his death by an admiring noble lady, and his pew, busy sprouting elm shoots. But the visitor could not even admire the spire without being reminded that Kyrle had paid for its pinnacles. Coleridge praised him as well as Pope, and claimed to have inscribed his *Lines on the 'Man of Ross'* on a window shutter of the Kings Arms in July 1794, though if he did they have vanished. The poem is not one of his greatest works, but Heath published it in his guides. Coleridge was a good deal more politically radical than Pope and began with a fine republican couplet: 'Richer than MISER o'er his countless hoards, / Nobler than KINGS or king-polluted LORDS'. He went on to recommend that 'If 'neath this roof thy wine-cheer'd moments pass / Fill to the Good Man's name one grateful glass', which the landlord, if he had known about it, or not been annoyed about graffiti on his shutter, might have used as an advertisement. The only person who seems deliberately to have avoided the general praise of Kyrle was the Revd Luke Booker, who chose to exalt his friend, the ironmaster John Partridge, whose tomb is in the church. Partridge gave away even larger sums than Kyrle – at least £50,000 in his lifetime – and still managed to die rich.[91]

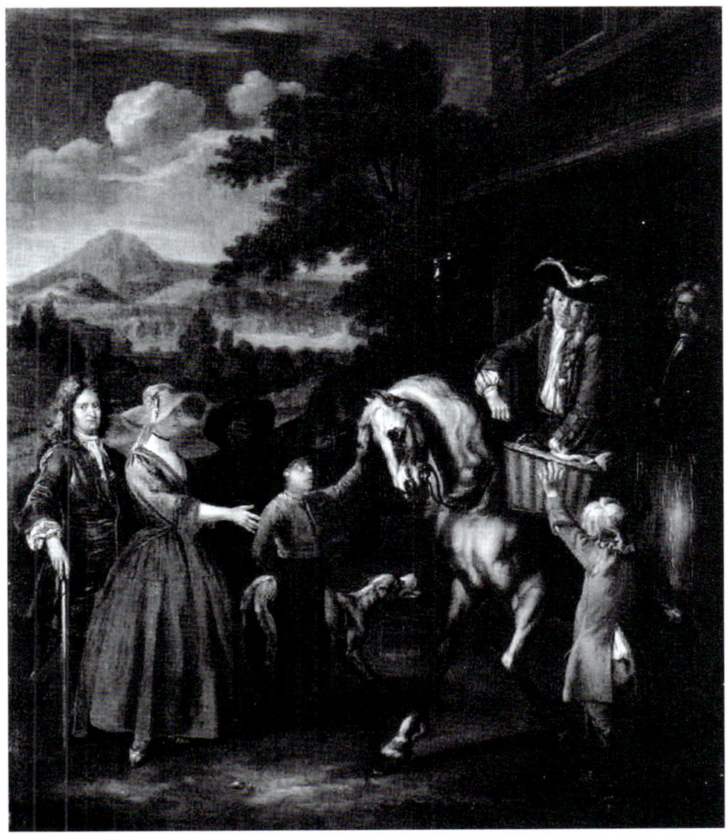

John Kyrle distributing bread to the poor by J. van Aken, c.1730. (Hereford Museum and Art Gallery)

Grose stayed at the Swan, and had no complaints, but an anonymous diarist in July 1776 complained of his or her inn that 'My bed was a good one but the dogs made a terrible noise and disturbed both Leycester & me.' Torrington, arriving for his second visit in a shower of rain in July 1787, found the town ill-paved, a complaint often repeated. He and his companion, an old school friend called Osborn, put up at the Swan and Falcon, as it had become, and took the required walk before dinner to admire the Prospect. After dinner ('salmon now every day'), they went to inspect the two available boats, and agreed to hire the larger, though they, like almost everyone, considered the trip expensive. They then 'made a ramble about the town', which may have meant a pub-crawl, 'and a long evening walk thro' corn fields; admiring the moon, and the goodness of providence, in a very religious and exemplary manner: with much discourse abt, Dr Hierchsell [*sic*], his rise, and genius.'[92] When they got back they found they had been bumped off their large boat by Lord V. 'who behaved very unlike a nobleman', using his wife's alleged ill health to push his own claim. The argument involved the boatwoman who 'made much clamour' (presumably because Lord V. was willing to pay extra for his bad behaviour). Torrington then went to find another boatman: 'his demands, however, were so exorbitant, and his manners so unpleasant, that we resolved to forego our intentions of the water scheme to Monmouth'. 'This dirty adventure', said Torrington crossly, 'fretted away our latter evening.' But the Ross women were handsome, and he slept 'well in a large good bed, better than the looks of the inn promis'd.' In the morning he walked down to Wilton Castle, and the owner allowed him to spend an hour inspecting it, before he and Osborn set off on horseback for Goodrich.

His is the first but by no means the last complaint about the bad language to be heard in the area. J.P. Malcolm, on his way from Gloucester in 1802, claimed the Severn boatmen were as obscene and improper as those at Wapping or Rotherhithe,[93] and Barber (1803), who took a very right-wing view of the working classes, said of the same boatmen that 'there being no competition for preference between [them], they are extremely rude in their manners, indifferent to the accommodation of the public, and by no means unpractised in various arts of extortion.' The passengers were just as foul-mouthed, according to Edward Collins:

> Where oft, the rude, and thoughtless passenger,
> Displays his talents, in a vulgar jest;
> Which, o'er the cheek of virgin modesty
> Spreads the deep crimson's lovely glow.[94]

Most later travellers were equally unimpressed by Ross. Mary Shiffner (1790) found it 'dull and dirty'.[95] Sophia Ward (1791) said 'the streets are narrow dirty and not paved [,] few genteel Families reside here [,] and Ross upon the whole seems much neglected.' But Thomas Mansel Talbot, who had travelled widely in Europe, arrived on the eve of the Ross Fair that same year and enjoyed himself: 'we had many a specimen of the produce of the soil in vast herds of cattle of a superior size & immense waggon loads of the finest Ryeland wool &c, besides great droves of Welch cattle & ponies. The crowds of people going to Ross from all parts was truly astonishing.'[96] Rutland, in 1797, thought it a poor town, though the church was pretty. Henry Skrine (1798), less critical than some, found it 'ancient and irregular'.[97] *The Cambrian Directory* (1801), which purported to be a guide to the best inns, among other things, had some difficulty in obtaining even a small room at the Kings Arms, and was snippy about its reliance on the connection with Kyrle: 'The landlord seems rather to depend on the custom of strangers, from this circumstance, than the accommodations the inn offers.' The town was so full of people wanting to take the Tour that it was recommended to book in advance. Though the walks were beautiful enough, the streets of the town were 'narrow, dirty and inconvenient'. Thomas Martyn, the same summer, writing at length about the monuments in the church, was especially struck by one to a lady 'who lost her valuable life by sleeping in damp sheets when travelling', though he makes no criticism of the sheets he slept in himself. He was so impressed by the intelligence and communicativeness of the church clerk, Mr Delahay, that he wanted to take him down the river as a guide, but in Commodore Evans of the *Friendship* found a more than adequate replacement.[98] Malcolm, in 1802, found the streets 'dreadfully rough and unpleasant, but the neighbouring fields and meadows give views truly beautiful.' Joseph Farington (1803) complained about his dinner at the Kings Arms: 'the fowls were tough and the wine very bad', and the landlord 'never made his appearance to us'.[99] Robert Parker (1804) found the same inn 'only tolerable, but the Landlady, Mrs Howells, civil, and neat in her cooking.'[100] William Mavor and his party, arriving at the same inn in 1805 'were much diverted by the attention which our carriage attracted; for we were followed by all the men, women and children, in the streets, an evident proof there is little travelling and less novelty in this place', about the first part of which he must, surely, have been wrong.[101] They were disappointed by the Prospect after so many 'hyperbolical descriptions we had read'. A.M. Cuyler (1807) thought the town had nothing to recommend it but the beauty of its situation: the streets were (once again) 'narrow, dirty and inconvenient' which he or she seems to have copied direct from *The Cambrian Directory*.[102] For Robert Bloomfield (also 1807) it was 'not a town to my fancy'. It had 'a kind of dreary look' which he attributed to the local stone. When he came to write his poem *The Banks of Wye* (published 1811) he was less grumpy:

> ... Here the mind,
> With all its luggage left behind,
> Dame Affectation's leaden wares,
> Spleen, envy, pride, life's thousand cares
> Feels all its dormant fires revive,
> And sees 'the Man of Ross' alive.

But Sir Thomas Cullum (1811) called it 'very mean, being built chiefly with a reddish coloured stone, &' – yet again – 'badly paved'.[103] He made a note in his memorandum book not to stay again at the Swan and Kings Arms (as it had now become) 'as we found their accommodation by no means equal to their charges.'

In July 1810 Louis Simond, born in France, but an emigrant to America ('a dark, gloomy-looking man' whose English wife, said a Scots lady who met them, was 'the plainest, worst-dressed woman' she had ever seen) arrived in Ross to take the tour. He found little to please him, and mocked the British tourist industry:

> There is no need for thought or foresight in travelling in England, – no care necessary, but that of keeping your purse well furnished; everything is done and arranged for you in the most convenient manner beforehand. We had not been many minutes in the inn at Ross, before the master, perceiving, no doubt, that we were people of taste in quest of picturesque beauties, called for our orders respecting a boat to go down the river ... The landlord knew exactly what was necessary for victualling of the vessel, and we found all ready in a basket in the boat.[104]

Catherine Sinclair found that this was an opportunity for squeezing the tourists. So unusual was the charge for the 'sandwich' her landlord put aboard that he 'of his own accord politely apologised, saying he really had so few visitors, it was absolutely necessary to make the most of those who came!'

Catherine enjoyed the river, but Simond found the Wye 'rather insignificant and tame' – but then he was a ship-owner and used to the Hudson. Sir Matthew Ridley (1813) was of the general opinion; the town was dirty and the houses ill-built and bad.[105] William Cobbett (1821), more used to rough travel, was also more enthusiastic: Ross was 'a good plain country town or settlement of tradesmen whose business is that of supplying the cultivators of the soil. It presents nothing of rascality or roguishness of look which you see on almost every visage in the borough towns.'[106] But Mary Anne Hibbert (1823) found her bed hard and

> did not sleep a wink for fear of not awaking in time, as … I knew by the look of the chambermaid that no dependence was to be placed upon her, & so it proved. She never appeared till we were getting into the carriages, & then a little pert 'please, miss, to remember the chambermaid' was answered by 'I always remember those who do not forget me. You were ordered to call us, & you did not, therefore I give you nothing'. The mistress who was standing by said 'Quite right, ma'am', so poor Madame Warming pan then went off with her tail between her legs, & I think the lesson will not be thrown away upon her.[107]

With which, in full consciousness of her own worth, Miss Hibbert went off to her boat. The fourth edition of Mark Willett's *Strangers Guide to the Banks of the Wye*, reported not only that ten feet of the church spire had fallen on the stormy night of April 4th, 1829, but that Kyrle's house was no longer an inn but shops. You could, however, sit in his armchair in the Nag's Head, which he recommended along with the King's Head, Swan and George.[108] In 1833 W.M. described Ross as small and ugly and reported that the town hall was 'fast [falling] into a state of dilapidation.'[109] Thomas Roscoe liked it but found Kyrle's summerhouse 'in a deserted and somewhat desolate condition.' But on a more cheerful note, Charles Greville, in 1839, found it a very pretty town, though the river (on July 3rd) was 'alas, in its muddiest state'.[110] And in May 1847 Jane Blanchard came on her honeymoon and stayed at the Royal where 'We had a very pleasant drawing room, spacious but not too large, with a beautiful landscape stretched before the window.' She and her new husband were amused by the waiters, who were much more talkative here and at Monmouth than they were in Southampton.[111]

Tour Boats

The point of Ross was never the town itself or its inns or the church or the dinner or the beds or even the omnipresent John Kyrle, but the Tour you took from it. The boats were fairly standard in design, though they got bigger as time went on in response to demand, with some large enough to take 14 passengers. Some were built by Thomas Skynner at Hereford, who advertised a new pleasure boat with oars and mast in September 1780: 'sails swift and draws but little water, will sail over the shallowest stream on the river Wye from Hay to Monmouth, at the lowest water.'[112] Like the barges, they had to be of small draught because summer levels were often very low. In 1785, for instance, the usual four-hour journey from Ross to Monmouth took eleven hours, the boatmen frequently having to get out and push the boat over the shoals. They had to get out again in September 1803, dragging and lifting Joseph Farington's boat with much good humour: 'One of them entertained the other by saying "it was like pulling a pig to market".' At other places they had to get into the water and lift it with poles. (John Gardnor published a print of 'Gotheridge' Castle [Goodrich] in 1792, showing a barge sailing downstream, laden with barrels, probably of cider, with a man at the prow with a pole to push them off rocks and shallows). If, as sometimes happened, a boat had to be lightened, the passengers encountered a new hazard as they were carried ashore on the backs of the boatmen. 'Unfortunately' said Farington, 'one of these assistants had by too repeated an application of his Bottle become a little unsteady & giving way under the weight of Mr Evans He was dropt into the water and with a narrow escape of falling upon his back into it.'

Torrington's boat in 1787 was rowed by the usual crew of three; two rowing downstream, the third steering; on the return journey the helmsman had to help haul and row the boat back up against the current. 'Our galley was well fitted up' said Torrington, 'with a carpet, wooden sides and awning, and lockers surrounding a table, at which 14 people might commodiously dine.' Sarah Anne Wilmot's boat in 1795 held ten, and had benches, she said, for four or five men to row. In her case there were the usual three, the third man acting as a tour guide as well as steering.[113] Dukes got, or imagined they got, the best treatment, and Rutland had a boat called the *Lively*, 'the best of those employed for parties' and his steersman 'had been forty years in this particular service', which sounds like George Evans. The distance to Chepstow was 38 miles by water and according to Leigh (1831) it was possible to do Ross to Monmouth in five hours and Monmouth to Chepstow in four, but not, of course, if you got out to look at any of the sights. *The Cambrian Directory* advised against such hurry and, ever zealous for good value, warned that the boatmen 'too frequently suffer [the] most interesting spots to pass unnoticed by strangers, merely from laziness, or to avoid the delay of a few minutes'. This is not a criticism found elsewhere. Leigh went on to say: 'Few persons, however, now pursue the voyage further than Monmouth, as the New Road from that town to Chepstow commands better views of the scenery than those obtained from the Boat.' The problem was that the low summer water left passengers gazing at the river banks rather than what was above them. The full two-day trip continued to be available, however, and the Blanchards took most of it in 1847.

There are detailed descriptions of tour boats in the diaries of Thomas Martyn and A.M. Cuyler. The *Friendship*, under 'our intelligent and communicative commander', Commodore Evans, was 'commodious', said Martyn, using the word used by Heath about Egerton's original boat. It had 'an awning of oiled cloth sufficiently elevated to admit you to stand upright.' There are disappointingly few pictures of tour boats, but the best, by Nicholas Pocock, shows four oarsmen and passengers actually sitting on the roof of what seems to be one of the large 'houseboats'.[114] (See colour plate 1.) William Coxe and Sir Richard Colt Hoare, whose boat seated eight plus the oarsmen, needed theirs against the sun, but in case of rain the awning had 'sides which let down and keep you completely dry.'[115] Roscoe was not the only person to describe his boat as 'not unlike a gondola, when its tarpauling [*sic*] was spread over the framework.' But Mavor had a problem in 1805: 'The use of a sail was proscribed, on account of the danger from eddying winds.' And though Mrs Blanchard sat with her new husband under theirs, feeling 'like King and Queen, of the river' as they set off in 1847, the scuds of wind came on so strong the boatmen had to take the awning down; the wind was turning it into a sail. Jane was glad then of her shawls, coats and plaid scarfs. The weather was so bad in fact that their boatmen declined to go beyond Redbrook, on the grounds of health and safety; of course they may just have been lazy. Under the awning was a table 'to draw or regale upon' as Sarah Anne Wilmot put it, and 'lockers to hold books, or *bottles*.' The books would include sketch-books and guide-books – Bloomfield took both Gilpin and Heath in 1807. The table also served as a dining-table if you didn't want to go ashore for your picnic. There were two benches for the rowers in front, and one behind for the steersman.

Cuyler describes two boats in 1807, one 'a large House-Boat, covered over, and having windows in the sides, which might be put up or down as occasion might require, with four boatmen and affording convenient room for twelve people', which sounds like the one Pocock painted. The other was a six-seater, requiring three boatmen. The price for the journey to Chepstow was £5 12s (£5.60p) for the Houseboat and four guineas (£4.20p) for the six-seater. The cost was creeping up. According to Shaw, in 1788 it had been one and a half guineas (£1.52½p) to Monmouth and the same again from Monmouth to Chepstow, plus ten shillings (50p) for 'provisions' for the men, and the same price is quoted by Heath in 1799, the *Cambrian Directory* in 1801 and Farington in 1803, though the boatmen then needed sixpence more – half a guinea in total (52½p). In 1801 Thomas Martyn had paid four guineas (£4.20) plus the half a guinea (52½p) for the boatmen. He did not regard this as excessive:

> But when we consider that the distance is 50 Miles and all performed by the labor [*sic*] of the Oar, that the Commodore has two Men to feed and pay, and that from Landogo [on the return upstream] they have to tow the boat near 32 Miles against the stream, to which if you add the wear and tear of the Boat and Tackle and consider that these Voyages are only made during the summer Months when the Weather is favourable it will not appear immoderate. The Traveller who prefers economy may forego this pleasure and by continuing his Post Chaise will shorten the distance full one half and reach Chepstow for about 35 shillings [£1.75p].

Heath goes on quoting three guineas (£3.15p) for the trip till his last edition in 1826, but in 1811 Simond paid £4 10s (£4.50p), plus 5s (25p) for pourboire. As well as an awning his boat had carpet on the seats, and perhaps was a large one. In 1824 Margaret Martineau travelled in one of the smaller boats, the *Prince of Denmark* (named for the actual prince who had recently visited) 'with two men to row and one to steer ... £1 2s (£1.10p) is the price of a boat from Ross to Monmouth ... they expected two to three shillings (10-15p) amongst them.'[116] In 1831 the price varied from £1 10s (£1.50p) to £2, depending on the size of the boat, for each section of the trip, according to Leigh, but 'the boatmen expect nothing but a trifling donation for beer'. Haggling no doubt entered into the individual price, though many tourists left negotiation to the manager of their hotel, who usually provided the picnic.

There was no set time for leaving Ross, though James Wathen urged the Misses Bird to make an early start in 1798 – 8am at the latest, which is when Bloomfield left. William Coxe and Sir Richard Colt Hoare started even earlier, at 7. Farington left at 8.45, Martyn at 10, the Blanchards at 10.30, and Shaw, in 1788, and Mavor, in 1805, at 3 pm. There was no tide on the first part of the tour, and the only advantage of an early start was that it gave you more time to wander about on shore.

In earlier editions of *The Excursion*, Heath warns his readers that they will have to walk a quarter of a mile down the hill from their inn to the 'meadow where they embark', which sounds as though there was no proper quay. The walk was not an inconvenience, as the path was easy 'being a continued descent' and the boatmen carried your luggage. Furthermore, the proprietor of their vessel accompanied the passengers 'so that the ear is not pained with the coarseness of language, too frequently heard from the navigators of public rivers', as Torrington's had been. By his final edition,

Heath was able to boast that whatever inconvenience there had been was now overcome 'by the *bel esprit* of the persons entrusted with its management, who have erected a flight of spacious stone steps, at the Dock Pitch, for conducting the *elegantly dressed Fair* in their way, to what a gentleman has designated "the *deceitful* stream".' And Willett said 'convenient boats and careful men' were available. There was always, however, one element no amount of *bel esprit* or care could do anything about: the weather. Gilpin himself suffered from Welsh Borders rain, which an anonymous diarist of 1776 said was like 'a great river poured through an immense Sieve. It falls in Spouts as in Italy and indeed in all mountainous countries.' There are many accounts of tourists getting soaked, like the poor Blanchards. However, Bloomfield's party of ten, one of whom had a clarinet, had sent their sociables (four-wheeled carriages with side-seats facing each other) on ahead to meet them at Monmouth and Chepstow. Ready for picturesque adventure, they were lucky:

The morrow came, and beauty's eye
Ne'er beamed upon a lovelier sky;
.... The boatman stript;
Glee at the helm exulting tript,
And wav'd her flower-encircled wand,
'Away, away, to Fairy Land.'

The First Day

This interesting voyage will afford an infinite variety of the picturesque, the pleasing, the tremendous, and the sublime of nature.

Mark Willett, *An Excursion*, second ed, nd, 26.

'The first part of the river from Ross', wrote Gilpin, 'is tame.' The only thing to see was the ruins of Wilton Castle, 'shrouded with a few trees'. Grose complained that a new house 'white and of the trimmest sort' had been built next to it, which didn't go with the dirty red stone of the castle. Louisa Anne Twamley, more than 60 years later, was still indignant about it. She experienced 'disappointment and vexation at the vile taste which has grafted a little, pert, formal, fresh-painted, Venetian-blinded, muslin-curtained "Cottage of gentility", upon the crumbling old towers and ivy-grown walls of the hoary castle', one of whose towers has been turned

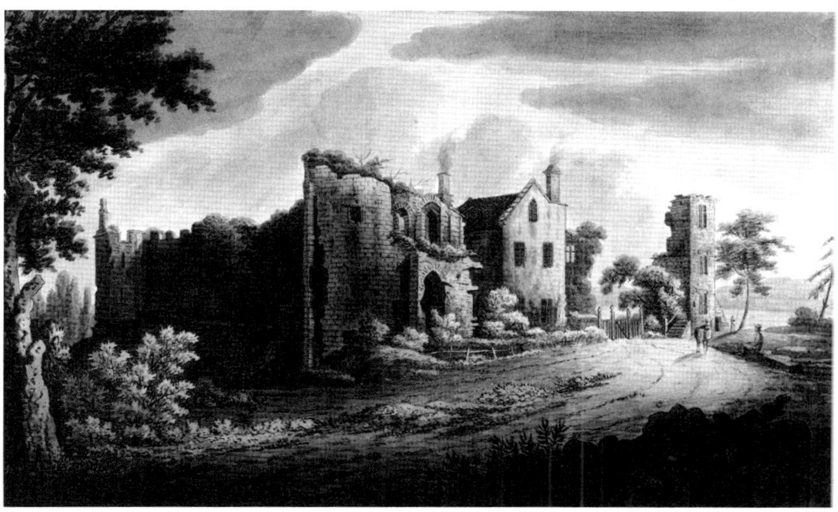

Wilton Castle by Sir Richard Colt Hoare.
(© Yale Center for British Art)

into 'a *thatched* summer-house, among similar travesties.' Not many people, other than artists, bothered to stop here, whether from aesthetic snobbery or eagerness to get to Goodrich, though some, like Henry Skrine, walked down from Ross and picked up their boat at the foot of the bridge. Bloomfield started working himself up to be political:

Who curb'd the barons kingly power ?...
…………..The fabric falls,
The rubbish of their splendid halls,
Time in his march hath scatter'd wide,
And blank oblivion strives to hide.

No doubt less inspired passengers were busy settling themselves, making sure their cushions were not damp, trying out their coloured glasses, checking the weather and the lunch boxes, and catching up on the reading of Gilpin which they'd meant to do the night before. Rutland's party found the river uncommonly rapid and swollen to a remarkable height after rain, which may have added excitement to the trip, but the water was so muddy that one of his two accompanying clergyman was unable to use the fishing-rod he'd brought. The boatmen, no doubt, were sizing up their passengers for tips.

The first sight of any interest after Wilton would have been the roving at Moor Meadow. A roving was a point at which the towpath crossed from one side of the river to the other when, for instance, the cliffs came too close to the bank for the bow-hauliers to be able to work their barges. There were at least eight rovings between Ross and Monmouth,[117] and where tourism and commerce met, tourism would have had to give way. Rogers, who travelled with Gilpin's own copy of the third edition of *Observations.*[118] and wrote some of his earliest verses on a blank leaf, was one of the most observant of all Wye tourists and noted that the white flowers on the water were known as 'greeds'. And he saw what passed for a timberyard somewhere under Pencraig. After that there was, at least for a time, a 'rope' at Glewstone. Bloomfield's party was entertained hereabouts, or so we must hope, by a fellow passenger:

Here, as the light boat skimm'd along,
The clarionet, and chosen song,
That mellow, wild, Eolian lay
'Sweet in the Woodlands,' roll'd away,
In echoes down the stream, that bore
Each dying close to every shore …

Music seems to have been as inescapable then as now.

Goodrich Castle

It would, however, have been but minor entertainment for those who had read their Gilpin and knew that the first great scene on the Wye was about to appear: Goodrich Castle on its bluff. The boatmen could rest on their oars while their passengers examined a view that Gilpin did not scruple to call '*correctly picturesque*' and which many painters sketched. When the oars were resumed, the boat came down to Goodrich Ferry, where the 'rope' cost a penny, though people rode through the water when it was low to save their money. It was possible to get a frugal breakfast and, Heath says, take advantage of the 'clean room' at Mr Davis's Ferry House where in summer strangers were frequently seen enjoying themselves under the shade of a fine spreading oak tree. (Those visiting Goodrich by carriage would find the same facilities at the Cross Keys.) A 'clean room' may have meant a reasonably decent privy, though eighteenth century notions of decency and privacy were not ours. Fosbroke, writing his first guidebook in 1818, found in the village of Staunton near Monmouth 'a very ridiculous relick of British antiquity. It was a privy in a populous part of the village, placed on the side of the high road, to which the door opens, apparently to invite or serve strangers ... Even at reputable village Inns on this tour, any door to these places is considered unnecessary.' It may have been delicacy that prevented any tour diarist from mentioning this, but it is more likely that no one expected anything else.

Gilpin did not climb up to the castle, as rain had set in 'and would not permit us to land.' He didn't mind the rain as much as some, writing that 'scenery at hand suffers less under such circumstances, than scenery at a distance; which it totally obscures', and 'the rain gave a gloomy grandeur to many of the scenes; and by throwing a veil of obscurity over the removed banks of the river, introduced, now and then, something like a pleasing distance.' This was certainly making the most of it, but keeping his boots dry meant he could give no description of the castle or its history for those who wanted them. Torrington and Osborn's horses crossed the ferry without terror and the ferryman guided them to the castle where Torrington, his mind often on money, thought that 'Were a cottage built near such a building, what advantage he the cottager wou'd find in fencing them from cattle; and by his attendance on strangers !' The castle had not then been tidied up, and Grose had already complained that 'The whole building is so surrounded with rocks & steep banks of trees, that it is impossible to draw a near view of it.' Rogers concurred: 'Elm and ash trees of considerable height have taken possession of its internal courts'. The mid-twelfth century keep, of a lighter-coloured stone than the rest of the castle, still made a great impression. By the time Greville came in 1839 there was 'A female custos, zealous and intelligent, whose husband ... was continually occupied in clearing away rubbish and exposing the remains of the old Castle.' This was Mrs Morgan. Comparison between the pictures of William Turner of Oxford and John Chessell Buckler (catalogue numbers 7 and 8) show how much work had had to be done.

Skrine took the path up what Willett called the 'craggy acclivity', passing the old prison with a door studded with nails, though Heath said this route was 'very incommodious for well-dressed women, being in part through fields of high grass in the season, and of steep ascent, but by taking a circuit of half a mile, a pleasant path leads to [the castle], with ease and convenience.' The old Court House was now a barn and granary. Once at the top, there was a hint of rural superiority in his cumbersome comment: 'The eye accustomed to the country round London, must enjoy a pleasurable relief, in contemplating the sublime terminations to many points of this view', and he went on to claim that, but for a lack of the fine skies which add such a lustre to Italian art, it would attract the pencil of a Gaspard, or even a Nicolas Poussin. He thought, though, the castle would be better for more ivy to cover its dingy red stone, but it was torn down and fed to the local sheep in winter.

According to H.L.V. Fletcher, the castle had floors of Irish soil, so no toad could live in it, and Irish timbers so spiders and cobwebs were kept away. They seem to have kept trouble away too, as it saw little if any action till the Civil War, when a 'roaring Meg' mortar played a part in its surrender to

Parliamentary forces, during which, a tale tells, Alice Birch and Charles Clifford were drowned while making their escape. They haunt it, allegedly, still. After the castle was captured its owner, the then Countess of Kent, was informed that she would receive compensation for the thorough slighting which reduced it to the ruin the tourists now enjoyed, but how much she got is not known.[119] 'We naturally indulged reflections on past scenes', said *The Cambrian Directory*, 'contemplated the traces of ancient splendour; and connecting what remains, with what is destroyed, we pondered on the vanity of human art, and the ravages of time, which exhibit, in this ruin, their completest triumph.' 'Pleasing melancholy' such as this was easily brought on by a ruin, and for the more democratically inclined tourist there was gratification in the idea of tyrannical medieval barons being brought low so that the modern middle-classes could enjoy the liberty to travel. Barber reported in 1803 that 'Until lately two ponderous helmets were shewn as belonging to [an Irishman called Mackbeth and his son], one of which held half a bushel'. He too, though not at all a democrat, could not resist a certain modern triumphalism: 'Thus it was in feudal ages, when every potent baron dared violate the strongest bands of society; when the property and freedom of humble individuals, and the honour of females, were subjected to the will of the contiguous power; and suffering innocence could only plead the wrongs that she suffered at the tribunal of the oppressor. But, alas! it is a principle of our being, it is a fact which ought to be treasured in the minds of Britons, that where power is without control it seldom fails to act unjustly.' Edward Collins, always ready to prose in verse on general themes, wrote:

> Obedience to some power must always be;
> Thrice happy land, where law is equity,
> Where feudal rights are all abolish'd,
> Where the prince enjoys his dignity;
> The wealthy peer his ancient honour;
> Talent oft meets encouragement;
> And the ingenious artisan,
> Not only just but liberal reward.
> And yon poor peasant in the midst of toil,
> However humble and obscure his lot,
> Appears content, for well he knows,
> The hard earn'd fruits for which he labours,
> Are sure to be his own;
> Nor fears the oppressive hand of power.[120]

Greater knowledge of the terms and conditions under which agricultural labourers worked might have made Collins less upbeat. But the image of a well-ordered and contented society was what most tourists, and native poets and artists too, wanted. It may have been reinforced by such occasions as the dinner recorded by Heath on May 1st 1804, given by the officers of the Archenfield Volunteer Infantry to the non-commissioned officers and private soldiers in the large court of the castle, with lots of cider and patriotic songs. Not so pleasing melancholy, possibly even some social discontent, may, though, have been felt the following morning.

Bloomfield spent an hour on shore at Goodrich, but he'd done his reflections on power and glory at Wilton so he chatted to Pollett, the boatman, who said 'he had often bought good cider for sixpence a gallon, and expected it as cheap this season', which was encouraging. Millicent Bant and Lady Wilson went butterfly hunting and 'found two Village Nymphs taking views of the Castle, who quizzed us'. The Blanchards rooted up some violets (they were there in May) but the roots of the lilies of the valley were too deep for similar spoliation, and they left their umbrella behind. They rested a few minutes in a cottage, where the children made a bad impression. They were 'dirty, shy, and yet desirous of being noticed.' The Franco-American Louis Simond, resistant to the charms of the Wye, complained, either here or more probably at Symonds Yat, that 'We were here beset by a great number of beggars, attracted, and in fact created, by the alms of travellers. The hopes of getting their bread that way has prevented honest exertions, and they have become wretchedly poor by pretending to be so. This is more or less the case wherever there is any sight to attract travellers.' Unlike most tourists, he was happy to include a drawing of a Welsh beggarwoman in his book (see p.18). But he was contemptuous of fellow-travellers: 'Wales and the Wye are visited by all tourists; we are precisely in the tract, and meet them at all the inns – stalking round every ruin of castle or abbey, – and climbing every high rock for a prospect; each with his Gilpin or his Cambrian Guide in his hand, and each, no doubt, writing a journal. This is rather ridiculous and discouraging.' He admitted, though, that 'Goodrich Castle is a very fine ruin', which became in the French edition of his tour (1817) 'Goodrich-castle est une ruine tres-bien ruinée.'

Mary Anne Hibbert had bad weather in 1823, but she and her companions were resourceful. They stopped at the ferry house and ordered 'a fire, dried ourselves & umbrellas and then drew a table to the window & with admirable philosophy began retouching some of our sketches of yesterday. We were soon rewarded by a gleam of sunshine & in pattens [overshoes with wooden soles on an iron base which raised your feet above the mud] began to scale the heights leading to [the] castle … our progress was impeded by sundry slight showers but on the whole we fared better than we expected, and after spending about two hours & taking two sketches amongst the ruins, we returned to our boat, ate some bread & cheese & began to think of enjoying ourselves when a storm came aptly enough to remind us of the instability of all human pleasures.' Rutland's party, equally rained on, let down the awning on all sides and also got on with their lunch.

Rutland says that 'no less than three pleasure boats had gone down the river before us' in early August 1797, but Prince Puckler-Muskau, who had, astonishingly, chosen to make the boat tour in December, was all alone. He found the winter river 'rather impetuous' at Goodrich ferry (to which he had walked, having sent the boat on ahead), and the ascent to the castle 'arduous'. His cap blew off as he entered 'as if the spirit of the place would teach me respect to the shade of its knightly possessor.' In summer and autumn, he complained, the Wye was never free from visitors, but 'as it probably never entered the head of a methodical Englishman to make a tour in winter ... during the whole day he found neither guide nor any sort of help for travellers'. The ladder for climbing to the top of the highest tower had been 'removed to winter quarters', so with the help of the boatmen and his servant, he constructed a Jacob's ladder to get there.[121] After he had 'duly grubbed into every hole and corner' he descended the hill on the other side and had breakfast in the boat as it travelled rapidly along on a rare nice day, the air as warm as April in his German homeland.

From the 1830s you could take 'a romantic winding path' from the castle to the gothic revival Goodrich Court, built by Edward Blore for Sir Samuel Meyrick between 1828 and 1831.[122] Meyrick had wanted to buy and repair Goodrich Castle itself as a home for his vast collection of medieval armour but the owners would not sell, so he bought the upstream bluff instead. Blore's towers and turrets look, to modern eyes, pure Disney, but they were described by *The Penny Magazine* as 'that admirable imitation of the antique' and 'the most perfect thing of its kind in England' and they embodied the anti-industrial, highly conservative attitude to modern life, typified by the novels of Sir Walter Scott, and which can be said to have reached its height with the Eglinton Tournament of August 1839, with its knights in armour, its Queen of beauty and drenching Scottish rain.

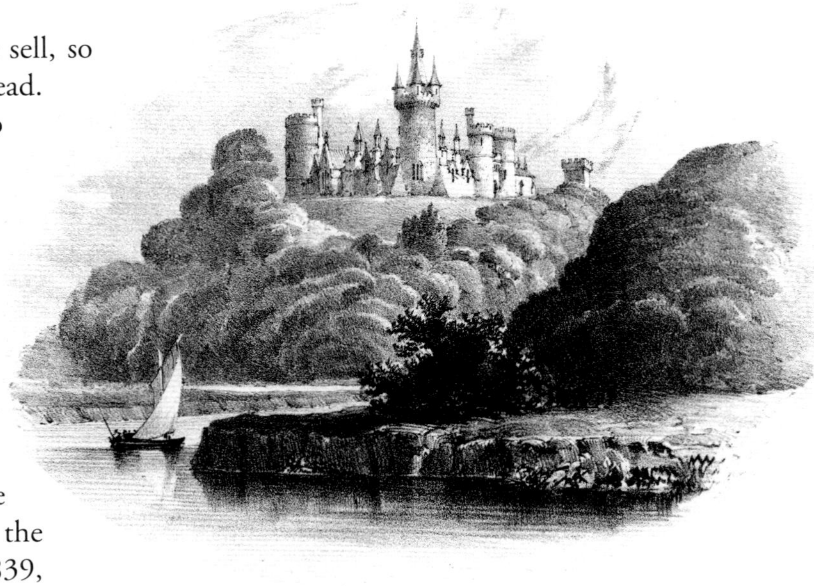

Goodrich Court, Drawn, Printed and Published by George Rowe of Cheltenham. (From a collection of his prints of the Wye Valley, Chepstow Museum)

The American Catherine Sinclair, visiting Goodrich Court in June 1833, 'rushed up' a steep hill from the river to see this 'amusing' but 'most eccentric' house. She was astonished:

> A gallery, like the great armoury at Dresden, has been erected within the house, measuring about eighty feet long, with more than fifty full-length figures in it, carved and painted to imitate life. The whole party is arranged along the wall, clothed in complete armour and placed in warlike attitudes ... In one room, a complete tournament was represented, with heralds, spectators and umpires, standing round, and two knights, mounted on wooden horses, not hobby-horses, nor were they at all like Madame Tassaud's [*sic*] waxwork exhibition ... though the family at Goodrich Court are Protestants, an ancient Popish chapel has recently been added in exquisite taste, with a screen of beautifully carved oak, and we were told that a kneeling nun is to be placed there, with a wooden monk to correspond ...

Each room was fitted up according to the taste of different periods and nations and she was particularly struck by an apartment devoted to an Indian Rajah and his Queen, and another to South Americans, but seeing no accommodation for the living felt 'it would appear rather awful to sit in an evening with 'our lanterns dimly burning', and 50 armed knights, frowning on every side, sword in hand.' The medieval mood was broken when the descent to the river proved no laughing matter. It had been raining heavily and 'if we had been standing on a mountain of butter it could scarcely have been more slippery!' Britton was less romantic: the court furnished 'a most impressive text and lesson for the historian and antiquary.' It was not everyone's view. 'At present its newness and sharpness make it rather striking than beautiful', said Twamley, who was shown round the collection by Meyrick himself, though she was not interested in weapons. Greville called it 'a strange kind of bastard castle', though 'admirably situated' and Wordsworth, for whom the castle was very important as the place where he'd met the little girl who had inspired 'We are Seven', was apoplectic at 'Sir

Meyrick's' rival. He called it 'a fantastic new castle set up ... as if to show how far modern art can go in surpassing all that could be done by antiquity and Nature, with their united graces, remembrances, and associations. I could have almost wished for power, so much the contrast vexed me, to blow away Sir Meyrick's impertinent structure, and all the possessions it contains.' He would no doubt have found more impertinence in 1847, when the Archaeological Association came on a visit. Meyrick hired Welsh bards and minstrels to perform for them during their meal in the banqueting hall. The following year he died, and just over a century later, in 1950, Wordsworth's wish was met when the Court was demolished.[123]

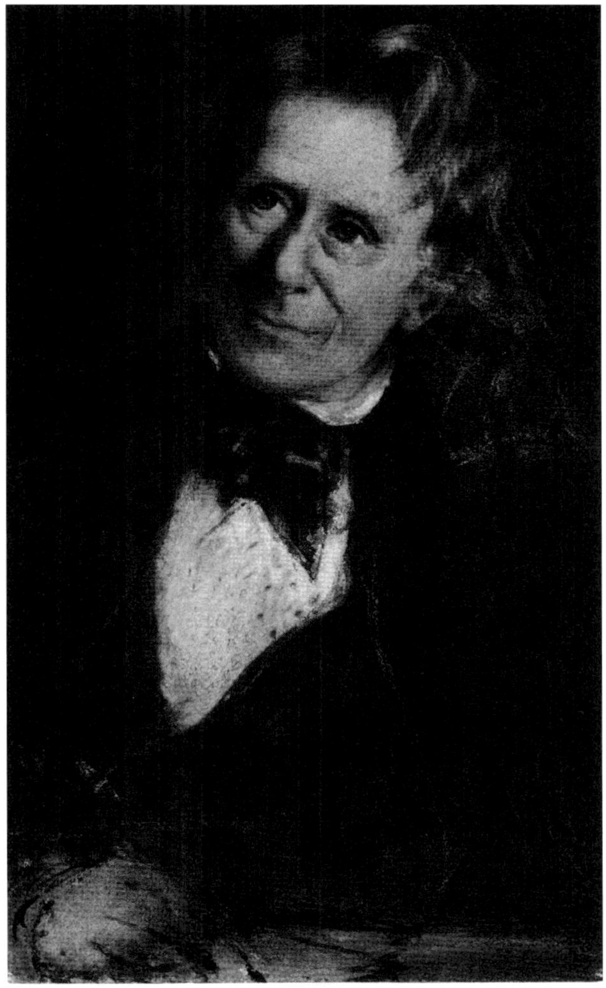

Joshua Cristall by an unknown artist (detail). (© NPG, London)

Visitors to Goodrich were reminded by their guide-books that the grandfather of Jonathan Swift, author of *Gulliver's Travels*, had been the Royalist vicar there during the Civil War, and helped the local blacksmith to make 'cats' – 'three-fanged sharp pointed pieces of iron' which they dropped in the ford to lame Parliamentary horses. There was a silver cup, left to the church by Dean Swift himself, author of *Gulliver's Travels*, and Heath gives the family almost as full a history as he does to Kyrle at Ross. From 1823 to 1841 you could have met Joshua Cristall, one the Wye's few locally based artists, in the village (catalogue nos 11-20 and 24). He lived at a cottage called Granton close to the church, and drew many pictures of local scenes, specialising in the fern-burners who worked on Coppet Hill. But most of those on the water tour skipped the village, and either went back to their boat at the ferry-house or walked on to the remains of Flanesford Priory, where it had gone on to await them.

Below Goodrich

The walk was not recommended by *The Cambrian Directory*, as it considered the reach below the ferry well worth seeing. Rogers commented on the anglers for salmon fry and grayling, knee-deep in the water, and he very much liked a basketmaker's cottage: 'in his little garden, which was almost a precipice, hung linen to dry on a line, and his threshold was strewn with heaps of rushes in the sun.' Mavor too liked the cottages visible from the river: 'for what real pleasure can arise from the contemplation of wild nature, however inviting her features, if the abodes of men and comforts of society are excluded?' Shaw commented on the coppicing of the woods here, and the lime kilns on the hills, and was fascinated by one particular building, 'a small hut by the water side carelessly heaped together'. It was a squatter's cottage, and he quotes the local tradition whereby if you could get a hut up, and a pot boiling on the fire, in twelve hours (some said a day), you had the right to stay there and live in it. Tourists were fascinated by this survival, though Heath, as we shall see, thought it nonsense. Shaw's shack, however legally or illegally raised, made a great contrast with Flanesford Priory where, said the *Cambrian Directory*, 'in many parts of the walls, the initials of names of persons, who have long since paid the debt of nature, and left behind no other memorial are carved with characteristic rudeness, shewing, to every passing stranger, the prevalency of that universal passion – the love of fame.'

From Flanesford there was a longish stretch down to Coldwell Rocks and Symonds Yat, with a few furnaces among the trees, whose smoke was always found attractive. At Bishopswood Twamley was taken with an ivy-hung boat-house, but there was nothing much else to stop for, unless, like Coxe, you wanted to visit Courtfield, home of the Catholic Vaughans, where Henry V was brought up and you could inspect the artificial hermitage and the folly. Shaw records 'a few fine deer were bounding on the ridgey banks', but the current Vaughan was a minor and the house was neglected and the gardens in a total state of decay when Heath wrote in 1799. However by 1803, things had improved; the heir had taken possession and was planning what became a 'very handsome mansion, compatible with the comforts of modern life', built by G.V. Maddox, the Monmouth architect. Mavor enjoyed watching the haymakers at work at Welsh Bicknor, 'among whom we thought we could recognise the parson of the parish or perhaps the curate, setting his flock a laudable example of industry.' This must have been a new appointment, as the previous vicar had been a notorious drunk, and one can tell Heath was glad when he died. Rutland enjoyed the 'delicious perfume' of the corn and hayfields. On the other bank, Lydbrook offered industry of a different sort. It was where the tramroad from the mines in the Forest of Dean met the river, and so the main centre for what Ireland called the 'sooty sable commerce' of the coal trade: 'With all the dark and dingy attributes of this place, involved as it is in smoke, and begirt with coal barges, it yet affords a very pleasing and interesting landscape'.

Lunch below Coldwell Rocks

All travel makes one hungry, and as they approached Coldwell Rocks people were beginning to get peckish after their often early start, and wishing, perhaps, they had taken advantage of a second breakfast at the Goodrich Ferryhouse. There was a spring below the rocks – there still is – which, said Skrine, often induced 'those who navigate the Wye for pleasure to take their cold collation' there, and his party 'dined pleasantly in our boat beneath a high hill crowned with wood, in front of a pile of rocks, which formed a magnificent contrast to the rich and tranquil scenes we had lately beheld'. Anne Cooper and her party were enjoying 'a meal enlivened by witt without gall & pleasantry without coarseness' there when two fishermen with coracles on their backs descended from the woods '& soon after we observed them paddling on the river, & throwing their flies with great dexterity.' When they'd gone, the party retired 'to a shade under a woody steep, & cooled our wine in the spring'.[124] Shaw called the place 'an amphitheatre of romantic beauties, beyond the power of words or canvas to express' and added 'We only wanted sun to paint the colours stronger.' Rutland said the cottages hung on the cliffs like bird-nests. Heath found in 1803 that a lime kiln had been erected, and its disagreeable effluvia were spoiling the view (and, presumably, the lunch). But Bloomfield went into raptures:

Noon scorch'd the fields; the boat lay to;
The dripping oars had nought to do ...
Here, in one gay according mind,
Upon the sparkling stream we din'd;
As shepherds free on mountain heath,
Free as the fish that watch'd beneath
For falling crumbs, where cooling lay
The wine that cheer'd us on our way ...

He liked his drink. The party was joined by some gleaners from Coppet Hill:

.... And here
They doubtless shar'd an equal cheer;
Enjoy'd the feast with equal glee,
And rais'd the song of revelry:
Yet half-abash'd [,] reserv'd, and shy,
Watch'd till the strangers glided by ...

Joshua Cristall's many drawings and watercolours of local men and women working in the fields sometimes show them pausing for refreshment, but it is unlikely that they were having as good a lunch as the tourists; perhaps, like the fish, they were hoping for a few crumbs. Class barriers were high at the time, but Margaret Martineau, who stayed in her boat and drifted quietly down as she enjoyed her dinner doubly 'from the novelty and the sweet stillness of the scene', was astonished to find that the steersman's son, who was presumably one of the oarsmen, was an artist. 'He showed us some of his drawings and was anxious for us to purchase one. He draws so well that I should think he must be a teacher of drawing. It seemed odd to hear our boatmen recommending me to attempt something more than pencil and to see him standing over me when I was sketching and telling me that I was beginning it too large. He was a very intelligent young man. His father was a careful and civil man.'

As well as food and drink and art lessons, the picnic site had other attractions. It had become a tradition for the barristers on the Oxford summer circuit (Rutland said it was judges who came on circuit from Bristol) to take the tour down the river at the end of the sessions, during which, no doubt after a good lunch, the boatmen named the most prominent rocks after the most prominent lawyers. This must have proved a successful scheme for gaining tips, for they tried it on non-juridical tourists too. Bloomfield, though now largely forgotten, was then at the height of his fame; his poem *The Farmer's Boy* (1800) had sold a phenomenal 26,000 copies in three years. When the boatmen decided to name one of the rocks after him, he was delighted:

In such a spot to leave a name,
At least is no opprobrious fame.

'Pleasing melancholy' could also be indulged here. In 1804 the 15-year-old John Warre, of the famous port wine family, went swimming after lunch – always inadvisable – and drowned in front of his parents, brother and sisters. Bloomfield was much affected:

– Hark! their shrieks!
The dreadful language horror speaks!

There is a lengthy description of the accident, the silver cups given to the would-be rescuers (and what happened to them),[125] and the full inscription of the monument to the poor boy's memory, in Heath's *Excursion*. (His own 12-year-old, drowned at Monmouth in 1808, had no such memorial.)[126] Alas, there were vandals about again, and Fosbroke reported in 1818 that some wretch had mutilated John Warre's memorial; but it is still there. Catherine Sinclair was told in 1833 that the family were seated in their carriage while their son, bathing at their suggestion, was drowning.

Symonds Yat

There was now a choice. From the picnic place to New Weir was four miles by water, though only a few hundred yards as the crow flew. You could therefore stay in your boat and be rowed round the Huntsham loop, in which case you would pass the western side of the village of Symonds Yat, (known as Coldnose, according to Rogers's boatman, because it never saw the sun); or you could get out and climb the steep cliff to the Symonds Yat viewpoint, then scramble down to the eastern. Some people, Luke Booker among them, suggested creating a short-cut via a tunnel under the rock, burning the spoil as lime, but nothing came of that. Gilpin, because of the weather and perhaps his age and corpulence, stayed in his boat, as did Coxe, which is what *The Cambrian Directory* advised, as there was good river scenery to be seen, and the boatmen only recommended the climb as they were lazy. Catherine Sinclair took a very different view. Her oarsmen were exhausted by the long row round, and her companion gave them some money to buy refreshments; quite devout, Catherine was pleased 'to find, that instead of buying spirits, they procured a quantity of bread and cheese to bestow on their families at home.' But most people crossed the river to where, according to Warner, 'The little cottages scattered at their feet, the neat residences of industrious labour, form a pleasing accompaniment; exhibiting simplicity contrasted with majesty.' This was the picturesque way of looking at it, but in 1795 Sarah Anne Wilmot showed a more humane one, expressing unusual concern for the cottagers' way of life: 'bread was too scarce & too dear for them to buy ... & of other meat they never bought any, they liv'd on potatoes & vegetables'. She was worried that too much corn was exported down the river 'in this time of general scarcity, it is an evil to be justly complained of, our greatest blessings may be perverted & become our heaviest grievances'. Free trade and protectionism were here in traditional battle. She later observed the custom of the local peasantry of cutting 'ferns ... which they burn to ashes, then wet & mix into paste, then work it in to balls which they sell for washing & whitening blankets & flannel, in spinning & weaving, of which the industrious poor find their principal employment & support'. Heath was more cynical: 'the inhabitants ... are always happy in the return of the summer season ; for they ... are ever ready to serve as guides ... well knowing, that the hand of an Englishman is ever ready to reward their attentions.' But an anonymous tourist in 1798 was more compassionate, writing that his guide

> was a haggard, decrepid [*sic*] old woman worn by age in attending strangers in creeping up these steep ascents; whether from the hope of reaping greater bounty for her toil or the severer pressure of real indigence, her garrulous tale of incidents were such as to excite our compassion in a larger gratuity than the merit of her services seemed to demand; there was mingled in her description

of woe, a strain of genuine calamity, that turns the heart to pity e'er it is ware; having furnished us with instruction to Redbrook she sighing left us with her blessing and turned toward her cheerless hut.'[127]

Bloomfield, who got lost going up, was rescued by the same old woman 'who led us over this isthmus, until our bones ached.'

Symonds Yat was pronounced Simon's in those days, according to Grose, though to the Blanchards 72 years later, it was Simmons. There were various theories as to which Simon gave it its name and what a Yat or Yatch (Grose again) was, the general opinion being it was derived from 'gate'. Herbs grew there in profusion: 'Wild thyme and various mountain productions scent the gale, and yield a rich fragrance to the smell'[128] and *The Cambrian Directory* was pleased to discover 'a very remarkable polysyllabical articulate echo, and we reckoned twelve distinct reverberations from the explosion of a gun, fired on this spot.' Anne Cooper's party were frightened by the way 'the Rock on which we sat, projected far beyond its base & seemed to hang over the river. The gentlemen crept forwards by turns to a tree which sprouted from the ridge, & made their companions shudder at their situation.' Perhaps their hair stood on end too. Sarah Anne Wilmot, though surrounded by 'all the charms that Nature can bestow[,] Wood, Rock, Mountains, Plains & Water', was again intrigued by the life of the locals: 'a young woman with a lovely infant in her arms & a boy of four years and seven months old were our guides; they were cloth'd in rags but clean & in the mother's face patient resignation sat personified. She had been married six years and seven months & had 3 children living – her husband earn'd 6 shillings a week which was all they could earn, as she had always had Infants to nurse & they pd. 5s a yr. to Ld. Gage for rent. Luxuries are purchased too dearly when misery like this pays.' The Blanchards were accosted by 'two hardy bonnetless girls', whom they commissioned to gather more wild flower roots for them. The sun was shining now, and 'the little birds seemed to enjoy its brightness for they carrolled away most joyously.' Jane was supremely happy and felt 'in such a peculiar degree what gratitude I owed to God for having given me such a husband.' Nonetheless, she felt in need of a rest, and went into the small school built in 1838 (now a much enlarged house). There the lame schoolmistress, who had a cheerful contented-looking face, though obliged to use crutches, and who was rather past middle life and plainly, almost meanly clad, made them welcome. By a move of her hand she made the 20 or so children rise. Jane, who may have been a schoolmistress herself, was extremely interested. The school cost the pupils a penny a week, and the only food they got was bread and water, and sometimes not much of the bread, but they were healthy and clean. Jane asked if they would sing for her, and they did, 'the old dame trotting up and down their ranks beating time with her bony fingers'. The song was 'Look up in the corner the little clock stands / And points to the time with its two little hands'. Jane slightly modified her impression of the dame when she noticed the cane at her side, and the pettish way she sometimes spoke. She then heard the children read, and was quite impressed. After another song, the Blanchards left, giving the old lady a few shillings with which to treat the children.

But it was the view not the school that people came to see. Gilpin, of course, didn't see it, but the politician and landscape gardener Lord Lyttelton (1709-1773) was an early visitor and was said to have been so fond of it that he came once a year to see it till he died. 'The course of the Wye', said an anonymous diarist, telling this story, 'twisting like a Snake is very Extraordinary and justifies the name of Vaga which was given it by the Romans.'[129] Booker, who claimed to have climbed Symonds Yat at least ten times by 1832, once bet a bottle of wine that he could throw a stone into the river on either side, but lost.

New Weir

After admiring the view, there was the alarm of another steep and slippery track down to New Weir, though as Heath said, 'going with gravity lessens the inconvenience'. Mary Anne Hibbert started by holding her female guide's arm: 'Laetitia followed with a stick to keep her footing, nevertheless she stumbled & fell. I then trusting to my own surefootedness gave her both woman & stick & proceeded alone boldly & fearlessly, but as usual pride had a fall. Not a severe one for the mud was soft, but the liability to such accidents certainly diminished the pleasure of our walk.' Twamley, who herself had fallen on her way up, gathered flowers. She too had a female guide who said 'Ah, Ma'am, you should come here in the summer, we've *hall* the *Horchises*!' Twamley admired the mules who carried fuel to the furnaces on Great Doward. They picked 'their way with unerring sureness of foot, and stepped into the ferry-boat with sagacious staidness'. Her guide lived at the bottom of the path, and they ate in her cottage, with blackberries as dessert.

Gilpin called New Weir 'the second grand scene on the Wye'. He was clearly influenced in his admiration by Whately's description:

> A scene at the New Weir on the Wye, which in itself is truly great and awful, so far from being disturbed, becomes more interesting and important, by the business to which it is destined. It is a chasm between two high ranges of hill, which rise almost perpendicularly from the water; the rocks on the sides are almost heavy masses; and their colour is generally brown; but here and there a pale craggy shape starts up to a vast height above the rest, unconnected, broken and bare: large trees frequently force out their way amongst them; and many of them stand far back in the covert, where their natural dusky hue is deepened by the shadow which overhangs them. The river too, as it retires, loses itself in woods which close immediately above, then rise thick and high, and darken the water. In the midst of all this gloom is an iron forge, covered with a black cloud of smoke, and surrounded with half-burned ore, with coal, and with cinders; the fuel for it is brought down a path, worn into steps narrow and steep, and winding among precipices; and near it is an open space of barren moor, about which are the huts of the workmen. It stands close to the cascade of the Wye, where the agitation of the current is encreased by large fragments of rocks, which have been swept down by floods from the banks, or shivered by tempests from the brow; and the sullen sound, at stated intervals, from the strokes of the great hammers in the forge, deadens the roar of the waterfall ...

No one ever improved on this description, and Gilpin borrowed much of it for his own: on the right 'its lower skirts are adorned with a hamlet; in the midst of which, volumes of thick black smoke, thrown up at intervals, from an iron-forge, as it's [*sic*] fires receive fresh fuel, add double grandeur to the scene.' Tourists had not yet learned to despise industry, and everyone enjoyed the forge's smoke and noise. 'The hammers that beat and shape the fiery mass', wrote one visitor, 'though the sound may be grating to the ear of sensibility, still be it remembered how useful are its purposes and how valuable is every part of *manual labour* that tends to produce the comforts and conveniences of life.'[130] Those comforts and conveniences required a great deal of wood to be

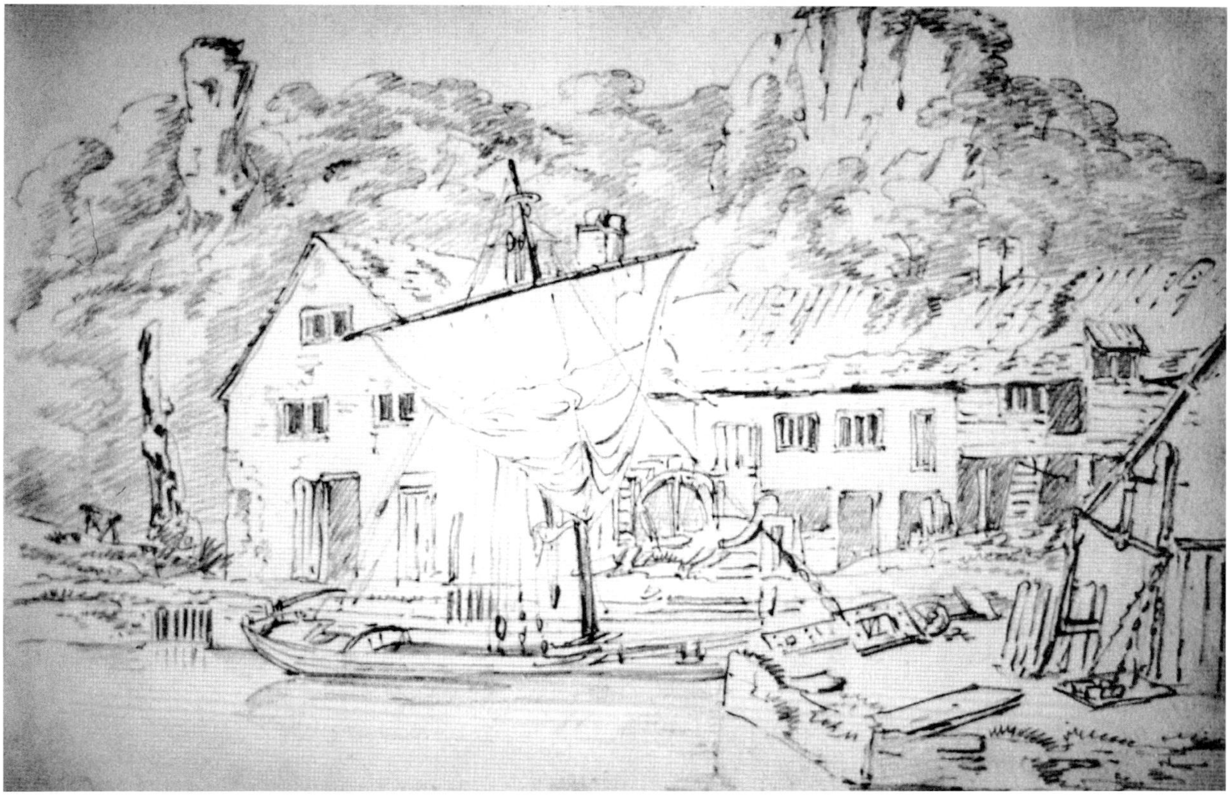

The Forge at New Weir by Joseph Powell. (Monmouth Museum)

burned to make them, and there were far fewer trees on the banks two hundred years ago than today, as can be seen from Wathen's views (catalogue nos 28 and 29). Trees were carefully coppiced every 14 years for charcoal, where they are now allowed pretty much to grow wild.

Heath printed a long document in his *Excursion* about the founding of the forge by George White in the late seventeenth century, though it is now believed there was industry there before that. It was taken over by members of the ironmaster Partridge family in 1753,[131] but it had been given up by 1815 'to the great loss of many industrious families'. Earlier Shaw, apparently oblivious to the local poverty, or possibly in favour of humility in workmen, wrote that the 'thinly scattered cots ... are richly recluse; no gripe of poverty, no perplexing care seem to disturb these quiet hamlets', which was, to put it mildly, obtuse. When Farington and his travelling companion John Hoppner waited in a cottage for their chaise to take them further on, the labourer was soon complaining about his wages. But, classically educated, Shaw likened the forge workers to the Cyclops who forged thunderbolts for Zeus, and ignored the many beggars. *The Cambrian Directory* did not: 'A disagreeable scene here generally occurs, and interrupts the pleasure of contemplation: a large assemblage of beggars, men, women, and children, on the banks, bare-footed, and scarcely a rag to cover them, followed our boat, imploring charity; and several almost throwing themselves into the water, to catch your money, which, every now and then, the bigger seize from the less. This idle crew subsist on the trifles they obtain from strangers; and as beggary is their professed trade, if their wants are not satisfied, they generally add insolence, with an oath, to their demands.'

This is third world behaviour, by tourists and natives alike. The fact is, as we have seen, there was a run of bad harvests at the end of the eighteenth century, and people were often hungry.

The falls were the other great attraction at New Weir, 'of no great height indeed' admitted Gilpin, 'but enough to merit the name of a cascade ... the violence of the stream, and the roaring of the waters, impressed a new character on the scene: all was agitation, and uproar; and every steep, and every rock stared with wildness and terror.' Bloomfield very much enjoyed shooting the rapids of the 'cascade':

> Here rush'd the keel like lightning by;
> The helmsman watch'd with anxious eye;
> And oars alternate touch'd the brim,
> To keep the flying boat in trim.

Rutland gave a graphic description of what it was like on high water:

> The boatmen now prepared us for shooting the fall, by removing all the bottles &c to a place of safety. We had first to go through a lock at one end of the fall, close to the left bank. We were kept some time in the middle of it, as the water ran in at one end as fast as it went out at the other; we could not open the last gate for some time. They were indeed in very bad repair, and we were pent up between the walls, while the women and children, who all flocked from the hamlet to assist, formed interesting groups. At last we escaped, and immediately shot the fall, which occasioned a very pleasant motion.

Later he said they went over rough water at the lower weirs 'almost with the rapidity of a bird'.

New Weir was an important fishery, and tourists came upon coracles below the falls. Rogers was struck by the Fish House (Farington drew it) – 'a long shed to hang the coracles in, & several barked trunks, on which the nets are spread'.[132] Gilpin himself was much impressed by the story of a man who, for a wager, had gone on a voyage from here in a coracle all the way to Lundy Island and back. When he returned after a fortnight 'the account of his expedition was received like a voyage round the world.' Anne Cooper's party met this adventurer's grandson, and Heath, investigating the story, discovered it was true and that the man's name was Luke Hughes, and 'he did not perform the voyage for a wager, but as a frolic'.

If some passengers had uneasy moments watching the coracle men, there were hazards on land, too. Either through the working of rain and wind, or undermined by men burning the rock for lime, from time to time a pinnacle would fall, 'thundering from rock to rock with a terrific plunge into the river', wrote Puckler-Muskau. His boatmen showed him the remains of one of these blocks and 'the monument of an unfortunate Portugese whom it buried in its fall'. Roscoe said some of the rocks here had also got names by the 1830s: they were called Ann, Mary and Elizabeth, presumably after English queens.

New Weir to Monmouth

Below New Weir, Gilpin found 'description flags in running over such a monotony of terms. High, low, steep, woody, rocky and a few others, are all the colours of language we have, to describe scenes.' Heath thought that it was better to walk than to navigate this stretch as 'a transitory view from the boat can convey but a faint idea of its beauty.' There wasn't much to see, though you could stop at Martin's Well. Bloomfield did:

> Bright as young beauty's azure eye,
> And pure as infant chastity,
> Each limpid draught, suffus'd with dew,
> The dipping glass's crystal hue.

Rogers seems to have been the only person to have remarked the Slaughterhouse Stream, where deer were shot when they came down to drink. Warner found a fine echo under Doward rocks, 'the *centrum phonicum* of which appears to be near a spreading beech-tree in the middle of the meadow.' And Ireland, not constrained by time, recommended climbing up to King Arthur's Plain for the view, and visiting a cave known as King Arthur's Hall. It was probably an old mine, said Heath, warning that the path which leads up to it was 'steep, stoney, and uncouth'. Exciting archaeological finds had been made there, including the bones of a giant man. There was always great consciousness of history, real and mythical, as well as aesthetics, among those who described the tour, and there was in fact an iron-age hill fort there, where the Bannerman family, builders of Wyastone, created view-points in the 1830s. Heath deplored the bargee squatters who had moved on to the Dowards with their 'numerous alien progeny' and whom – and here the hostility goes back to the first Poor Laws in Britain and forward to contemporary tabloid xenophobia – the local ratepayers would have to support. The squatters, he frothed, had the outrageous nerve to rebuild their cottages after they were legally knocked down; Shaw was quite wrong about squatting; it required an uninterrupted possession for *sixty years* before a cottage could become a freehold. Heath omitted these remarks from later editions, but Mavor seems to have read them in 1805, for he observes of the Doward cottages that 'from what we heard, they are not all the abodes of innocence and simplicity.'

As the boat approached Monmouth there was Hadnock on the left, but in Willett's fourth edition it says that the house where Dr Griffin, one of the major supporters of David Williams's *Monmouthshire*, had lived, had been taken down and the materials sold. Heath, in mellower mood now, described one Signor Rossignol, 'celebrated for his imitations of the feathered tribe', walking out there at night 'for the purpose of comparing his notes with those he imitated', waking the blackbirds and thrushes and nightingales 'till he had called forth the song of every bird in the wood.' On the right came Dixton with its pretty church, regularly flooded. The river, said Heath, could 'suddenly swell to a boisterous and overwhelming sea; rising many feet in a short space, sweeping everything before it ... and exhibiting one continued scene of terrible grandeur.' He describes the floods of 1795 and the melting of the frozen river in 1814 when the ice was 18 inches thick. It melted 'with a noise equal to a tremendous crash of thunder'. Tours were not undertaken when the river was frozen, of course, but given the river's unreliability and the boatmen's capacity for liquor, there were surprisingly few accidents to tour boats. There was a very nasty one, though, at Chepstow in September 1813, when a boat returning from Tintern with a family of nine, two servants and three boatmen 'ran foul of a hawser that was in a most neglectful manner extended from a brig to one of the piers of the bridge' and only five people were saved. For most tourists, though, the first half of the tour, 'an uninterrupted day of rational enjoyment', as Bloomfield called it, ended safely at Monmouth, in his case at half-past seven in the evening, after eleven and a half hours on and off the water.

'It is not very large but it is pretty well built & there seems to be an air of trade & plenty amongst the Inhabitants' said Jeremiah Milles of Monmouth. He was there on Saturday July 17th 1742, which was market day, and the town was 'so crowded that it seems to be the resort of all the inhabitants of South Wales.' Thomas Gray, though he had never heard of Monmouth before his visit in 1770, said it lay 'in a vale, that is the delight of my eyes, & the very seat of pleasure', though he was probably too much of an aesthete to enjoy the pleasures Grose discovered five years later. Grose was staying with one of the Rooke family at Newland in the Forest of Dean, and though he found Monmouth 'a melancholy indifferent Town' as he passed through for the first time, he enjoyed it a good deal more when he returned with a party for an evening's entertainment which began at the Pleasure Garden created by John Tibbs, landlord of the Beaufort Arms:[133]

> After sending for Miss Jenny Rooke & some other young Ladies from the School, we went over a Bridge & through some fields to a Kind of Vaux Hall, called the Farm, Kept by one Tibbs, here we saw several of the Monmouth beauties at least Goods reputed such. Among them were Miss Davis Miss Bullock, Also Mrs Powell & a Mr Griffin[134] son of Admiral Griffin who tho not otherwise Corpulent has a pair of Legs far exceeding in size those of Bright of Malden[135] it is said to be occasion'd by a Scorbutic Humour.
>
> The prospect from the farm is Delightful & the day being fine & the wheat in Shock standing on the Ground, the Ladies Dancing on the Turf & the Musick, one of them a Welch harp, playing al Fresco exhibited a truly Pastoral Scene. From this place there is a fine View of the Town of Monmouth the castle & Bridge with that of the Hill which overlooks it. The Price of this Entertainment is two shillings to Strangers for which they have tea Coffee & Musick. The Town is Literally what it is called, but Inclosed by a Clip'd Hedge with Borders in which are a Variety of Flowers some Turf & Gravel Walks & after Rainy Weather if the Miller pleases a Cascade is made at the Bottom of the Walk by the spare Water. Here the ladies danced till ½ after seven when we repaired to the Theatre a miserable hovel decorated with Shocking Scenes & Lighted with farthing Candles & Train Oil ... the play was not finished till 12 & after a Slight Supper at the Kings Head where we Inn'd we retired to Rest abt two. [136]
>
> Tuesday. At abt 11 after Breakfasting at our Inn, the Major & I walked to draw Monnow Bridge near it is a very Ancient Chapel, whose Arches are Circular & decorated with Zig Zag mouldings.

The ancient chapel was St Thomas's Overmonnow. Grose missed the other great Monmouth festival, the annual Mayor's Feast to which everyone who was anyone contributed. 'When the clock told the hour of dinner', wrote Heath, 'forth went the cooks, with their large pewter dishes, bending beneath the weight of the delicious gammon, the savoury haunch, and famed sirloin; so that the ground floor of the market house ... appeared to the eye ... as the *grande salle de manger* for the whole of the inhabitants of the county of Monmouth.' The feast turned the day into a riotous holiday, as a result of which it was discontinued, and Heath was obviously sorry.[137]

Rather surprisingly John Wesley visited Vauxhall in 1784. Though he had 'hardly seen such a place before' he did not disapprove of the dancing, found the walks 'full as beautiful in their kind as even the hanging woods at Brecon', and seems to have been unworried about the likelihood of the 'Bowling-green House' being burned up at the end of the world. Torrington, who had preceded him in 1781, also enjoyed the social life of Vauxhall: 'Here when the weather permits, the company of all the neighbourhood meet, every Thursday, at 5 o'clock in the evening; and dance till 9 o'clock upon two bowling greens, from which the views are delightful'. The sort of views he meant were not so innocent as those of Wesley: 'surely this must be a famous place for cuckows!' A later writer was more romantic: 'Imagine a small but very neat House plac'd in the midst of Hay and Corn Fields; the Roads thro' wch are nicely gravell'd & border'd on either Hand, by a thick Plantation of Pinks wch added ten thousand Perfumes, to the natural Sweetness of the Air'. He (or perhaps she) felt wonderfully cut off from the real world 'excepting a few Villagers who are seen stealing thro' the Bushes on the other Side of the River'.[138] Natives in the way again.

Dancing ladies were not the only entertainment for Torrington: 'I saw the parade of the Monmouthshire militia, this evening, and a stout body of men they are', though 'It is a plague to be in an inn with troops, for the officers employ, and occupy the whole house' as a result of which he slept badly. Always keen to know the price of things, he got up early and went to the market, where 'there were store of kids of six weeks old, at 5 shillings [25p] price, and of old goat at 2 pence [about 1p] per lb; with plenty of salmon.' Venison was in abundant supply, allegedly from the local gentlemen's parks, though he assumed it was mostly poached. But things were not as cheap as he had hoped, and when his landlord (who seemed 'tolerably intelligent') told him it would cost the

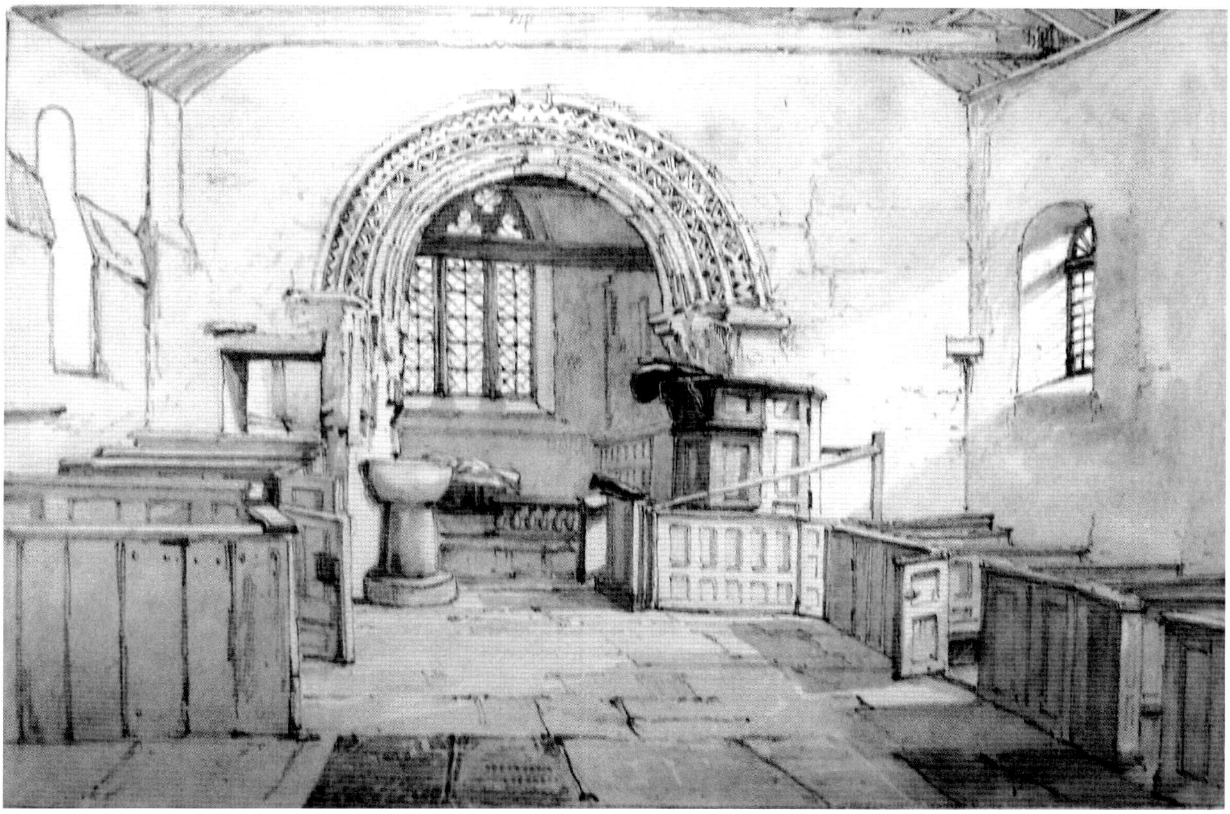

Interior of St Thomas's Overmonnow by George Orleans Delamotte, shortly before its restoration in 1830-31. (Reproduced by kind permission of Mrs J.E. Harding-Rolls © Gwent Record Office)

usual guinea and a half [£1.52½p] to take a boat to Chepstow, and he'd do better to ride and save his money, he took the advice. Welsh, he noted, was as much understood and spoken in Monmouth as English.

When Torrington returned in 1787, he and Osborn 'seated ourselves on a bench in the bowling green, in perfect contentment of ourselves, and the evening, and with lavish encomiums on the surrounding prospect: here we stayed an hour, commenting on the happiness of lovers in such a place, where denials cou'd neither be given, or taken.' Torrington decided this time they should take a boat. Next day they had time to visit Raglan, come back, walk round the town (and in Osborn's case eat mutton chops) and visit Owen Tudor's bookshop (his son Thomas was then two years old) before they set off at 2 pm, 'laden with baggage (like a Calais embarkation)'. Still sharp about the price of pleasure, Torrington noted that his inn charged him as much as 'other inns upon greater roads'. He feared he wouldn't find in the sophisticated south 'the simplicity of manners, and cheapness of living, that I met with in Nth. Wales.'

Another who enjoyed Monmouth's social life, this time on a Sunday, was Barber, in 1803. He joined the promenade 'where many a squire of little manors eyed us with much more inquiry than cordiality.' Perhaps there had been too many tourists sizing up the local beauties. Barber found the women attractive – 'But who would leave London to describe female beauty?' – but not everyone was so pleased with them. Millicent Bant was happy enough going into St Thomas's Overmonnow, with its good doorway and arch, and its font 'like a thick Punch bowl' (though the rest of the church was 'a perfect Dunghill'). But her travelling companion Lady Wilson, going alone to church on Sunday, met with a specimen of Welsh hospitality to strangers which she didn't care for at all. She 'was first in the Pew & seated herself on a small Cushion of which there were three. A Dame in Pattens with her two daughters soon entered ... seeing her Ladyship on one of the cushions and probably in the corner usually occupied by herself she looked as black as thunder, pulled out an Hassock, and down she flounced. When the sentences began Lady Wilson got up and turning towards the Parson did not suppose what was going on behind her, but when she set down, found her Cushion was flown.' Millicent went with her to Evensong, and 'The Dame was going to play me the same trick, but being on the watch, I turned round, caught her in the act and she relinquished her prize.' Natives 1, Tourists 1.[139]

Monmouth was not just for the traveller passing rapidly through. For Luke Booker, vicar of industrial Dudley, 'released from the arduous duties of a populous parish, surrounded by mines and manufactories', it was his regular summer holiday resort for many years. By 1831, according to *Leigh's Guide*, Chippenham Meadow rather than Vauxhall had become the favourite evening promenade. The races, which coincided with the assizes, had been held there for many years, only to be suspended in 1784 when the militia was embodied on account of the American War of Independence. But when the militia returned, they were revived.[140] Twamley didn't attend the races, but said the 'concourse of gay and busy people, added considerably to its beauty.'

Wyndham had found Monmouth a very large and handsome town, its streets spacious, and decently built. 'They are frequently adorned with good houses, which are inhabited by families of fortune', he noted approvingly. Walpoole thought it had 'one of the most handsome Gothic churches in England', but St Thomas's had nothing of remark. The town was populous and well-built. *The Pocket Vade Mecum* agreed: 'the streets are wide, clean, and well-paved, and contain many good houses', though the Wye here was not so charming or so romantic as at Chepstow. Shaw said

'The general white complexion of the houses gives it a neat and animated look', though he thought Monmouth had once been much more flourishing than it was now. That was in 1788, and the town must have been going very rapidly downhill if Sophia Ward's description in 1791 was right; she found the streets narrow, the houses dirty and the paving wretched, 'the number of respectable [houses] being but small'. She did, though, like the Town Hall. Jeremiah Milles did not. It suffered from bad proportions and want of good furniture, though it was the clumsy statue to Henry V which brought most derision (though Bloomfield thought it noble). Twamley complained in 1838 that 'In Monmouth every thing has, or is made to have, some relation to its favourite prince', just what people felt about Ross and Kyrle.

Sophia also approved of 'a row of decent almshouses'. She went to look at the wharf and noted that 'a horse load of Coals – consisting of 2 sacks weighing 300 [three hundredweight] sells from 15 to 18 pence per load when sold from the barge 10s a Ton.' Everyone looked at the remains of the castle, and followed Gilpin in remarking how it was humbled into a farmyard. 'The transmutations of time are often ludicrous', he wrote. 'Monmouth-castle [*sic*] was formerly the palace of a king; and birth-place of a mighty prince: it is now converted into a yard for fatting ducks.' It was one of his most repeated phrases: Puckler-Muskau was playing a variant on it fifty years later. No one put it better, though people kept trying.

Tourists did not have much to fear from crime, and confinement in Monmouth gaol was not rigorous, though not comfortable either: 'The sheets my Chum and I lay in, were as coarse as a Nutmeg-Grater, and the Colour of the Owner's Face, which I cannot compare to anything, except damag'd Gingerbread' wrote James Parry, who was awaiting trial there in the late 1730s. He paid 10s a week for his board, with another 2s 4d for ale or cider, and spent his time playing fives and abusing the gaoler's wife for drinking the prisoners' liquor without paying for it.[141] At least he escaped the always lurking danger of gaol fever. John Howard, reporting on British prisons in 1780, said that the Monmouth gaoler and several of his prisoners had recently died of it, after which the survivors were new-clothed by the Duke of Beaufort.[142] The new County Gaol was completed in 1790, and Ireland was impressed: it 'frowns over the country, and impresses the idea of rigorous confinement and the impossibility of escape.' But there was 'only one solitary inhabitant, and he a prisoner for only a very trivial offence.' By 1804, said Heath in his Monmouth guide, only four prisoners had been executed, one for murder, two for burglary, and one for stealing cattle. Chepstow was just as safe. Willett boasted that, though a populous seaport, it was policed with two petty constables, which should make the traveller 'entertain the highest opinion of our morals and native placibility of temperament.' Drunkenness was the most likely cause of any trouble. Heath records a custom that applied generally on the Severn, but on the Wye only at Monmouth. When hired for a barge trip, a man was given a pint of ale, called a 'mugging': 'Hence, when a man is a little – "how came you so?"– we say he has been mugging himself.' If he failed to keep his side of the bargain, he could be jailed for three months, a serious mugging indeed. If the master failed to keep his, he had only to pay the man's wages.

Samuel Ireland liked Monmouth, but a cross and anonymous diarist of 1796 thought it 'an old bad Town; nothing to see from, or in it', but though 'the Inns and Houses all look very dirty ... we got tolerable beds.'[143] Wigstead was of much the same opinion: 'The town dirty, and the buildings irregular', but *The Cambrian Directory* was another that thought the town 'neat and well built'. St Thomas's, Overmonnow, was not so well built, though; it had had to reduce the number of services because of the damp and the decayed state of the pews. Sarah Anne Wilmot, on her first visit, damned both the inn and the town with faint praise, 'tolerably' being her favourite word. Monmouth is a 'tolerably good town' and the inn is 'very dirty, but tolerably good fare'. Cooke was the only guide to recommend the Dragon rather than the Beaufort Arms.[144] Barber attributed the town's 'thriving appearance ... to the numerous gentry that are induced to fix their residence here from the pleasantness of the situation.' The more one tries to make sense of such very different opinions, the more likely it seems that they depended on the individual tourist's digestions. At the Royal Hotel, the Blanchards' digestions rejected the tea and coffee, which tasted of the bad water, and drank lemonade instead. (This is probably a slip of the pen for the King's Head.)

When Sarah Anne Wilmot came on her second trip, in August 1802, she and her husband had the personal attention of Heath, now established as the chief authority on and guide to the local scene. He took them to the Kymin, about which he issued a separate very detailed pamphlet, to see not only the extensive view across to the Black Mountains, but also the small circular banqueting pavilion used since 1796 by the local gentry as a club for weekly cold collations, provided by each member in turn. (Booker, the regular visitor, was invited to join them). The Duke and Duchess of Beaufort had visited in 1799, following the presentation of colours to the Monmouth Volunteer Infantry, which reminds us that the Napoleonic wars had already been going on for six years, something some tourists, perhaps, were hoping to forget. The duchess was the daughter of Admiral Boscawen, and she and the duke came again in June 1801 to see another, more splendid and patriotic building – the Naval Temple, erected by the duke to celebrate British naval victories of the last half century (catalogue no. 87). It was opened with a public breakfast and dancing, and among its earliest visitors was G.W. Manby, who had a little adventure there with 'a woman in affliction'. 'I soon found myself imperceptibly seated by her side, her hand enclosed in mine, and, stimulated by sympathy, urging a recital of her woes.' This was delightful melancholy indeed.

The following year, in a brief lull in the war and the week before Sarah Anne's visit, Nelson had come down the 'little gut' of the river in a boat garlanded with laurel leaves, with Sir William and Lady Hamilton and others. They were on their way to west Wales to inspect Milford Haven and to have a holiday, but Nelson took the opportunity to eye the woods for ships' timbers, and later drafted a report on the Forest of Dean. He had been made a Freeman of the Borough, and everyone was ready for him – he had a sharp eye for publicity and may have chosen arrival by boat for its dramatic potential – but to general disappointment he expressed disingenuous surprise at his welcome and declined to stay and be fêted. He did however let the town celebrate him with a banquet on his way home, and the Buckstone was whitewashed for the occasion, so it looked like a Welsh cottage without a chimney. Every remark he made at the banquet was carefully noted. ('*I hate the French* !' he said to Philip Hardwick, who had erected the Kymin pavilion.) Lady Hamilton sang two patriotic songs to great applause. Next day Heath accompanied Nelson up the Kymin and watched as he scrutinised a picture of the Battle of the Nile in the Naval Temple. Disappointingly, and perhaps crushingly, he made no comment. The party then walked through nearby Beaulieu Grove, a wood with equally splendid views in all directions and seats from which to admire them. (The wood was soon coppiced and the seats vandalised.) Later in the day Nelson and Lady Hamilton came into Heath's shop to get guide-books, which was one of the greatest moments of his life. 'This', says Liz Pitman, 'perhaps explains why Sarah's lively pencil sketch of him in her Wigan journal shows him strutting proudly forward with his hat in his hand, umbrella under his arm, his long, beaky nose looking positively luminescent.'[145]

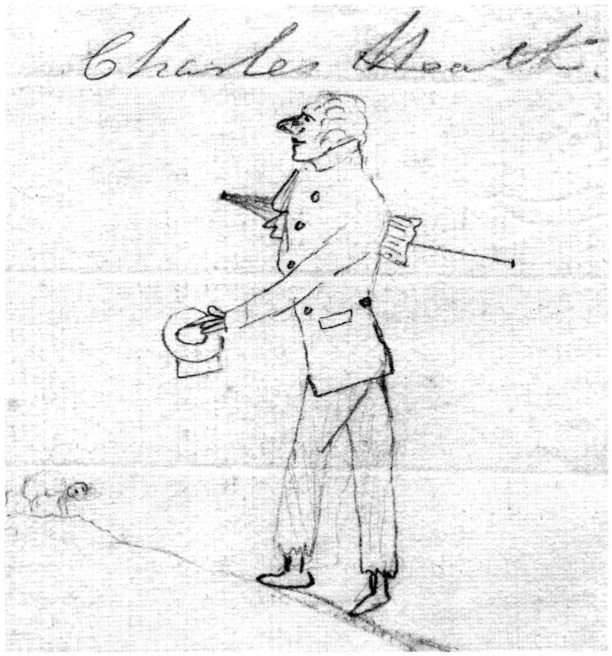

Charles Heath by Sarah Anne Wilmot (1802).
(Wigan Archives Services, WLCT)

Sarah, who had been sad, now cheered up and felt she was seeing 'all the wonders of the World – the scenery is rich beyond description, & by the attention of Mr. Heath we had the advantage of seeing the curiosities of the Country much better than by ourselves'. As well as the Kymin, there was the Buckstone, still wearing its whitewash from the previous week. It was 'an immense Rock 38 yards in circumference at top about 30 feet high standing on its own irregular base of 9 feet to the earth – its appearance is so tremendous that a number of the people at Monmouth assembled with 16 horses & strong Iron chains which they fasten'd to the slender base & then by every means urged the horses so attached to throw it down, but all in vain ... it is said it has the property of a rocking stone & can be moved with hand but that is not true!' Actually, says Liz Pitman, Sarah was wrong, it was a logan stone, that is, a stone which was so finely balanced that it could be rocked to and fro simply by pushing it gently. Logans were 'made much of by 18th century antiquarians', according to Geoffrey Grigson. They thought they were put in place by Druids who used them for divination and other magical powers, though 'less credulous people have amused themselves by using logans to crack nuts'.[146] It was true that people were always trying to push this one over, as Booker records:

Full oft the prodigy has brav'd
Rude violence, and yet been sav'd
From all attempts of Goth and clown
To hurl the ponderous Wonder down;
And still, for ages, may it prove
The solemn guardian of the grove!

Alas, the Goths and clowns had the last word in 1885, when the Buckstone was tipped from its plinth, allegedly by a group of travelling actors from London. For Sarah it had displayed 'one of those unanswerable proofs of the Power of the Divine Architect which no human Being can Comprehend or dare to imitate', and such was the public outcry at the desecration that the stone was put back, though it no longer rocked.[147]

When Puckler-Muskau came to Monmouth he, like Nelson, felt in need of a guide-book, so he went into Heath's shop where he found the family, including two pretty daughters, just having tea. They were very welcoming, and he thought Heath 'unusually loquacious, for an Englishman'. Although the family tried to stop him, Heath questioned the German closely 'about the continent and about politics'. The conversation, one-sided or not, went on for half an hour, at the end of which Heath gave him a guide-book and refused to take any money for it. Things did not go so well at the inn, where Puckler-Muskau was convinced his purse and pocket-book with £10 in it had been stolen by the coffee-room waiter. The inn-keeper, 'a most disagreeable-looking fellow', took offence, saying there'd been no theft in his house in the last 30 years, but if the Prince wanted, he would send for a magistrate and have the place searched, adding with a sneer that Puckler-Muskau's own luggage would have to be searched too, and if nothing was found, he would have to pay the costs and give him, the landlord, compensation. Puckler-Muskau left, thinking he'd escaped a den of thieves. He told Heath what had happened. The pretty daughters offered to lend him £5, which touched him deeply, though he declined. When he got to Chepstow, he was disconcerted to find purse and pocket-book in his dressing-gown, and wrote at once to Heath, apologizing and sending £2 for the maligned waiter.

From this time on the Kymin and the Buckstone were considered pretty much essential additions to the tour, though interest in the Naval Temple waned after a period of peace. Leigh records in 1831 that it was 'now going to decay'. Many tourists, though, had to skip them, as they were whisked off to Tintern first thing in the morning – Bloomfield's party started at 6 am:

> Ten hours were all we could command;
> The boat was moor'd upon the strand,
> The midnight current, by the side,
> Was stealing down to meet the tide;
> The wakeful steersman ready lay,
> To rouse us at the break of day.

And off they went.

The Second Day

Monmouth to Tintern

Whatever time the tourists started on their second day, the main attraction was Tintern Abbey, and the extensive woods on each side of the river were generally ignored. They were coppiced, which meant that 'What is this year a thicket may the next be an open grove', said Leigh, noting eight separate woods between Monmouth and Chepstow. 'The woods, consequently, exhibit but little grandeur, as the trees are not suffered to attain their full stature.' This was not Heath's view; he thought a coppiced wood 'appears scarce distinguishable, at some distance, from the most luxuriant crops', and the different tints add to the 'wonderful variety so peculiar to these scenes'.

If you were bored by woods, there was always life on the river. Gilpin liked 'the light vessels gliding past us. Their white sails passing along the sides of woodland hills were very picturesque.' *The Cambrian Directory* paraphrased and added to this: 'The rude hail of the boatmen, as they passed, was re-echoed by the rocks, and the dingy white sails of the vessels, which soon disappeared round some bold promontory, were particularly picturesque.' But Skrine, on a bad day, found the river 'so rough from strong gusts of wind, that we found it difficult to proceed; for the stream is naturally very rapid, and this part of the river abounds in dangerous shallows.' *The Penny Magazine*, almost 50 years later, noted 'a barge or two, making their way against the stream, had to tack and manoeuvre in a curious manner' because of shelves and ripples.

However it wasn't long before there was something interesting to look at – the tinplate works at Redbrook on the left bank[148] and the paper mills of Whitebrook on the right. Skrine liked the 'poor villages diversifying the scene with a scanty show of ragged population' and described Redbrook as a 'beautifully romantic spot'. An anonymous diarist wrote in 1798 that it

> was the most bustling little place imaginable, every face looked busy and quiet was here wholly banished by the reverberating strokes from the iron-works. The inhabitants appeared one whole family of Cyclopes nearly [or newly] grilled in daily smoke and flame: The degradation by excessive labour in many classes of the poor was added to in the condition of the workmen there. The lot of humanity must be miserably cast, when chain'd to severe toil hourly broil'd in acquiring bread to sustain precarious health! Yet these workmen of Vulcan amidst expression which we pitied appeared determin'd to feed the parching heat in themselves by copious draughts from the refreshing can; for we learnt that the bread of the publicans at this village depended solely on the demand of those at the forge for beer. On a superficial scan of the degrees of condition in our species we were prompted to acknowledge the favour of destiny which had so differently allotted our portion of earthly economy, in placing us so remote from these metaphors of Etna.[149]

That was unusually vivid and honest. Another writer wrote a detailed description of the process by which copper was refined and rolled, involving the use of sulphur and arsenic. as a result of which 'a thick yellow smoke hangs over the works wch is very unwholesome as well as detrimental to vegetation'.[150] But when Manby came in 1801, Lower Redbrook's tin works were 'all in gloom, and a mournful picture of misfortune' owing to a law suit.

Ireland left his boat here and went to look at St Briavels Castle, 'patched and cobbled, like a worn out shoe' (Fosbroke) from which the Forest of Dean had been ruled for centuries. Until 1819 there was a Whitsun scramble for bread and cheese in the church, after which 'this disgraceful scene' (Leigh) was moved to the churchyard. The Blanchards, obliged to leave their boat at Redbrook because of the high wind and water, waited for a fly in a cottage, and again got the children to sing for them. After the performance they asked them what they would do with a penny if they gave it to them. 'Buy some sweet stuff', they said. Jane was firm: 'We told them how much better it would be to buy something that would last a long time which after a time they quite understood and said "they should buy a hymn book instead".' There was a maypole on Penyvan Hill beyond Whitebrook, and though it was May, it's doubtful the stormy weather allowed the Blanchards a glimpse of any of the celebrations which went on there. Though Heath claimed 'The return of this pleasing season is not distinguished openly from any other part of the year', Willett, no slouch at circumlocution himself, said Whit Monday 'presents no inconsiderable assemblage of dancing fauns and faunesses ... who foot it away to the scraping of the fiddle or tinkling of the harp, and regale themselves, not with nectar, but with cakes and ale'.

The next place was Bigsweir, the home of the Rooke family, relatives of the Admiral Rooke who captured Gibraltar for the nation in 1704. Grose considered it

> one of the Most Romantic Situations conceivable, Close to it runs the River Wye & Surrounded with Lofty Woody Steeps & opposed to it on the other side of the River is Landogo a Small Village on the side of an Almost perpendicular Slope, whose houses seem deposited by Accident & whose small Church is of a piece with & Does not shame the rest of the Buildings. The Hill is coverd with a most beautiful Verdure. On it is a Gulley formed by Floods & in Rainy season there is a sort of Waterfall. The side of this hill is so steep that Mill Stones are used to be slid down a Path[.] A Remarkable Story is told of the Effects of one of them which in its Descent Overthrew a Horse. Nothing can be more Romantic than the Coup D'oeil here, The Lofty Hills & Sloping Banks are wooded to the Waters Edge, but as they are every where equally coverd the Eye is fatigued with a continued Sameness of the Trees which are mostly underwood & Close together when view'd at any Distance [they] seem scarcely more than fern or Plantations of Box.

Twamley, 60 years later, thought Bigsweir house 'looked somewhat forlorn and forsaken, but yet had an old-fashioned stateliness in its gardens and terraces.' She considered it, though, much superior to the Florence, the 'modern residence' of one of the Rooke family just upstream, 'a fanciful Anglo-Swiss cottage ... presenting a great contrast with the ancient mansion, which, by the way, loses nothing by comparison.' Roscoe found the Florence 'tasteful'. There was no bridge here, or anywhere else between Monmouth and Chepstow, till the turnpike trust built the elegant iron one in 1825-1827.

Torrington, like Grose, thought Llandogo 'most picturesque ... with a little chapel, and numbers of detach'd cottages creeping up a wooded hill'. Warner loved it: 'a lofty hill, whose indented side is mantled with deep woods, through which a multitude of small cottages, sprinkled over the declivity in an artless, whimsical, and picturesque manner, shew their little whitened fronts, and strongly impress the imagination with the idea of its being fairy land, the romantic residence of Oberon, Mab, and their fantastic train.' He was being disloyal to Gilpin here, as Gilpin disliked whitewashed cottages. Willett went further; he thought the annual whitewashing gave an appearance of neatness and cheerfulness, and contributed to the health of the inhabitants, and considerably heightened the picturesque effect of the diversified landscapes.[151] The famous Cleddon shoots were not often to be seen during the tourist season, and had to be taken on trust, but by the fourth edition of the *Strangers Guide* a circuitous path had been made up the side of the falls, and there was a guide to show them. Torrington bought a botcher here[152] of 3 or 4 pounds, 'to add to the quantity of provisions we were cajoled to send aboard, for ourselves, and our crew.' It was another chance for him to grumble about the cost of everything: 'this, with their charge, the beer, &c, &c, makes water travelling shamefully expensive'. But he could make a joke of it: 'This river, said our boatmen, is call'd Wye, sir; yes, answer'd I, but my voyage on it will not make me *wiser*.' Bloomfield had an optical illusion of the river running downhill here, and later wrote an indifferent poem on 'The Maid of Llandoga'. Twamley was grumpy. She thought the beauty of Llandogo greatly exaggerated, with its 'small, not too clean-looking cottages.'

Grose 'embarqued at ... Udnalls [Hudnalls, below Bigsweir on the Gloucestershire bank] on board a barge like kind of boat navigated by two men with large oars which they rowed standing.' This was clearly not a tourist boat. He was told the boats had to be strong because the river was full of large stones and sunken rocks and weirs. The next place was Brockweir, where sea-going vessels transferred their cargoes to barges and loaded oak bark for tanneries, hoops and faggots.

By the 1830s, villas were appearing along the river and *The Penny Magazine* praised 'a number of white, comfortable-looking cottages and elegant little villas scattered about the hills' here. Gilpin had clearly lost the battle against whitewash. Willett recommended landing and walking up the Passage Hill to the Devil's Pulpit, from which there was an excellent view down on the abbey. The effect of the tide was now beginning to show and Skrine was obliged to wait for it 'as the shoals beyond that spot are impassable except at high water, and our boatmen were fatigued with their exertions against the wind. – Unfurling our canvas awning, we enclosed ourselves in the boat, and excluded all objects during the time of dinner, to protect ourselves from the cold.'

It was somewhere round here that Wordsworth started his famous poem, usually and wrongly known as *Tintern Abbey*, though the abbey is in fact not mentioned. The full title is *Lines composed a few miles above Tintern Abbey, on revisiting the banks of the Wye during a tour, July 13, 1798*, and even that is not strictly accurate, as his own account of its composition makes clear: 'I began it upon leaving Tintern, after crossing the Wye, and concluded it just as I was entering Bristol in the evening, after a ramble of four or five days (10th-13th July) with my sister.' Many people have tried to pin down the exact spot where he started composing, using such clues as 'steep and lofty cliffs', 'these plots of cottage-ground, these orchard-tufts', 'these hedge-rows, hardly hedge-rows, little lines of sportive wood run wild; these pastoral farms', and so on, all of which could apply to anywhere between Whitebrook and Brockweir. Leitch Ritchie (1841), who called Wordsworth 'the great Druid of the Wye, the poet of nature internal and external' thought it was at Lyn Weir below Brockweir. The website of the local Area of Outstanding Natural Beauty says it was at Llandogo. In fact Wordsworth was composing the poem in his head as he walked along, and as poems are not required to be topographically accurate, it seems foolish to claim any one place as 'it'. What is clear is that the memory of his first walks up and down the Wye, in 1793 and 1798, remained with him all his life. He urged his wife Mary to go to Tintern in 1812, though he couldn't accompany her. As the boat trip (£4 10s from Ross to Chepstow) was too expensive, she rode, spending the night at Monmouth. 'What divine villages !' she exclaimed. In 1836 he urged Henry Crabb Robinson to start his Welsh tour with the Wye, and two years later told his daughter Dora 'if you can see Tintern and Piercefield without injurious fatigue, do so.'[153]

Tintern

Tintern was, at first, barely accessible by carriage from either side of the river, and for Jeremiah Milles in 1742 it was well off the main road from Chepstow to Monmouth (or, as John Ogilby's *Britannia* (1675) described it, from Bristol to Chester). Most early tourists, as has been said, were rowed up to Tintern from Chepstow and back again. Most later ones from Chepstow came along what Heath (1828) called the 'fine broad driving way', that is the new road begun in 1821, from which, said Cliffe, as you descended, the abbey suddenly burst upon you, like a gigantic stone skeleton. Before this, people hired horses and rode, or walked as the Wordsworths did. The then shortest route was along the road through St Arvans, where you branched off towards Penterry, before turning right and plunging down the steep, slippery and stony track which came out at what is now the Abbey Hotel. This 'road' has never been metalled, and anyone wanting an idea of what eighteenth century travel in Monmouthshire could be like, is recommended to wear walking boots before attempting it. There were equally steep ways down along the Angidy brook which brought you out at the ironworks, and there was the road from Trellech which came out at Tintern Parva.

Torrington, on his first visit, came down the Angidy valley: 'I descended into immense woods, with a rippling stream on my right hand, heard but not seen; and, embowered with lofty wood, here and there a cottage appear'd, with scarcely ground sufficient for their small garden and apple trees. ... To this succeeded the incessant thump of furnace hammers, which might appal (in the night) a stouter heart than Sancho's, by their 'dreadful note of preparation'; and terrified poor Jock [presumably his horse] most exceedingly.' Shaw came down the same 'hollow and uncouth tracks, seldom attempted by any carriages but those of the natives ... we entered a profound dell for several miles; a gurgling brook winding through the umbrageous cavity which supplies a number of large iron works above the village.' (Webb, 1812, said there were 22 water-wheels on the Angidy.) The track was 'a way formed for the speedy conveyance of ore which is brought on the backs of mules from the mines a few miles distant. But we soon found without the possibility of turning that such roads were not calculated for carriages or even the safety of horses unattached to any weight; it was comprised of an entire succession of rocky shelves, many of considerable depth, and the high embankments on each side were compressed in such a manner, as scarcely to admit the action of the wheels, so that caution being more indispensable than expedition, we did not accomplish the whole 11 miles in less than 4 hours'.[154] The main Chepstow-Monmouth road sounds no better: 'From the Abbey I rode back to Chepstow and attempted to reach Monmouth the same night but meeting with a vile road and being caught in a very severe shower I was under the necessity of resting my head in a very sorry Alehouse at a place called Trelagh [Trellech] 5 miles from Monmouth where I philosophised at escaping a worse situation as I might have lost my way in the dark. I believe mankind in general feel happiness more or less as they draw comparisons by others'.[155]

The approach from the Gloucestershire side was no easier. A few days after his barge trip from Hudnalls Grose came again, riding this time from St Briavels, to make drawings. He dismounted at the top of the hill, 'the road being not only excessively steep, but full of rolling stone.' Even travel by boat wasn't always easy. Approaching Tintern downstream, Anne Cooper's party met the tide coming up, and had to be towed against it. Many tourists got out at Tintern Parva, then called simply Tintern, as opposed to Abbey, where, said Grose, 'the Church, the Remains of a Castellated Mansion some Adjoining Cottages with the Turn of the River & the Neighbouring Impending Hills form a most Picturesque Appearance'. Grose was a much travelled man, and the church, he thought, 'somewhat Ressembles the Pocket Cathedral in the Isle of Wight near Steephill.' The ruined mansion was variously known as the Abbot's House, or the Great House, or Mr Fielding's House. Grose drew it and was told it had formerly belonged to Rhees Mawr. Willett, whose father's garden adjoined it, remembered from his childhood finding cannon balls there. The visitor then approached the abbey round the great bend.

The industry of Tintern fascinated some as much as the abbey itself. Indeed in 1665 Marmaduke Rawdon, one of the earliest recorded visitors, found it far more interesting. All his biographer had to say about the abbey (working from Rawdon's journal) was that it was 'a famous place in former times, as by the walls and some arches yet standinge appears.' More exciting were the 'iron furnases, where the iron is first melted before itt is beate by the mills into barrs' and the wire works 'wher they draw wire from little iron barrs into severall sieses, a curiositie worth the seeinge. The fire of the furnace where they melt the iron is soe greate, that, lookinge into the hole where the nosell of the bellowes are, itt lookes like the sun in a hott day att noone.'[156]

There had been wireworks on the Angidy since the 1560s, with new works being added as late as 1803.[157] The most exciting were at Abbey Forge at the bottom of the stream, especially at night. Grose stayed at the Beaufort Arms (nothing to be had but eggs, but the bed was far from bad) and is the first visitor to record the thrilling night view: 'Out of the Window where I spent the Evening & which was a very tollerable Room I saw a Kind of Fireworks occasion'd by the Sparks which ascended from the Forges, which having a high Dark Mountain for a Back Ground & the hight [*sic*] being rather cloudy exhibited a pleasing Appearance. A Continual Din of Hammers is to be heard here a very Considerable Iron Work being carried on by a Mr Tanner. When they have water sufficient they Work Night & Day, this Iron Work was lately rented by a Mr Jordan.' Warner must have watched from the same window of the 'very comfortable inn, kept by Mr Gething, the antiquary and historian of the village'.

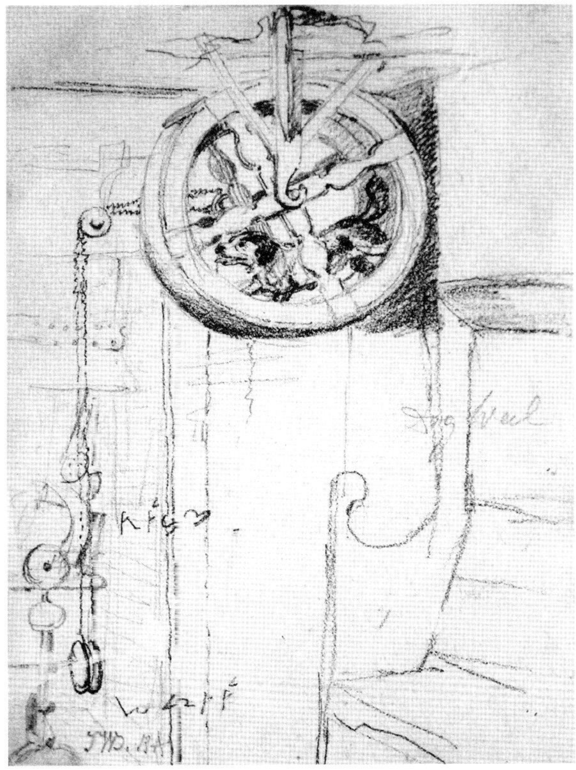

Dog-wheel turnspit at Tintern pub by James Ward. (Private collection)

> The extreme heat of the last night (Aug 30th) effectually prevented us from sleeping, and we passed the greater part of it at our window ... both for the sake of a balmy and refreshing breeze that gently whispered without, and in order to enjoy a scene perfectly new to us, highly gratifying to a warm imagination. Immediately opposite to the room in which we were lodged, stands a large iron forge, one amongst the many that are constantly worked night and day, in the valley of Tintern. The wide folding-doors were thrown open, and as they faced our window, the interior part of the edifice, with its huge apparatus, and the operations carried on by it, were displayed to our view. Here the dingy beings who melt the ore, and prepare it for the bar-hammer, were seen busied in their horrible employment, all the detail of which we clearly discovered by the strong illumination cast on them from the flaming furnaces.

Britton had a rather different experience at the inn in 1798.

> I was aroused from a sound sleep by remarkable sounds of water rushing through the room, and leaping from stair to stair in its descent to the lower floor. Mr and Mrs Gethin ... bringing lights, relieved me from all doubts and alarm, by showing that the water from the sloping garden at the back had forced a passage through the door-way, across the room, and down the stairs in a new sort of cascade. In the morning, the waters of the Wye were seen and heard rushing over their rocky bed in torrents; and a scene of much grandeur was presented to a person who had only known the Thames, the Medway, the Loddon, and the Avon.

Shaw was more interested in metallurgy than dramatic night-time effects, and wrote at length about the different ores and types of iron and how it was produced, but Coleridge preferred the inn. He'd had a hard day. Travelling with his Bristol publisher Joseph Cottle, the poet Southey, and a couple of girl-friends, they'd started late and got thoroughly lost as night fell. Cottle, who was riding, dismounted, whereupon Coleridge 'who had been more accustomed to rough riding than myself ... without speaking a word put his foot in the stirrup and mounting, determined to brave at all hazards, the dangers of the campaign'. The dangers were real; he nearly went over the edge of a quarry. When they did finally reach Tintern, they asked where was the hotel. '"Hotel" ! "Hotel" ! Sir ? Oh, the sign of the Tobacco Pipe ! There it is over the way.' Southey and Cottle thought the forge a 'real spectacle of sublimity', but nearly fell in the mill-pond, so perhaps Coleridge was wise to stay by the fire. However after dinner he joined the party to visit the abbey by moonlight, as many people did. It's not known what they'd been drinking, but they upset the roosting jackdaws.

Puckler-Muskau had stopped on his way down the river to look at 'an immense water-wheel' (possibly the one painted by Joseph Powell, catalogue no. 47). 'This wheel had the power of eighty horses; and the whirling rapidity of its revolutions, the frightful noise when it was first set going, the furnaces around vomiting fire, the red-hot iron, and the half-naked black figures brandishing hammers and other ponderous instruments, and throwing around the red hissing masses, formed an admirable representation of Vulcan's smithy'. Vulcan and Cyclops and other mythical smiths were constantly invoked. The David Tanner, mentioned by Grose, was 'once one of the most eminent Iron Masters in this part of the kingdom', having forges at Lydbrook and Redbrook as well as Tintern, and others in the western part of the county. Torrington said he 'pays daily 1500 workmen, most of whom earn from 18 to 20s pr week', which is remarkable, if true, but Torrington, as we shall see, could be gullible, and the 1500 is likely to have included the workers' dependents. Some idea of the effect of the industrial revolution on local life can be gained from the pay agreement between masters and men in the wireworks after a 'convulsion' following the introduction of new methods of work in 1747. 'Such was the spirit of resentment against the intended innovation, that the Introducer was compelled to conceal himself at a distance from the spot, till their fury was abated ... to prevent his life from falling a sacrifice to their mistaken opinion of an injury to their trade', said Heath in his 1801 *Tintern*. He was no sympathiser with radicalism, and omitted this from later editions. A curiosity worth the seeing here, as Rawdon noted more than a century earlier, was the drawing of lengths of wire. The expert wire-worker Joseph Laban could draw a 1,000-yard length of wire from a square inch of iron. His descendents, according to Willett, were still working there in the 1830s. Oddly, though, no one else mentions it. At the ironworks Tanner went bust in 1798, in what Heath delicately described as 'the late arduous times of commercial difficulties'. No doubt this added to the number of local beggars.

The forges and furnaces, however fascinating, were always secondary to the abbey, both in age and their place on the eighteenth and nineteenth century tourists' list of essential sights. Gilpin set the tone for all later travellers: the abbey was 'esteemed, with its appendages, the most beautiful and picturesque view on the river.' Once again he leaned heavily on Thomas Whately, as Heath noted snidely. Whately was very theoretical, laying down picturesque principles more precisely than Gilpin ever did, but with the emphasis on their practical exercise in landscape gardening. He said that 'Whatever building we see in decay, we naturally contrast its present to its former state, and delight to ruminate the comparison', but added that feelings of regret, veneration or compassion could arise from fake ruins as well as real ones. At Tintern where 'maimed effigies, and sculpture worn with age and weather, Gothic capitals, carved cornices, and various fragments, are scattered about, or lie in heaps piled up together', they suggest 'every idea which can occur in a seat of devotion, solitude and desolation.' He also said 'the shed of a cottager, amidst the remains of a temple, is a contrast both to the former and the present state of the building: and a tree, flourishing among ruins, shews the length of time they have lain neglected.'

Gilpin praised the abbey's setting on 'a gentle eminence in the middle of a circular valley, beautifully screened on all sides by woody hills, through which the river winds it's [*sic*] course; and the hills closing on it's entrance, and on it's exit, leave no room for inclement blasts to enter. A more pleasing retreat could not easily be found.' Though a good Anglican he could see why 'a man of warm imagination, in monkish times' might have been tempted to join the Cistercians. Tintern was 'a very inchanting piece of scenery' and its abbey 'a very inchanting ruin'. However – there is always a 'however' or a 'but' in Gilpin – the abbey 'does not make that appearance as a *distant* object, which we expected.' This is a criticism made over and over again by later visitors, no doubt with their Gilpin in hand. 'Tho the parts are beautiful, the whole is ill-shaped', he said, adding – infamously – 'a number of gabel-ends [*sic*] hurt the eye with their regularity; and disgust it by the vulgarity of their shape. A mallet judiciously used (but who durst use it?) might be of service in fracturing some of them.' So for him the abbey was not ruined enough. He recommended the view from the road as best – something else regularly repeated by those following in his ample wake. (He was slightly taller than average, athletic, corpulent but not unwieldy; and 'his figure apostolical, his head bald.')[158] He doesn't seem to have taken the ferry to see the abbey from across the water, one of the most popular views, though Grose drew it, coming from the Gloucestershire side and sending his horse over while he worked. Colt Hoare also sketched it while Coxe examined the abbey.

From a nearer point of view, said Gilpin, 'when the eye settles on some of it's nobler parts', the abbey looked better. 'Nature has now made it her own. Time has worn off all traces of the chissel: it has blunted the sharp edges of rule and compass; and broken the regularity of opposing parts.' He followed Whately in disliking all signs of modernity in a ruin and approving of ivy, even in such large quantities as festooned the abbey. (Colt Hoare said that the 70-year-old ferryman with a bottle nose remembered when the ivy was constantly cut and carried away by people to burn and feed to cattle in winter, as at Goodrich. But it was cut no longer, and the following year he praised the aisle for being 'overhung with ivy in the most picturesque manner'.)[159] Gilpin also liked 'the mosses of various hues, with lychens, maiden-hair, penny-leaf' and other plants which 'add the richest finishing to a ruin.' The great moment then came, when Gethin, the custodian, unlocked the west door, throwing it open to collective gasps. Even Gilpin was almost satisfied. 'When we stood at one end of this awful piece of ruin ... the eye was above measure delighted with the beauty, the greatness, and the novelty of the scene.' It would, however, have been more picturesque if it hadn't been tidied up. 'Yet as the outside of the ruin, which is the chief object of picturesque curiosity, is still left in all it's wild, and native rudeness; we excuse – perhaps we approve—the neatness that is introduced within. It may add to the beauty of the scene – to it's novelty it undoubtedly does.' Visitors debated this issue for at least the next 70 years, *The Cambrian Directory* waxing particularly hot for the opposition. But everyone commented on the magnificence of the first sight of the interior:

> On opening the gates of the Abbey the coup d'oeil is very grand; its extent the peculiar lightness of its shafts and elegance of its several parts, together with the decorations of Ivy, moss & Shrubs which wave through the windows, form a most picturesque and justly celebrated ruin. The surrounding scenery also conspires to its effect, being composed of romantick dingles and fine wooded slopes with occasional protrusions of naked rock together with a majestick river flowing in full pride beneath.[160]

Grose, though, complained that the abbey wanted 'that gloomy solemnity so essential to religious ruins; those yawning vaults and dreary recesses, which strike the beholder with a religious awe, and make him almost shudder at entering them, calling into his mind all the tales of the Nursery.'[161] Torrington agreed. He wanted the duke to plant 'cypresses, etc.' in the ruins. He was shown the abbey by a boy 'who knew nothing, and by a very old man who had forgotten everything; but I kept him with me, as his venerable grey beard, and locks, added dignity to my thoughts; and I fancied him the hermit of the place.' The desire for gloomy vaults and dreary recesses continued, the American Jacob Green (1831) lamenting their absence. He also complained that no one would sell him fragments of the abbey for love or money.[162] Torrington had further suggestions:

> At some trifling expence, the surrounding cottages and orchards might be removed; and then the abbey would stand nobly back'd by woods, and open to the water: at present it is shamefully block'd up. The way to enjoy Tintern Abbey properly, and at leisure, is to bring wines, cold meat, with corn for the horses; (bread, beer, cider, and commonly salmon, may be had at the Beaufort Arms;) Spread your table in the ruins; and possibly a Welsh harper may be procured from Chepstow.

More puritanical tourists pondered the wickedness of (Roman Catholic) monasticism. Sulivan, highly critical of the superstition of the past and 'pious imposition', nonetheless acknowledged that abbeys and monasteries did keep useful records. But there were still too many 'useless drones' about for most visitors, though the more generous, like Grose, who found 'a parcel of beggars' there in 1775, 'four of whom demanded charity of us, in the literal sense of the word', noted they lived in slummy buildings 'now patched up for Dwelling Houses [but which] yet have Indisputable Marks of having once been Part of the Monastery.' He was shown the church by 'an old woman who picks up a tolerable livelyhood [*sic*] by the parties which constantly come hither from Bath and Bristol.' This may have been the same old woman who had captivated Gilpin by her poverty and wretchedness. 'As we left the abbey' he said, 'we found the whole hamlet at the gate, either openly soliciting alms; or covertly, under the pretence of carrying us to some part of the ruins, which each could shew; and which was far superior to any thing, which could be shewn by any one else.' He allowed the old woman to show him what she claimed had been the monks' library. 'She could scarce crawl; shuffling along her palsied limbs, and meagre, contracted body, by the help of two sticks ... and pointing to the remnant of a shattered cloister, told us, that was the place. It was her own mansion. All indeed she meant to tell us, was the story of her own wretchedness.' Gilpin did not expect to be interested but he was. 'I never saw so loathsome a human dwelling.' Thanks to his *Observations*, this old woman became something of a celebrity, but by the time Samuel Rogers visited in July 1791, she had died in the workhouse. Rogers left Tintern late:

> It was now near ten [at night], and the gloom was awful. It was here that I met a figure which I at first thought was an ancient tenant of the abbey. It wore a flannel gown which hung like a hood over the head. Not a lock of hair appeared over a pallid but striking countenance. A small black beaver hat was in one hand, and the other held a staff. I asked with some degree of hesitation the way to Chepstow, when it appeared to be an old woman. My question drew an appeal to my charity. She was returning home from the surgeon with a strengthening plaster and could scarce crawl ...

'Could scarce crawl' must be a memory of Gilpin's account of his old woman. Later tourists were less compassionate, being thoroughly fed up with the beggars they'd already met on their tour. 'At the door, were many cripples, produced for our charity', said Torrington, making Monmouthshire sound like modern India, though Rutland said the ones at Tintern were the poorest and most ragged set of inhabitants he had ever beheld. Barber was unsympathetic. He disagreed with Whately, disliking, as did many others, the 'train of miserable cottages engrafted on the offices of the abbey', and approving of the Duke of Beaufort's tidying up:

> In our different walks between the inn and the abbey, we were regularly beset with importunities for alms: the labouring man abandoned his employment and the housewife her family at the sight of a stranger, to obtain a few pence by debasing clamour This system of begging we found to arise from the late distresses, particularly that of the preceding year [1801], which, bearing on the great class of the people with an almost annihilating pressure, entitled them to the sympathy and assistance of those whom fortune had blessed with prosperity: they had strained their aching sinews to meet the exigence, yet their utmost exertions proved inadequate to the means of support. Thus situated, alms or outrage formed their alternate resources; but, happily, in the benevolence of the affluent they found an asylum. This pressure was fast withdrawing, but its effects remained; they had tasted the sweets of indolence, of support without exertion; they no longer felt the dignity of independence (for the odium of begging was withdrawn by invincible necessity); and they continued the unworthy trade without remorse.

Apart from Neath, this was the only place Barber came across 'the unworthy trade', in which case he was lucky, as beggars, as we have seen, abounded up and down the river, and it is clear from Gilpin, Grose, Rogers and others that their presence was not, as Barber thought, due to the recent run of bad harvests alone. Some, like the great propagandist for the gothic, John Carter, writing anonymously in *The Gentlemen's Magazine*, thought the problem went back to pre-reformation times. 'Without the portals, poor hoveled creatures demanded charity ... which once was doled to their forefathers in daily gifts.' He goes on to mock Gilpin via 'touristical perambulators full of refined notions and high taste [who] spouted off their several opinions by way of giving hints for the improvement of the natural defects and present condition of the edifice.' One of these wanted not merely to take a mallet to the gable-ends, but a hammer to the west front. 'The mullions of the west window, he also maintained, required a few judicious strokes; its tracery was too perfect and formal; and wanted variety.' Another so disapproved of the gothic he called for a cannon to knock down large parts of the church. Carter was equally savage about those who praised the ivy though they could see the effect of 'its sapping devastation', and a man who wanted to clear away all the stone 'rubbish' lying about and cart it off to help build the new wall round Piercefield. Artists are sneered at, too. 'This abbey-church, to artists who are skilled at taking views of our Antiquities, is considered by them as the chief model in the land for enriching their scenic knowledge, and ensuring pecuniary rewards from their well-sketched imitations of its various parts.'[163] Full-scale satire on Gilpin had, though, to wait for Dr Syntax's appearance in 1809.

Almost everyone seems to have been hungry by the time they'd seen the abbey, specially Torrington, who was keen on food as well as economy: 'It is always my rule to stop (if possible) about noon, at second-rate inns, and take the family fare; as one commonly dines much better in that way, and at half the expence of an order'd dinner.' On his first visit to Tintern he dined in the kitchen of the alehouse on salmon, and tolerable ale, with an 'impudent, talkative fisherman' boasting about his catches. Salmon up to 60 lbs, he was told, were sold at threepence a pound. On his second visit, six years later, he wanted to eat in the abbey, 'but the day was too cold and ungenial' so he again ate in the alehouse, this time food he'd brought with him. 'And we drank of our own bad wine: nor did the landlady seem dissatisfied, as I thought she wou'd, at this introduction of dinner, and wine; but attended us with assiduity, and cheerfully brought of her ale before us.' He was still hankering for a musical accompaniment. 'Musick in a fine day, or by moonlight, must sound nobly in the abbey.' He should have been there in August 1799, when the Beaufort family came down from Monmouth by water, accompanied by the band of the county militia in another boat (nearly 20 performers) who provided national, popular and other airs 'with little intermission, the whole of the voyage.' Heath reported that while the aristocrats looked at the abbey, the bandsmen, whose leader was a foreigner 'as well as unacquainted with the place', devoured the picnic brought from Troy house, instead of 'administring [*sic*] a mental entertainment to those whom the charms of their art had attracted to these walls.' Heath kept changing his account of this occasion, and later added that as the Beauforts returned to their boat, the band struck up 'Rule Britannia', which

> when the chorus parts united, the sound of the horns, added to the loud clangor [*sic*] of the cymbals, produced an effect in these high, rocky, woody and confined regions, far beyond the power of language to express, adequate to its just reward. It was highly amusing to the company witnessing the workmen leaving their employments in the woods, – hurrying to the shores of the river, – and standing with mute wonder and astonishment, on hearing the fine 'Concord of sweet Sounds', as the barge gently glided on the bosom of the peaceful Wye.

Torrington's alehouse may have been the Anchor, but the Beaufort Arms, where George Gethin was the inn-keeper, was more popular. (It is very probably Gethin in the background of catalogue no. 51). Heath said (1801) that you could get (again) a clean room and frugal fare there, and Mrs Gethin would arrange your repast while you looked at the abbey. Barber and Gethin got on especially well, perhaps sharing views on beggars and begging. Gethin 'extraordinary as it may seem, unites unaffected civility and kindness with upwards of forty years initiation into the business of an inn-keeper, and, as the neighbours say, a well-lined purse.' If he had really been there since the early 1760s, he had flourished with the tour. Barber wanted a shave and Gethin recommended the local blacksmith, but after the first few strokes of the razor Barber fled in terror. Gethin usually had the key to the abbey, but not always. Warner complained that a man on the other side of the river had got it – 'an inconvenience which is not recompensed by the civility of the ciceroni, [*sic*] who has none of the obliging attention of our host at the Beaufort Arms.' This man had it again the year after Barber visited and a boy had to be sent for him, while the waiting party ordered dinner.[164] Collins warned visitors in 1825 that 'a prohibition has recently been issued that prevent the inspection of the Ruins, at least the inside of the building on the Sunday.' No one else mentions this, so the prohibition must have been brief. Willett (fourth edition) described the landlord as 'the loquacious Cicerone of the Abbey'. It was then a Mr Payne who showed visitors the ruins.

By 1815, in Heath's sixth edition of *The Excursion*, a Mr and Mrs Mitchell had taken over the Beaufort Arms, providing the same services, but there seems to have been a less satisfactory period in between. An anonymous gentleman was received there in 1808 with most unwarrantable and disgusting insolence, and spent the night in a fisherman's cottage instead. The fisherman 'took great pains in explaining to us his art of fishing, and held a free and unrestrained conversation with us, which pleased us very much. Old threadbare representations of various parts of the sacred writings were closely stuck over our bed-room. We were obliged to sleep in one bed, which was perfectly clean and neat, and afforded us a comfortable and sweet repose.'[165]

Sarah Anne Wilmot, on her 1802 tour in heavy rain, made 'a few slight sketches', then sheltered at the Anchor, 'where the good woman boil'd us some potatoes, made us a good fire & we dry'd our shoes etc. & having eaten our Cold Collation the sun gave us a Cheer'. Cheer was sometimes needed as melancholy was not always pleasing:

> On our egress we met Mrs & Miss Hammet & Mrs Henley who were travelling in order to relieve the melancholy state of Miss H's mind, who had a misfortune to lose her only brother & sister in the spring of this year; they had brought a cold collation with them from Chepstow with an intention of dining in the abbey – After making our obeisance we retired to the Inn, where the ciceroni soon after joined us and with much apparent concern expressed his regret that so beautiful a young lady as that we had left should be so dejected, and his surprise to find, after we had retired, that the same scene which had a few minutes before inspired us with admiration and delight should have caused in her a profusion of tears. Probably the recollection of having formerly visited this place in company with the whole family or some train of reflection excited by the scenery, occasioned an excess of grief, which her prudence could not restrain.

The writer added a footnote in pencil: 'I have since heard that the family had spent a day together at the Abbey the preceding summer, when the brother had carved with a knife the several initials of their names on the bark of a tree adjoining the entrance the sight of which had caused this severe emotion.'

Many liked to picnic in the abbey like the Hammets, among them Bloomfield and his friends. 'Most of the party sat down and took sketches of the interior; but I found it above my reach, and so gave vent to my feelings by singing for their amusement and my own the 104th Psalm.' This contains appropriate verses on wine making glad the heart of man, and getting meat in due season. 'We took a hearty, but hasty breakfast; and I rather think the Welsh girl who waited upon us was not sorry to get rid of her company', he added. Mary Wordsworth had bread and cheese. The amateur composer and musician John Marsh and his party were splendidly conned in 1808 by the boatmen before tucking in:

As we approached the Abbey we found that according to ancient custom, the first person that discovered it, forfeited half a crown to the boatmen, which I therefore afterwards paid & set down to the general account, with a guinea for the boat & rowers. – On our arrival there we carried a provision basket Mrs. Smith had brought with us, to the Abbey, where we borrowed a table from an adjoining cottage & had a very good cold collation of Veal pye, Chicken & tongue, with some Wine & water, after which we explored the ruins.[166]

Webb deplored the way water tour parties ate in a once sacred building, but in vain. Twenty-five years later Twamley noted that stones were set in all the chief viewpoints to serve as seats and even tables for people to draw on and picnic. She was disturbed by 'Where *can* John have put the sandwiches?' from a party who had come for the express purpose of 'lunching' in the abbey. She felt it had become too much of a 'sight'; 'The various, and sometimes too obvious contrivances which have been adopted for the safe passage and ascent of visitors to every part of the Abbey, by means of platforms, rails and ladders, annoy, even while they accommodate us, by the evidence they bear of the solemn old place being one of the 'show' family.' The railings, which can be seen in some drawings and prints, had been put in by the Duke of Beaufort so tourists could 'traverse the greater part of the transept at a considerable height from the floor', as Roscoe did (as they are doing in catalogue no. 56). The difference between sensitive tourists and vulgar trippers was offensive to Catherine Sinclair in 1833 when:

our solitude was invaded by a cargo of passengers, landed at Chepstow from on board the Bristol steam-boat, who rushed in with sketch-books, eye-glasses, parasols, best bonnets, McIntosh cloaks, baskets of provisions, and every sort of modern luxury considered essential to the full enjoyment of beautiful scenery or ruined abbeys; and before we could hurry away, the ivy-mantled walls were crowned with a wreath of beaux and young ladies in full flirtation, while the long aisles rung with laughter and merriment, causing a ludicrous mixture of tragedy and comedy in our own feelings of sympathy with past and present times.

But in spite of trippers and railings, and 'the ignorant garrulity of the man who shows the abbey' (*Penny Magazine*), people went on admiring it. Twamley wrote 'There is a pure and beautiful symmetry – a calm, venerable and solemn character about this place, that must be *felt* to be understood.' And on Greville, in 1839, the abbey produced 'an impression similar in kind and equal in amount to that which I felt at the sight of St Peter's.' The only person who seriously disagreed was Louis Simond, who was jaundiced about the whole tour. For him Tintern was like 'Westminster Abbey with the roof off', and it confirmed his view that 'upon the whole the beauties of the Wye itself fell rather short of the descriptions of Gilpin and other travellers.'

People usually spent at least an hour at the abbey before moving on, but the boatmen were always anxious about the tide. Booker wrote a poem on leaving, published by Heath in *Tintern* (1803):

No troubled waves infuriate foam beside
Me and my Fellows, while thro' scenes so fair
We pass, on waters soft as zephyr's kiss. –
Oh, may we thus, at life's *last* eve, repair,

Peaceful, to that eternal ocean, wide
Opening to fairer scenes – the realms of bliss!

Tintern to Wyndcliff

Torrington, with the boastful fisherman as steersman, spent the last part of his voyage listening to the boatmen 'telling miraculous stories; and in hunting a duck for half an hour.' He was less amused when 'By the wind meeting the tide, the water began to be too rough for me; but my company spoke lightly of it; after bragging of their skill in swimming.' When he came for the second time, his feelings were unmixed: 'the evening was cold and miserable, but we lay for some time upon our oars, gazing.' What upset most people was not the waves but the colour of the water now it was tidal, and the 'ouzy' and 'sludgy' and 'sedgy' banks. Gilpin was particularly disgusted, seeming to have expected a river as silver and clear as one in a painting by Claude. Greville, 70 years later, and looking down from the Eagle's Nest on Wyndcliff, said 'The Wye ... is an eyesore in the midst of such scenery: it looks like a long, slimy snake dragging its foul length through the hills and woods which environ its muddy stream.' Manby, however, who had hitched a lift with a boat-party of ladies, thought the whole voyage to Chepstow 'as nature's Lyceum to exhibit her beauties, capriciousness, and sublimity.'

The view from the Eagle's Nest was the widest on the tour; you could see the fields of the Lancaut peninsula running down to where the Wye made its grand curve under Piercefield cliffs before turning sharply below Winter's Leap to head along the final stretch to Chepstow. You could see the castle on its bluff, and beyond it the meeting of the Wye with the Severn, and the Bristol Channel busy with ships. Beyond that lay Gloucestershire and the Cotswolds, Somerset and the Mendips and on a clear day the Quantocks. 'The grouping of this landscape is perfect', said Puckler-Muskau. 'I know of no picture more beautiful'. So it was well worth the unpleasantness of landing, as Gilpin did, on an ouzy beach, and the labour of a steep climb. The steepness was lessened after 1827 by the construction of an 'easy, regular zig-zag' path – the 365 Steps – by Beaufort's agent, who also rebuilt the Eagle's Nest rather higher up. (Both sites remain). At the same time there was built 'a pretty little toy of a cottage, containing a huge walnut-tree slab, being the section of an ancient tree that stood a few years back in Chepstow moat, and was blown down by a storm', said Thackeray, who somewhat perversely preferred the view from the bottom of Wyndcliff to that from the top. 'The little rooms, nay chandeliers, of this cottage are all daintily covered with moss and the cottage is hidden from the road by a thicket of laurels; here parties may picnic at their leisure, and passing it ... we heard from the thicket the sound of a Welsh harp, a very old, feeble and unsatisfactory instrument, that performed for a considerable period a certain tune called 'Poor Marianne', that the British public has probably heard ere this.'[167] Music again, even here at Moss Cottage (see picture overleaf), where Mr and Mrs Vaughan would give visitors the most marked attention in 'these regions of pleasure', Heath said, and look after their horses while they made the climb. Collins said one of the rooms was made out as a wigwam. Baker mentioned ravens, and said the nightingales were 'more numerous and more melodious than in any other part of the kingdom.' Mary Anne Hibbert thought nothing could be more picturesque or beautiful than the path itself, as it wound up the rocks in an easy ascent with occasional glimpses through the trees of the lovely view. It was 'covered with moss and stones here & there to prevent you slipping. There are seats too at intervals all the way up. The air was heavenly and it was altogether a

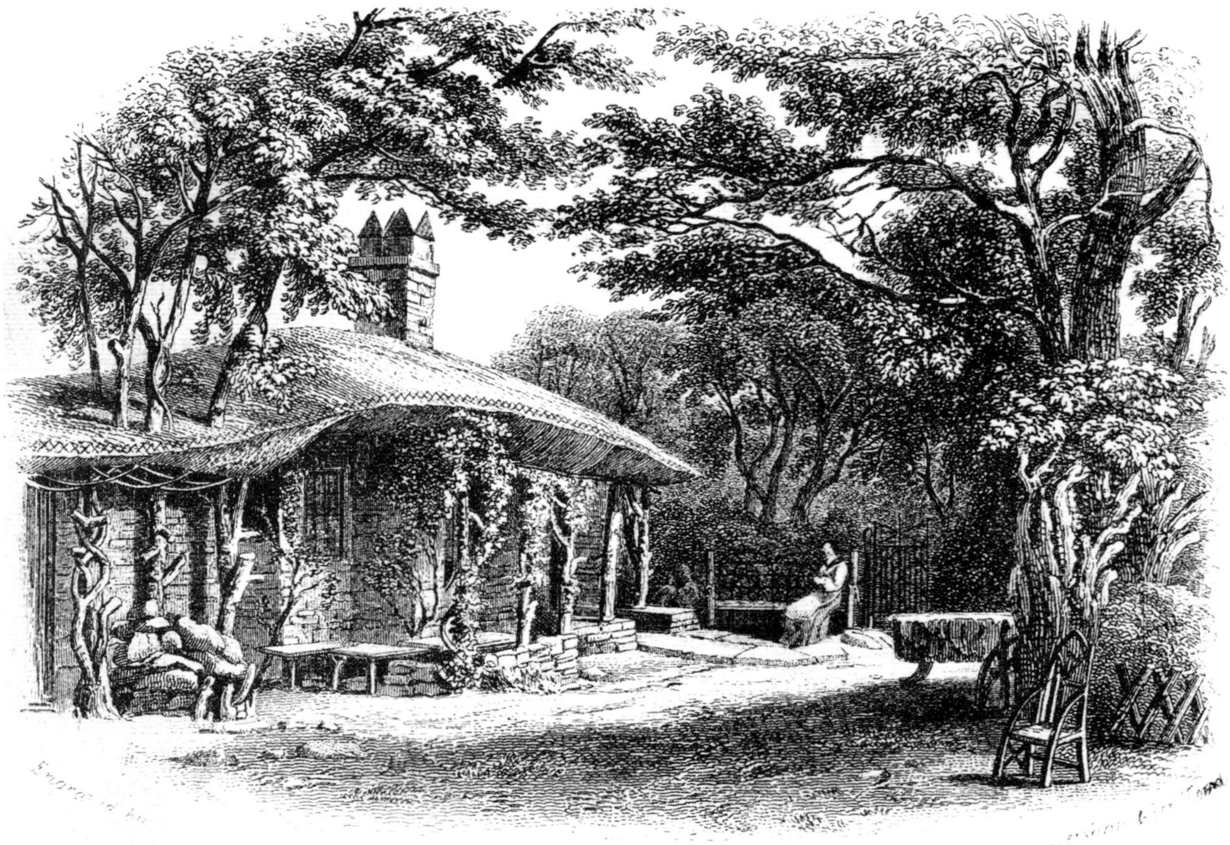

Moss Cottage, engraving by Kershaw and Son, nd. (Chepstow Museum)

walk of exquisite enjoyment.'[168] *The Penny Magazine*, less athletic perhaps, pointed out there was an easier climb from behind, up what Fosbroke called 'a giant with a hairy skin of wood and a head with enormous teeth of rock.'[169] Earlier he had denounced the fir-trees at the summit. 'Who but a barber in the picturesque would have curled and powdered Windcliff [*sic*]? Will it never be known, that firs are fit only for single trees and shrubberies; that they look like funereal plumes stuck in the ground, and stand only, like tombs, to show the burial of the picturesque ... Windcliff should have only forest trees. If the rage for firs continues, England will soon resemble Norway.'[170] William Mason agreed: firs were 'those swine of the vegetable race'. Fosbroke thought that Wyndcliff, like Snowdon, should be visited at sunrise or seen through a Claude-glass.

Piercefield

The tourists who'd made the climb to the Eagle's Nest then descended to walk through the 300 acres of the famous grounds at Piercefield. But many stayed in their boat, disembarking at Chepstow, and then walking upstream, perhaps the next day, to see them. Rutland, most unusually, got out at the Piercefield cold bath and climbed the 'steep ziz-zag path that led through the thick of the woods into the garden on the top of the ridge.'

Piercefield, as has been said, was the creation of Valentine Morris, and his principal architect, said Heath (1826) – we would probably say builder – was Charles Howells, a mason who kept the pub at Pont-y-saison on the Angidy brook. They constructed an extensive network of paths for the visitor to follow along the three miles of clifftops. As well as the views cut through the woods, there were seats at which to stop, and buildings to admire When Bishop Pococke visited in 1756 he was shown round by the gardener, who pointed out the projecting rock on which Morris had been standing moments before part of it crashed down the cliff to the river. Work was still going on; he saw a small Druid's Temple under construction. Dodsley (1759) listed 23 scenes, views and buildings beautiful 'beyond description'. Edward Knight listed 26 in 1760, by which time the Temple was finished.[171] There were also a Chinese Bridge and a Chinese Seat, an Orangery and Cascade, though Arthur Young, visiting in 1767, found the last missing. He wrote a long and ecstatic description of the scenery, and was equally enthusiastic about Morris himself, who 'has always people ready to attend whoever comes, to conduct them every where, and not one of them is suffered to take anything; yet they shew all with great readiness and civility.' Whately, in 1770, very much admired the lawns and 'these romantic scenes', which is where Gilpin may have got the idea that the views were not picturesque, but extremely romantic 'and give loose to the most pleasing riot of imagination.' He thought Morris's shrubberies, though, were paltry. 'It is not the shrub which offends: it is the formal introduction of it.' Everyone thereafter followed him in dismissing the shrubberies, though Sulivan, in 1778 and therefore before the *Observations* were published, found them boring all on his own. He also thought the house, of which there is only one distant representation, was indifferent and whimsically placed. An anonymous diarist in 1777 or 1778 was more generous; it was 'an old mansion, added to and repair'd, rather neat than costly; and exhibits the appearance of a plain comfortable Dwelling'.[172] But the *Pocket Vade Mecum* (1785) called it 'an inconsiderable edifice, unworthy of its situation', Torrington dismissed it as of no account, and it was described by Anne Cooper as 'by no means adequate to the situation, irregularly built and unequally elevated.' Later Heath said (1813) 'The house was a very indifferent residence for a family of fortune before Sir Mark Wood purchased the estate.' Perhaps Morris was planning to build a new one when the landscape was finished, but by 1772 he was catastrophically in debt after a very expensive but unsuccessful attempt to become MP for the county, and, handing his estates over to trustees, he went off to be lieutenant-governor of St Vincent in the West Indies where he hoped to recover himself.[173] Alas, he did not. When he returned to England in 1782 his wife had gone mad and his walks were neglected. George Cumberland and Charles Long found the place deserted, and 'put up our horses in the solitary stalls of his once busy stable' and walked about without a guide. They found tourists had been taking advantage of Morris's absence to plunder his fruit walls and conservatories.[174] Two years later, imprisoned for debt, Morris was forced to sell Piercefield to George Smith, a Durham man who opened the Monmouthshire bank, with John Curre of nearby Itton, in 1787.

Smith's arrival was welcomed by Edward Davies, who added a quatrain to his poem:

With joy I hear these walks again look gay,
And a new lord, of polished taste, obey:
The fairy spot revives beneath his care,
And is once more the fairest 'mongst the fair.

He was too optimistic. Smith had already employed John Soane on his Durham estate, and now got him to draw up plans for a new mansion. A start was made, and the roof was on, when Smith's bank crashed on the outbreak of war with France in 1793. Smith was forced to sell Piercefield the following year to Sir Mark Wood, a nabob and MP who, with Joseph Bonomi, considerably altered Soane's design, adding a portico and wings. Bonomi also designed the interiors. 'Col Wood is building a very large House of white stone which is brought from Bath' wrote a diarist in 1796; ' [it] was only begun 13 months ago and the Col expects to get into it in 5 weeks – gave 39,000£ for the Estate. The House is to cost more than 20,000 pounds and the walks 1000£ to put them in repair: then remains the Garden Green House and Hot House to do – so much for East India Money.'[175] The new house was still not completely finished when Rutland visited in August 1797.

Wood did not enjoy his new house long. In 1802 he sold the estate to Nathaniel Wells, the son of a white plantation owner in St Kitts and his black house slave Juggy. According to Farington, who got it from the gardener, Wells was 'a civil intelligent man' and had paid £95,000 for the estate, so Wood did pretty well out of it. Farington thought the house 'a specimen of very bad taste in architecture', though 'the view from the front is beautiful.' The lodgewoman spoke very highly of Wells who was 'a Creole of very deep colour, but Miss Wells (his sister) is fair.' Wells was very particular about knowing visitors' names, and didn't like trespassers. He, like all previous owners, soon found the estate a burden, and in 1819 tried to sell it. According to Collins in 1825, there was an idea the estate should be bought by the nation and given to the Duke of Wellington. Wells was still trying to sell it when Puckler-Muskau came a few years later. According to Puckler-Muskau's coach-driver, Wells had nearly sold it to a man who wanted it for his son, but the son had gone off with an actress and the sale had fallen through. Now Wells, who had a numerous family, was in debt. In the end he stayed on till his death at Bath in 1852, after which the house had several owners. It continued to be lived in till the 1920s before being abandoned and left in its current ruined state, with the parkland developed into the race-course.[176]

Torrington, on his first visit in 1781, arrived early. He knew Mr B--- who was then leasing the house for £40 per annum, without grounds or garden, but he didn't want to meet him, so asked the gardener to show him round. He thought the place grand, romantic – and good for a picnic. 'In these shades one might pass a happy day, and dine as I had before proposed in Tintern Abbey; for there is a well near the Elm Walk, that would serve to cool wine in; and the grotto or cave will protect from bad or sultry weather.' The gardener sold the fruit of the garden and hot-house 'which wou'd add much to an entertainment in the woods.' Torrington was moved to write a mildly erotic poem, then walked on to the Lovers Leap, 'well rail'd; so that none but the very desponding would take it: I have never heard that it was attempted: the first leap would cure the most heart-felt pangs.' But the walks had been sadly neglected in Morris's absence: 'It is to be lamented that this fine place is suffered to run into neglect which is but too evident since Mr Morris left it', wrote a visitor in 1781,[177] and Torrington found some of the walks 'almost impassable, viz the zig-zag walk to the water, and that to the cold bath'. He thought old people should be allowed to go round in carriages 'and how highly it wou'd repay the gardener to keep a garden chair with a small horse; as it is so profitably and agreeably practised at Mr Hamiltons at Pains-hill.' The trees of the Elm Avenue, 'tall and beautiful, are now mark'd and number'd; so that I tremble for their approaching fate.' (He was right to do so, for when he returned in 1787 the axe had 'done much havoc'.) After his second visit he felt Piercefield was 'a very fine thing to see, but not a desirable place to inhabit

... being for ever on an exhibition, and in a glare; and so famed, that an owner, and his servants become shew men, with an eternal 'Walk in Gemmen'.'

Tourists enjoyed exercising their critical faculties and picturesque vocabularies here. Wyndham, for instance, said 'among the many awful prospects ... these of the Wye are the most sublime'. Torrington found them 'noble and romantic'. Ireland considered that only Claude Lorrain could do justice to the views. Skrine thought Lovers Leap 'a frightful precipice, darkened below with wood', and Bloomfield wrote of a fearful complacency 'down which the eye descends'. Barber said Morris 'engrafted the blandishments of art upon the majestic wildness of the scene without distorting its original character.' But there were worries about his successors. Shaw, who found half the grounds were grown wild in 1788 and 'not at present displayed', and the rest only shown once a week, was very dubious about the alterations George Smith was making; recent research has shown these involved quite extensive widening and straightening. 'Whether his new models will be more valued than the originals, time and taste must determine; many of the beautiful serpentines, I fear, from what we now observed, will be thrown into strait lines.' This was against all picturesque principles. But one of the seats 'may be called a front box of one of the compleatest theatres in the universe ... Here wants no painted canvas to express its scenery, nature's sweet landscape is quite enough.' Shaw's description is one of the very best, and most people agreed with him about Smith's changes. David Williams, who had been shown round the grounds by Morris himself in happier times, thought it was 'extremely difficult to place a modern house in anything like harmony with the grounds' and criticized 'a disposition to ornament [which] has been gradually encroaching on the interesting objects that are crouded on this enchanting spot.' This is presumably a crack at the nabob Wood:

> Superb gate-ways, white paling, spruce hedges, lawns by mowing rendered bald and insipid, artificial banks, new plantations, meandered walks, with verges nicely edged, and curvatures fatiguing by their correctness – these are the evils to be apprehended at Persfield; of which the author has perceived some of the symptoms: for opulence is strongly tempted to expence, and expence is generally employed to deprive natural objects of everything that can give them spirit and attraction.

He also sneered at Gilpin, who 'had probably fatigued his sensibility at Tinterne'. Like everyone else, Williams had suggestions for improvements: 'a finer river; a cascade in a solemn and woody precipice; a characteristic edifice for the proprietor; a solitary urn, in an appropriate spot, with only the simple inscription, "To the memory of Valentine Morris." would render these ornamental grounds unrivalled in Great Britain.' Whately would have approved this last, recommending that 'sometimes a solitary urn, inscribed to the memory of a person now no more, but who once frequented the shades where it stands, is an object equally elegant and interesting.' And pleasingly melancholic, one might add. Wigstead was alarmist: 'I earnestly hope, we shall not in a few years, see little Chinese temples, flaming dragons, and sea horses, peeping through the vistas, (now so beautifully engrossed by nature in her unattired loveliness) such decorations serve only to distract the eye, and raise the pitying sigh in the breast of the true taste.'

The new house was a stately mansion, said Skrine approvingly, but the grounds, open only once a week under Smith's brief tenure, were still only open twice a week under Wood, so many people missed them, including Warner. Barber had trouble with the gate-keeper: he went a mile and a half from Chepstow to 'a capital lodge with iron gates and palisadoes' where he met 'a well-grown lad [who] stared at us through the rails, with more than the usual stupidity of boys brought up at a distance to towns.' The boy's grandfather appeared 'and, if intellect were hereditary, the boy might presume on his lineage with more chance of correctness than many of higher birth'. Eventually, though, it became clear that as it was a Saturday, Piercefield was closed and would not be open again till the following Tuesday. So Barber and his companion rode to St Arvans, left their horses with the blacksmith and went in through a back gate. No one attempted to stop them, and they wandered all over. The Giant's Cave had lost 'That giant with the goggling eye, Who strides in mock sublimity' (Bloomfield), a victim, according to Heath, of frost. 'Now in impotence alone he frowns', said Collins, though a culverin (a small canon) stood outside the cave for making echoes. Willett was anxious that tourists came upon the cave from the south, where it was 'dark, gloomy and obscure', not from the north, where the effect was spoiled by a gleam of light. He later dropped this advice. Britton, like Barber, ignored the owner's wishes and 'To save time, and the distance of a long circuitous walk, I ventured, with some qualms of conscience, to trespass through a hedge, and by an unbeaten track, across the Park'. Farington, who'd brought a picnic, chose to dine at the cave, but 'Not having knives and forks and glasses we sent to Piercefield House and were furnished with them', which seems unusually civil of the proprietor. On open days you were supposed to leave your carriage at the main lodge, and meet it again at the Fishpond above St Arvan's, after your walk. (Collins advised making sure there was someone the other end to let you out to where carriage or horses were waiting, or you'd have to walk all the way back again.) Or

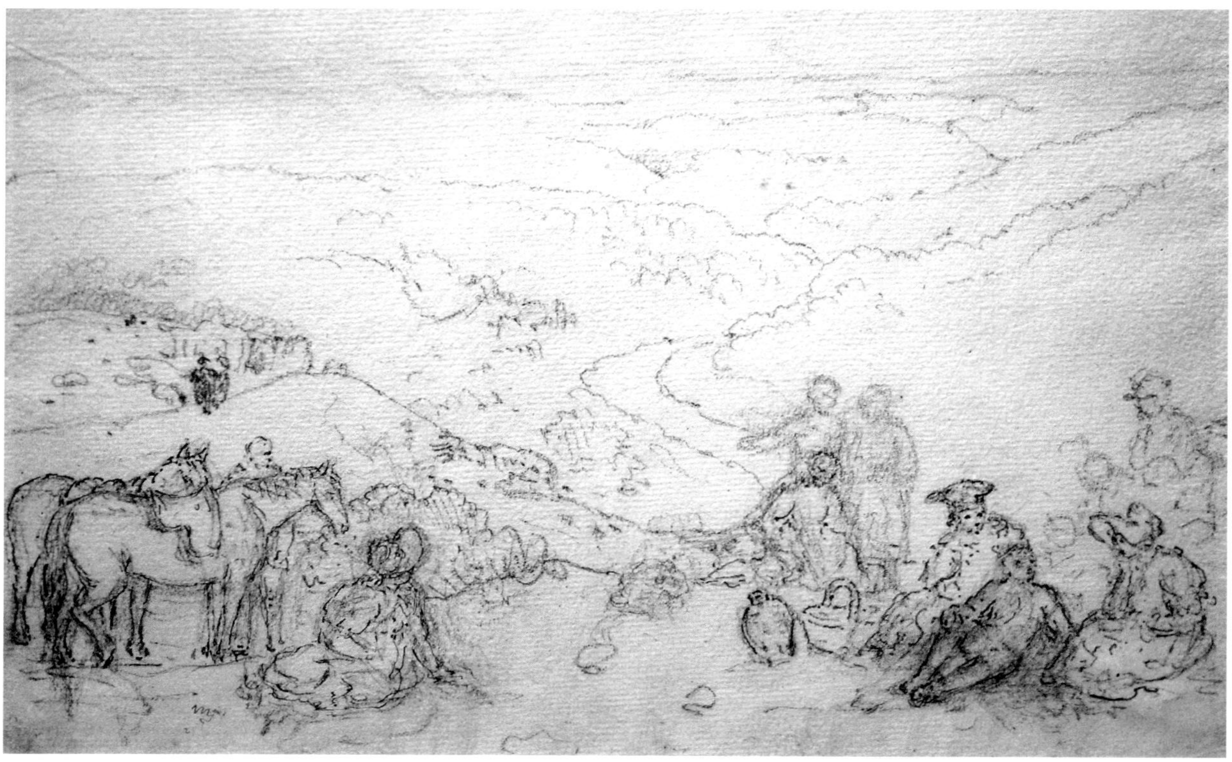

A Picnic at Piercefield by Thomas Tudor. (Private collection)

you could park horse or equipage at the Squirrel Inn at St Arvans (Heath, *Tintern*, 1823). When the fourth edition of Willett's *Strangers' Guide* was published (dedicated to Wells) the grounds were closed, but he listed nine Grand Views, though the Druid's Temple had gone. It was said Wells never refused entry to anyone who wrote for permission to visit, but Catherine Sinclair reported that travellers felt extremely ill-used at not being admitted 'to lionize the beautiful grounds'. There was, she was told, a new owner who 'desirous to avoid the odium of causing such an exclusion' remained anonymous and entrenched behind his park walls. She was misinformed. Wells, in financial distress, was hoping to sell the estate, or at least to build some 'superb villas' in his demesne, but nothing came of these plans, just as nothing ever seems to come of the many modern ones to restore the ruined house today. Perhaps it should be left as it is, a picturesque ruin.

Many travellers were interested in the echoes that could be created at the Giant's Cave by firing the culverin, swivel guns or a pistol. Young said you could bounce the sound back and forth across the Wye up to nine times in favourable weather; Anne Cooper said thirteen. Manby, who himself travelled with a flute to play to the birds, joined a party with a bugle-horn which produced even more satisfactory reverberations. One of Bloomfield's friends had a clarinet, as we know, and the writer of a 1798 *Welsh Tour* had a fellow traveller, also with a flute, who 'raised some of the sweetest sounds, which ever struck my ear.' Collins heard music rising from tour boats below:

> The softly breathing flute by skill attun'd.
> At intervals breaks on the attentive ear,
> Thus with thanksgiving join'd to melody,
> The soul enjoys serenity and peace.

Or perhaps not. Cumberland noted the howlings of foxes; perhaps a comment on the music.

There is always a grouch in every tour party, and Simond continued to play the part at Piercefield. The view was not, on the whole, equal to its reputation, and he didn't like the way what some people called the *ferme ornée* of Lancaut had 'everything going on in the way of husbandry, picturesque or not'. He compared the house unfavourably with Stourhead. But he liked the grass shorn by 500 sheep – 'this is all beautiful' – and he took an interest in local prices: rent of good arable land or coppiced wood, was from 30s to 40s an acre, and it sold at 30 years purchase; labourers got 2s 6d a day plus small beer – 'twenty years ago ½d, since when price of land has doubled, so no one suffers but stockholders and mortgagees.' Butchers' meat was 9d a pound, a good fowl 4s 6d; fuel was cheap. Doctor Spiker, in 1820, was another grumbler. Though he at first called the house 'a superb villa with a very extensive park', as he got nearer he became more critical. The third storey was a clumsy addition, and the house as a whole only looked good from a distance. The Druid's Temple was not a success, and the park was neglected and the walks choked up with weeds and bushes Perhaps he was cross because he couldn't examine the grotto as it was 'full of gay ladies and gentlemen'.[178]

As time went on, the criticisms got sharper: people had described Piercefield too often. For Leigh, in 1831, 'The walk ... has a degree of tediousness and too much sameness in many of its parts, not withstanding the general variety which enlivens it.' Though Puckler-Muskau thought it 'without question the finest [place] in England, at least for situation', Twamley agreed with Leigh about the 'sameness of an artificial walk of such length becoming very wearisome'. She was determined to be unimpressed: 'Piercefield is the only beautiful place I know, the reality of which did not surpass the expectations I had formed.' Perhaps the views across the Wye had become overgrown – they would have needed constant attention. She scoffed at the house: 'A fine handsome mansion placed in a commanding situation, looking about with all its windows, and seeming to say "Am I not an exceedingly good-looking house?"' And she didn't like the Grotto or Giant's Cave – 'all such small trickery upon grand nature, such tinkering of tinsel upon gold – are my aversion.' She then fell off her high horse by quoting a Coleridge poem which she thought was about the view from Wyndcliff, but was in fact about the view from the other side of the Bristol Channel.

Final Stretch to Chepstow

Those who stayed in their boat instead of climbing Wyndcliff sometimes stopped below Winter's Leap, like Anne Cooper. 'At the foot of these rocks, near a bason formed by the tide we cast anchor & prepared our dinner. A dinner of cold meats is soon dispatched. When we had finished our repast, we endeavoured to climb the rocks. The gentlemen succeeded but my strength was not equal to the attempt: The banks were slimy & steep, the stones were rough & pointed, & the danger of retreating overcame the pleasure proposed in the ascent.' Everyone got back in and proceeded to Chepstow, passing under the bridge. Bloomfield, not always to be relied on to have the correct response, here did so:

> And shall we e'er forget the day,
> When our last chorus died away:
> When first we hail'd, then moor'd beside
> Rock-founded Chepstow's mouldering pride:
> Where that strange bridge, light, trembling, high,
> Strides like a spider o'er the Wye ...?

The bridge he admired was replaced by the elegant iron one in 1816 costing £17,850. Spiker said workmen were still removing the old piers in 1820. *The Penny Magazine* denied the usual guidebook description of the new bridge as 'elegantly light and airy'; it thought it 'massive and grand'. Safely under it (and remembering the accident which had killed so many there, no doubt), passengers disembarked, said Willett, at the upper or Packet slip, or the lower slip on the Back.

Chepstow

Those coming out of Piercefield by the Alcove got a fine view of Chepstow Castle, a variation on which Paul Sandby was to make famous through his 1775 aquatint (catalogue no. 85).[179] Those who continued by boat had an equally good view of it from below. They often left its exploration, and Piercefield, to the morrow. It had been a long day. Grose, for instance, didn't get to Chepstow till 6 pm as there had been a strong wind against the oarsmen all the way from Tintern. Like everyone else he disliked the low banks of mud and slime, and when he got up at 7 next morning and crossed the bridge to draw the castle from the other side, 'We found it very difficult to get along the river's side, the mud of ouse being extremely slippery.' But he found the town attractive, with 'many very neat houses almost all of them whitewashed over [and], two or three good inns.' He stayed at the Three Cranes, but when he returned a few weeks later, 'The house being full I slept at a Sadlers next door to the inn.' Monmouthshire was 'about' rebuilding its side of the bridge, which had the loose planks (to accommodate the very high tides) which had excited visitors since at least Marmaduke Rawdon in 1665. There had been an extraordinarily high tide in 1703, and people were still talking about it in 1742 when Jeremiah Milles came for a night. He thought the church 'a clumsy Gothick building', but was very impressed by a walnut tree near the churchyard, the finest he had ever seen, ten feet in circumference, and with boughs spreading 110 feet from one extreme part to the other. No one else mentions this walnut, and it may have been another tree chopped by a merciless vicar. The text to Sandby's first aquatint described another very high tide in 1738, when 'one man lost above 130 head of Cattle, which with other damages it did there ... were computed at 7 or 8000£.' There were further great tides in 1768 and 1799, and always the prospect of another, so crossing the bridge could give the visitor another of those safe frissons which were so highly valued.[180]

Rawdon arrived on market day 'where they had abundance of hogs and sowes with their litters of pigs, to be sold in pens, as they sell sheepe in Smithfield'. Torrington found the town crowded for the wool fair in 1781. He thought the women handsome, having 'fair skins, with very long eyes, and noses' which he regarded as essential for female beauty. He managed to get a room at the Three Cranes, at whose door he found 'a bevy of Welsh squires intoxicating themselves; and round the market-place, plenty of puppet-shews, balance masters, &c. &c. but the heat of the weather prevented my going to see them.' After drinking two pint basins of tea, he walked to a stone 'gazeabout, half a mile distant' and looked across the Severn. Two ladies were already there, doing their gazing at a boat carrying someone very dear to them, so he hurried away 'not to interrupt the luxury of their grief' – not such pleasing melancholy, perhaps. On the quay he saw immense piles of oak bark for export to Ireland, and nearly 21 miles of iron water pipes, like cannon, each 9 feet long and weighing about eight hundredweight, which were being exported to France (with permission) 'but whether for the Paris aqueducts, or the Kings water works is not known'. Torrington was either the victim of a local jokester, or it was not tea he had been drinking in his two pint basins. Tanner, who then leased the Tintern iron-works, was in fact sending about 40 cannon of exactly that size to Woolwich Arsenal that very month. He, along with other iron masters, was (almost certainly with malice) accused of trading with the enemy, and he may have been sending water-pipes to France as well. But 21 miles of either cannon or water-pipes is not remotely credible.[181]

Torrington was on safer ground at the churchyard where a rat-catcher offered him a 'cunning receipt to kill rats, or to cure horses of the staggers', but he preferred a beautiful Pontypool snuff-box as a souvenir. He was interested in surviving customs, and noted that the Chepstow maypole, like all the others he'd seen, was 'well hung round with garlands'. Morris dancers, he learned on his second visit, 'yet existed in the Forest of Dean, whence they issued, as formerly, at Whitsuntide; and ... in every antient device; (except that of the hobby horse;) the Maid Marian, and the Clown being preserv'd: – as forests still retain, with their wild looks, some wild manners, these will, probably, extinguish at the sale of the Crown lands.' This was not so: Heath reported in 1815 that the Morris dancers still went about 'decorated with ribbons that might vie with the rainbow for variety of colours, and other ornaments – entertaining the neighbourhood with their grotesque humour.'[182] But Torrington was disappointed by a lack of wildness on the Wye: 'As yet every charge has been very dear, and we have found no country manners, hear no strange dialect, mett [*sic*] no harper, or any ridiculous difficulties.' But he disapproved of the churchyard being 'overun, as most others are, to the disgrace of decency &c, with rampant nettles', and he was very dissatisfied with his accommodation. He was at the Three Cranes and suspected tourists were imposed upon because both it and the Beaufort Arms were leased by same person: 'Nothing cou'd be worse, or more imposing than our inn at Chepstow; the stables were a wretched dungeon; everything bad, and charged high, and this arises from its being the only inn.'

Sulivan, in 1778, had found little good to say about the town: 'Chepstow, if ever it was a populous and beautiful town, has now very little the remains of either; the houses are poor and dirty, the streets narrow, and the inns so wretchedly bad, that travellers would do well to continue there no longer than merely to procure a change of horses.' But in 1791 Sophia Ward had no complaints about the George, or the town: 'it is a Charming Town well paved – and the houses kept in good order ... saw a number of ships lying here – some a building – & every appearance of much Industry and trade.' Samuel Rogers had no complaints either. It must have been nearly midnight when he arrived after his night walk from Tintern, but Chepstow kept late hours, and 'I was regaled with songs by a cheerful young man of the town who was entertaining the landlord's daughters – fine girls, particularly the youngest – in the bar'. Sarah Anne Wilmot thought the town was prettier than Monmouth, with houses that are 'white with parapets & mostly sash'd, the inhabitants look neat & comfortable.'[183] Baker, a terrible snob, recommended the Beaufort Arms because it was built by the duke. It was 'furnished with every convenience and accommodation. But there are other Inns that will be found convenient for the frugal traveller.' He, like most tourists, was fascinated by the bridge, and the well in Mr Evans's house in Castle Street, which ebbed and flowed contrary to the tides. Willett gloomily reported accidents: a horse fell off the bridge in 1801, and in 1803 two horses fell down the cliff, but survived.

Sir Christopher Sykes was of Sulivan's opinion. He found 'a poor miserable town, without even a book or station[ers] shop it seems to be supported by travellers to Wales and to see Piercefield.' The people were ignorant: 'As I walked to the church I observed to a Gentn that it was much anterior to the Castle. Yes tis the Church is very antient it was built about the time Julius Caesar came over.' Sykes 'now judged that I was in Wales.' Church attendance didn't meet his requirements: 'The Church was ill attended both Morning and Evening every corner is crowded with seats, but few in them, many quite empty.'[184] The churchyard, according to an anonymous diarist of 1796 had been 'much disfigured by the Parson – having just lopped a Row of Lime Trees, that did form a most agreeable shade, sold the Tops for 5 Guineas to make Matts and by cutting the trees at this season ... the <u>Parson</u> will have killed the trees (Oh fye!)'. Also the water in the town was bad.[185]

And so the tourists went on, alternately ecstatic and grumbling. Barber thought the town 'an irregular-built trading place, but where the well-furnished houses and opulent establishments of many of the inhabitants engaged in business prove the success of their commercial enterprise' and he had an excellent repast at the Beaufort Arms, which Wigstead thought very ill-sited. Cooke was impressed that the merchants were rich enough to import their wines from Oporto, and that the salmon fisheries brought in £300 a year. Farington had the excitement of a parade of the Volunteers who marched from the castle to the church. 'Two Captains of the Navy were also here for the purpose of exercising Sea fencibles [volunteers]. Everything indicated universal preparation for War.' He was right; it was 1803 and the brief peace between England and France was over, which meant, among other things, continued demand for travel within Britain. His bill was: 'dinner 2/6d, wine 5/- a bottle, bed each night 1/6d, breakfast 1/3d, Tea 1/3d.' He reckoned his daily expenditure was ten shillings, including tips, and said this was 'the first time of wine being charged pr. Bottle', which must mean he was used to paying for it by the glass. Daniel Carless Webb dined at the Beaufort Arms and found good accommodation combined with civility and moderate charges. The Revd Edmund Butcher recorded road rage. His driver had an altercation with that of a loaded wagon which he described as 'a canvas-covered mountain'. It looked as though a battle of whips might ensue, so he made his driver back up.[186]

A popular after-dinner entertainment was to walk to the castle by moonlight. Zouch Turton, the Duke of Beaufort's agent, forewarned of Rutland's coming, accompanied him there. 'Every breeze was hushed: the moon had risen, and her silvery beams diffused their splendour over the embattled towers and mouldering fragments, while other parts remained immersed in dark shade.' Bloomfield's party 'spent a delightful and social evening at the Beaufort Arms, and retired to rest, but not till we had walked to the castle by moonlight, where we found an owl hooting lustily from the battlements of Marten's Tower.' But Simond sulked because he couldn't get a copy of Cobbett's *Political Register*, of which nobody in Chepstow had heard.

When steam-boats began a regular service from Bristol in September 1822, there was a multitude of carriages always in waiting to carry passengers to Piercefield, the Wyndcliff and – since the new road from St Arvans to Tintern had opened the year before – Tintern Abbey. The two-day tourists from Ross were now hugely outnumbered by the day-trippers from Bristol. The *Gloucester Journal* reported on July 21st 1827 that Chepstow and its vicinity were resorted to that summer more than usual and though travelling accommodation had more than doubled, the demand for lodgings was greater than could be supplied, and 'Sociables, phaetons, cars and pony-chaises for visiting Piercefield and Tintern Abbey, are increased at least tenfold during the last three years.'[187] It got worse: on March 21st 1856 the steamer brought no less than 700 of them to Chepstow.[188] Willett recommended these 'shoals of flying visitors' to The Beaufort Arms. The town was extremely healthy, he said, having 'no pernicious vapours arising from manufactories, marsh, effluvia, or stagnant water', and there were 'hot and cold sea-water Bathing-rooms, in Bridge Street, very conveniently fitted up, and replenished with water every tide.' Earlier editions noted that

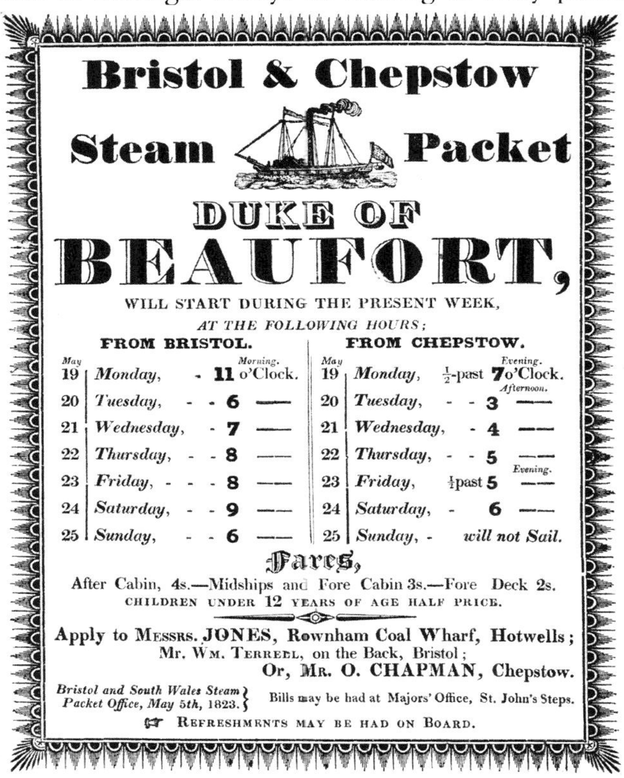

Advertisement for the Bristol and Chepstow Steam Packet, Duke of Beaufort, *May 1823. (Chepstow Museum)*

the castle had had recent 'laudable improvements', made by the duke's agents, including a neat gravel walk to an eminence above it with excellent views, but he considered the acrostic epitaph on Henry Marten's grave, much quoted in other guide-books, abominable. The town had 4,000 inhabitants now, gas lighting, a 'very handsome Market House, with an Assembly Room over it', and a theatre. Thackeray liked the George, 'one of the cleanest, neatest, cheerfullest, fresh salmon-givingest Inns to be found anywhere', and enjoyed the 'suburb along the river' with 'a few sailors lounging about with the fair companions of their leisure hours, and a few tradesmen smoking pipes at little inns, an hostler in a white jacket, who has come out to give the *dawg* a bathe, some street boys swinging about on the bars of the dock, furthermore, a boat in the course of building.'

It rained too hard for any sight-seeing the first day Thackeray was at Chepstow, and when he 'indiscreetly scrambled' up the hill across the river he had to take shelter in the Bonny Thatch, whose bar was 6 feet 2¾ inches high between the beams and 9 feet square. Here he settled happily down with a policeman drying his wet shins, and 'a pretty little coquette of a landlady's daughter, a pretty maid and a landlady who had been pretty once', plus two wet ladies, an old dog, a dozing landlord, a carter, a tipsy labourer and a tramp who'd served with Nelson, now selling matches. The price of a room there was a guinea week. 'Think of that! At six hours from London, in the face of a beautiful landscape, in a little quiet shady hedge inn, with the Chepstow town and castle before you, with the Wye running under them, and on the Wye the best salmon that was ever eaten in the world.' And lunch of cheese, butter, bread and excellent hard cider, was only 4d. This wasn't the reaction of a tourist in search of the picturesque, more that of a holidaymaker in search of a bargain. Twamley and Catherine Sinclair also crossed the river to look at the double-view from the cliffs above Lancaut, the latter finding it an inconceivably long walk, perhaps because she took it 'under a deluge of rain'. She thought the Bristol Channel looked exceedingly muddy, 'like a concentrated London fog'. Wisely, perhaps, given how exhausted the vocabulary of description had by then become, Twamley refused to wrack her brains for more words to praise the view.

Whatever they thought of the town, and whatever their reason for travelling, everyone liked the castle, Puckler-Muskau calling it 'a ruin the most sublime that the imagination of the finest painter could conceive.' He was amused, though, by the financial arrangements. 'In the least ruinous part of the castle lives a woman with her family, who pays the Duke of Beaufort, the possessor, a rent, for permission to show the ruins to strangers, of whom she consequently demands a shilling. You see that in England "on fait fleche de tout bois" [you can make arrows from every sort of wood], and that an English nobleman with an income of sixty thousand a-year, neither disdains to take the widow's mite, nor to lay strangers under regular contribution.' He went first at twilight, coming back next morning when 'a blooming girl was my guide, and formed a graceful contrast to the blackened towers.' She gave him a neat summary of the regicide Henry Marten's imprisonment here after the Civil War. Showing 'a horrible hole', she said 'Here Marten was put at first, while he was wicked; but when he became serious, he was moved a storey higher; and at last, when he was *religious*, he had the room with the beautiful view.' Rawdon, visiting just before Marten was imprisoned was impressed by 'about 50 pece of ordnance' kept there. He recorded the long-held view that the castle (like the church) had been there since the time of Julius Caesar.

Over a century later Torrington found the castle, which had ceased to function as a military base in 1690, very overgrown with ivy, valerian, fox glove and red and white ladytire. People were still finding cannon balls in the rubbish, and memories, or legends, of the Civil War abounded. Heath (1813) told the exciting story of how the Parliamentarians, in revenge for the Royalist commander's obstinate resistance to their siege, had 'mangled his body in the most horrid manner, – and that the soldiers wore his remains in their hats, as trophies of their victory.' Though he rather pooh-poohed the story as typical propaganda of the time, he still recorded it. Perhaps he got it from the man who showed the castle to Torrington on his second visit who was 'very voluble, and ignorant'. Marten's tower was now a receptacle of sail cloth. Shaw's guide was the elderly Mrs Williams, the last of the three very long lives on which the castle had been rented in the early eighteenth century:[189] 'she was born here where she still resides in comfortable apartments, and makes a good subsistence by the fruits of the garden, peaches &c. which are plentiful on these warm walls when other places fail.' She told Penhouet in 1797 'that, from her infancy she had discovered little or no difference in the Ruins' and she had known two of Marten's servants. She was then in her eightieth year, and Marten had died in 1680, so it was quite possible. Barber was very impressed by the door-knocker: 'we thundered at the portal for admission with a cannon-ball suspended by a chain ... a pretty smiling damsel, conjuring all her rosy dimples, bade the gate, or rather made it, revolve on its creaking hinges, and welcomed us into the castle.' He fancied her; she was 'our fair guide' and 'our gentle conductress' and wore taper heels. He found the deserted works of a glass-house and a dog-kennel, and other people too felt the castle was not properly looked after. They liked their ruins ruined, not lived and worked in. 'The lover of antiquity must regret', wrote Webb in 1812, 'that the beauty of the ruin is deteriorated by the building of insignificant works and sheds, together with unseemly pig-styes, which I am convinced, from his Grace of Beaufort's well known and judicious taste, on consideration he will rectify, and order these venerable ruins not to be disgraced by such appendages.' He thought the castle should be cleared and fenced, and the custodian housed in a neighbouring cottage. But Spiker found a greenhouse still there in 1820, and apartments rented to the poor, and Twamley, in 1838, complained of the custodian's pert little dimity curtains, quite wrong for a castle. The cannonball knocker had gone and there was only a simple latch and a young and rosy (but ignorant) girl to open the wicket. Thackeray met what was probably the same ignorant girl, only he called her 'a little prim damsel'. She said the castle was closed as it was a Sunday, but soon changed to 'The castle is not shown on Sundays, *unless to those who are going away*', and let his party in. Twamley expressed the common view that it was an excellent thing that noble dens of titled and licensed tyranny were now ruins and there were no more dungeons. Roscoe was equally not 'a lover of any thing of feudal tyranny, darkness, and oppression of soul and body – that iron vassalage of by-gone days – God forbid!'

Several artists painted and drew the rocks and islands below Chepstow at the very bottom of the Wye. Ireland, for instance, drew Red Rocks and wrote about Hardwick Cliff and Thornwell and the 'mouth of the Wye, where we found the tide uncommonly rapid, and where if the wind is brisk, the waters are troublesomely rough.' But the artists were working, and the tourists were not. The tour and their holidays over, and full of confidence that they had now seen the sights and got the right moral and aesthetic opinions about them, they headed home to England, taking the Old Passage across the Severn from Beachley to Aust or the New one, a little further down the river, from Black Rock to Redwick – unless, like Gilpin, they continued into Welsh Wales for further adventure. Bloomfield gave thanks on their behalf:

Pollett, farewell! Thy dashing oar
Shall lull us into peace no more;
But where Kyrl trimm'd his infant green,
Long mayst thou with thy bark be seen;
And happy be the hearts that glide
Through such a scene with such a guide.

The artists, meanwhile, kept sketching. In the months and years ahead they would turn their sketches into pictures.

Catalogue

We have tried in this exhibition to combine illustrations of the main sights of the Wye Tour over the period 1770-1850 with paintings which show the development of watercolour from the 'tinted drawings' of earlier artists to the much more ambitious work of later ones, intended to compete artistically with oils. We have included very few prints for lack of space (though many can be seen elsewhere in Chepstow Museum), but there is no doubt that the demand for illustrations for the numerous published *Tours* and *Guides* was a very powerful economic factor behind much topographical landscape painting. That was not, of course, the landscape painting of Claude and Poussin, which referred only rarely to real places, but the accurate depiction of sights the reader might have seen and of which he or she wanted a record, something which persists among tourists to this day. However, as artists in the 1790s began to develop the art of watercolour, and invented new techniques for its use, they became less interested in literal depiction and more in letting their feelings for a scene dictate what they painted. This, which is part of the history of romanticism, was seen as an artistic advance and led to the disparagement of 'mere' topography, but the two strands continued side by side, and there is no reason why we today should share the aesthetic snobbery of the early nineteenth century. As well as masterworks by Paul Sandby, Michael 'Angelo' Rooker, J.M.W. Turner, Samuel Palmer and others, we have selected several paintings by amateurs, since these often give information not to be found elsewhere, and tell us what interested tourists rather than artists. We have also chosen works by three local watercolourists of very different artistic quality: James Wathen, Joshua Cristall and Thomas Tudor. We believe that paintings of the Wye valley contributed significantly to the great period of British watercolour art.

A standard format has been adopted for the description of the pictures on the walls, all of which are watercolours. The name of the artist, with dates; the title of the picture, with date where known; whether signed or not; measurements of the image in millimetres, height before width; where it is held, with accession number and other relevant information. Watercolour can mean a number of things, and, where the holding museum or gallery wishes, a more detailed description is included. Mounts and frames are those of the public or private owners. In the eighteenth and early nineteenth centuries watercolours were often framed to the edge of the image, like oil paintings, and in exhibitions pictures were usually hung very close together, not separately as they are today. With little space available, and with pictures of many different kinds of frame and mount, we have hung the exhibition more on eighteenth than twenty-first century lines.

1. WILLIAM COLLINS (1788-1847) (attributed). *From Winter's Leap, c.1834*
Unsigned. 610x853 mm. (Private collection)

A tour boat is passing below the cliffs at Winter's Leap, site of an alleged jump by the royalist Sir John Winter to escape his parliamentary pursuers during the Civil War. The locals on the cliff top are clearly exaggerating their surprise at seeing tourists – Wye tours had been running for more than sixty years. Across the river is the Piercefield estate, whose walks were one of the highlights, and down river is another – Chepstow Castle. The fishermen, working barges, known as trows, and sheep being brought to graze on the horseshoe bend show how the search for the picturesque was only a minor part of the river's life. In the distance is the Bristol Channel with one of the steam packets whose service from Bristol to Chepstow began in 1822 and brought a great change to the Wye Valley; trippers rather than tourists. William Collins travelled in Wales with his young family in 1834, visiting Chepstow and Tintern among other places. The party included his eldest son Wilkie, named for Collins's friend the painter David Wilkie, and later to be the author of *The Woman in White* and *The Moonstone*. William seems the most likely of the Collinses to have painted this picture, though it could possibly be later and by his second son Charles Allston Collins (1828-1873).

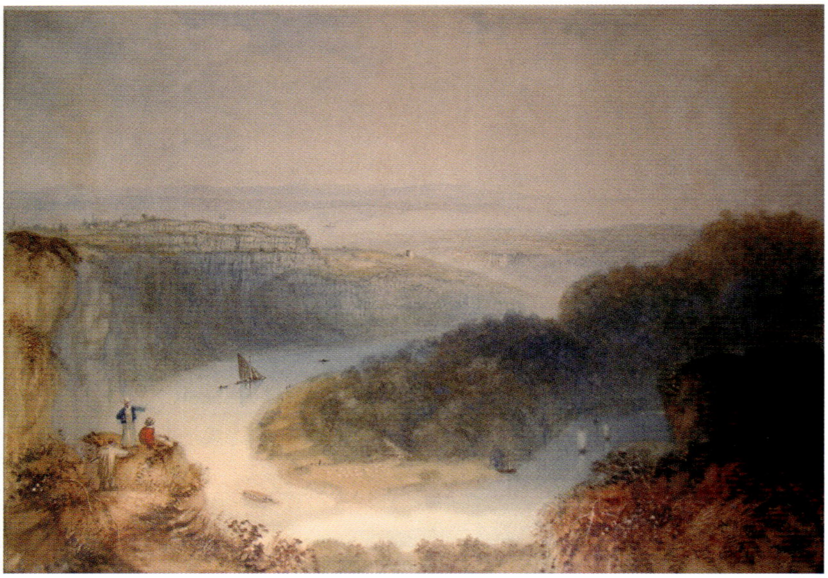

2. CORNELIUS VARLEY (1781-1873). *The Market Place, Ross, Herefordshire*
Signed Cornelius Varley 1803 and inscribed 'Drawn on the spot'. 296x457 mm. (Victoria and Albert Museum 108-1895)

The Market House was built in the reign of Charles II, and was regarded by Samuel Ireland (see no. 94) as in 'the worst style of saxon architecture', though many admired and drew it, including William Gilpin. On the right is the Crown and Sceptre, still in business. The buildings on the left were known as Underhill or Under Hell, and included the Boars Head. They were pulled down in 1862 to make way for the new road. Cornelius was the younger brother of John Varley (see no. 5). They travelled together in north Wales in 1802, and the following year Cornelius came to south Wales with Joshua Cristall (see nos 11-12) and William Havell. There is a very similar picture by John in NMW, drawn from slightly lower down the street. Though John's version is dated 1809, artists very often kept their sketches for years before working them up into finished pictures.

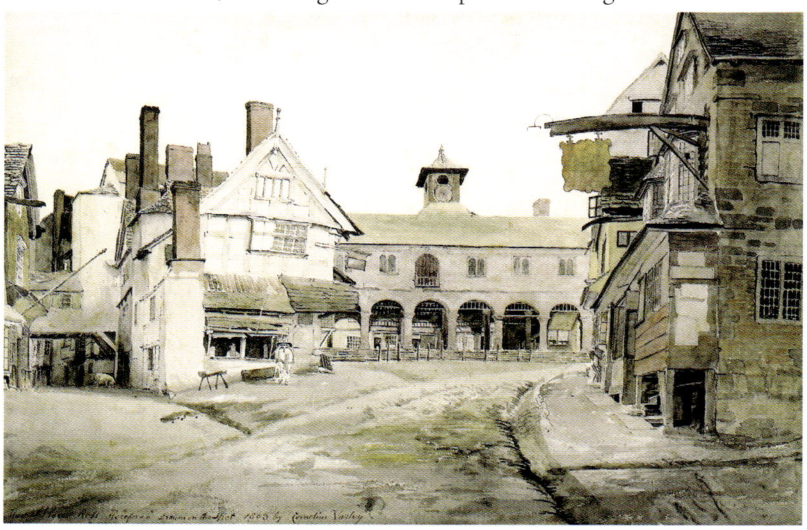

3. JOHN 'WARWICK' SMITH (1749-1831). *The Ruins of Wilton Castle on the Wye July 1788*
Unsigned. 142x222 mm. (NLW PB 424 TH/6)

Note the tour boat in attendance. Smith grew up in Cumberland, where his father was a gardener to William Gilpin's aunt, and he was trained by the family to draw. He very probably accompanied Gilpin down the Wye in 1770, making a copy of Gilpin's journal (see no. 91), though if he made drawings on the trip himself they do not seem to have survived. In 1776 he went to Italy for five years, under the patronage of Lord Warwick, hence his sobriquet. He painted many watercolours of the Wye from 1784 onwards, often noting the weather and hour of day he made them.

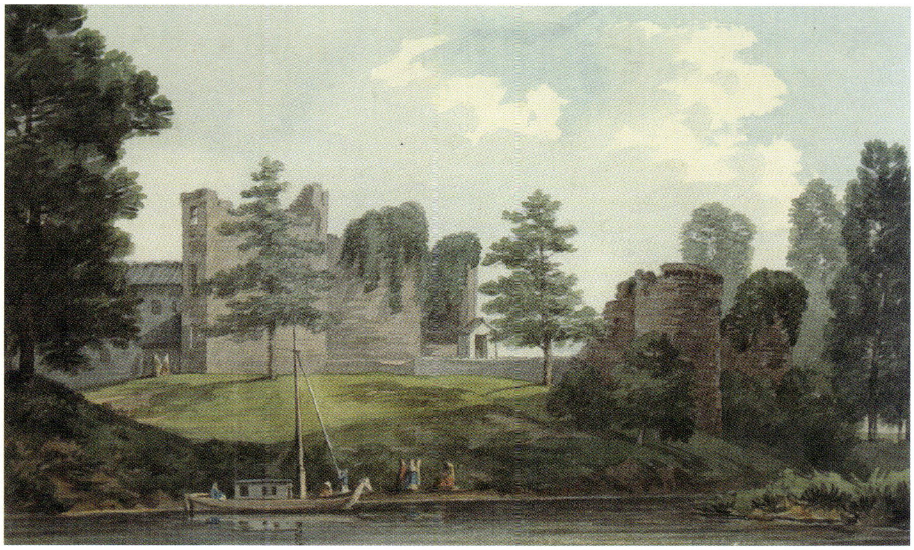

4. JAMES WATHEN (1751-1828). *'N. View of Ross, from the Wye [...] August 4th 1797'*
There is a frontispiece to the collection of Wathen's drawings, dated 4th April 1804 which is signed, but individual sketches are not. 144x230 mm. (Herefordshire Archive Service S 40, Part I, 48)

Wathen's sketch shows the town spilling down the hill from the church, with what remained of the elms planted by John Kyrle, 'The Man of Ross'. The lower branches of the trees were trimmed so as not to block the view from the Prospect of the loop of the river in front of the town, with the Black Mountains in the distance. A vegetarian and teetotaller, James Wathen was born and died in Hereford, where he at first followed his father's career as a glover. After the death of his mother in 1801, and with the help of an inheritance from an uncle, he devoted the rest of his life to drawing, walking (up to twenty sketches and forty miles a day respectively) and travelling as far as India and China. At home, known as 'Jemmy Sketch', he often volunteered his services as a guide to Wye tourists. Though not a talented artist, his pictures contain much detail of the Wye valley not otherwise available, and it is a puzzle why so few apparently survive.

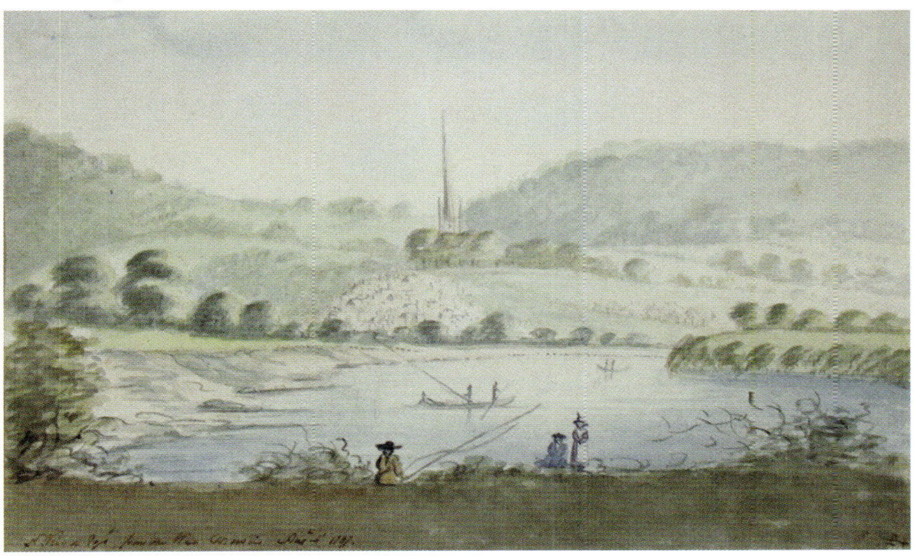

5. JOHN VARLEY (1778-1842). *Approaching Goodrich castle, 1833*
Signed. 362x468 mm. (NMW A 18569)

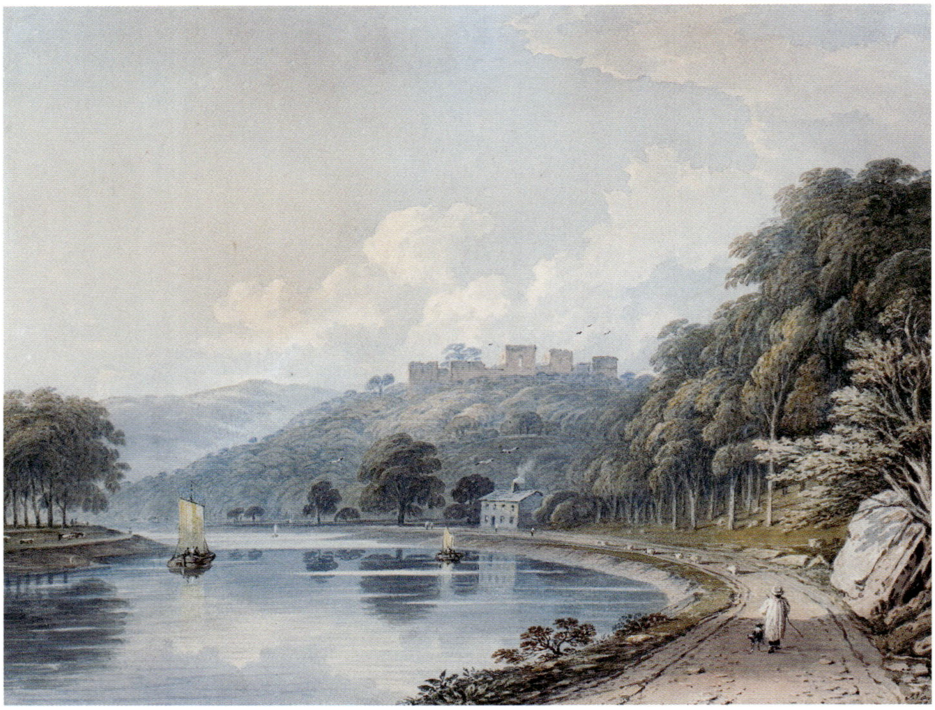

John was the eldest of three artistic Varley brothers (see no. 2). In 1804 he was a founding member of the Old Water Colour Society. As he grew older, and further in time from the sketches he made in his youth, his pictures became less topographical and increasingly idealised, as in this and his view of Tintern Abbey in Chepstow Museum (Plate X). Here he draws attention to the ferry house, where the hungry tourist could get (perhaps a second) breakfast and use the 'clean room', after which he would be ready to attempt the not very arduous climb to the castle.

6. WILLIAM TURNER of Oxford (1789-1862). *Goodrich Castle Keep,* c.*1813*
Unsigned. 294x412 mm. (British Museum 1867 4.13.669 Binyon 1)

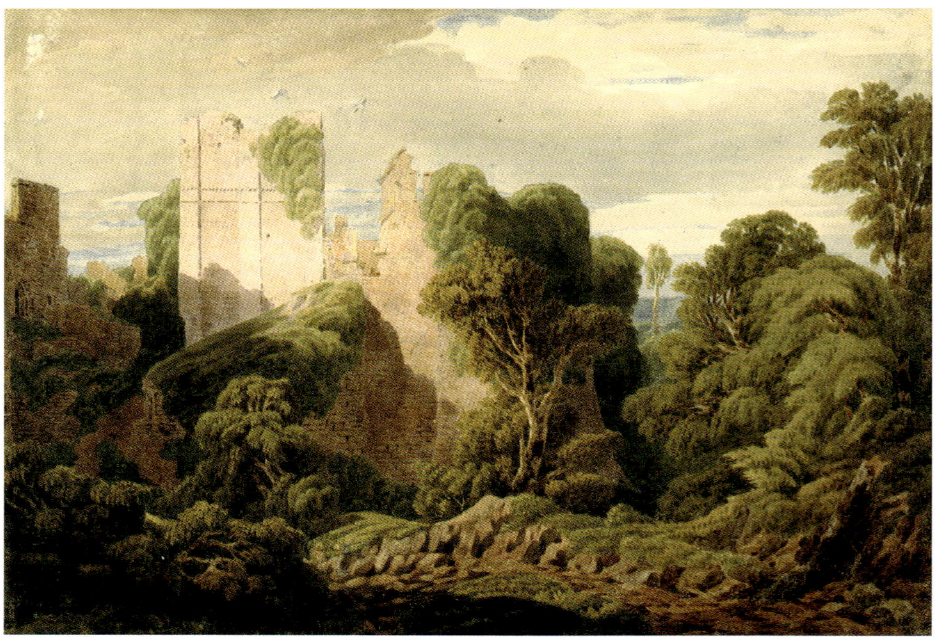

Both Francis Grose and Samuel Rogers (1775 and 1791) had commented on how overgrown the ruins at Goodrich had become, and Turner's version of the castle, with trees growing wildly in the ruins, is very different from that of John Chessell Buckler (nos 7 & 8). A pupil of John Varley (see no. 5), William Turner is known as 'of Oxford' to avoid confusion with J.M.W. Turner (see no. 55). He visited the Wye in 1808, and it is presumed that this painting is based on sketches made then. (Another watercolour of Goodrich is dated 1813.)

7-8. JOHN CHESSELL BUCKLER (1793-1894). *Goodrich castle chapel, 1827* and *North View of the Keep, Goodrich castle, 1827*
376x276 mm and 270x383 mm. Signed. (Hereford Museum & Art Gallery, 3021 and 3024)

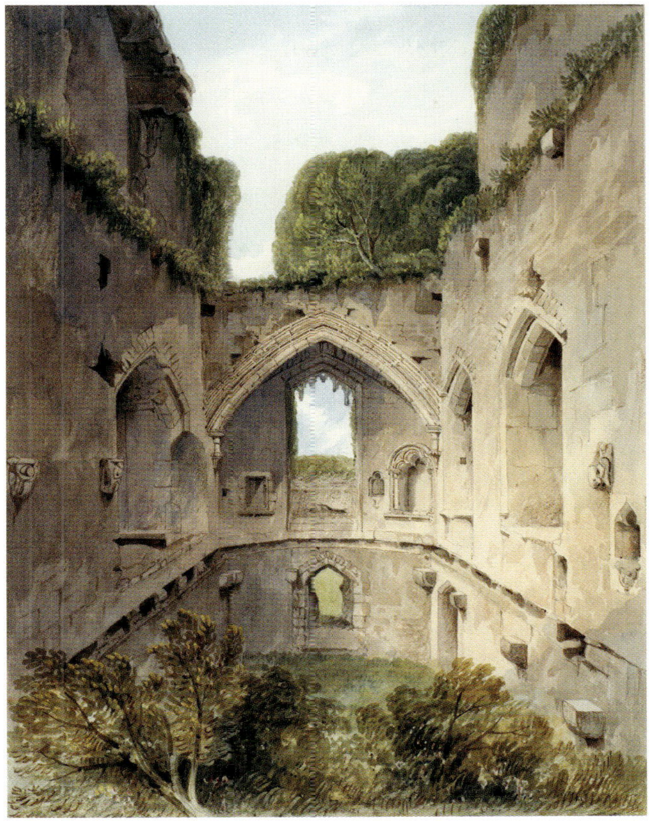

Three generations of the Buckler family were artists and architects. John Chessell Buckler was the son of John (1770-1851), a hugely productive and meticulous draughtsman. He studied drawing with Francis Nicholson, but his architectural training and the influence of his father are obvious in the series of watercolours he made of Goodrich Castle in 1827, of which these two are fine examples. The castle had clearly been tidied up since William Turner of Oxford was here fifteen years or so earlier (see no. 6). Though the chapel is still full of bushes, paths have been made past the Norman keep. Buckler also drew scenes in Chepstow. He took over his father's practice about 1830, working with his brother George and later his son Charles Alban Buckler.

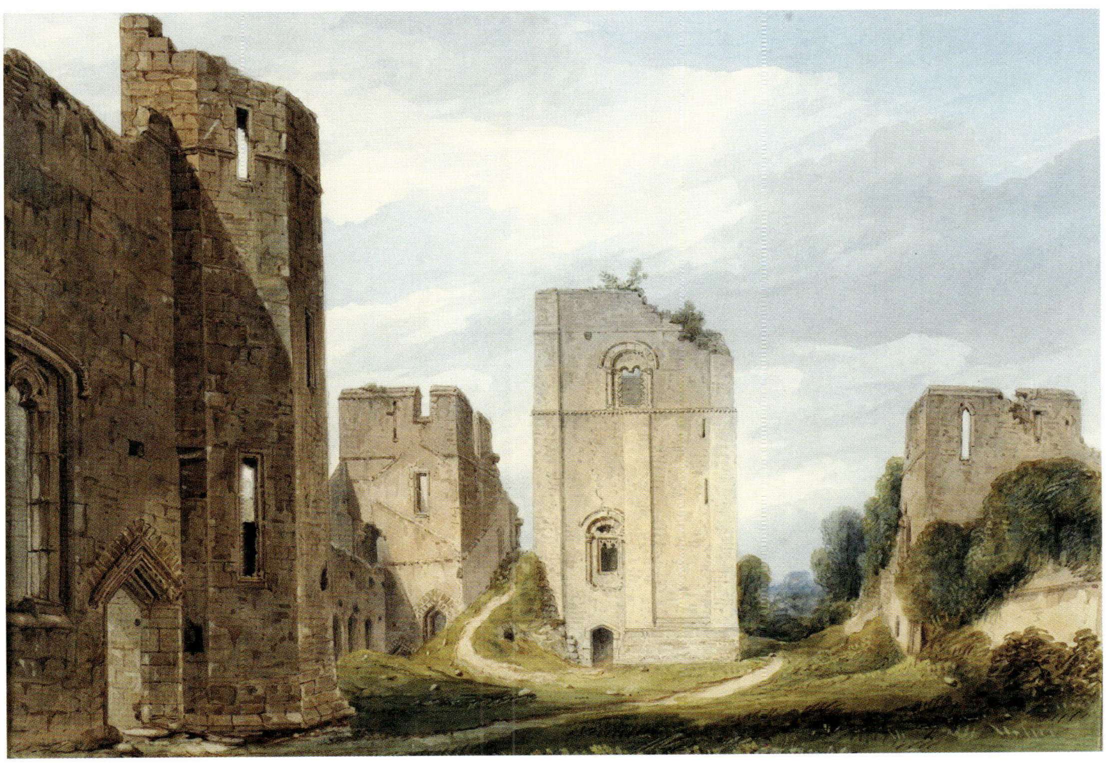

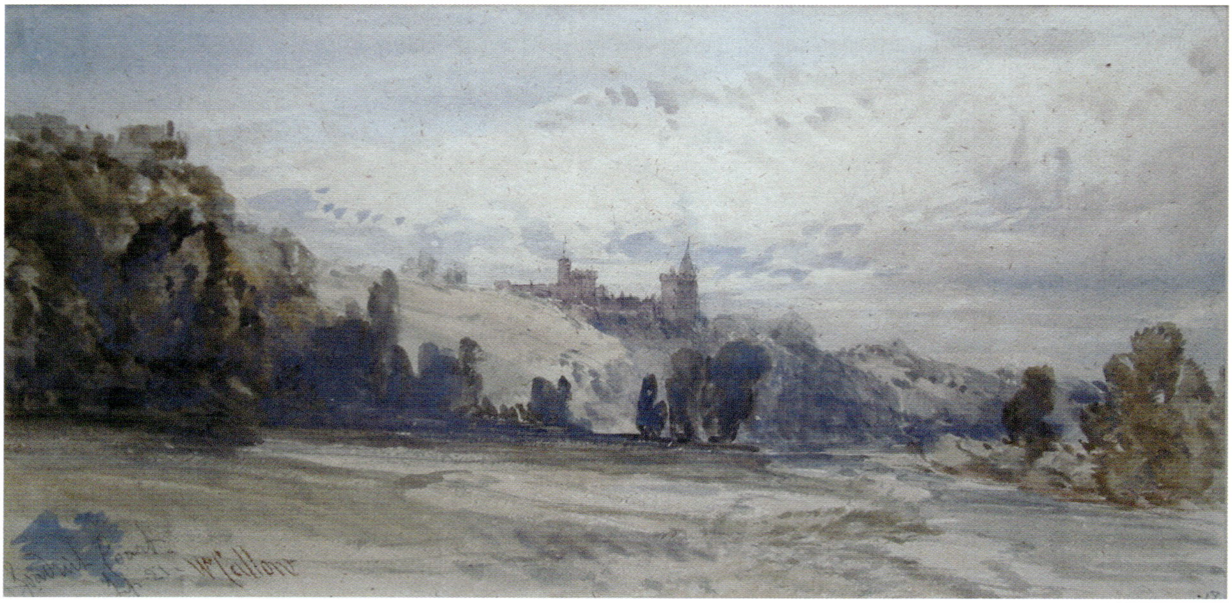

9. WILLIAM CALLOW (1812-1908). *Goodrich Court, September 21st (1848)*
Signed. 180x305 mm. (Private collection)

This is an on-the-spot sketch for a more finished version made in the studio, and shows Goodrich Court, the gothic extravaganza designed by Edward Blore for Sir Samuel Rush Meyrick (1783-1848). Much admired by some, it was completed in 1831 and housed a huge collection of armour, but Wordsworth said he would have liked 'to blow away Sir Meyrick's impertinent structure, and all the possessions it contains.' In 1950 his wish was met when the Court was demolished. Callow was a pupil of Theodore Fielding, brother of the better known Antony Van Dyke Fielding. As a young man he shared a studio in Paris with Thomas Shotter Boys, and taught drawing to the children of Louis Philippe. He returned to England in 1841 and toured the Welsh marches in the autumn of 1848.

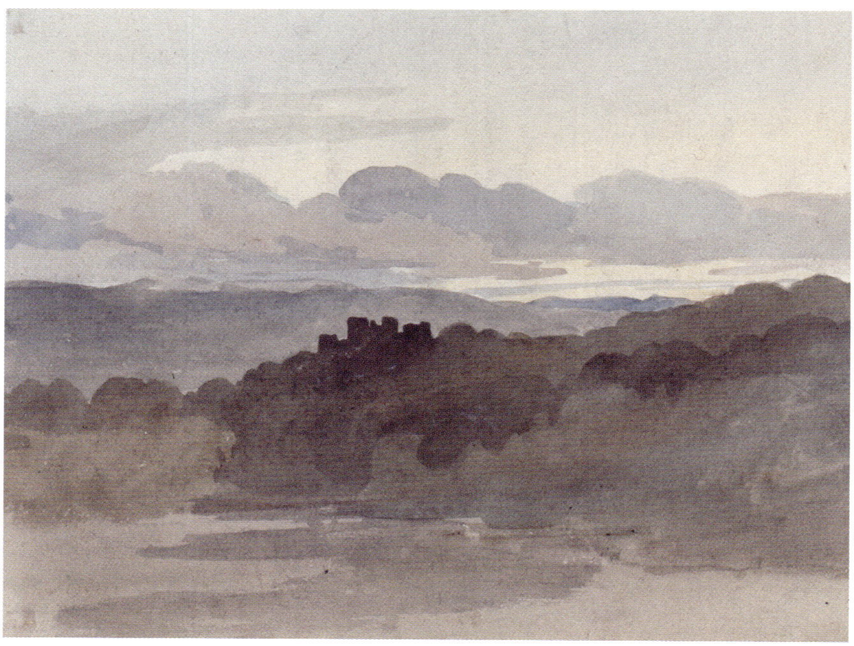

10. DAVID COX (1783-1859). *Goodrich,* c.*1815*
Unsigned. 177x241 mm. (Private Collection courtesy of Andrew Wyld)

Cox came from Birmingham where he studied under Joseph Barber and painted scenery for the local theatre. He moved to London in 1804 where he became a pupil of John Varley (see no. 5). In 1814 he settled in Hereford till 1827, making frequent visits to Wales, particularly the north. This evening view of Goodrich Castle from the river, painted about the time he moved to live in Hereford for twelve years, contrasts happily with his teacher's morning view.

11-12. JOSHUA CRISTALL (1767-1847). *Granton cottage, Goodrich* and *Goodrich cottage*
Unsigned, but dubious initials J.C. 158x263 mm and 142x199 mm. (Dyer Collection)

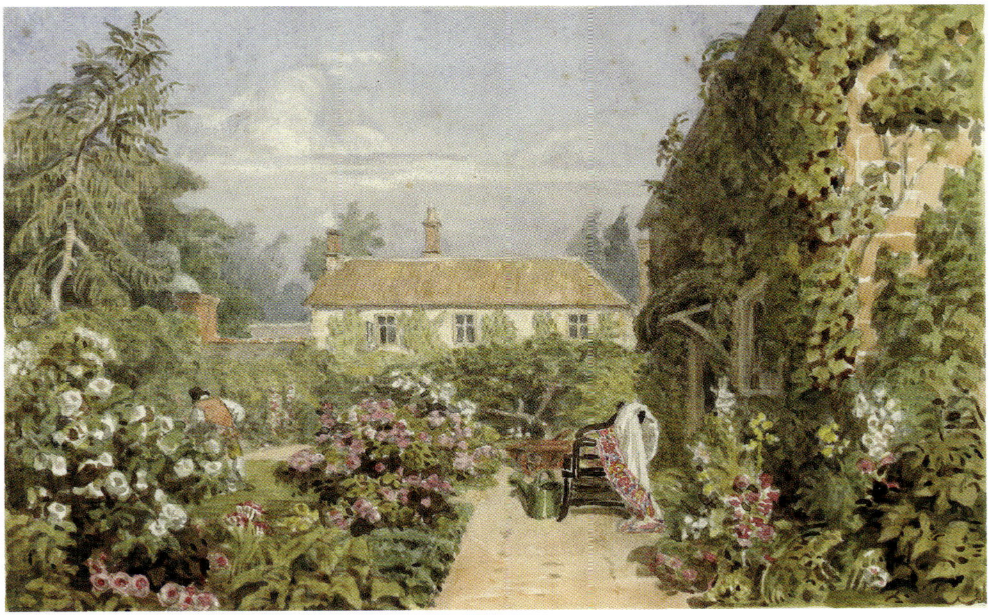

Cristall was born in Cornwall and grew up in London. He entered the RA in 1792 and first came to the Wye with John and Cornelius Varley in July 1803. (Cornelius painted him sketching a Wye scene under an umbrella.) The visit left its mark, for twenty years later, aged 56 and after a rather struggling career, he moved to Goodrich, living from 1823 till 1841 in Granton cottage close to the church. (It is now a bed and breakfast.) The smaller cottage is thought to have been his studio. His wife had run a school for young ladies in Paddington, among her pupils being the Lovett sisters who had become like the Cristalls' own daughters. They now lived with their father at Hellens in Herefordshire, and it was their local presence and that of Sir Samuel Meyrick (see no. 9), also a patron of Joshua, that seem to have brought Cristall back to the Wye. From Granton he looked across at Coppet Hill, where there was a hamlet of fern-burners, who earned a small living from the coarse soap they made from the ashes. As a young man he had spent much time tracing engravings of classical drawings, the influence of which is apparent in his many studies of the women who worked there, whom he tends to turn into Arcadian peasants. Over the years he did many pencil drawings and scarcely different watercolour versions of the same people and scenes. Perhaps he was planning to incorporate the figures into one of his major neo-classical works like his *Nymphs and Shepherds Dancing* (Hereford Museum) or *Scottish Figures at a Fountain* (Dyer Collection). If so, it seems never to have materialized. He also did drawings and watercolours of the landscape about Goodrich, always tending to idealize the pastoral life. He died in London, but his body was brought back to Goodrich where he was buried next to his wife on the north side of the church. Wind and weather have sadly made the inscription virtually illegible.

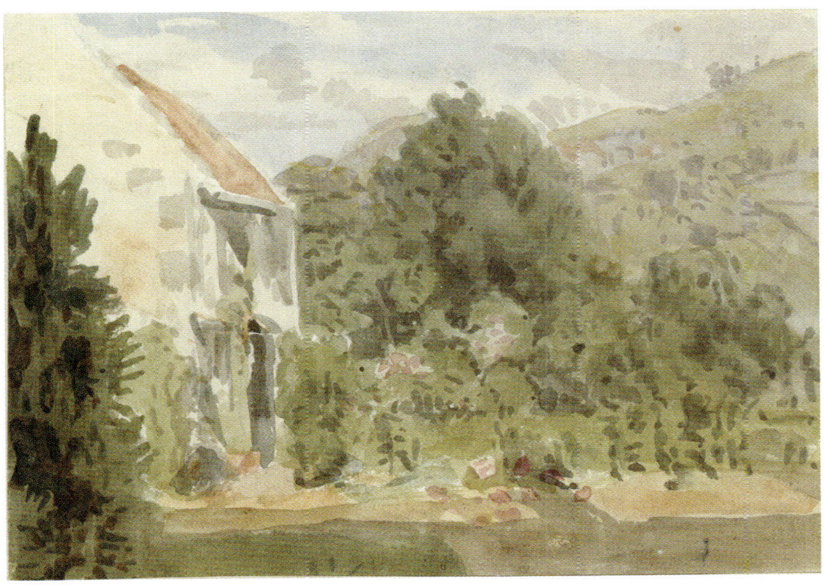

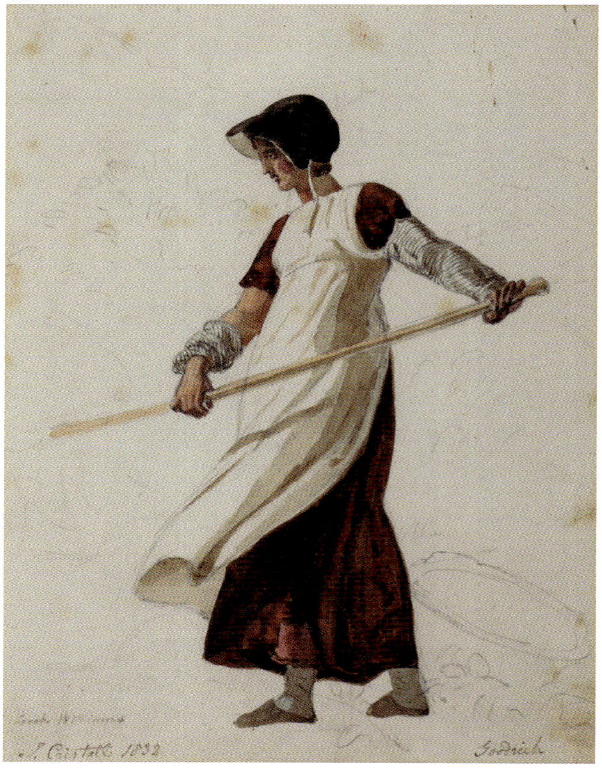

13. JOSHUA CRISTALL (1767-1847).
Sarah Williams, Goodrich, 1832
Signed. 232x173mm. (Private collection)

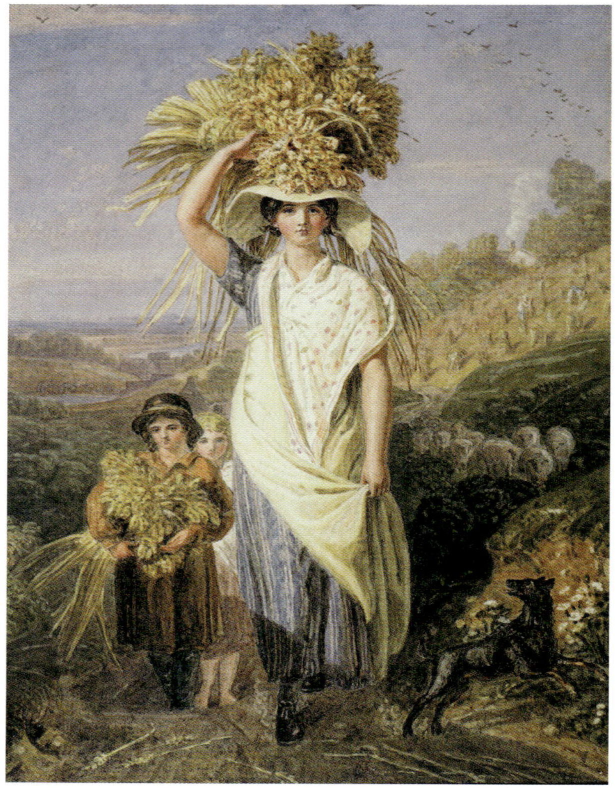

14. JOSHUA CRISTALL (1767-1847).
The Gleaners, 1831
Signed. 356x263 mm. Haworth Art Gallery, Accrington (Hyndburn Borough Council), Gift of Alfred Hitchon, 1946. (Image © Haworth Art Gallery / The Bridgeman Art Library)

Another version of this watercolour, in the Dyer Collection, names the woman as *Betsy Southern, Coppet Hill 1826*.

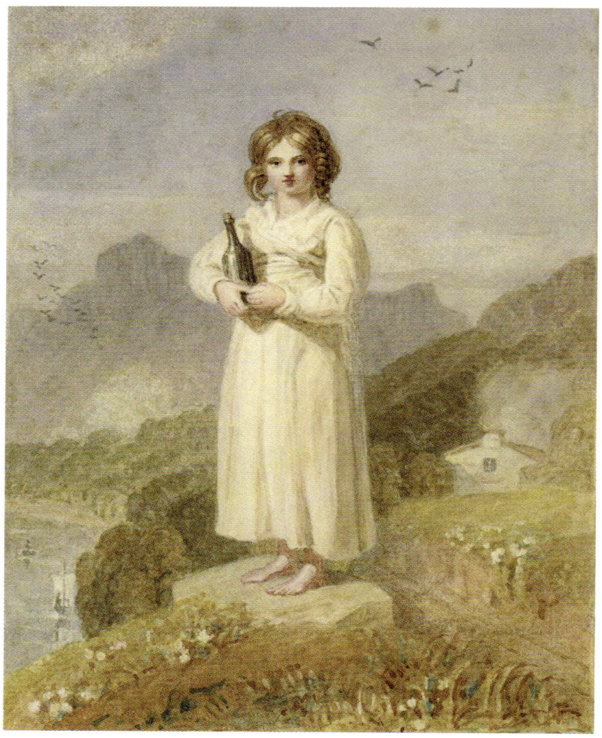

15. JOSHUA CRISTALL (1767-1847).
Girl with bottle at Symonds Yat rock, 1842
Signed. 237x185 mm. (Dyer Collection)

The river can be glimpsed below. The Dyer collection also has a slightly smaller version of this picture, dated 1836.

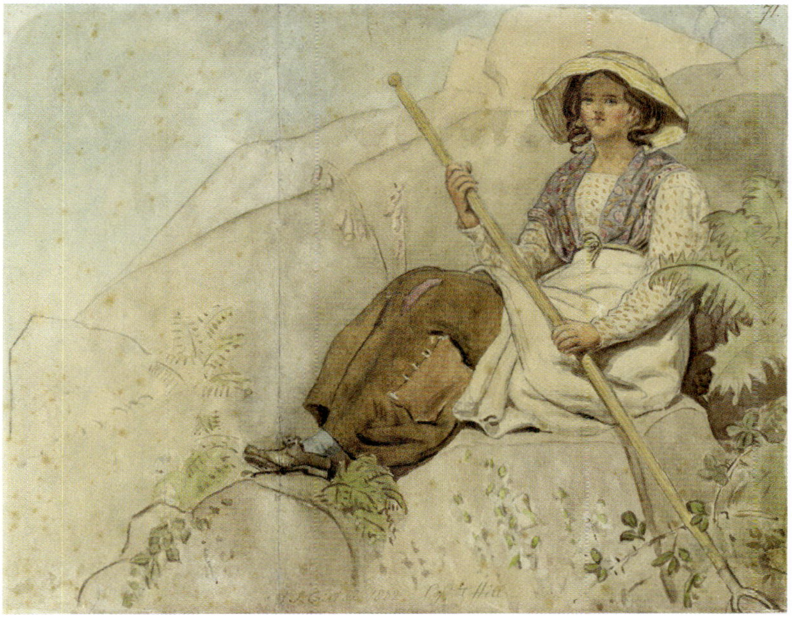

16. JOSHUA CRISTALL (1767-1847).
Country girl seated with pitchfork, Coppet Hill, 1832
Signed. 237x300 mm. (Dyer Collection)

On the back is a pencil sketch of no. 17, only with the pitchfork over the girl's right shoulder. It is the same girl in both pictures, with the same hat, same patch on her skirt, same colourful top, and very probably the same pitchfork.

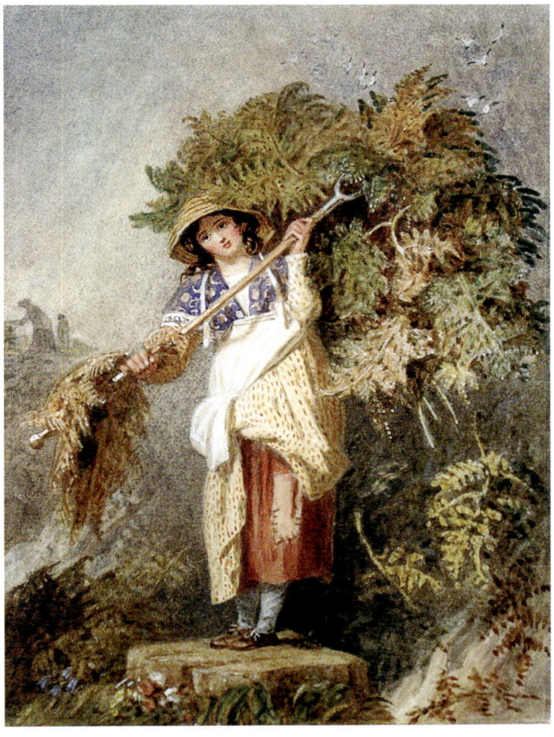

17. JOSHUA CRISTALL (1767-1847).
Girl Harvesting Bracken, 1829-1831
Unsigned. 275x195 mm. (New Art Gallery, Walsall. 1973.030.GR.)

Another version of this picture, in the Dyer Collection, is dated 1830.

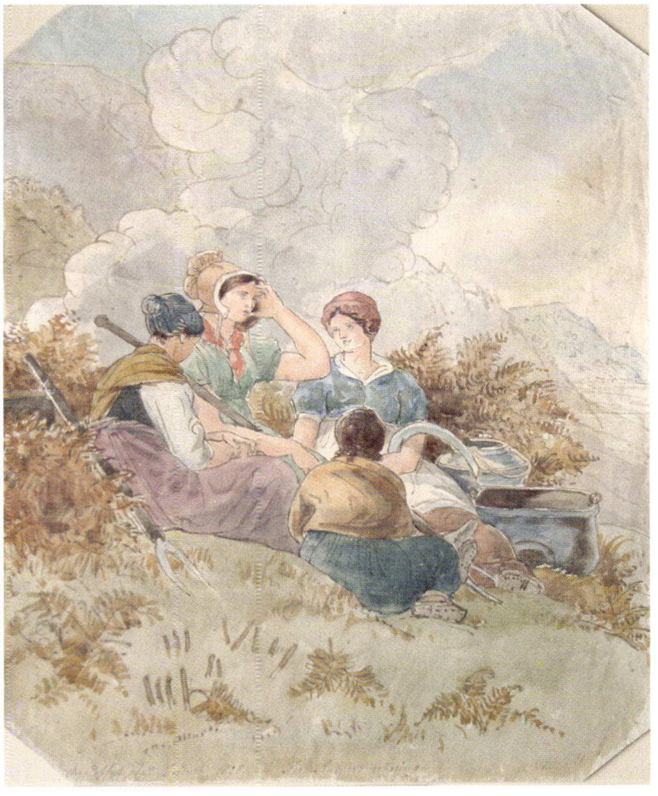

18. JOSHUA CRISTALL (1767-1847).
On Coppet Hill Goodrich Fern-burners reposing 1828.
Unsigned. 393x313 mm. (Dyer Collection)

The paper is watermarked Bevan and Swayne 1825.

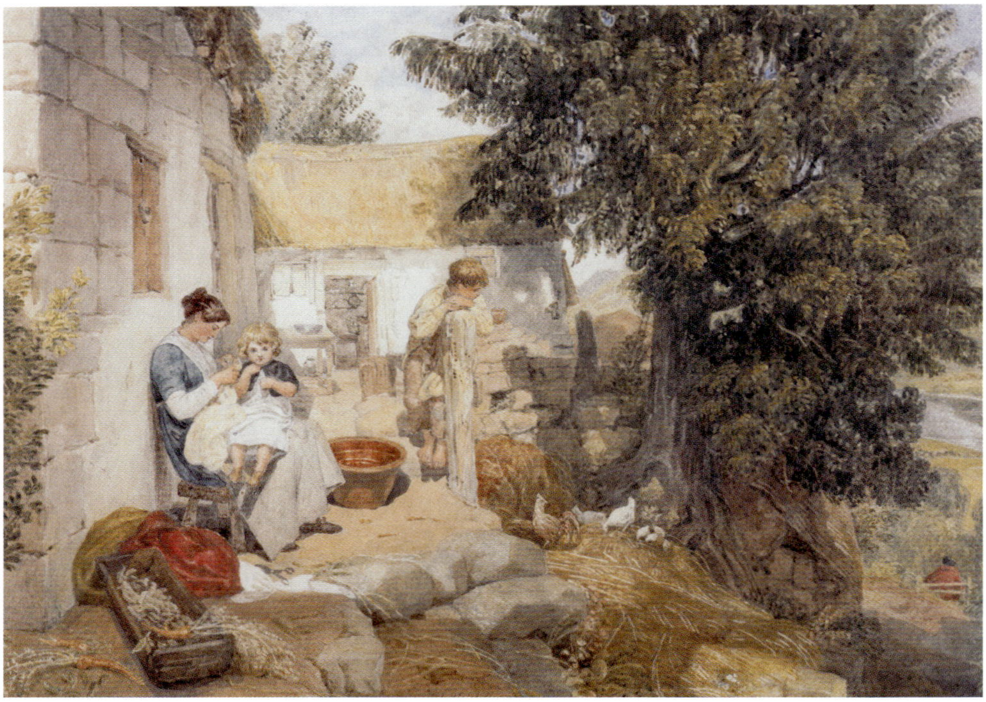

19. JOSHUA CRISTALL (1767-1847). *Cottages near Symonds Yat with country figures, 1825* Signed. 560x595 mm. (Bolton Museum and Archive Service BOLMG: 1947.31)

With the river so close, this stone-built cottage may be one of the ones under Coldwell Rocks where the inhabitants were always, for a consideration, ready to offer their services to guide tourists up to Symonds Yat rock.

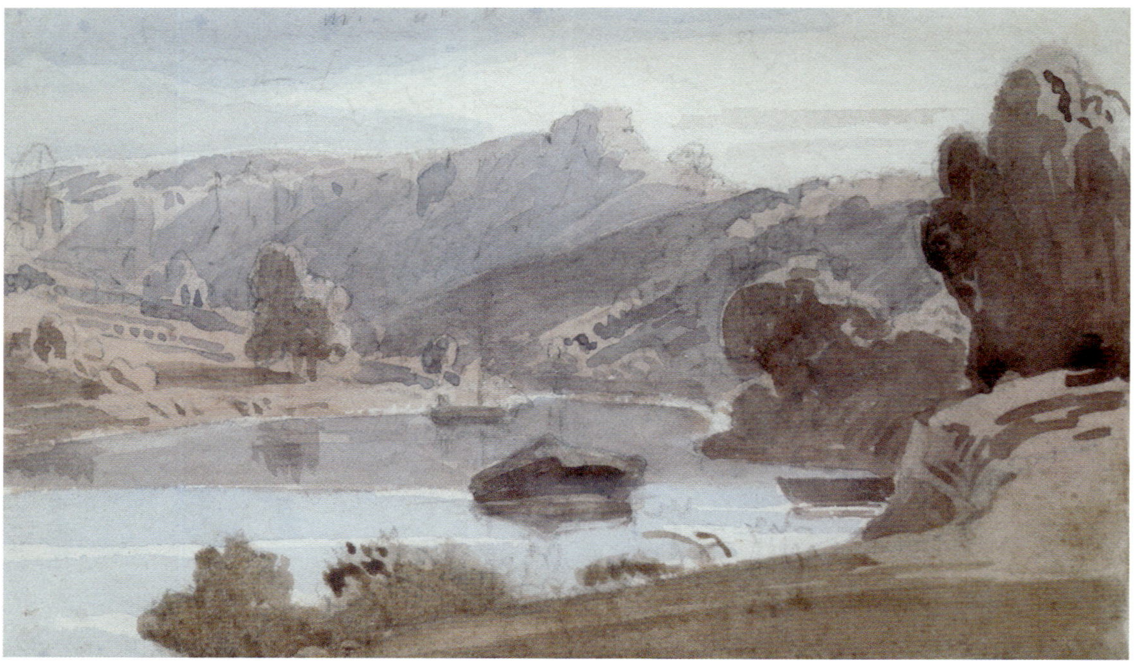

20. JOSHUA CRISTALL (1767-1847). *View of Coldwell Rocks from the river*
Unsigned. 167x100mm. (Private collection)

This picture belonged to George Clive of Perrystone Court, one of Cristall's Herefordshire patrons. There are, as with most Cristall paintings, other versions of the scene, one of which is in the National Gallery of Scotland. Both J.M.W. Turner and Michael 'Angelo' Rooker also drew this view.

21. MICHAEL 'ANGELO' ROOKER (1746-1801). *Symonds Yat, 1788*
Signed. 297x470 mm. (Private collection, courtesy of Andrew Wyld)

This picture shows the top of Symonds Yat Rock, looking down to the river below. Rooker's father was an actor as well as an engraver, and Rooker, like many painters at the time, began his artistic life as a theatrical scene painter. He was a pupil of Paul Sandby (see no. 61), who is supposed to have given him the name 'Angelo'. He came to the Wye valley in autumn 1788 (see no. 82, dated October), and painted many scenes here, exhibiting several of them at the RA in 1789. One of the very best landscape artists of the period, he combines topographical accuracy with a limpid, classical light, perhaps all the clearer for him coming so late in the year.

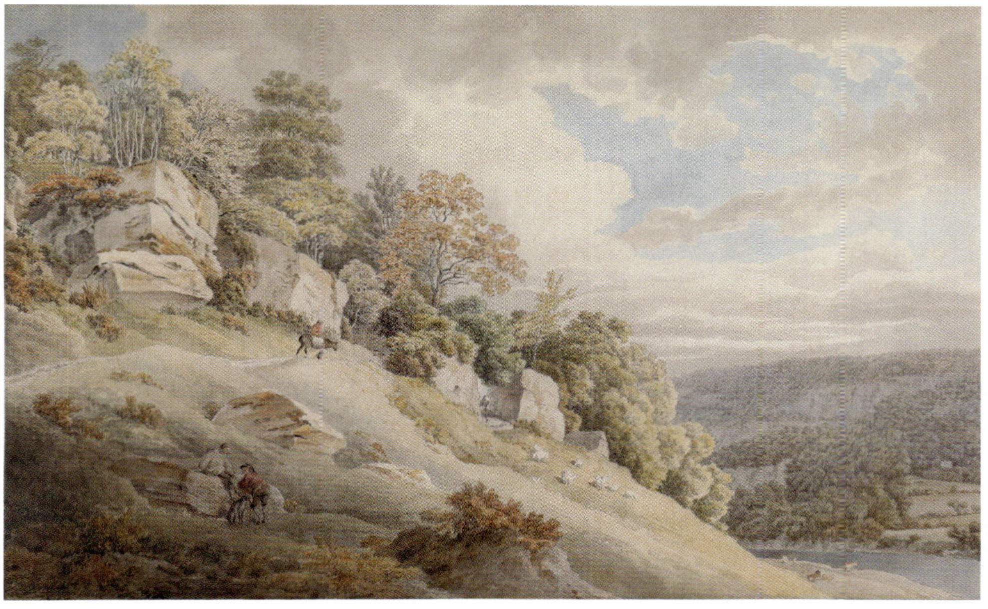

22. WILLIAM DAY (1764-1807). *View on the River Wye, North of Chepstow*
Signed and dated W. Day 1788. 356x531 mm. (Victoria and Albert Museum P.140-1929)

Day's picture is of the Wye, but a good way north of Chepstow. It is of Symonds Yat Rock, seen from near river-level, looking up. Day, who travelled down the Wye in 1788 with John Webber, trained as a geologist, which may explain his interest in the cliffs behind the surprisingly florid vegetation. Note the tour boat crossing the river, perhaps after lunch.

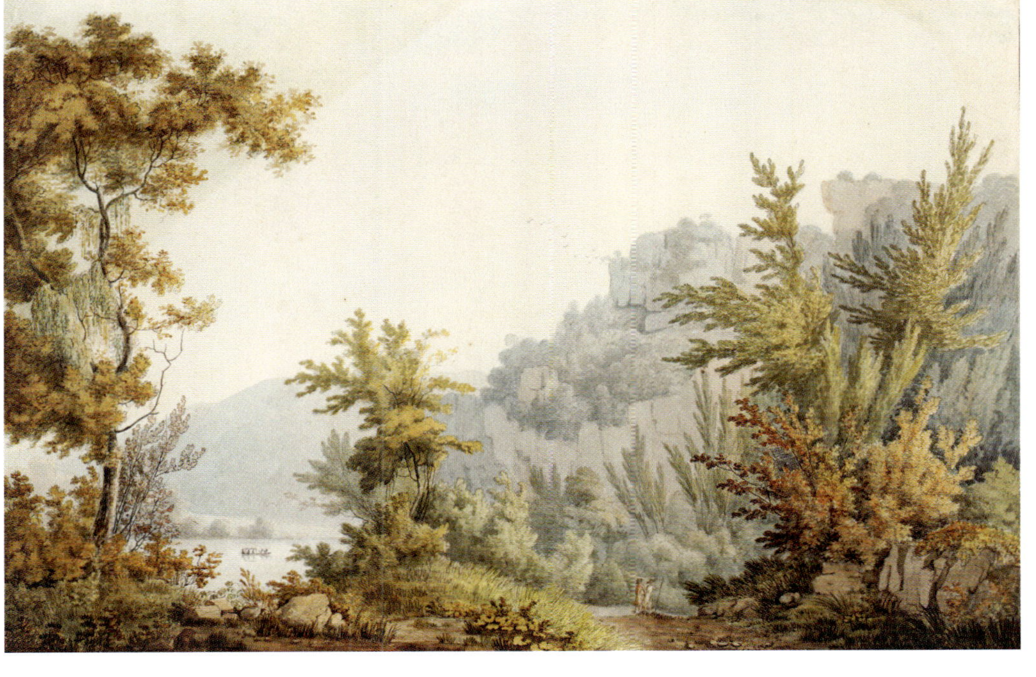

23. THOMAS RICHARD UNDERWOOD (1772-1836). *Symonds Yat*
Signed. 182x252 mm. (Hereford Museum & Art Gallery, 4858)

This shows the view from the top of Symonds Yat Rock, looking across to Coppet Hill. Underwood, another geologist, was draughtsman to the Society of Antiquaries.

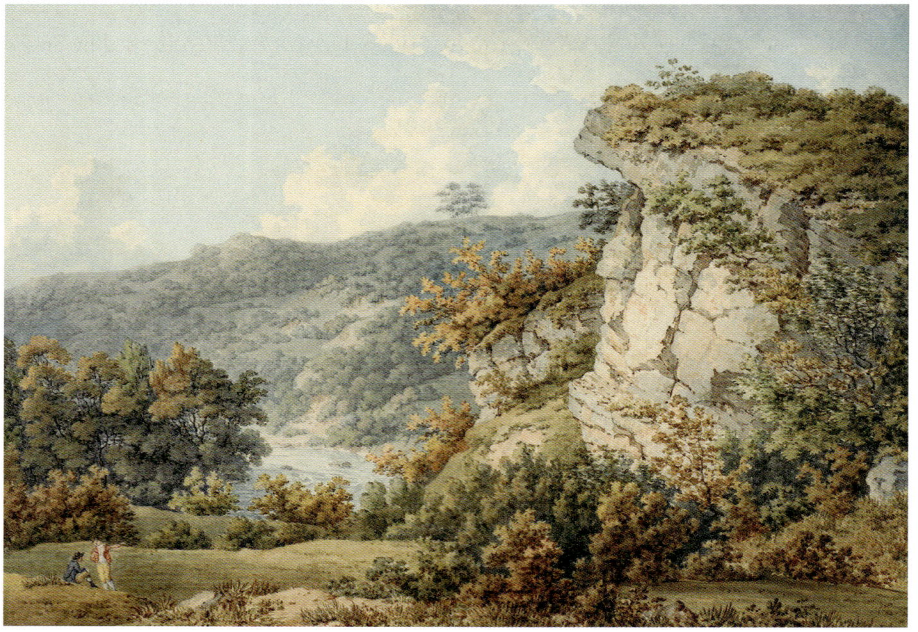

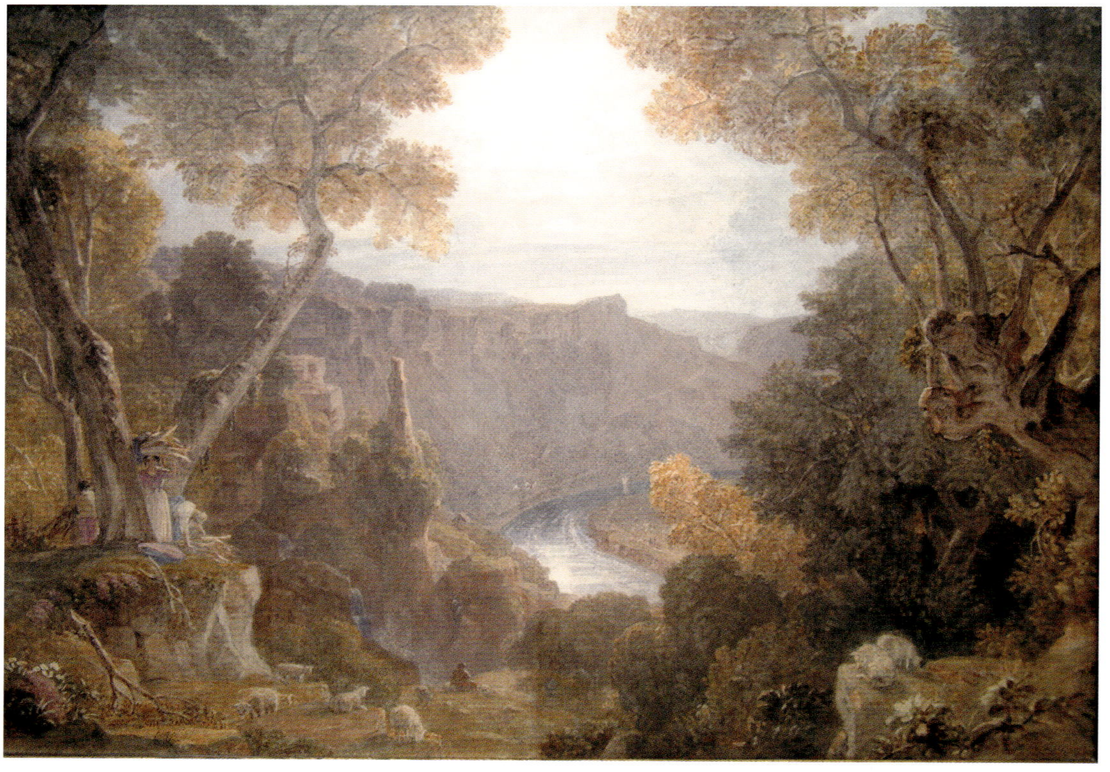

24. JOSHUA CRISTALL (1787-1847). *New Weir from Symonds Yat*
Signed J. Cristall, 1837. 670x480 mm. (Private Collection)

The prominent rock went under various names, such as the Longstone. This late example of Cristall's work, with sheep and shepherds in the foreground, shows typical pastoral idealization. (See nos 11-12.)

25. THOMAS HEARNE (1744-1817). *Symonds Yat on the River Wye, Herefordshire*
Signed Hearne. 242x346 mm. (Whitworth Art Gallery D.1924.81 : Bequeathed by Sir Edward Tootal Broadhurst, 1924)

The painting shows the Longstone prominently on the left, with pack mules below and men towing a barge upstream towards the lock through which they had to pass because of the weir. Across the river is the forge whose noise and smoke gave much delight to William Gilpin. Hearne published *The Antiquities of Great Britain* between 1777 and 1781, a key work in making the country's sights better known. In 1794 he travelled down the Wye with Sir George Beaumont, who was to be one of the founders of the National Gallery.

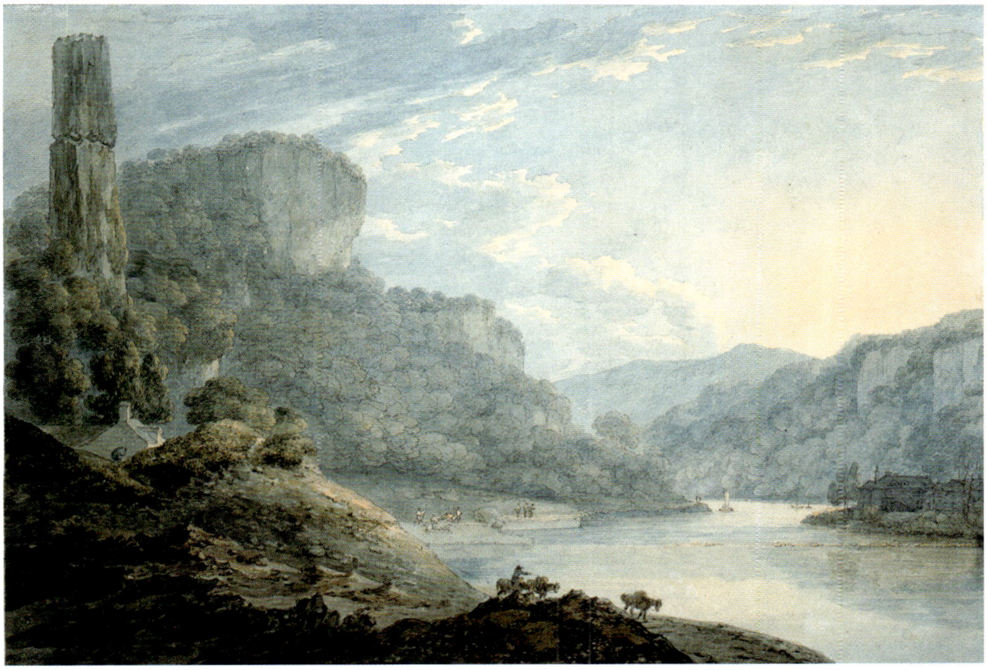

26. MICHAEL 'ANGELO' ROOKER (1746-1801). *New Weir*, c.*1788*
Unsigned. 305x474 mm. (Monmouth Museum)

Rooker's picture shows the smooth water above the weir before it falls, and the leat leading to the forge. (See no. 21.)

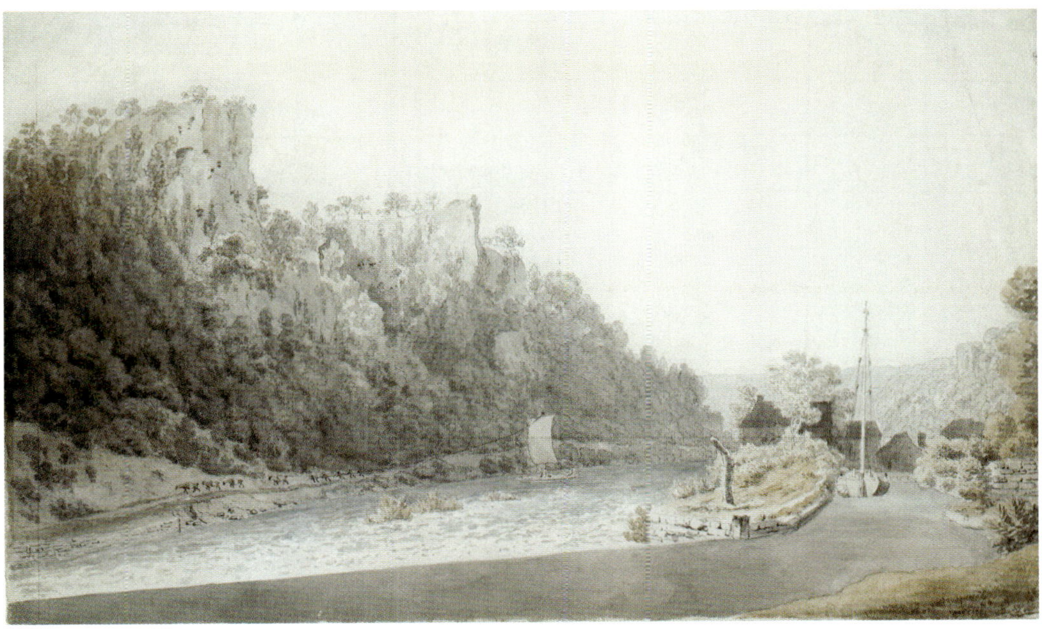

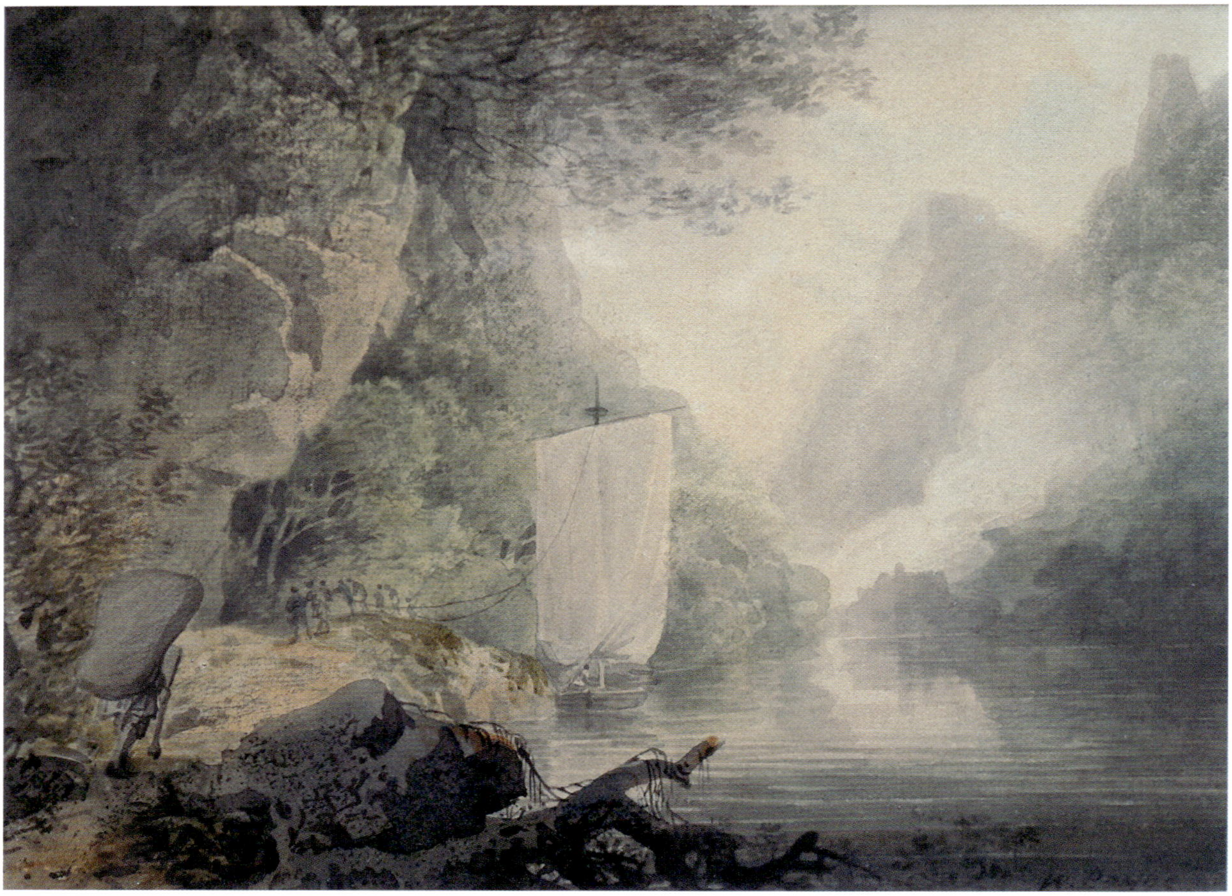

27. WILLIAM PAYNE (1760-1830). *New Weir with coracle man and barge*
Signed, and inscribed on original backboard label: 'View upon the Wye. 1791. by W. Payne'. 164x125 mm. (Private collection)

In this busy picture, Payne shows a man carrying a coracle on his back, a sight which always delighted tourists, a barge with its sail, pack horses, and the forge. He started life as an engineer in the naval dockyard at Plymouth, moving to London the year before this picture was painted. He painted many Wye scenes over the years, less interested in topographical accuracy than in making charming pictures like this one.

28-29 (opposite). JAMES WATHEN (1751-1828). '*Near New Weir Wednsdy 1 o'clock, 30 Aug' 1797*' and '*New Weir from Works taken from the opposite side the Wye Sunday 12 clock 9 June 1800*'
166x258 mm and 158x258 mm. (Herefordshire Archive Service S40/55 and 56)

The Wye makes a great loop at Coldwell Rocks towards Whitchurch and back again to Symonds Yat, and the earlier sketch has written in pencil 'New Weir the opposite side the Wye to Coldwell – To cross over the Rock on foot from the opposite side is – 200 yards by Water – 4 miles'. Looking from the forge across to the Longstone towering above the cottages, it shows bow-hauliers bringing a barge up to the lock on the right. The second sketch, drawn from near the lock, shows the size of the New Weir forge, with its row of workers' cottages above. There were many fewer trees on the banks two hundred years ago; this is because they were then much more carefully nurtured, specially through coppicing, for fuel for the forges. (See no. 4.)

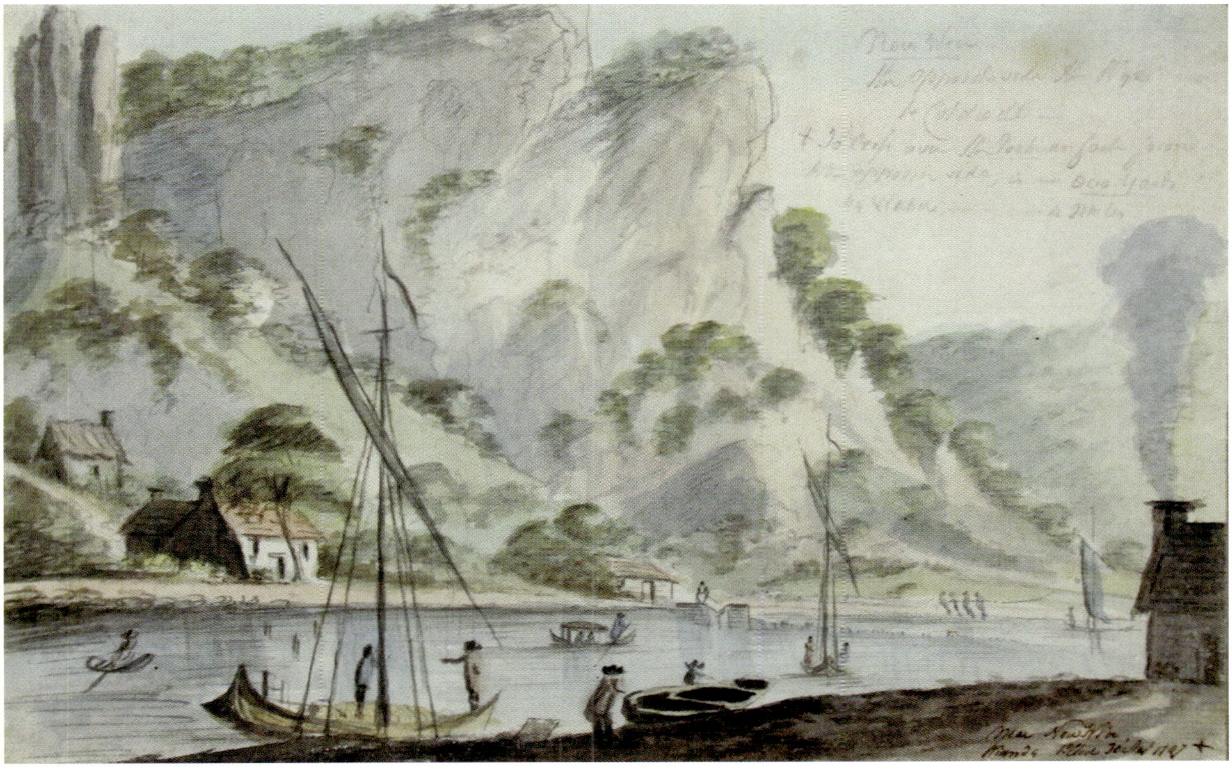

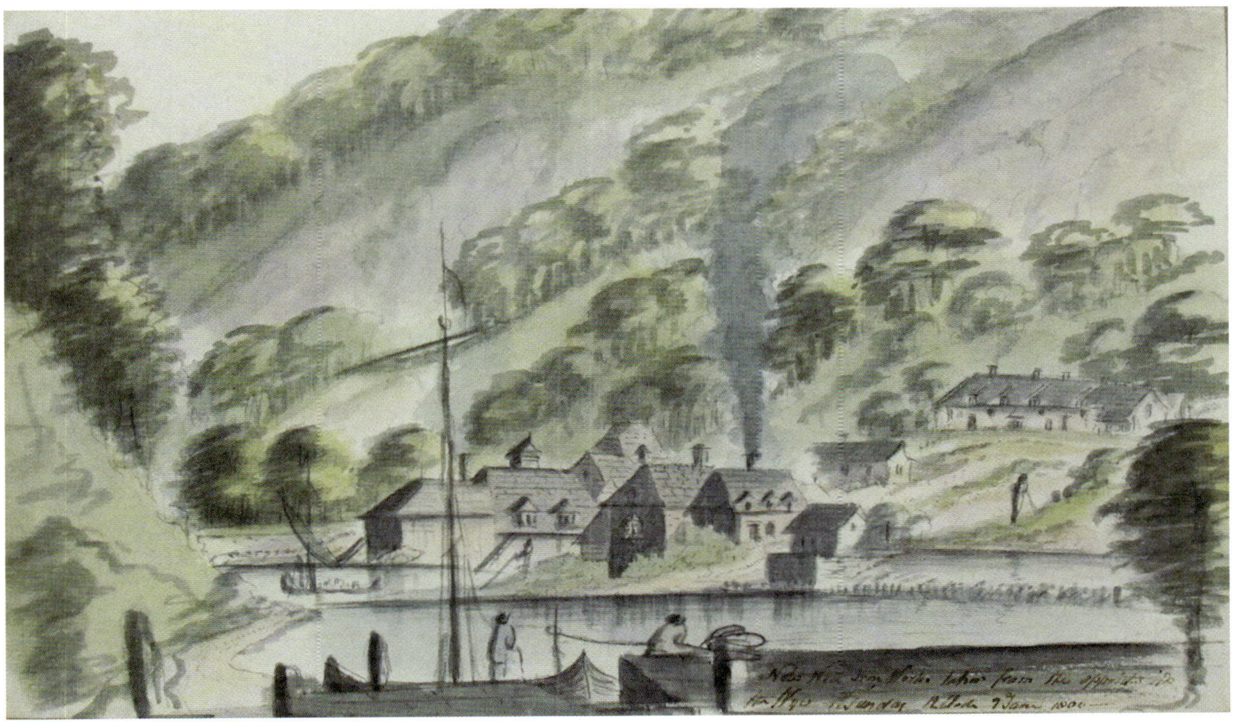

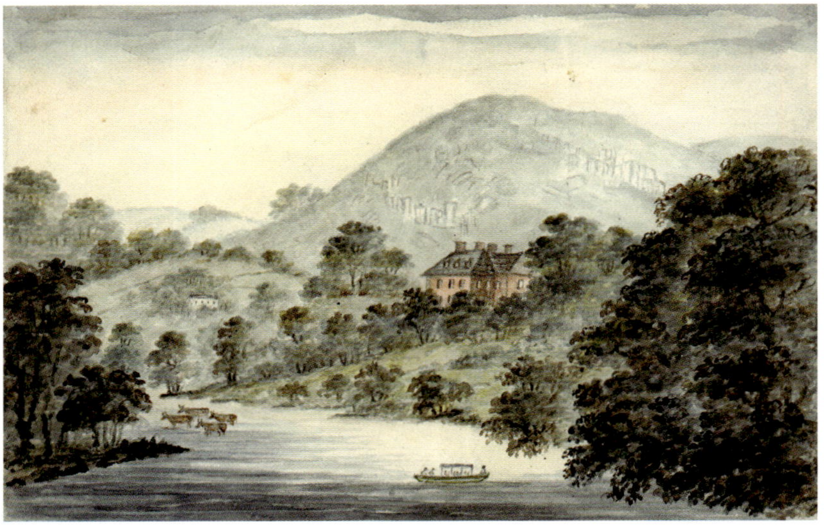

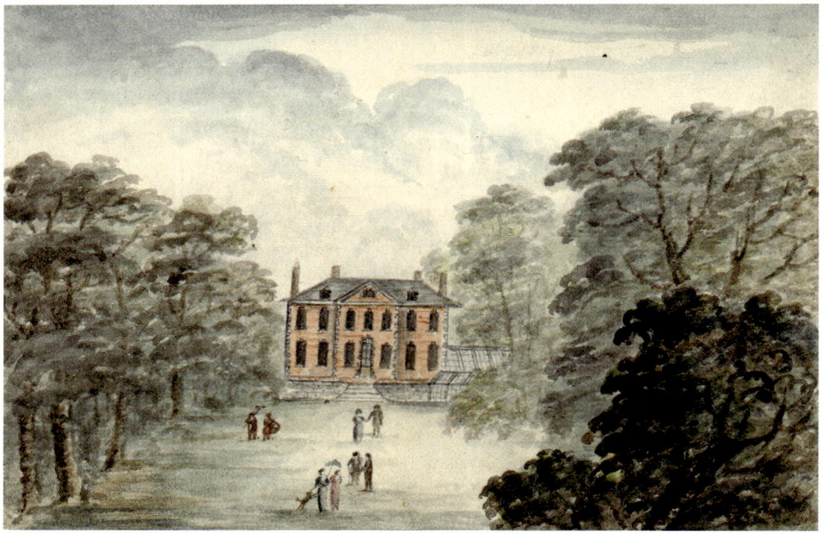

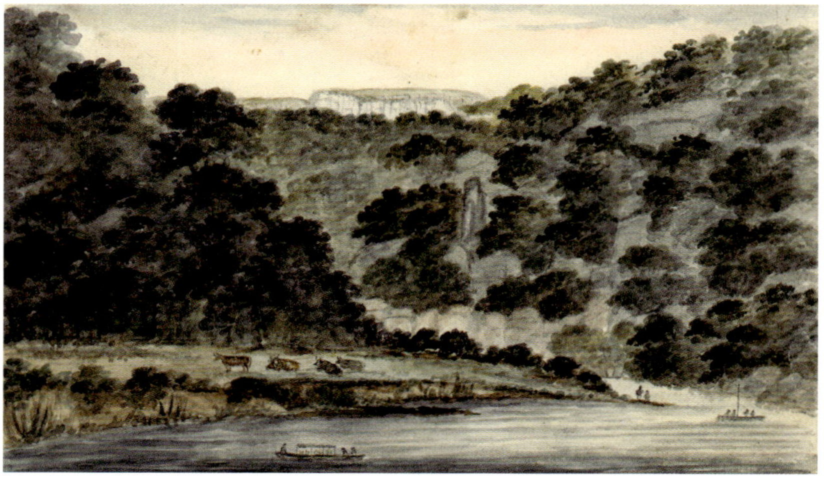

30-32. JOHN SAVERY (dates unknown). *A sketch of Hadnock taken in a boat on the River Wye by J.S. 13 Sep 1819; Mr Partridge's House taken from Chippenham, June 1819 by John Savery*; and *A sketch going from Monmouth to the Wear* [sic] *taken on a boat on the Wye 13 Sep 1819 by J.S.* 127x187 mm, 130x193 mm and 131x213 mm. (Monmouth Museum)

Monmouth was the hub of industrial activity in the area; Hadnock, across the river from the town, was the home of the Griffin family, who at one stage owned the ironworks at New Weir, leased for many years by members of the Partridge family, of whom William Partridge was one. His house overlooked Chippenham, the forty-five acres of meadow between the town and the rivers Wye and Monnow. At one stage in possession of Bishopswood Furnace, he acquired a large estate in and around Ruardean, and died in December 1819, shortly after Savery's picture was painted. (Unpublished article by John Evans.)

Nothing is known of Savery, except that he sketched Tintern in June 1818 and Monmouth and the Wye in September 1819. He may have been a tourist, but since he was in and around Monmouth in both June and September in successive years he was more probably a local amateur. His quick sketches, however naïve, show what interested people at the time, beyond the sublime and the picturesque.

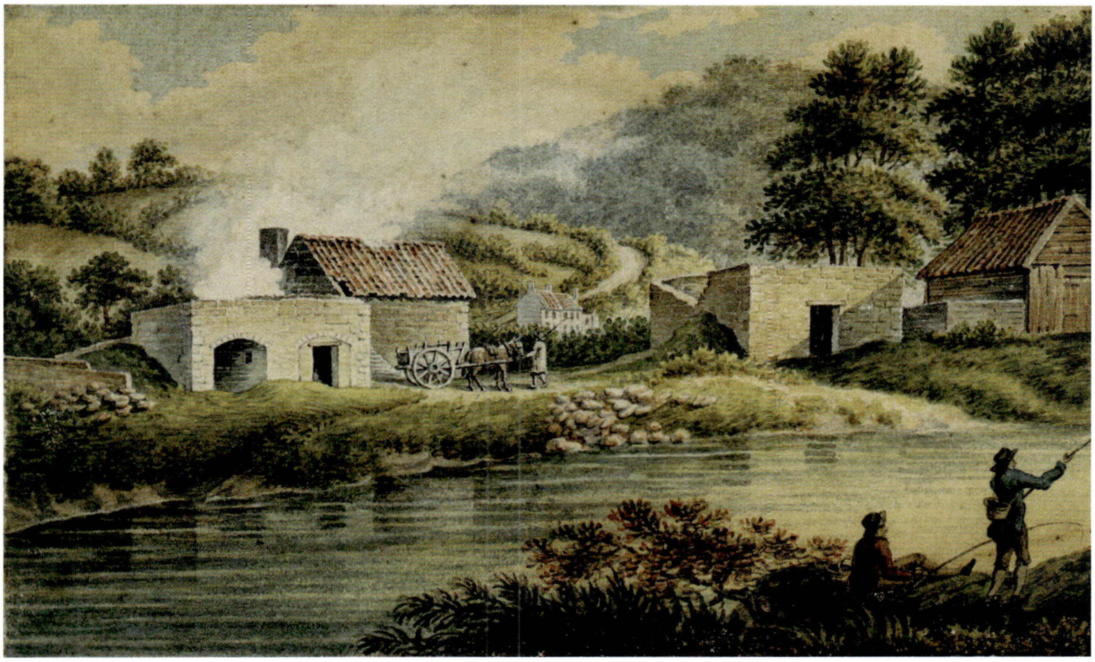

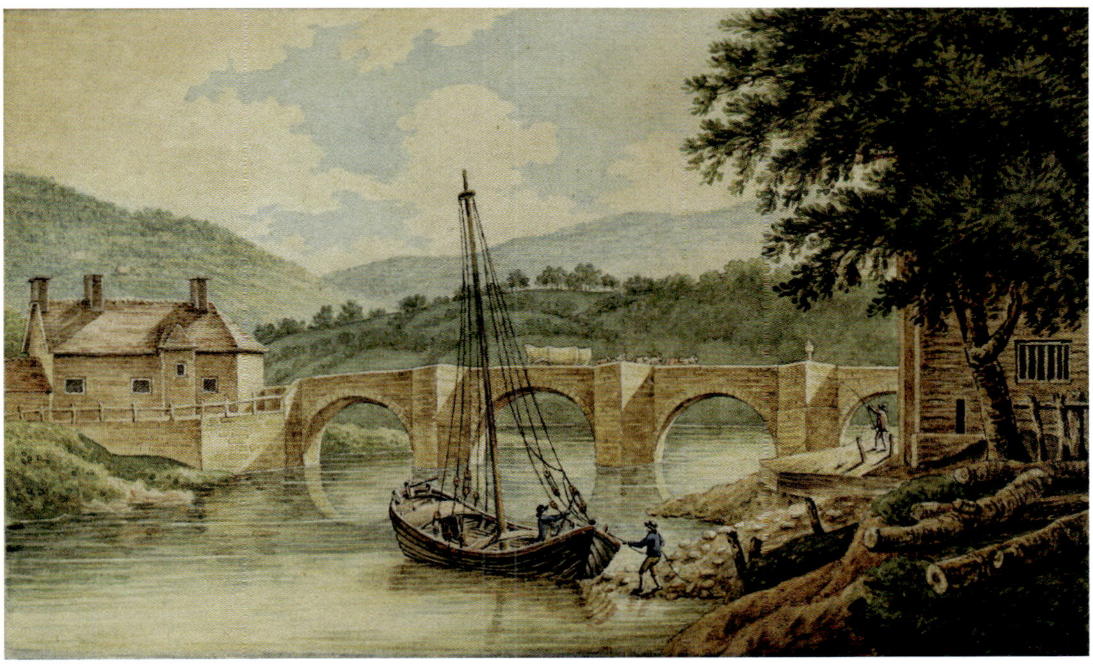

33-34. J.H. FIDLOR (fl.1796-1808). *Lime kilns, near Monmouth Bridge, fishermen in right foreground on grassy bank, 1797.* Pen and grey ink and watercolour. Signed. 102x163 mm. And *Wye Bridge at Monmouth; timber lying in right foreground beneath tree, 1796.* Pen and grey and black ink and water-colour. Signed. 102x163 mm. (British Museum PD 1939.0502.3 and 1939.0502.2)

Very little is known of Fidlor except that he exhibited four Wye views at the Royal Academy in 1797, these two paintings perhaps among them. Lime was burned extensively in the area as a dressing for fields as well as for mortar, plaster and render.

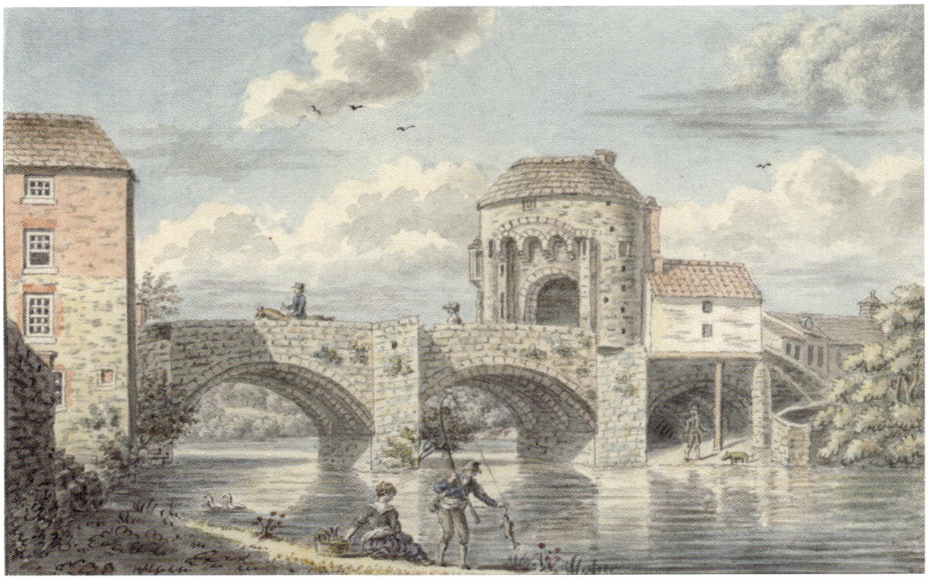

35. JOSHUA GOSSELIN (1739-1813). *Monnow Bridge and Gate at Monmouth, 1808*
Unsigned. 150x188 mm. (Monmouth Museum)

Gosselin was a lawyer, antiquarian and watercolourist from Guernsey, who first painted Monmouthshire in 1784. Later his daughter came to live near Usk, where he paid her and her family several visits. His paintings, of which this is a particularly charming late example, only came to public light in 1999.

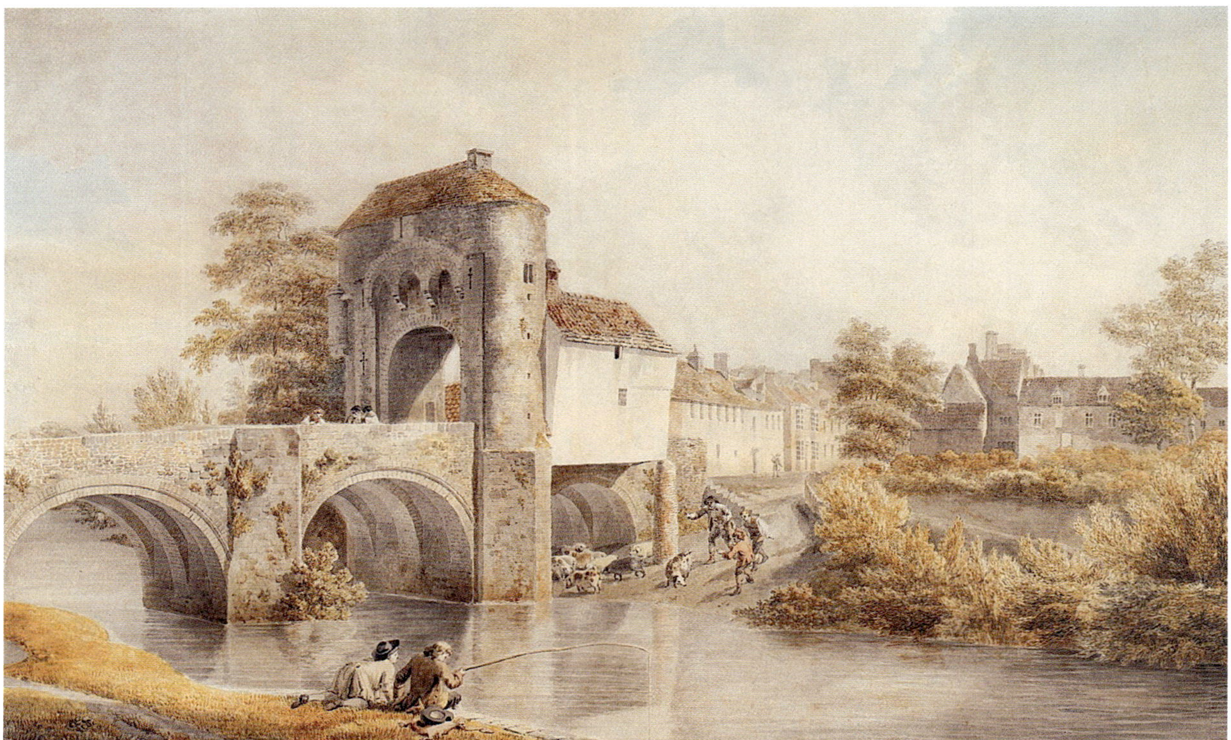

36. MICHAEL 'ANGELO' ROOKER (1747-1801). *Monnow Bridge and Gate,* c.*1788*
Signed. 290x455 mm. (Monmouth Museum)

Monnow Bridge was a very popular subject with visiting artists. (See no. 21.)

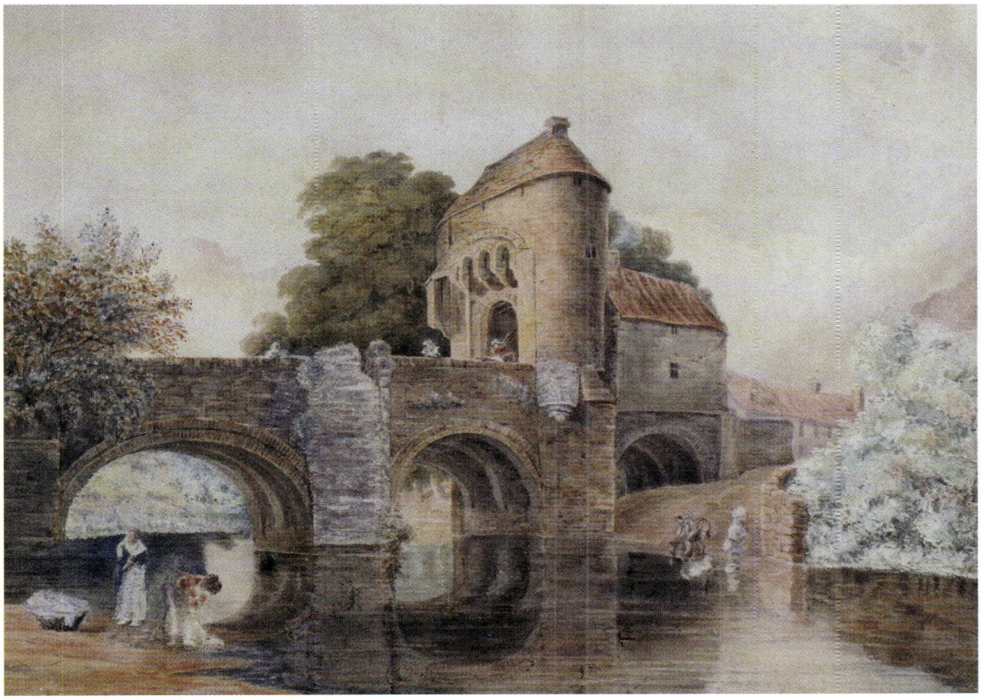

37. THOMAS HEARNE (1744-1817). *Monmouth, Monnow Bridge, c.1794*
Unsigned. 283x380 mm. (Newport Museum & Art Gallery NPTMG : 1945-22)

Where Gosselin and Rooker show animals being watered on the Monmouth side of the river, and fishermen on the Overmonnow bank, Hearne more realistically, paints washerwomen on both. (See no. 25.)

38. MICHAEL 'ANGELO' ROOKER (1746-1801). *Bridge at Monmouth with St Mary's Church in the Background, c.1788*
Signed. 272x369 mm. (Victoria and Albert Museum 118 – 1892)

The bridge across the Monnow from the town to Vauxhall was known as Tibbs Bridge, as John Tibbs, the landlord of the Beaufort Arms, had a farm there which he converted to a Public Mall and Tea Garden, with a bowling green where dances were held in the summer. The prospect, according to Francis Grose in 1775, was delightful. For two shillings a stranger could get tea, coffee and music while the ladies danced. The structure at the town end of the bridge is a barrier against cattle. The railings seem very spruce and new. Compare no. 39.

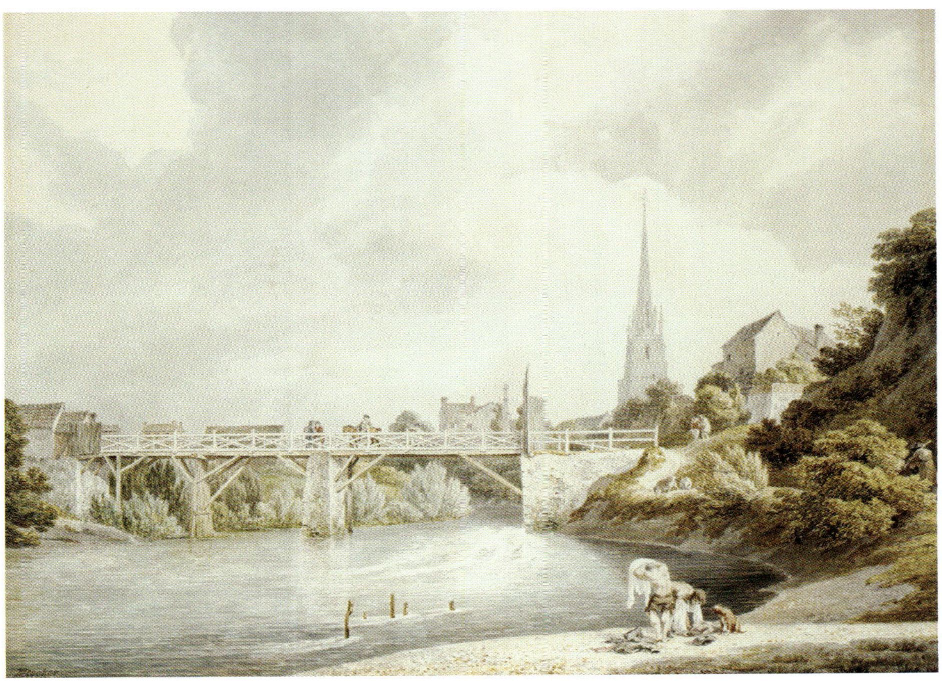

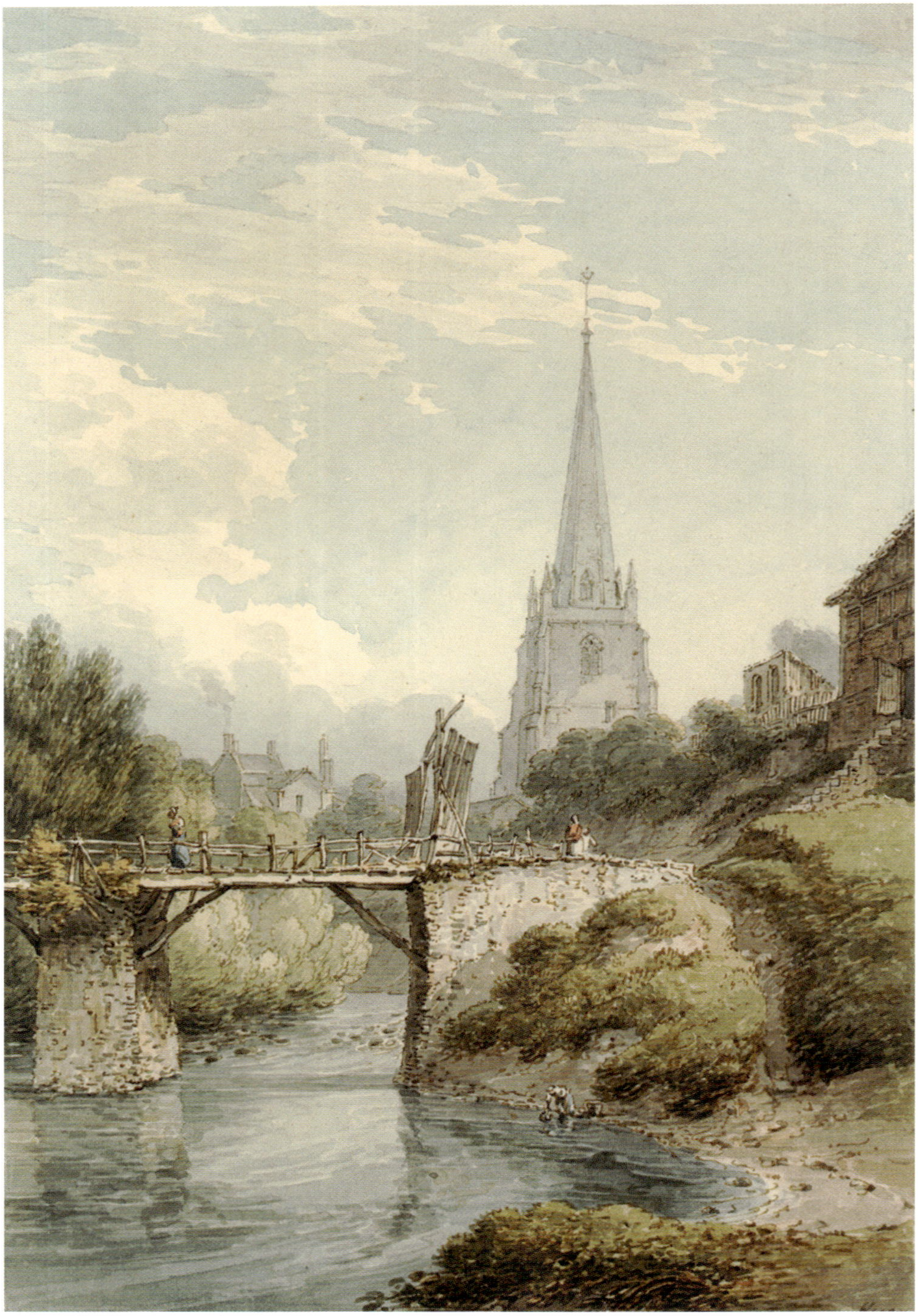

39. THOMAS HEARNE (1744-1817). *Near Monmouth; a stream flowing between high banks into the foreground under a Footbridge, 1794*. Pen and brown ink and watercolour. Unsigned. 216x143 mm. (British Museum PD 1859, 0528.212 (Binyon 8))

Tibbs Bridge seems have become very dilapidated since Rooker's visit in 1788 (no. 38). (See no. 25.)

40. THOMAS TUDOR (1785-1855). *Monmouth from the West, 23 August 1811*
Tudor did not sign his pictures. 116x484 mm. (Monmouth Museum)

This is Monmouth viewed from Vauxhall, with the castle on the right, Castle House in the middle and the church to the left. Priory Street had not yet been built. Thomas Tudor was the son of Owen Tudor, a Monmouth bookseller. His aunts ran the girls' boarding school at Castle House. As a boy, with his father and his brother John, he contributed architectural plans and sketches to William Coxe's *Monmouthshire* (1801), and he continued to draw all his life, though his main business was as a land agent. He trained at the RA, where he exhibited from 1809 to 1819. He built himself Tudor House in Wyesham, across the river from Monmouth, where he had a fine collection of paintings which he exhibited in Monmouth in 1840. It included a Van Dyck, a Reynolds, a J.M.W. Turner and a Joshua Cristall. Cristall, who lived nearby at Goodrich (see nos 11-12), was a friend.

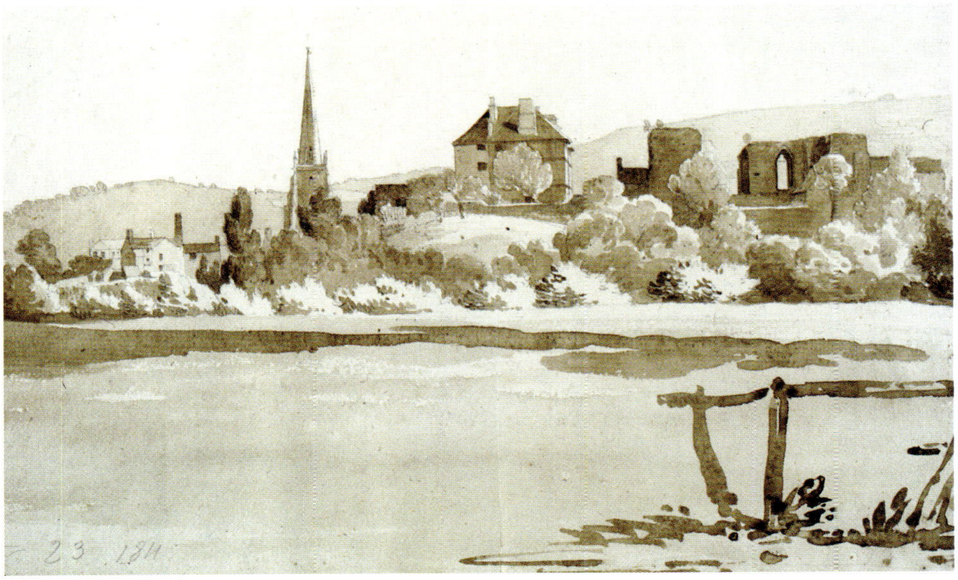

41. JOHN or THOMAS TUDOR (1785-1855). *Monmouth Castle and Castle House, with the river Monnow*
Inscribed on reverse 'Monmouth Castle taken from the banks of the Monnow' and inscribed John Tudor. Sepia drawing on paper, 1810. 140x200 mm. (Newport Museum & Art Gallery NPTMG : 78-178.2)

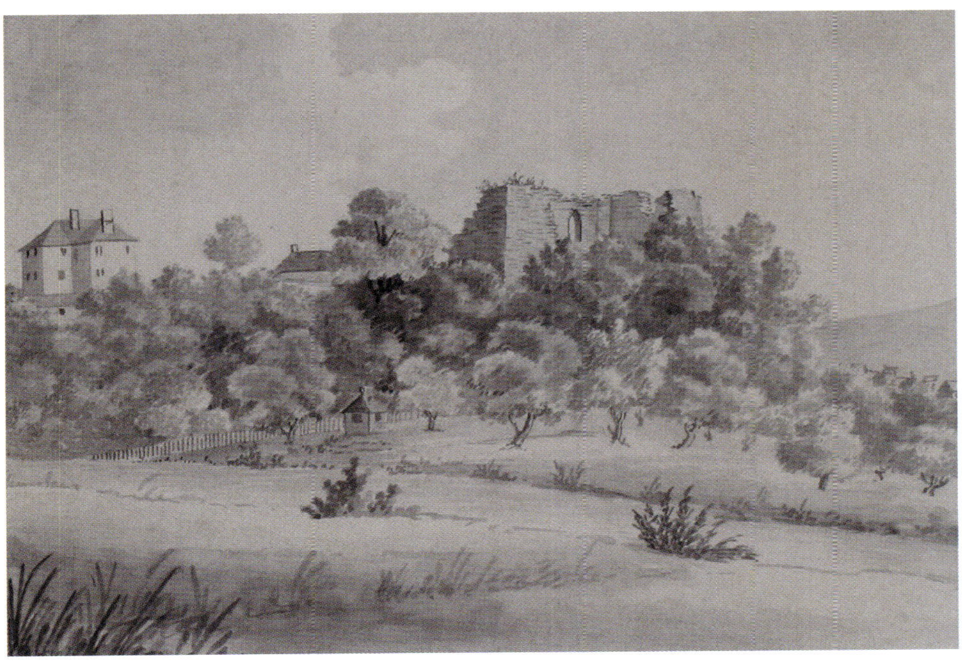

Little is known of John Tudor, Thomas's elder brother, though he exhibited fifteen pictures (and Thomas seventeen) at the Royal Academy between 1809 and 1819. John seems to have lived in London, while Thomas remained in Monmouth. Neither became a professional artist. It is extremely difficult to distinguish between their work as very few of their paintings are signed, and they drew many of the same local scenes (compare no. 40).

42. THOMAS TUDOR (1785-1855). *Monmouth Quayside,* c.*1810*
177x101 mm. (Monmouth Museum)

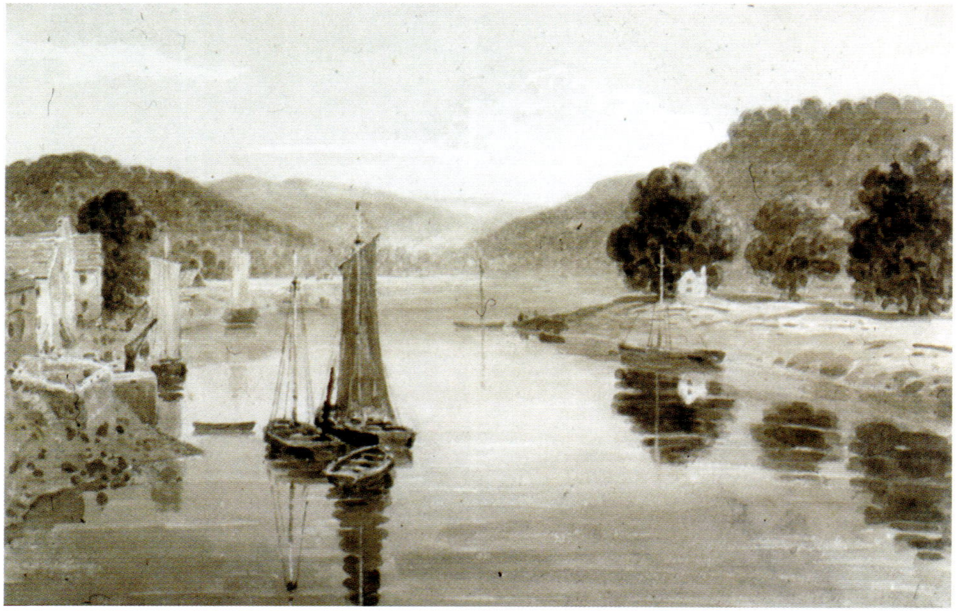

A view from the bridge, with trows heading upstream. On the left is now the site of the Monmouth Rowing Club.

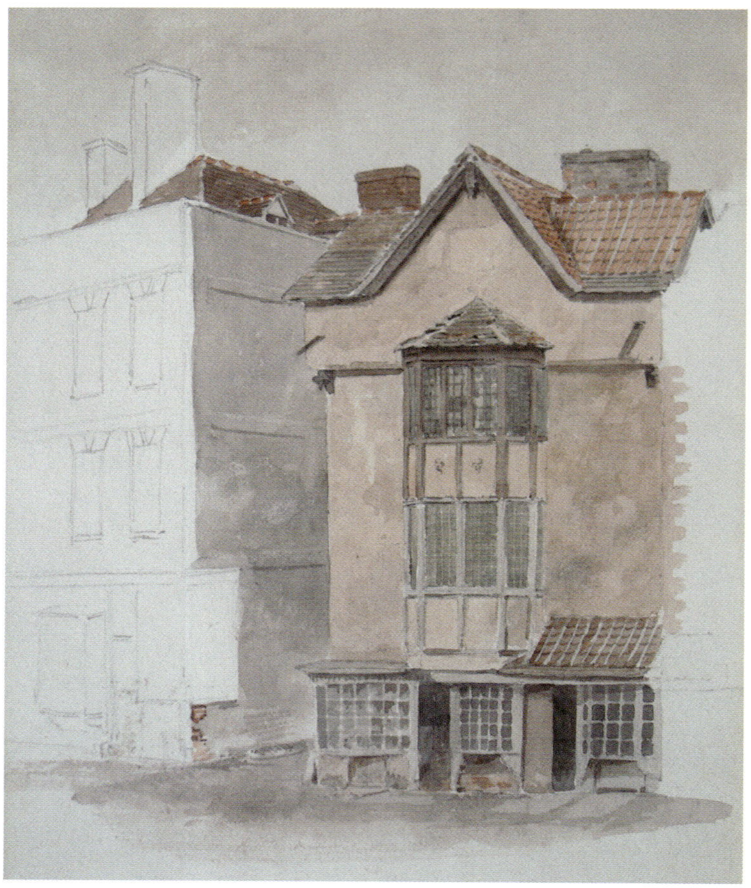

43. THOMAS TUDOR (1785-1855).
No. 1 Agincourt Square, Monmouth, c.*1810*
212x168 mm. (Keith Kissack Collection)

No. 1 Agincourt Square first figures on a street map of 1610, though the house is dated 1624 on the apex of the western gable. For most of the nineteenth century it was an ironmongers, before being restored and given a shop front. It was restored again in the 1980s, having served as a shoe shop for sixty years or so. Since then it has been a butcher's and an antique shop. At the time of writing it was empty.

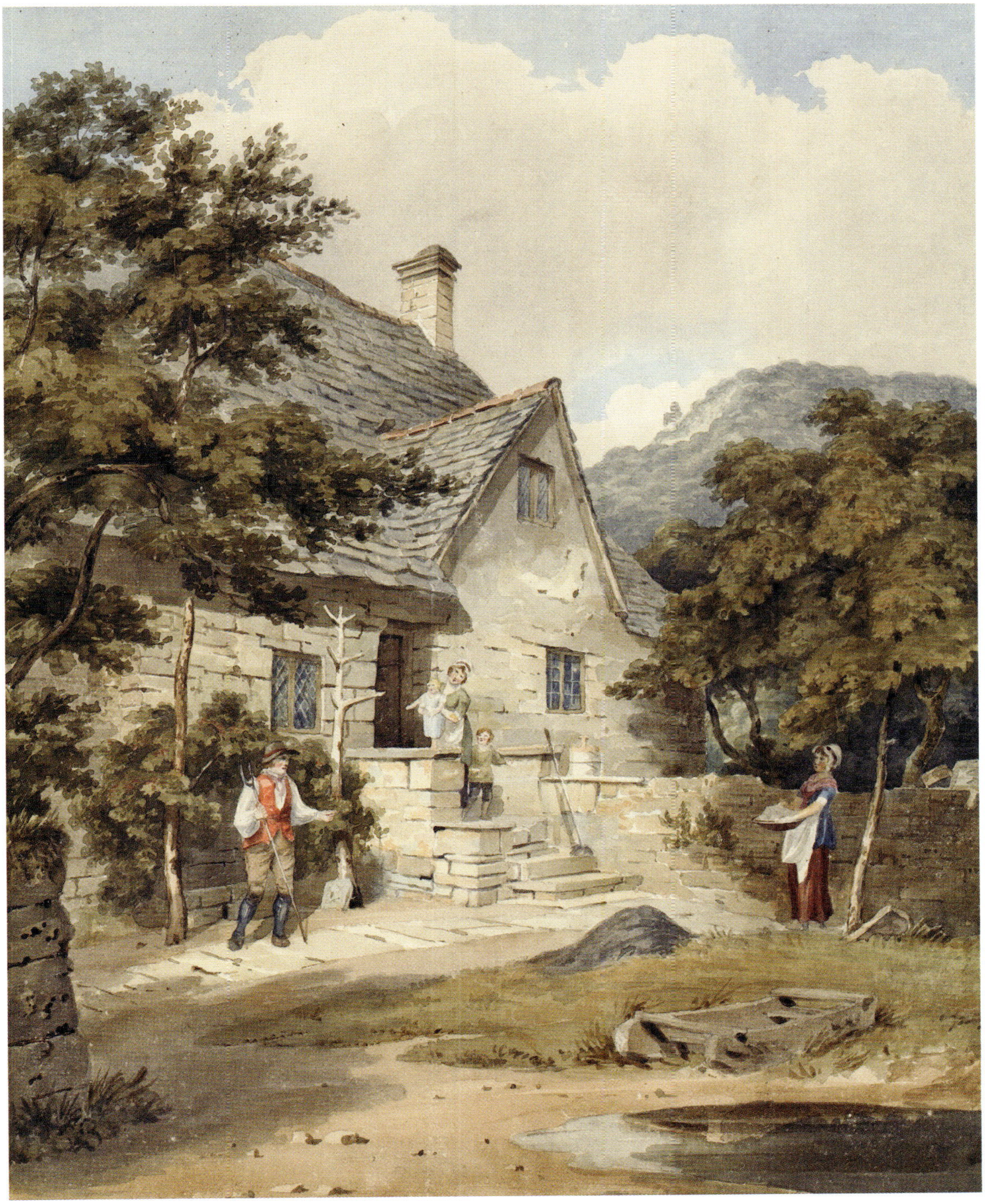

44. GEORGE SAMUEL (*c*.1760-1823). *Tintern, Monmouthshire*, *c*.1815
Unsigned. Watercolour on paper. 353x279 mm. (Fitzwilliam Museum, Cambridge, no. 1707)

Samuel, who had the misfortune to be killed by a falling wall, showed landscapes at the RA from 1786 till his death. He exhibited a picture of cottages at Tintern in 1810 at the British Institution, and a print of this watercolour was published in 1815.

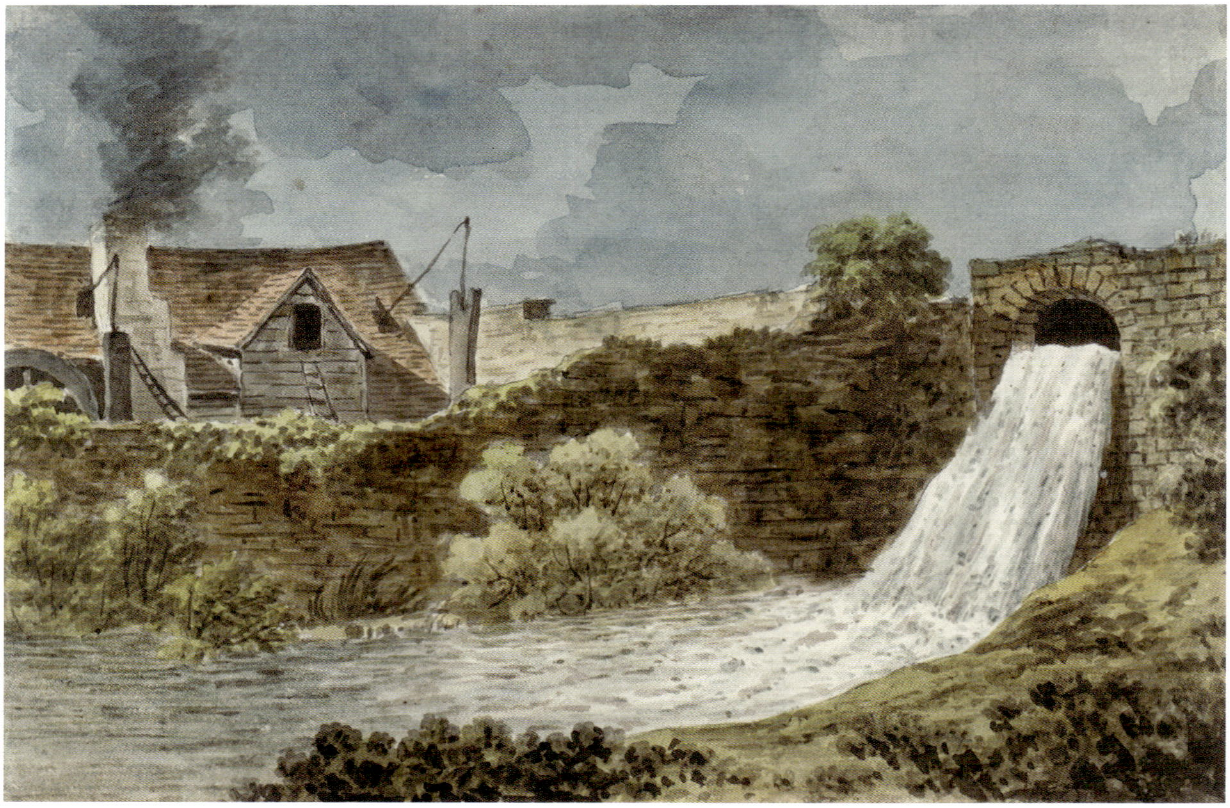

45. JOHN INIGO RICHARDS (1731-1810). *Ironworks, Fenton, Monmouth*
Pencil and watercolour on paper. Signed. 143x210 mm. (Tate TO9345. Purchased as part of the Oppé Collection with assistance from the National Lottery through the Heritage Lottery Fund 1996)

The writing on a painting is never necessarily that of the artist, and as there is no Fenton in Monmouthshire, and there were only copper works at Fenton, near Swansea, the title would seem to be a later addition, with 'Fenton' possibly a misreading for 'Tintern'. Research by John Evans suggests this picture is of part of the middle wireworks in the Angidy valley. Tourists were often as entranced by the industry at Tintern as by the abbey, and there are several descriptions of the excitement of the furnaces by night.

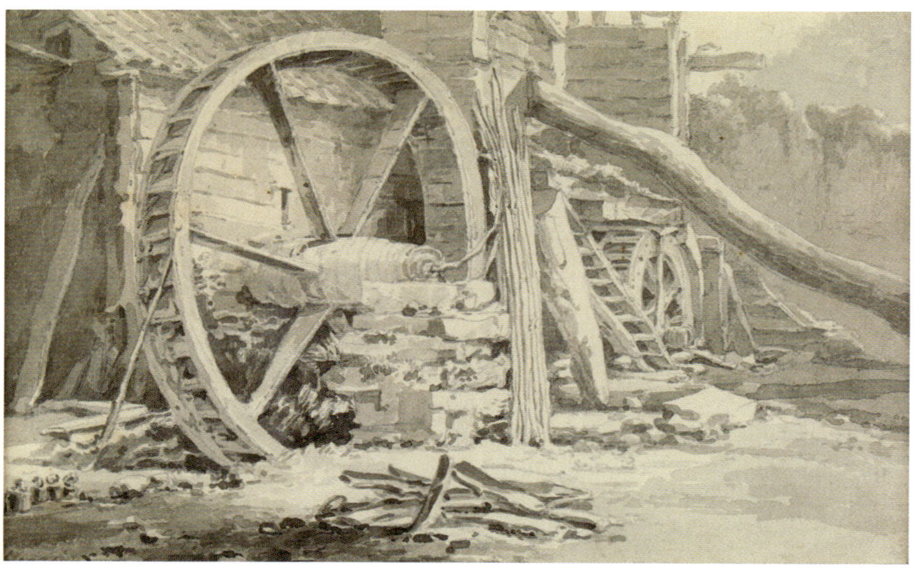

46. THOMAS HEARNE (1744-1817). *Iron Forge at Tintern, c.1794*
Signed. 110x175 mm. (NLW PB 01260)

This is Hearne's drawing for a well-known engraving. (See no. 25.)

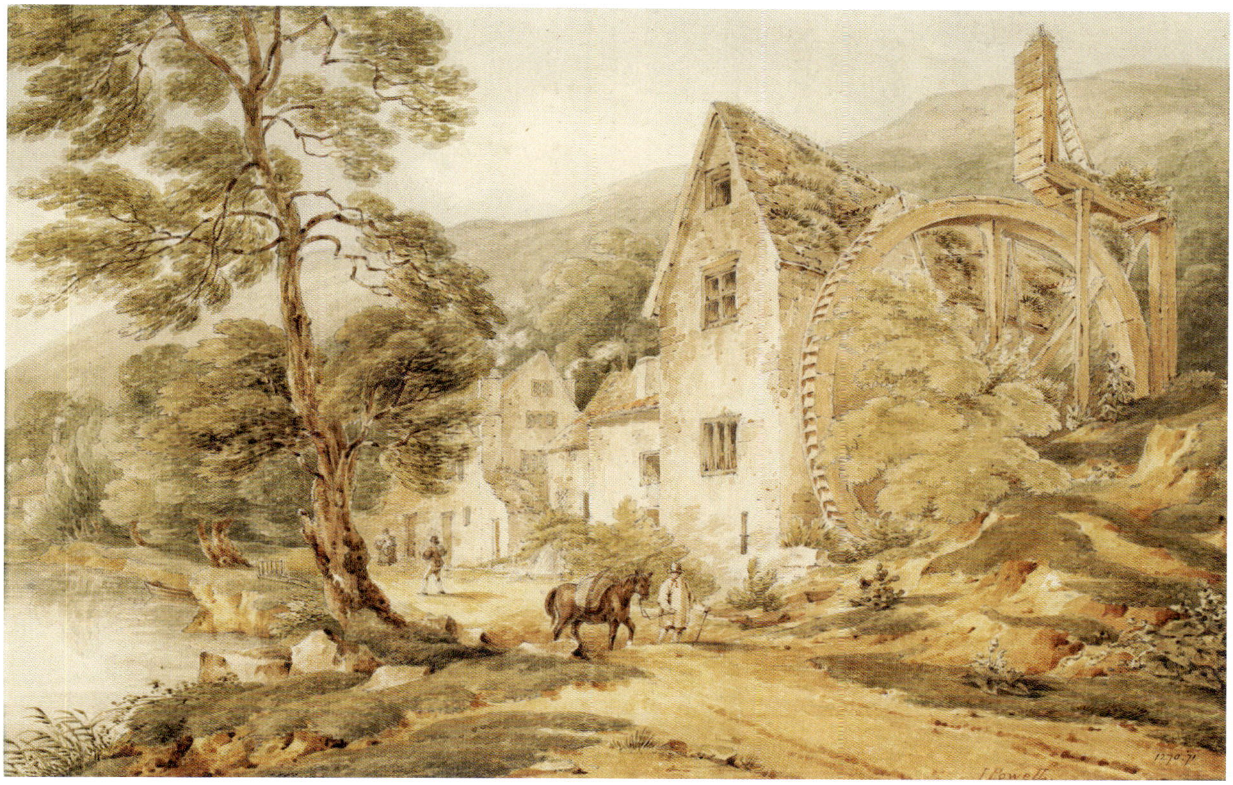

47. JOSEPH POWELL (1780-1834). *Mill at Tintern, Monmouthshire*
Signed J. Powell. 308x460 mm. (Victoria and Albert Museum 1270 – 1871)

This gigantic waterwheel was at the bottom of the Angidy valley. Powell, who exhibited at the RA from 1796, travelled upstream from Chepstow. His sketchbooks, on which this and a similar painting in the British Museum are based, are watermarked 1801.

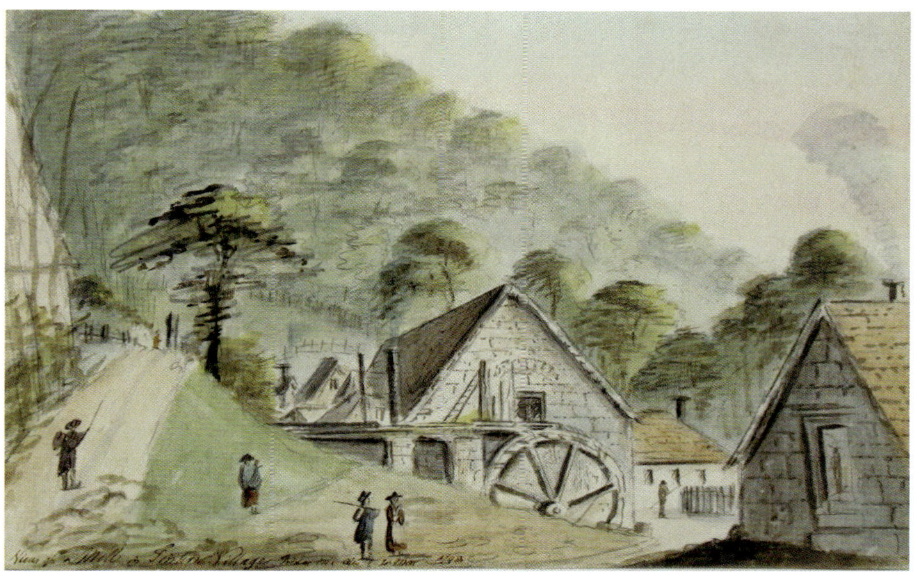

48. JAMES WATHEN (1751-1828). *'View of a Mill in Tintern Village Friday [??] clo 20th May 1798'* 162x255 mm. (Herefordshire Archive Service S40 Part II, 67)

This mill was probably in the Angidy valley also. (See no. 4.)

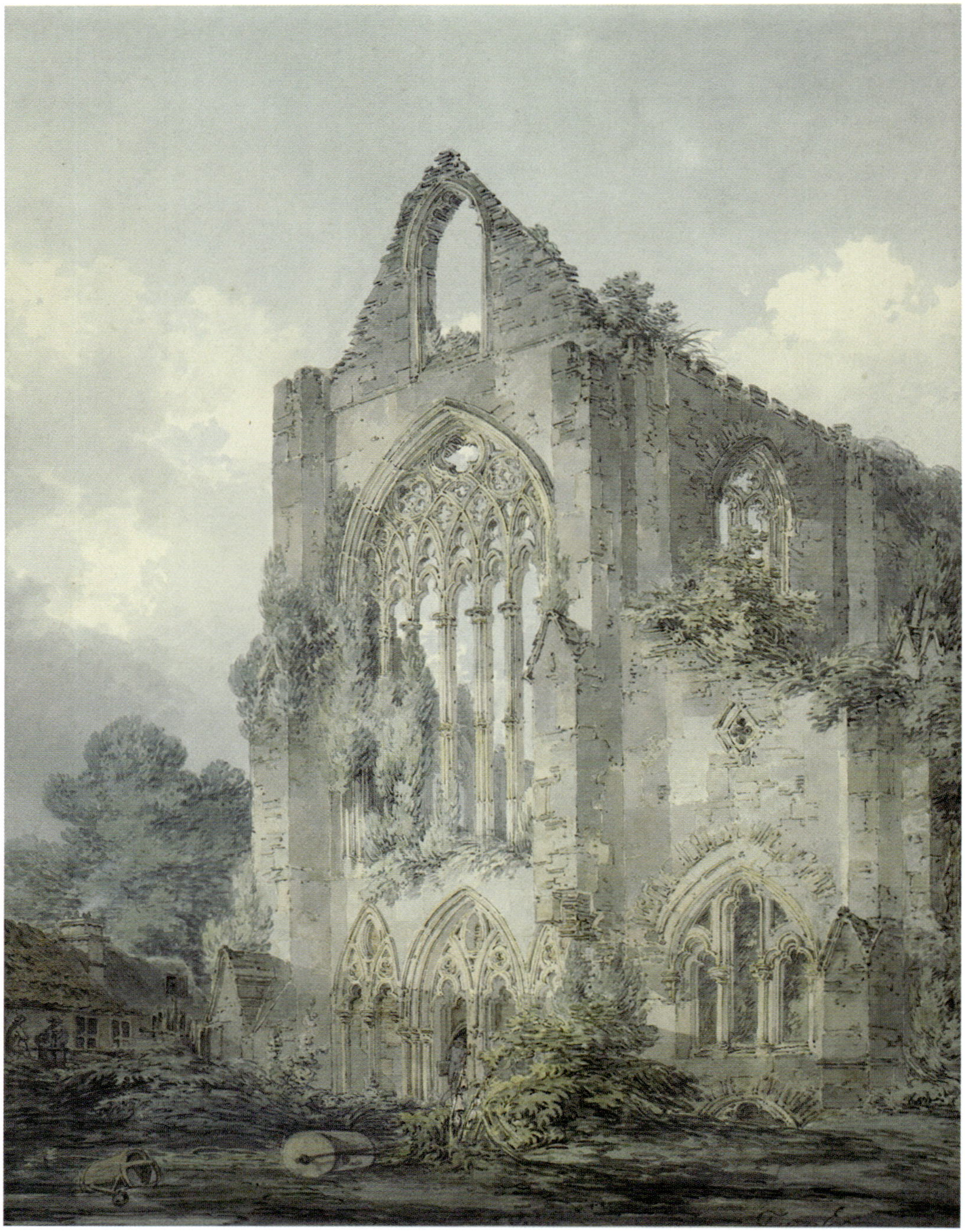

49. JOSEPH MALLORD WILLIAM TURNER (1775-1851). *Tintern Abbey. West front; the ruined abbey, c.*1794. Watercolour over graphite. Signed. 419x316 mm. (British Museum PD 1878,1228.41)

Turner was only 17 in 1792 when he visited the Wye valley for the first time and made the pencil sketch on which this picture is based. He came again in 1798, travelling upstream from Chepstow. He made use of the sketches he made on these trips many times in later life (see nos 50 and 76 and the Courtauld Gallery's watercolour of Chepstow Castle, Plate XIII), each time developing his painterly language. The sketchbooks are now in Tate Britain.

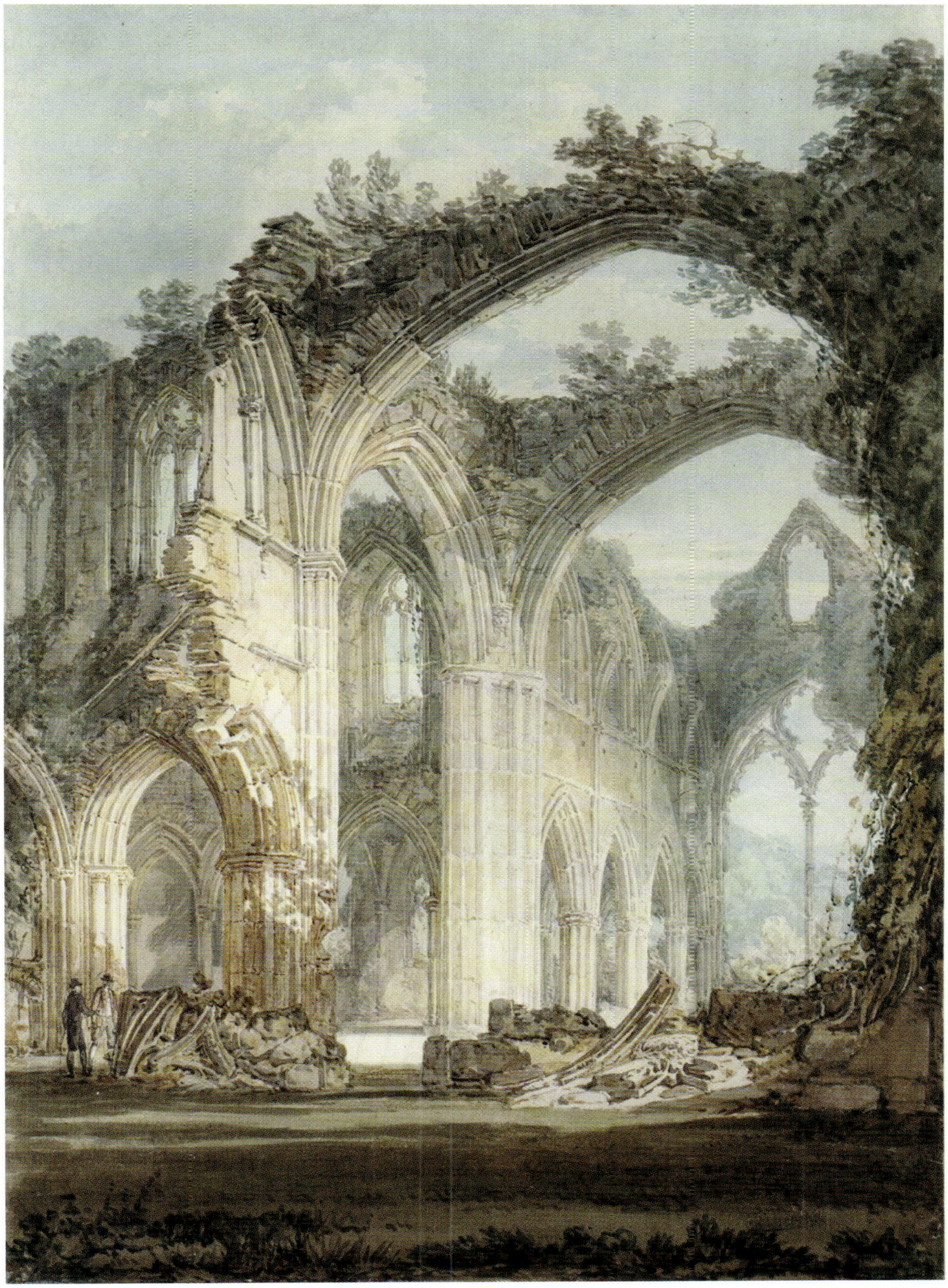

50. JOSEPH MALLORD WILLIAM TURNER (1775-1851). *The Chancel and Crossing of Tintern Abbey, Looking towards the East Window,* 1794. Unsigned. Pencil and watercolour on paper. 358x255 mm. (Tate D 00374 : Accepted by the nation as part of the Turner Bequest 1856)

Like the painting of the West front, this is based on a sketch from Turner's 1792 tour. It is a study for the more finished version in the V & A. Turner has very much flattened the crossing arches, below which lies rubble from the choir screen.

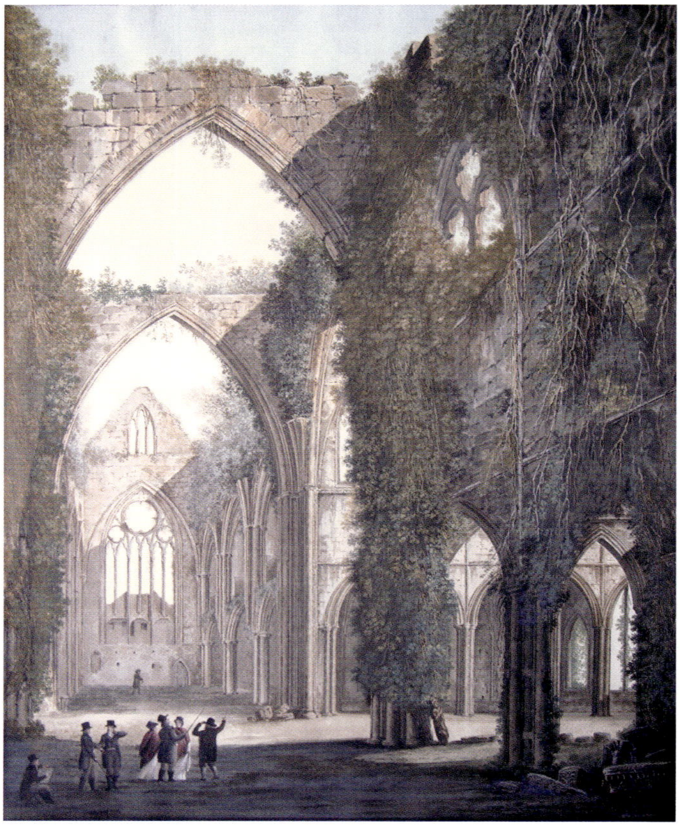

51. AGOSTINO AGLIO (1777-1857). *Tintern Abbey Interior, September 1806*
Signed and inscribed on a loose sheet behind the painting: 'Interior of Tintern Abbey taken from nature & painted by Augustin Aglio in the September 1806 – the present View is taken from the North Side in the interior.' 600x480 mm. (Private collection)

The abbey was kept locked at this time, and the figure in the background with the keys may well be George Gethin, landlord of the Beaufort Arms, whose responsibility they were. The man sketching, while the rest of his party look at the ruins, may be a self-portrait of Aglio himself. Born in Cremona, then under Austrian rule, and where his father was a lawyer, Aglio welcomed Napoleon's invasion of Italy in 1797, and followed him to Rome. But he soon became disillusioned with his hero and began to study painting. He visited Greece and Egypt with William Wilkins, RA, the architect of the National Gallery, who brought him to England in 1803, where he seems to have turned his hand to every sort of artistic endeavour. He painted other scenes in south Wales in 1806, and was later responsible for large-scale decorations in major Roman Catholic churches in London.

52. EDWARD DAYES (1763-1804). *Tintern Abbey, Monmouthshire, and the River Wye*
Signed Edw.Dayes 1794. 253x392 mm. (Whitworth Art Gallery D.1899.8 : Gift of Mary Worthington 1899)

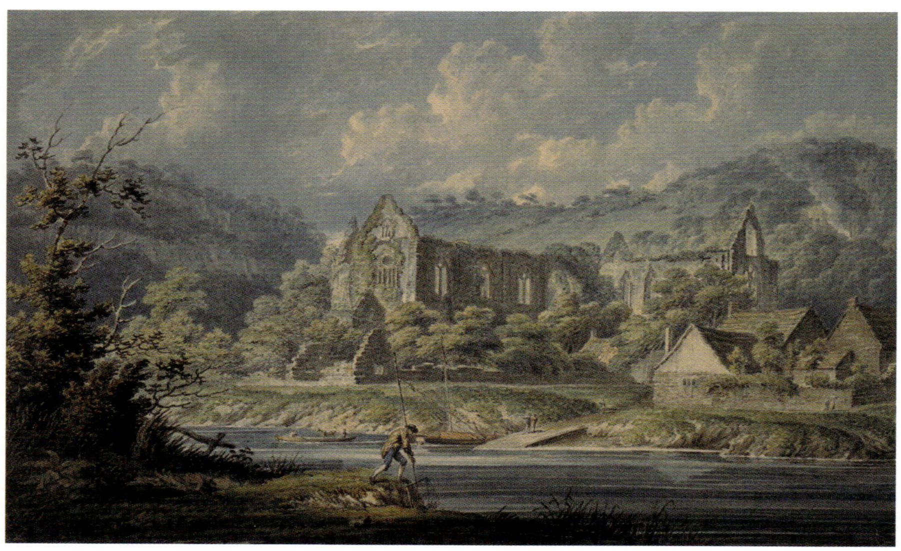

This is one of the standard views of Tintern Abbey, taken from across the river, with the landing place for the ferry next to the inn. Dayes exhibited at the RA from 1786. He was very highly regarded and had a great influence on both Thomas Girtin and J.M.W. Turner. But he was of uncertain temperament, and committed suicide. He made a series of watercolours of the Wye, engraved by Francis Jukes between 1797 and 1802, of which this is one. The prints are among the most beautiful made of the Wye.

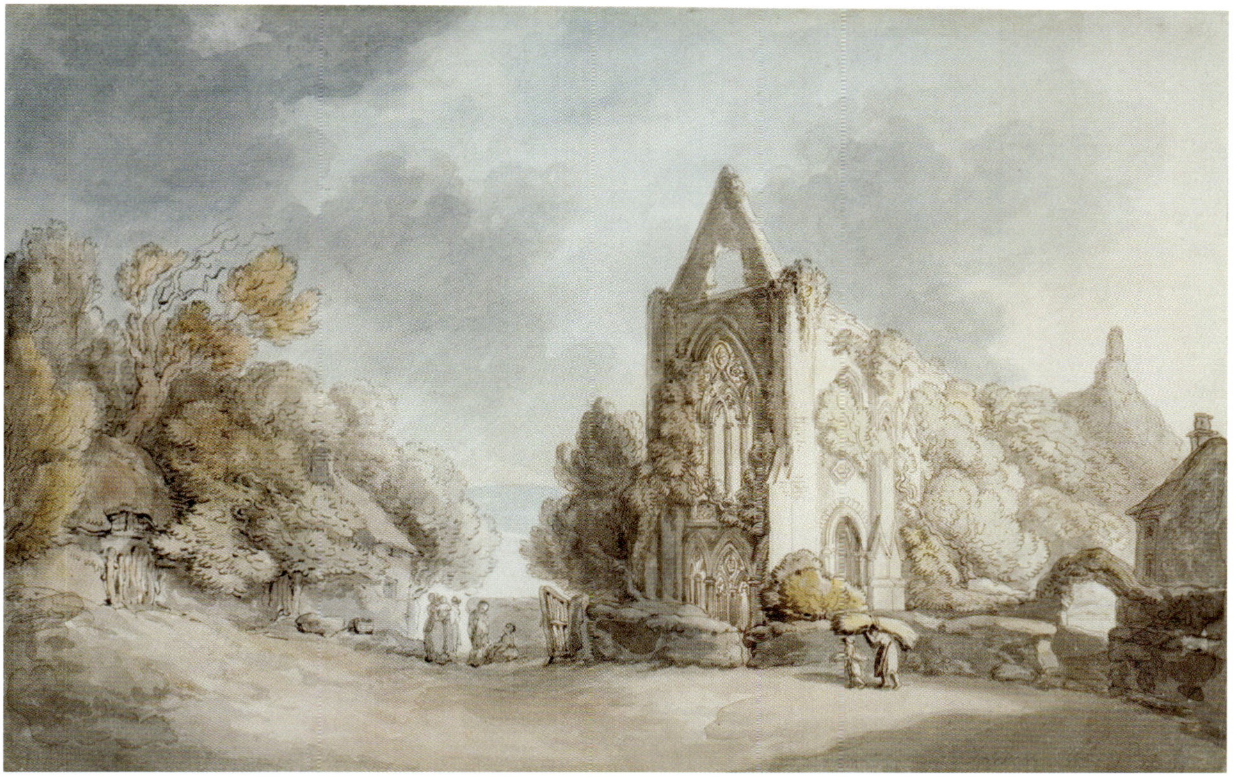

53. THOMAS ROWLANDSON (1757-1827). *Tintern Abbey S. Wales*
Unsigned. 283x435 mm. (Whitworth Art Gallery D.1996.23 : Given by George Ainscow in 1996)

Rowlandson travelled round Wales with Henry Wigstead in 1797, finishing at Chepstow and Tintern. Best known as a caricaturist, he seems less impressed by the abbey than most artists.

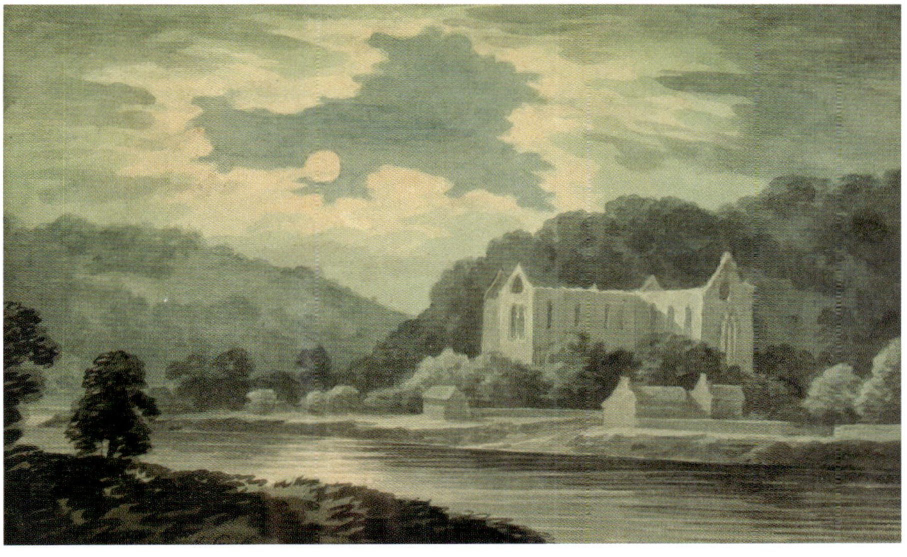

54. JOHN 'WARWICK' SMITH (1749-1831). *Tintern Abbey by moonlight, 1789*
Unsigned. 135x212 mm. (NLW PG02297 TI/7)

Moonlit views of Tintern were always popular, often with the moon shining through the east window (compare nos 55 and 56). Smith, though, has taken the opportunity to show a standard view of the abbey under unfamiliar conditions, with the moon peeping between clouds. (See no. 3.)

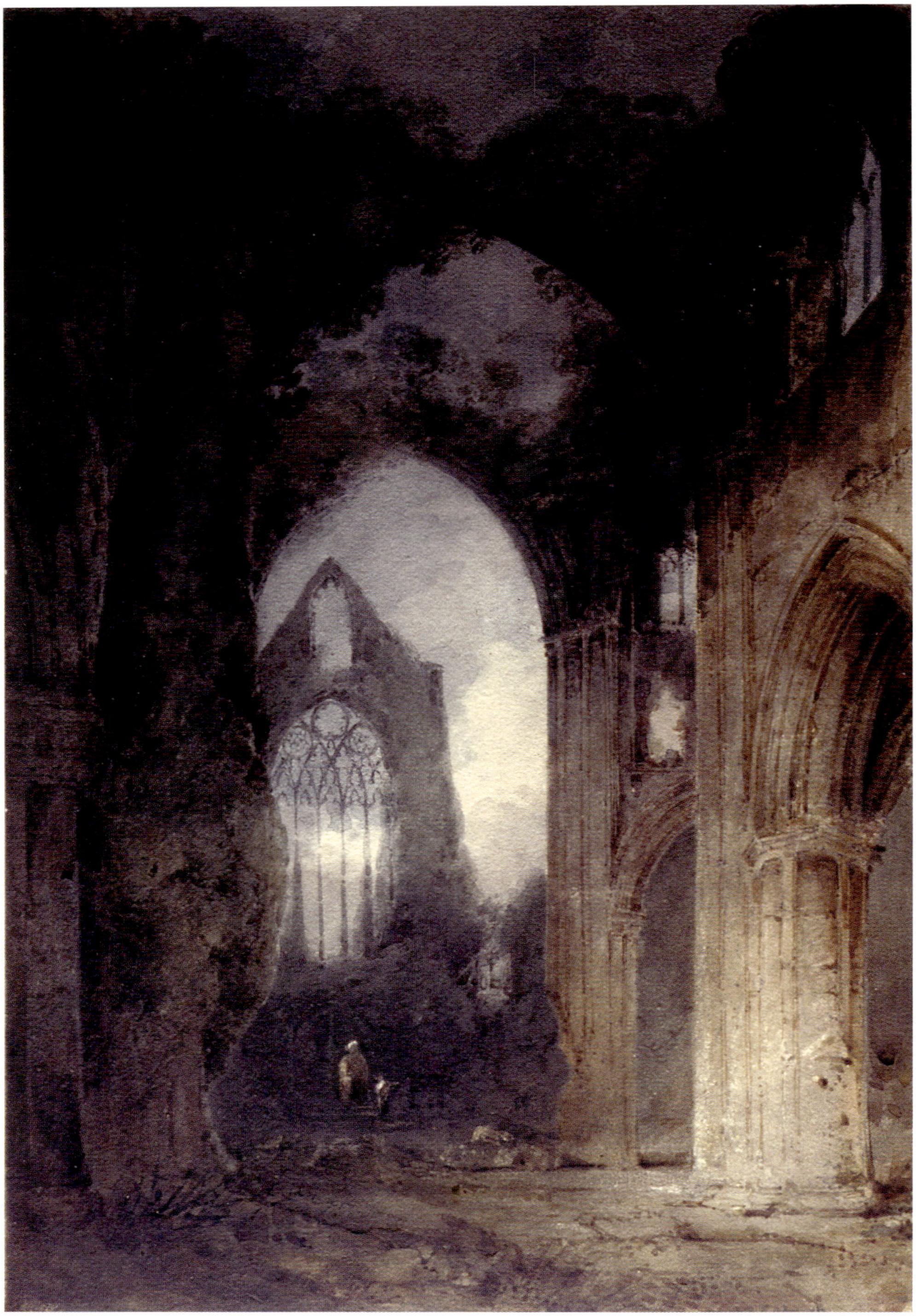

55. JOHN SELL COTMAN (1782-1842). *Tintern Abbey by Moonlight. c.*1802. Signed. 391x264 mm. (Private Collection courtesy of Andrew Wyld)

Cotman, the Norwich artist, came to the Wye in 1800 and again, with Paul Sandby Munn, in 1802. This painting was done from sketches made on his first tour.

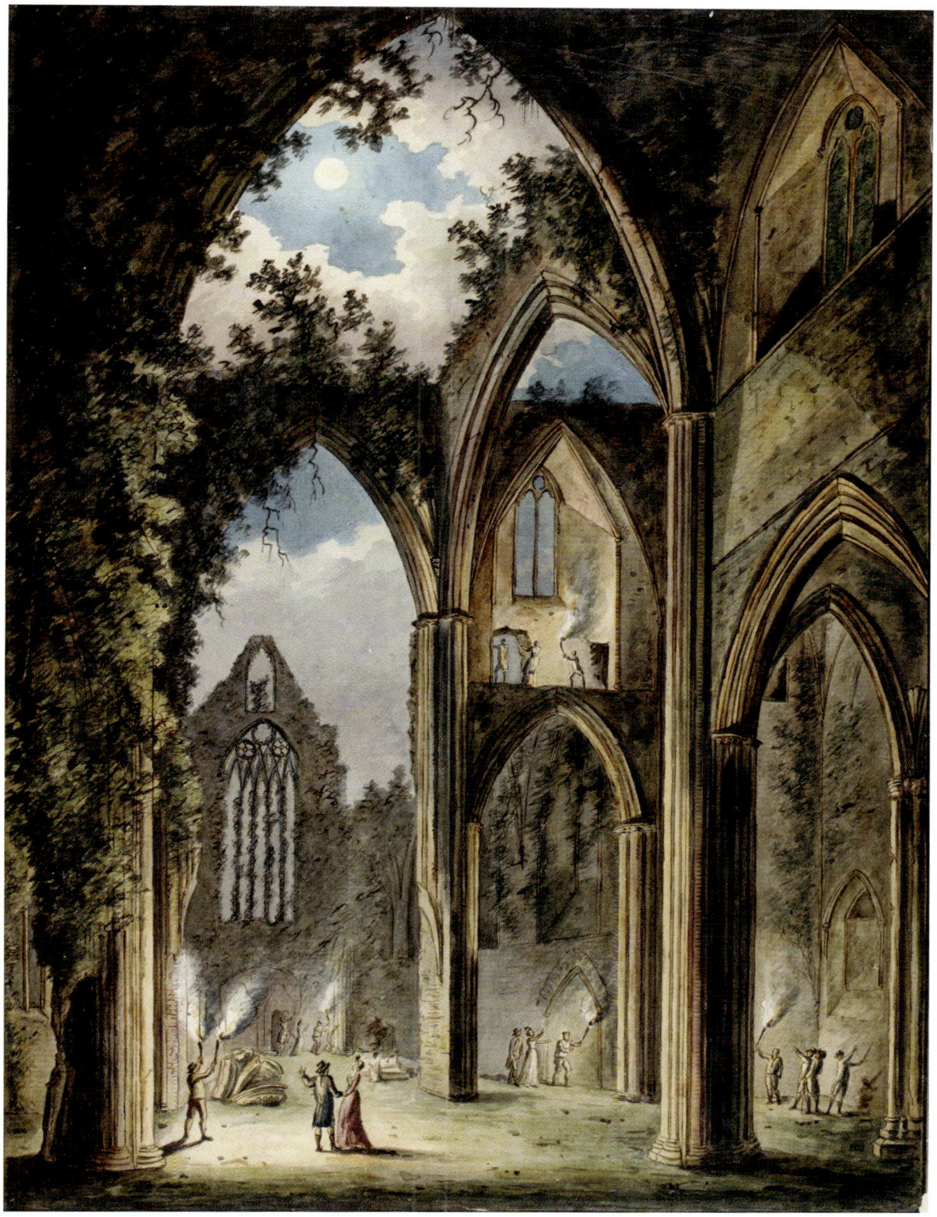

56. P. VAN LERBERGHE (fl. *c*.1801-1805). *Interior View of Tintern Abbey, in South Wales*
Watercolour and pen and ink. Unsigned but inscribed 'An Interial View of the Tintron Abbey, in South Wales, seen by moonlight' in pencil. 538x397 mm. (The British Library Maps K.Top.31.16.f.)

This painting has only just been identified (by Felicity Myrone of the British Library) as being by Van Lerberghe, of whom little is known except that his books and pictures were sold in June 1802 after he had left England – perhaps hoping to take advantage of the lull in the Napoleonic wars after the Peace of Amiens. As the sale went on for nine days he must have been rich. His picture shows that *lumière*, if not *son*, was available at Tintern from the early nineteenth century. There was criticism of the Duke of Beaufort for allowing the erection of railings etc so that tourists could scramble about the ruins.

57-58. SAMUEL PALMER (1805-1881). *Tintern Abbey. c.*1835. Unsigned. 283x492 mm. (Victoria and Albert Museum: Presented by Mrs J. Merrick Head. E.1902-1919) and *Tintern Abbey from near the Chepstow Road, looking towards Monmouth. c.*1835. Graphite and watercolour heightened with bodycolour on paper. Signed: SP. 301x458 mm. (Fitzwilliam Museum, Cambridge. Acquired with a contribution from the MLA/V&A Purchase Grant Fund, no. PD4-2005)

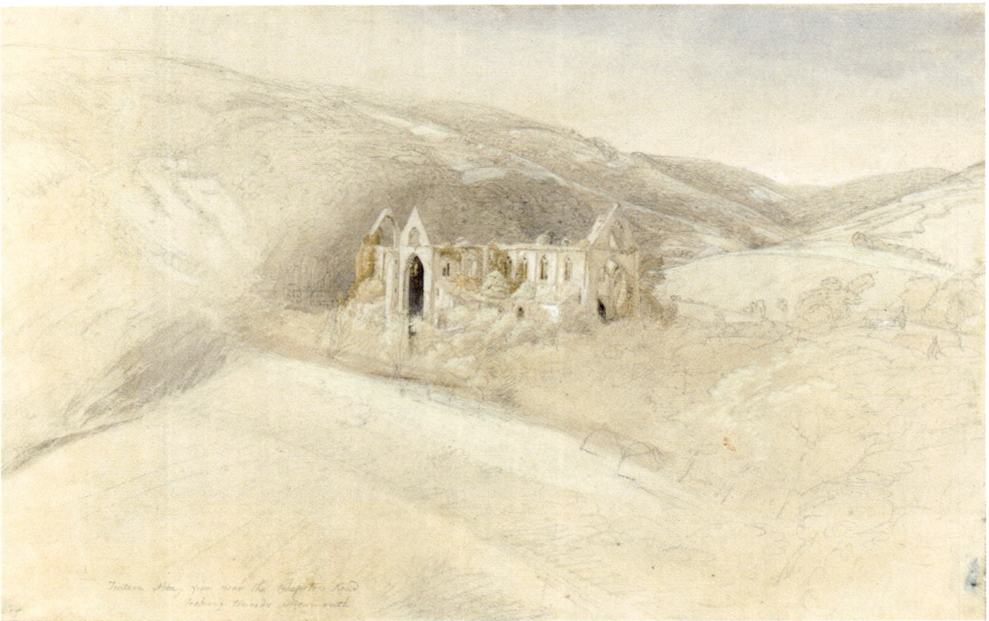

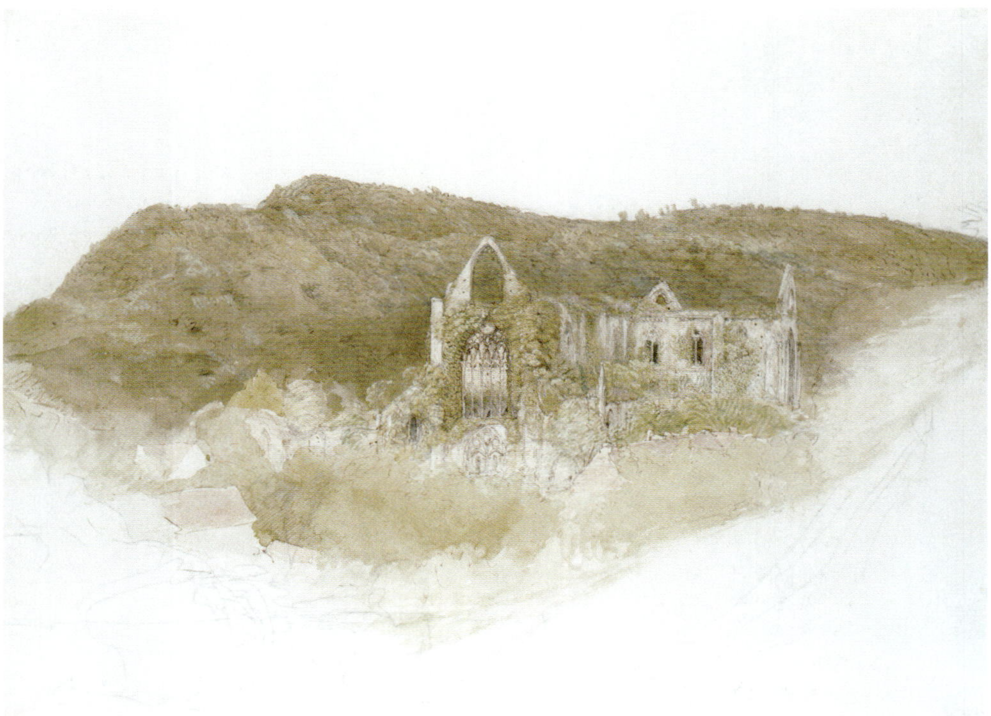

An intense mystical artist, Samuel Palmer's much admired early work, very much under the influence of William Blake, was painted at Shoreham in Kent in the 1820s. He came to Wales after that famous period was over, and shortly before his marriage and Italian tour. He was not impressed by most of the Wye Valley, but he liked Tintern very much, describing it as a nook for which he would give 'all the Welch mountains, grand as they are'. He wrote of the abbey that it was 'the highest Gothic; trellised with ivy, and rising from a wilderness of orchards, and set like a gem amongst the folding of woody hills'. He added: 'I feel here a most grateful relaxation and am become once more a pure quaint crinkle-crankle goth – If you are a Goth come hither, if you are a pure Greek take a cab and make a sketch of St Paul's Covent Garden before Breakfast'. He stayed painting at Tintern till he ran out of money.

59. JOHN LAPORTE (1761-1839) *Meeting of the Wye and Severn, Monmouthshire, Wales*
Unsigned. 249x299 mm. (Whitworth Art Gallery, D.1924.5: Given by A. Watson in 1924)

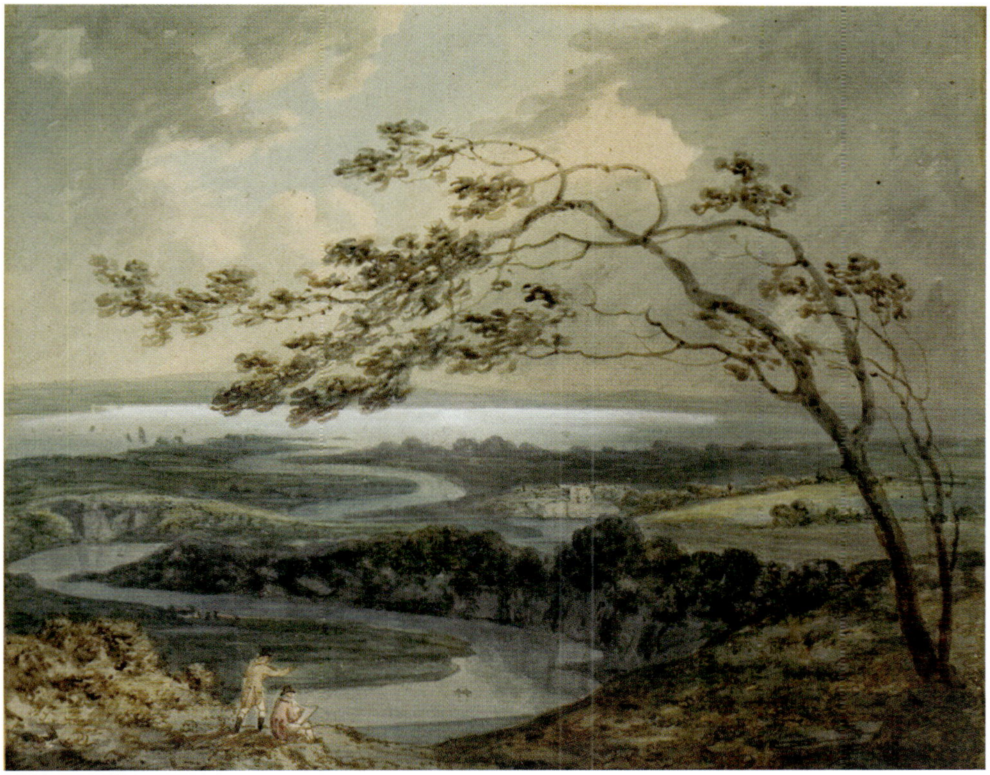

The view is from the old road from Chepstow to Tintern behind Wyndcliffe, looking back to Chepstow and the Severn. Anyone who wants to know how appallingly bad an eighteenth-century road could be should try walking down it to Tintern. Laporte was a drawing master at the Addiscombe Military Academy. Among his private pupils was the celebrated patron Dr Thomas Monro. He exhibited at the RA from 1779, and published instruction manuals on water-colour painting.

60. JAMES WATHEN (1751-1828). *'Persefield House from the Lawns Tuesday 4 o'clock 17 July 1798'*
140x256 mm. (Herefordshire Archive Service S40 Part I 69)

The Piercefield estate was bought by Colonel Valentine Morris in 1740, and it was his son, also Valentine (1727-1789), who made the walks for which it became famous. The original house was 'an inconsiderable edifice, unworthy of its situation' and when George Smith, a local banker, acquired the estate in 1784, he got John Soane to design him a new one. When Smith went bankrupt Sir Mark Wood, a very rich nabob and MP, bought the unfinished house, and employed Joseph Bonomi to add the portico and wings and to do the interior. In 1802 Wood sold the estate to Nathaniel Wells, son of a white plantation owner from St Kitts and his black house slave Juggy. (See no. 4.)

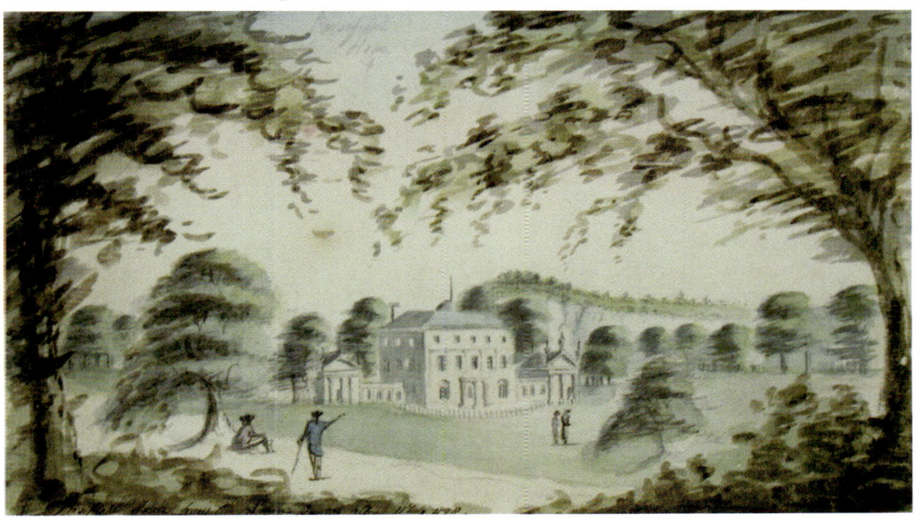

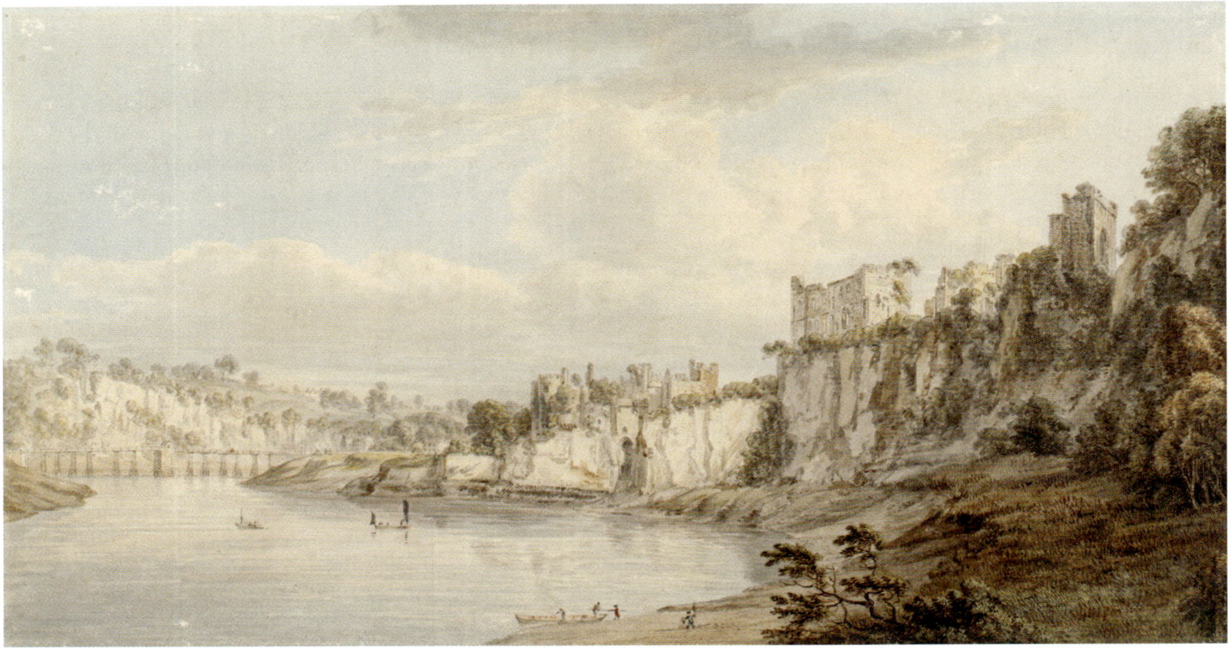

61. PAUL SANDBY (1731-1809) *Chepstow Castle*
Signed P. Sandby 1775. 293x524 mm. (Victoria and Albert Museum : Parsons Bequest. 613.1870)
On the back of the watercolour, in pencil, is written: *This drawing was done for Chas Price/I purchased it at the Bernard sale at/(Gravesend) 21 Feb 87 – Paul Sandby retouched it for/me Nov 88 – & said in His humourous Manner/ 'He in red by the Boat Mr Greville. He in blue going/down to (harbour) is me up to my knees in mud'….Nov 88.*

Paul Sandby and his brother Thomas (1717-1798) began their careers making maps and military drawings of Scotland for the duke of Cumberland after the suppression of the 1745 rebellion. Founder members of the Royal Academy in 1768, like many other artists of the period both taught in military establishments, but thanks to his many prints Paul was recognized as the leading topographical artist of his time. He toured south Wales in 1773 with Sir Joseph Banks and others. This and no. 70 are the earliest watercolours in the exhibition. The prints based on them can be seen in the cases.

62. SAMUEL HIERONYMUS GRIMM (1733-1794). *The Whole of Chepstow Castle – in Monmouthshire – from a Meadow on the opposite side of the River Wye,* c.*1777*. Unsigned. 176x261 mm. (NMW A 11742)

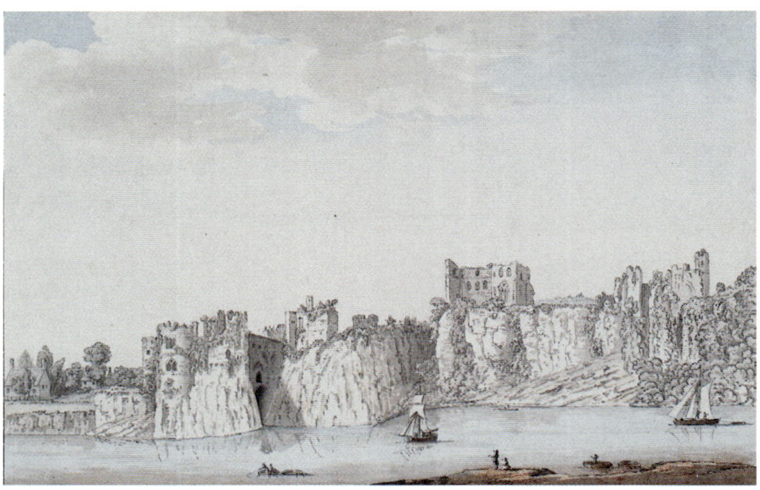

Grimm was a Swiss who moved to England in 1768, where he made a successful career, being employed by Gilbert White to illustrate *The Natural History of Selborne*. White described his technique: 'He first of all sketches his scapes with a lead-pencil; then he pens them all over, as he calls it, with Indian ink, rubbing out the superfluous pencil-strokes; then he gives a charming shading with a brush dipped in Indian ink; and last he throws a light tinge of watercolours over the whole.' Grimm toured Wales with Henry Penruddocke Wyndham in 1777 to illustrate the second edition of Wyndham's *Tour in Wales* (1781).

63. MOSES GRIFFITH (1747-1819). *Chepstow Castle and Bridge, Mon., at low tide, May 1778*
Unsigned. 245x375 mm. (Newport Museum & Art Gallery NPTMG: 56-51)

The old bridge was of wood, as pictured here. Francis Grose said that Monmouthshire was 'about' rebuilding its side in 1775, but there is no sign of that here. The planks of the bridge were loose, so they could rise and fall with the exceptionally high tides of the Wye, something which frightened horses but fascinated tourists. Of poor parents, and lacking many of the basic skills, Moses Griffith was taken up at the age of 22 by the grandee antiquary Thomas Pennant of Downing in north Wales. 'The drawings marked Moses Griffith', wrote Pennant in the preface to his *A Tour in Wales 1773* (London 1778), 'are the performances of a worthy servant, whom I keep for that purpose. The candid will excuse any little imperfections they may find in them; as they are the works of an untaught genius.' He goes on to recommend Sandby's aquatints for the more discerning.

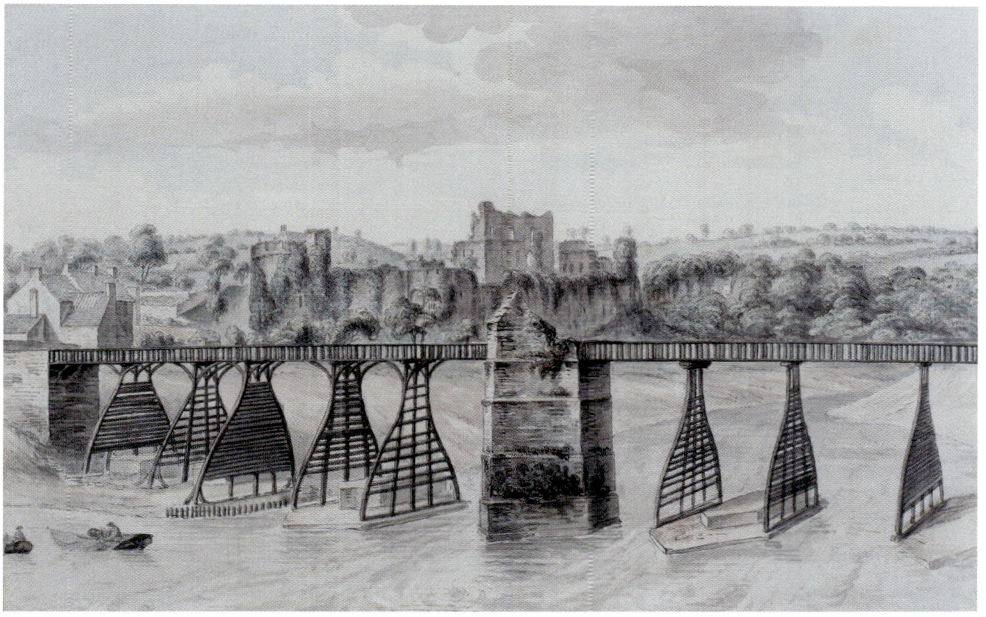

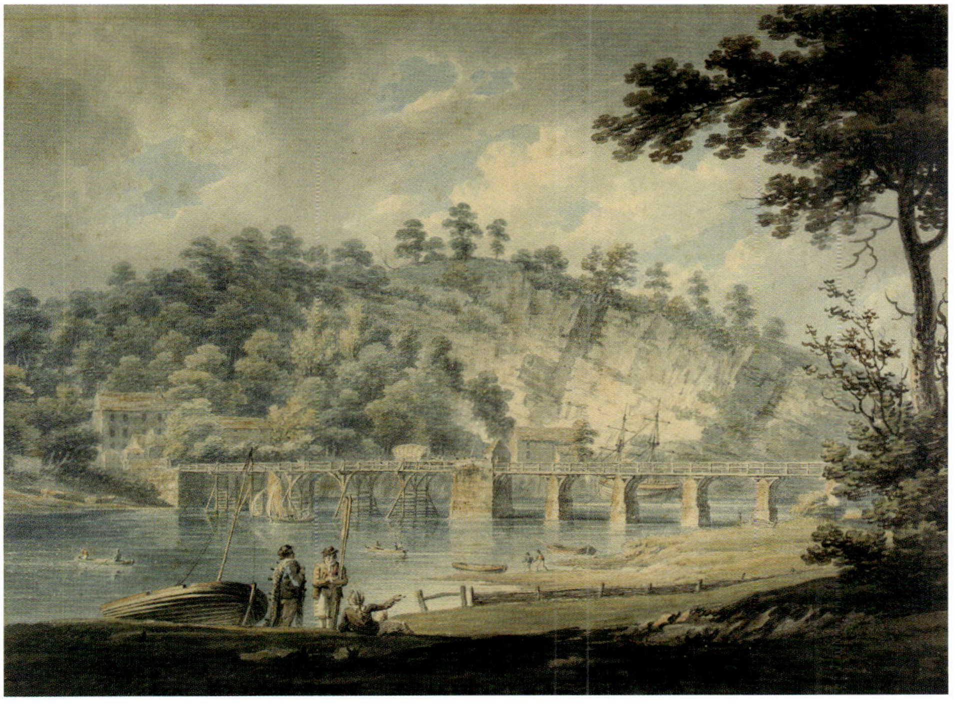

64. EDWARD DAYES (1763-1804).
Chepstow Bridge, 1795
Signed. 327x426 mm.
(NLW PB 04670 TF/4)

The bridge is seen from below the castle, with a wagon passing over the still wooden Gloucestershire side to the Monmouthshire side which had been rebuilt in stone a few years earlier. A trow has lowered its mast to pass under it on the ebb tide and there is a sea-going vessel beyond. Compare no. 65, Michael 'Angelo' Rooker's very similar view of seven years earlier.

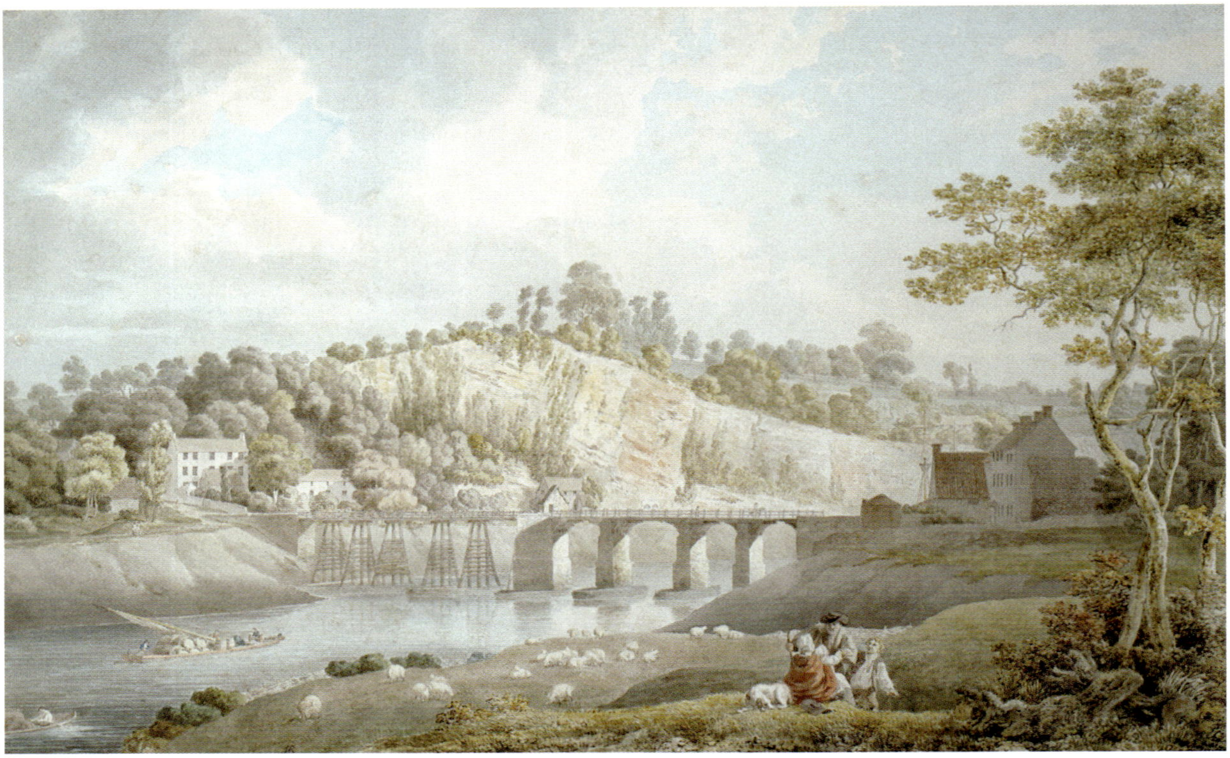

65. MICHAEL 'ANGELO' ROOKER (1747-1801). *Chepstow Bridge. c.*1788
Signed. 302x508 mm. (NMW A 3342)

This picture was probably exhibited at the RA in 1789, though there is another version in Norwich Museum. It is one of Rooker's most picturesque Wye views, with the tree to the right, the pastoral scene in the foreground, and the limpid light which was his trade mark. The building on the Gloucestershire side of the bridge is still there, but the empty clifftop is now covered with houses. (See no. 21.)

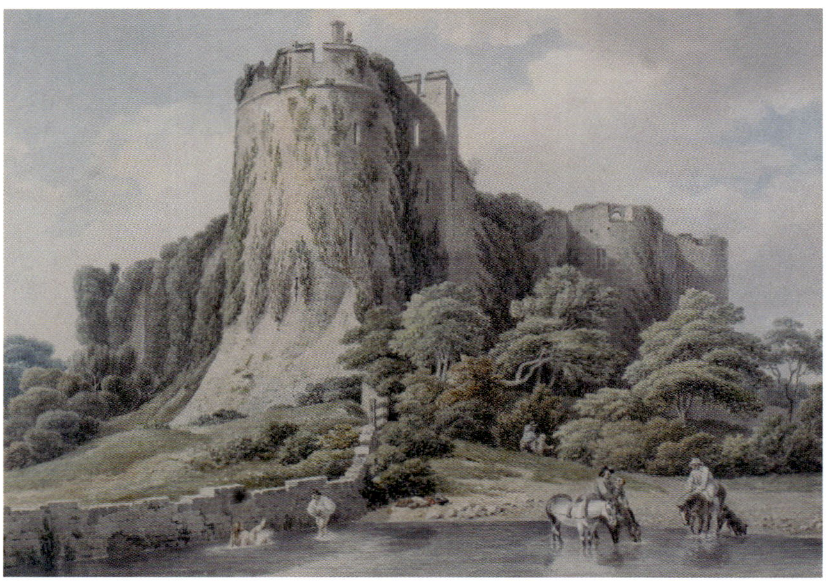

66. MICHAEL 'ANGELO' ROOKER (1747-1801). *Chepstow Castle, 1788*
Signed. Inscribed on reverse: 'This view taken in October 1788'. 258x360 mm. (Newport Museum & Art Gallery NPTMG : 1959-56)

There was a large pond in front of the castle, not finally filled in till the 1960s, and many pictures show horses being watered there and boys bathing. Rooker has chosen to emphasize the grandeur of Marten's Tower, where the regicide Henry Marten was imprisoned after the Civil War, perhaps to give the viewer a shudder at the power governments still had to punish. (See no. 21.)

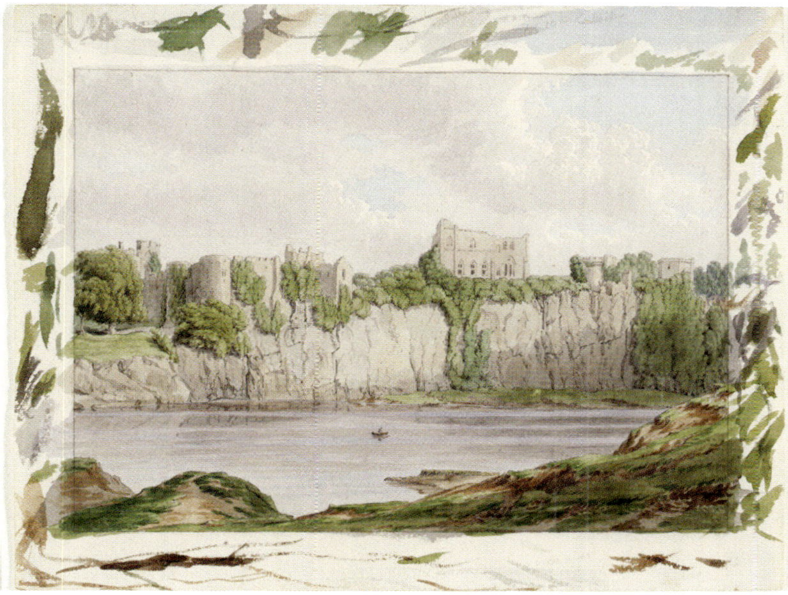

67. WILLIAM TURNER of Oxford (1789-1862). *Chepstow Castle* Unsigned. 230x315 mm. (Victoria and Albert Museum P.8 –1977)

Turner's view of the castle from across the river is a standard one, but the picture is fascinating for showing the artist trying out various colours in the margin. (See no. 6.) Watercolours are not done all at once, as the artist usually has to wait for one colour to dry before adding another. As a drawing master Turner's method was to take a watercolour through all its stages, giving it to the pupil to copy after each lesson. Was this perhaps originally a teaching aid?

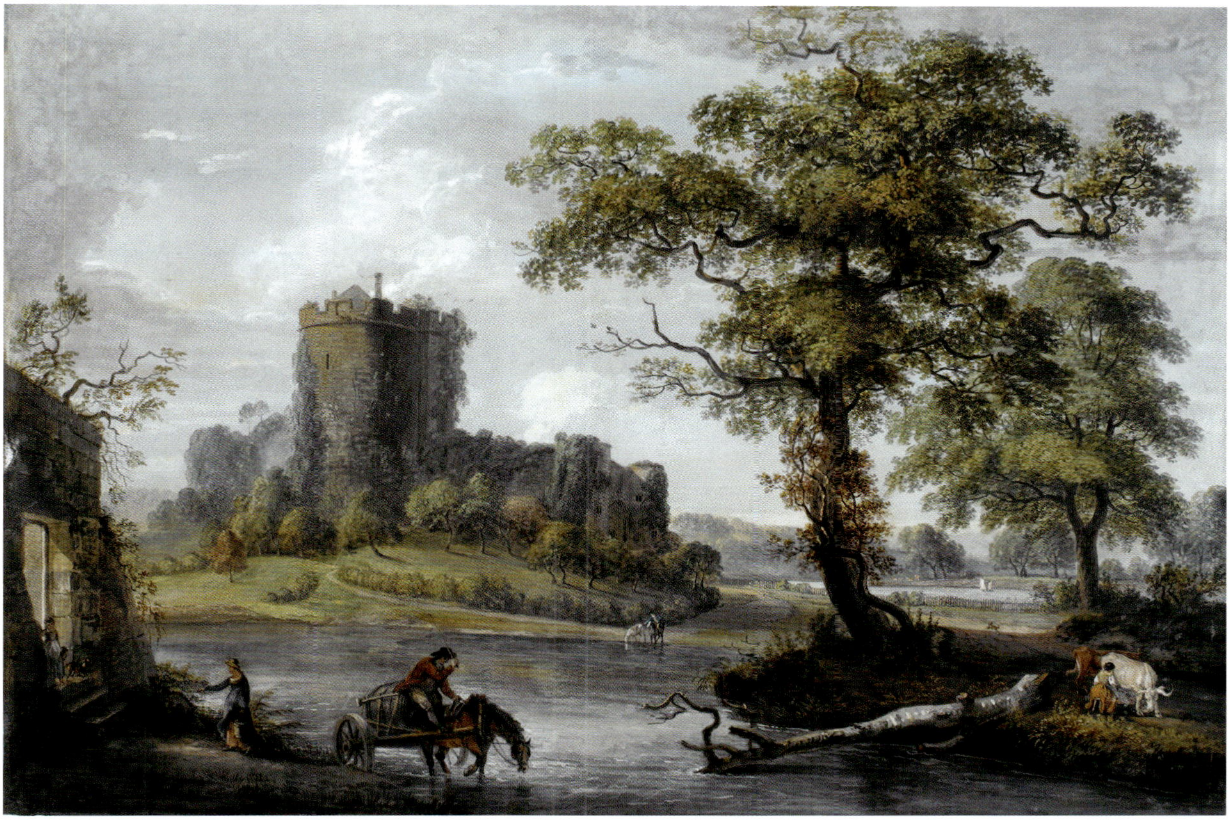

70. PAUL SANDBY (1731-1809) *Chepstow Castle, c.*1775
Signed. Watercolour and bodycolour on paper. 667x952 mm. Fitzwilliam Museum, Cambridge (no. 629)

There is another version of this view in the Yale Centre for British Art. The aquatint made from it, Plate III of Sandby's third set of views, dated September 1st 1777, is in one of the cases.

68-69. JOHN WHITE ABBOTT (1763-1851). *Part of Chepstow Castle, Monmouthshire*
Signed, J.W.A, May 31st 1797. 134x189 mm. (Victoria and Albert Museum : Given by John McGregor. P.5 – 1930); and *Chepstow Castle, Monmouthshire.* Signed JWA. June 16. 1827. 212x229 mm. (Private Collection)

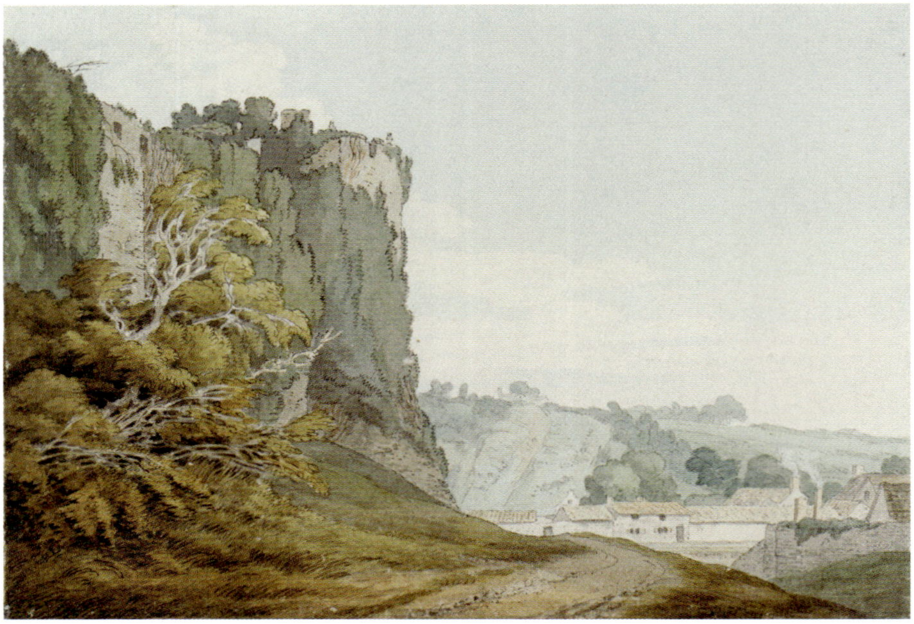

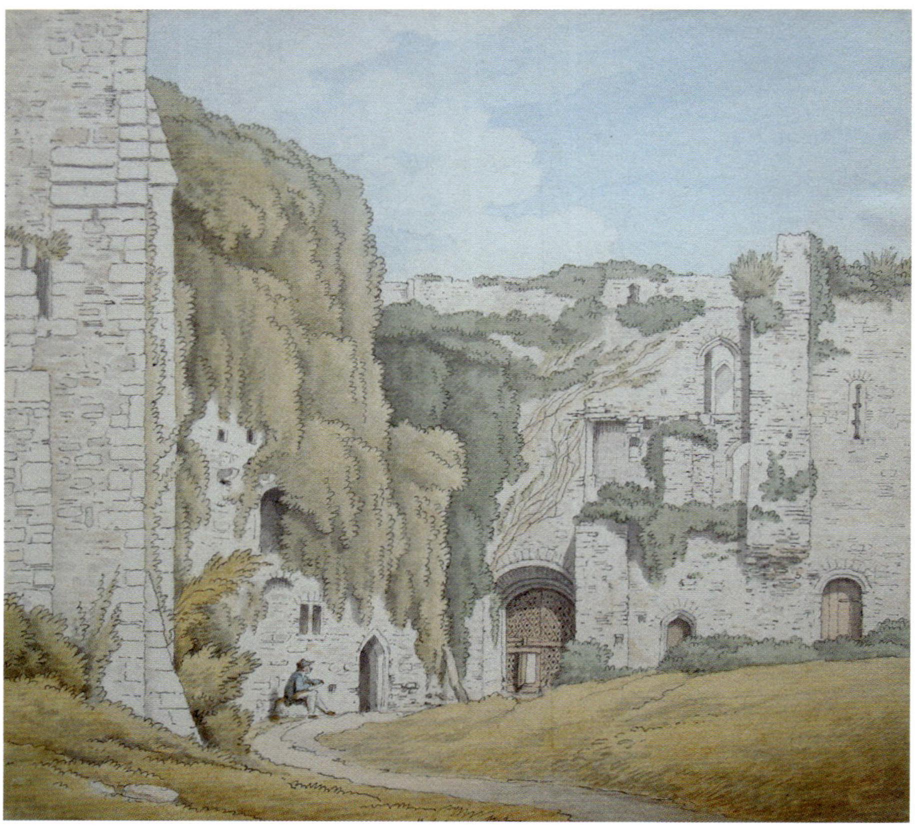

The exterior view of the castle is unusual, taken from the Dell and looking over the lower town to the cliffs on the other side of the river, with no sign of the river itself. The later painting is of the entrance from the lower bailey inside the castle. Though the castle had not been used as either a prison or a military base since 1690, tourists still felt it a rather awe-inspiring place. For some, though, it wasn't frightening enough and they complained about 'insignificant works and sheds, together with unseemly pig-styes' within the walls. The figure on the bench may be Abbott himself sketching. The two pictures were painted thirty years apart, but his style has not appreciably changed in all that time. He is still using the pen outlines and light washes he learned from his friend and teacher Francis Towne, who after his travels in Europe in 1780-81, spent at least part of the next twenty-five years in Exeter where Abbott was a surgeon and a leading figure in the cultural life of the city. Unlike Towne, Abbott, who exhibited occasionally at the RA, never went abroad. He inherited a Devonshire estate from his uncle in 1825, and became a Deputy Lieutenant of the county in 1835. A great many of his drawings have appeared on the market in recent years.

71. DAVID COX (1783-1859). *Wyndcliffe on the Wye*
Signed D. Cox 1831. 270x371 mm. (Victoria and Albert Museum 1112-1866 (EGM))

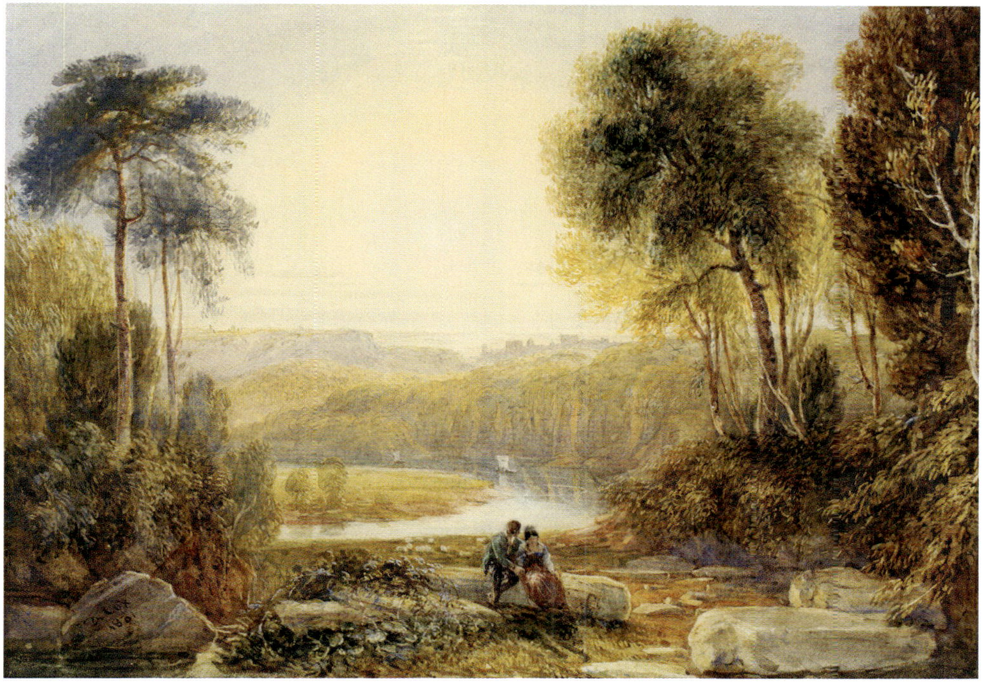

Cox's first sketch of this view, to which he frequently returned, was made in about 1810. It is from the Monmouthshire bank of the river, looking across to the Piercefield woods, with the Llancaut peninsula below, and Chepstow Castle in the middle distance. The fact that Cox kept harking back to it suggests he may have felt it gave a glimpse of paradise on earth; especially when he includes, as he sometimes does, a rainbow. (See no. 10.)

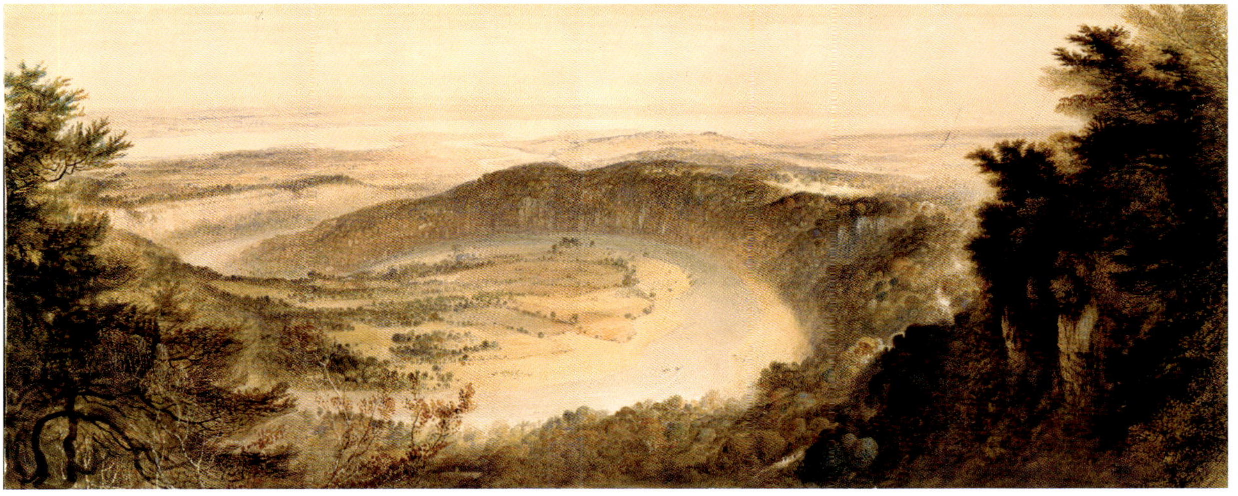

72. JOHN MARTIN (1789-1854). *The Wye Valley, View from Wyndcliffe looking towards Chepstow*
Signed Martin 1844. 303x721 mm. (Whitworth Art Gallery D1957.10 : Donated in 1957)

It is not clear when John Martin first came to the Wye. He exhibited at least four highly romantic watercolours of Chepstow, Piercefield and the Llancaut peninsula between 1845 and 1850, one of which is now in the collection of Chepstow Museum. But *The Plains of Calypso* of 1833 is clearly based on a similar view of Piercefield cliffs to the one in this painting. He went in for grand biblical scenes, floods and disasters and the Piercefield cliffs seem to have appealed to his profound sense of drama.

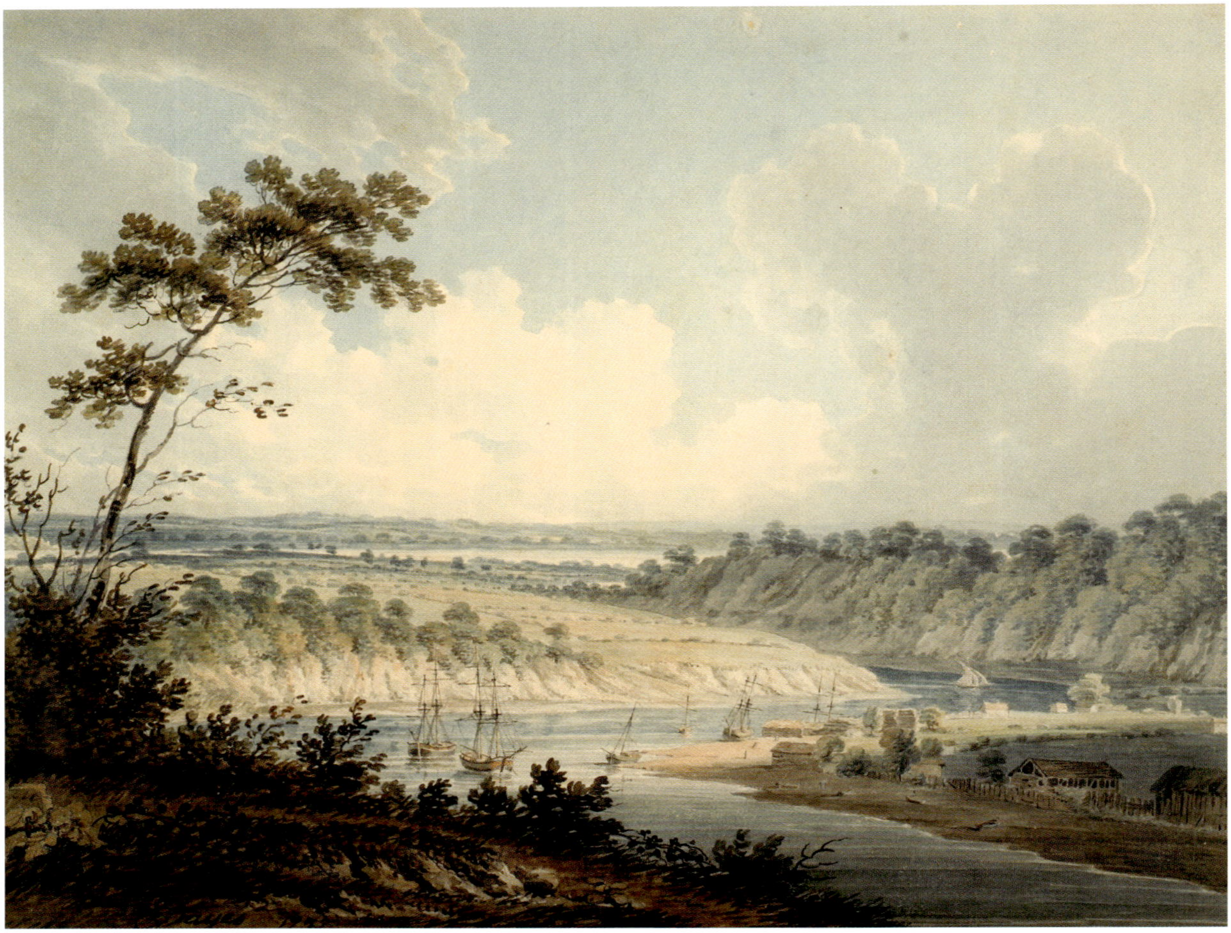

73. EDWARD DAYES (1763-1804). *Chepstow shipyard below the bridge, 1795*
Signed. 322x422 mm. (Hereford Museum & Art Gallery, 3255)

There were sixteen aquatints in Edward Dayes's *Views on the river Wye* (1797-1802), which are among his most ambitious compositions. He took his role as a drawing master very seriously, and his 'Essays on painting', published in *The Philosophical Magazine* for 1801-2, emphasized the importance of the artist's moral role as a teacher. His career was going badly by then, and though he said landscape painting should be governed by the intellectual process of selection rather than the mere imitation of nature, he attacked the landscape of 'effects' which was then being popularized by a new generation of artists led by J.M.W. Turner and Thomas Girtin. The tree on the left of the picture is a somewhat token gesture towards the picturesque tradition. Few tourists ventured below the town of Chepstow, and more interesting than the tree is the way Dayes takes the viewer past the confining cliffs on the right and out to the Bristol Channel – and by implication to the open sea and the wide world beyond the river. In this way his is quite a classical painting.

Chepstow had always been a thriving port, with an important local trade across the Severn with Bristol. Wine was imported from at least the fifteenth century, and timber, oak bark (for tanning), cider and corn were exported as well as the valuable products of the Wye's many iron forges. Great stacks of oak bark, stripped from trees in the Forest of Dean, stood on the bank awaiting shipping to Ireland. As can be seen from Dayes's view which is taken from below the bridge on the Gloucestershire side of the river – like those of John Varley and Thomas Rowlandson in Chepstow Museum – there was also a considerable ship-building industry. In fact there were three shipyards, known as the Upper, Middle and the Rock, by the time of Dayes's picture. In the 1820s regular steam packets began bringing great numbers of trippers to the town.

74. WILLIAM PAYNE (1760-1830). *The Confluence of the Wye and the Severn at St Twrogs Chapel (Treacle Rock)*
Signed. 188x268 mm. (NLW PE 00470)

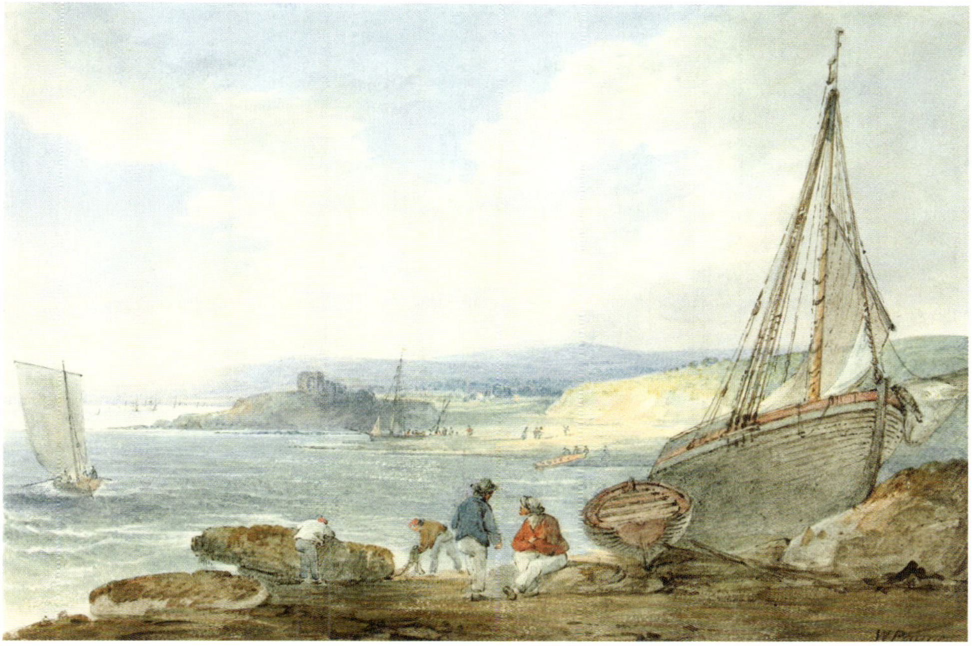

At the mouth of the Wye is a rock on which there once stood a small chapel to St Twrog, allegedly a hermit of the early Celtic church, whose name, like the walls of his cell, crumbled over the years to Tecla or Treacle. The charm of the scene in Payne's picture owes much to it having been painted at high tide. At other times the 'oozy banks' of which Gilpin complained would have made it much less attractive. (See no. 27.)

75. SAMUEL HIERONYMUS GRIMM (1733-1794). *The Passage House at Aust in Gloucestershire – called the Old Passage – a[cr]oss the Severn,* c.*1777*
Unsigned. 193x275 mm. (NMW A 14714)

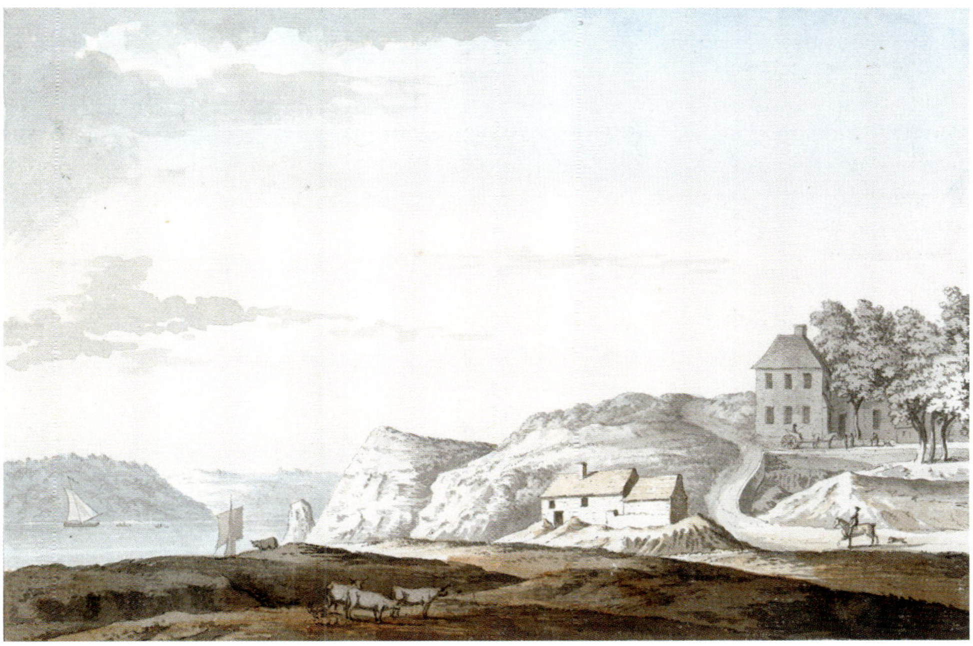

Travellers on their way back to England could take the New Ferry from Black Rock, a few miles below Chepstow, or the closer Old Ferry from Beachley to Aust. The passage could last a few minutes or several hours, depending on the weather, the tide, the mood of the ferrymen, the number of cattle on board and whether or not they got frightened. This view is looking upstream at the ferry house on the far side of the Severn. (See no. 62.)

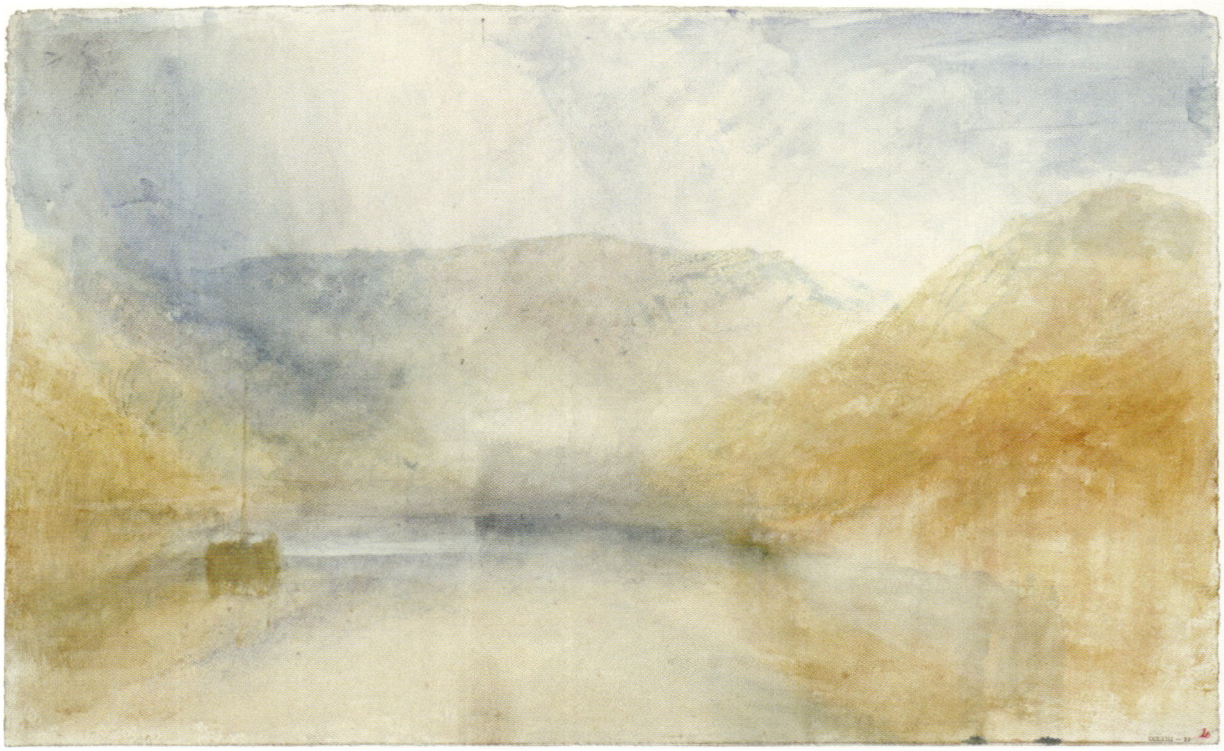

76. JOSEPH MALLORD WILLIAM TURNER (1775-1851). *Tintern Abbey, Monmouthshire, c.*1828
Watercolour on paper. Unsigned. 306x487 mm. (Tate D 25142. Accepted by the nation as part of the Turner Bequest 1856)

The view is of the abbey from upstream. Turner was a restlessly adventurous artist, always experimenting with new ways to make pictures, and he made a great many preliminary studies, often of a very original kind. A most interesting early example of this is Plate no. XIII.

Turner was very young when he first came to the Wye, crossing from Aust to Beachley and walking upstream as far as Monmouth, before heading into Welsh Wales. Later he was perhaps more interested in the grand and 'sublime' views of the mountainous north. As he only once visited anywhere in Wales after 1798, the Wye sketches belong to the earliest and most strictly topographical period of his life – though he was already ignoring strict accuracy as can be seen in his flattening of the arches of Tintern Abbey in Catalogue no. 50. But like many artists of the time, he depended on engravings of his work as a source of income, and he included two views of the Wye valley, *The Junction of the Severn and Wye*, and *Chepstow castle*, in his *Liber Studiorum* of 1811-1812. An inveterate collector and storer of images to be reordered and reused, Turner preferred to work in his studio rather than from nature, and when he was commissioned to make new pictures to be engraved for Charles Heath's *Picturesque Views in England and Wales* (1826-1837) he returned to his sketches, now more than thirty years old, to make them. (This Charles Heath [1785-1848] was different from the Monmouth printer [see nos 97-99]. He was an engraver and printer and occasional artist in his own right.)

Still trying out new ideas, in this sketch Turner here was not making a precursor of twentieth century colour-field abstraction, but one of the many Colour Beginnings he experimented with for the pictures to be engraved; they were preparatory essays in the chromatic layout of an 1820s composition. Andrew Wilton has written about the *Picturesque Views* as 'a new manifestation of the form, transformed by the mature Turner into a medium of great range and expressive power, uniting the elements of topography, history and genre into a potent commentary on the world in which he lived, and creating from the old forms a fresh language of watercolour which was to revolutionise yet again the practice of his contemporaries.' By this time 'mere topography was generally designed by connoisseurs, but the popularity of books of views shows that people still wanted to know what places actually looked like.'

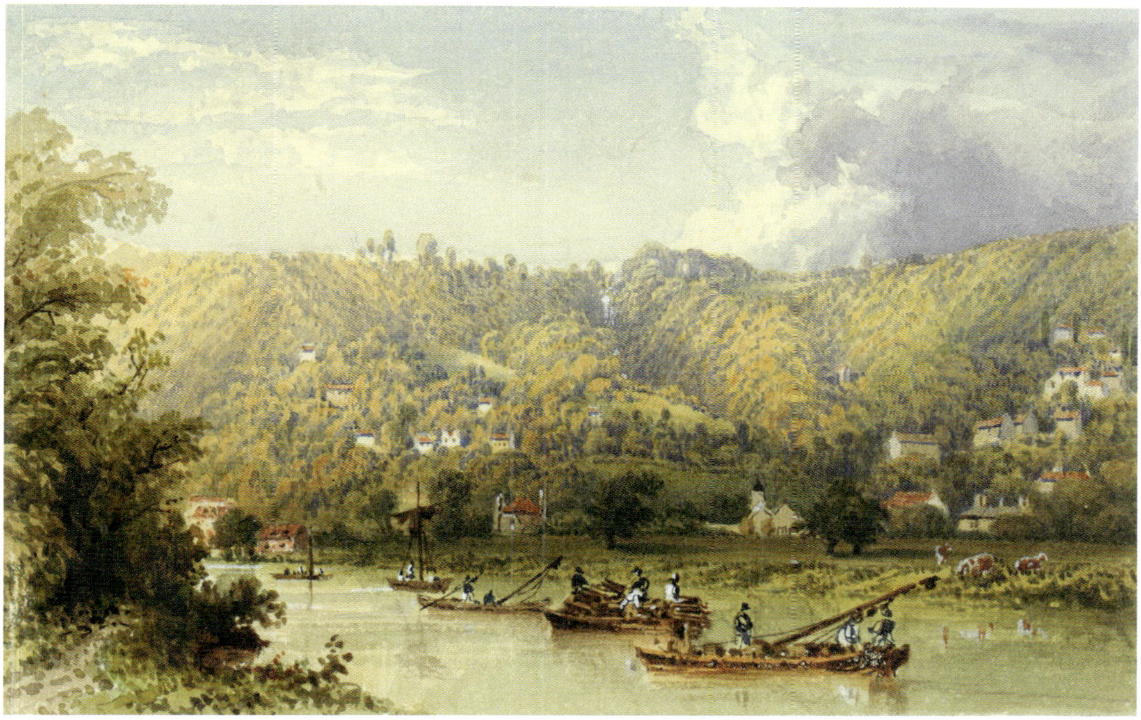

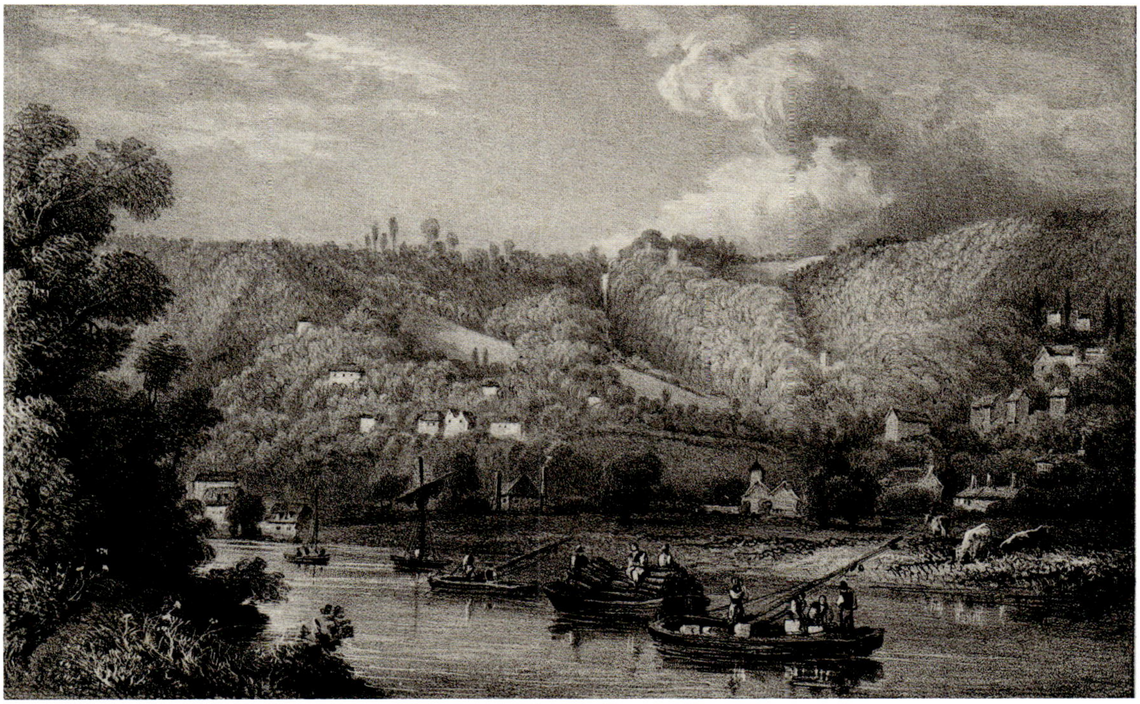

77-78. WILLIAM HENRY BARTLETT (1809-1854). 100x155 mm. 280x236 closed. (NLW Sketchbook DV59. PA 08473)

Watercolour of Llandogo with Cleddon Shoots, with instructions to the lithographer. Shown with finished print.

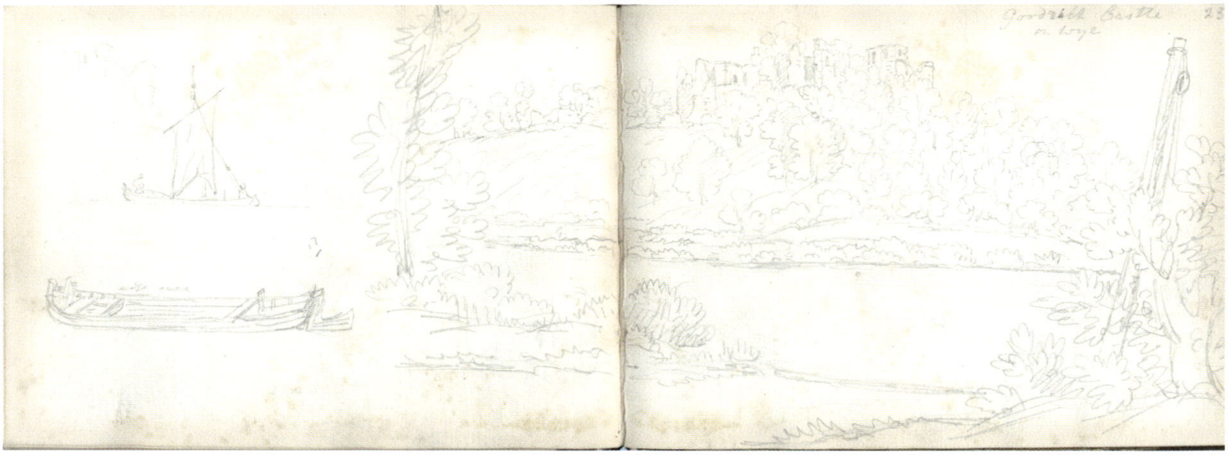

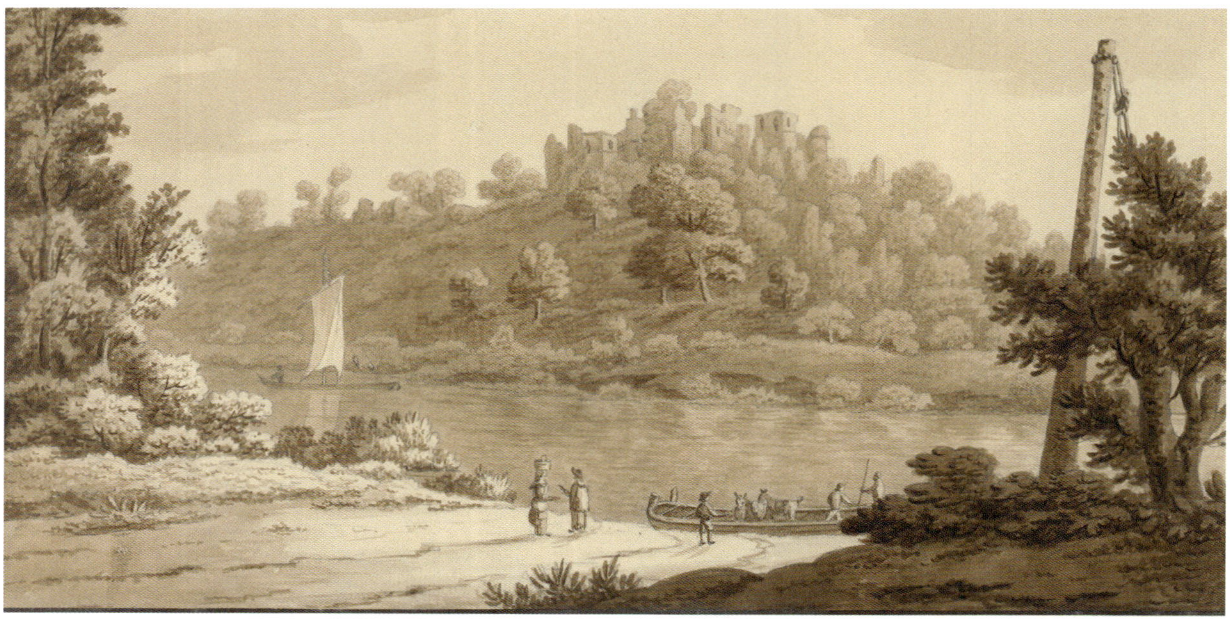

79. SIR RICHARD COLT HOARE (1758-1838). Drawing of Goodrich Ferry, with boat. (Cardiff Central Library, SB 38)

Colt Hoare was making sketches in 1798 and 1799 for William Coxe's *Monmouthshire* (1801). Extra illustration of finished drawing (Yale Center for British Art, Paul Mellon Collection).

80. GEORGE ORLEANS DELAMOTTE (1788-1861). *Coracle man,* c.*1820.* 255x210 mm. (NLW Sketchbook DV 271)

George was the younger brother of the better-known William Delamotte. He was patronised by the Rolls family of the Hendre, near Monmouth. This is one of more than twenty sketches he made of Welsh characters. A pencil drawing of Tibbs Bridge, on which the background of this watercolour is based, is dated October 20th, 1817 (West Glamorgan Archives).

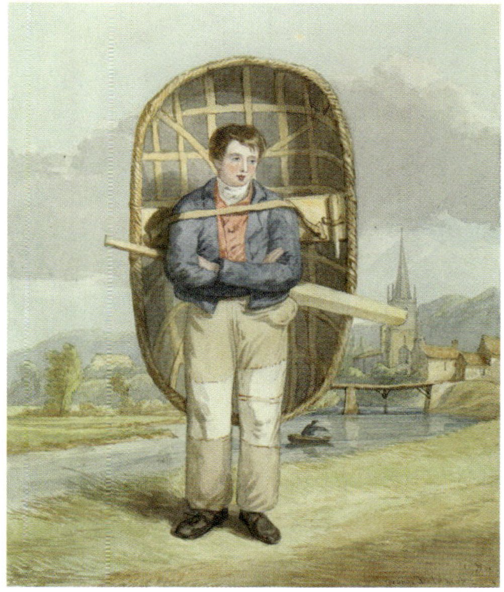

81. JOHN MARTEN (fl 1782-1808). *Wynd Cliff on the Wye* 182x536 mm. (NLW Sketchbook DV 393 PE 04891)

The view from Piercefield of Wyndcliff and Llancaut. Marten was based in Canterbury.

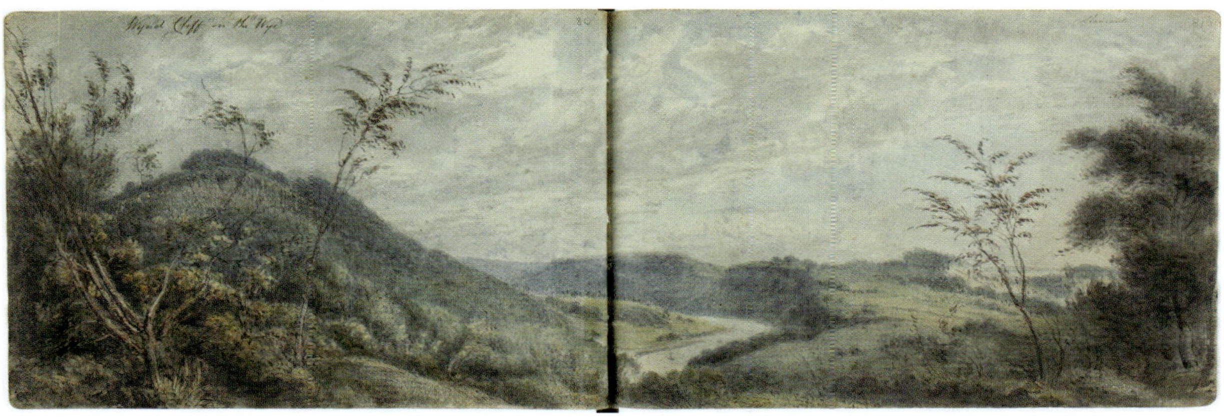

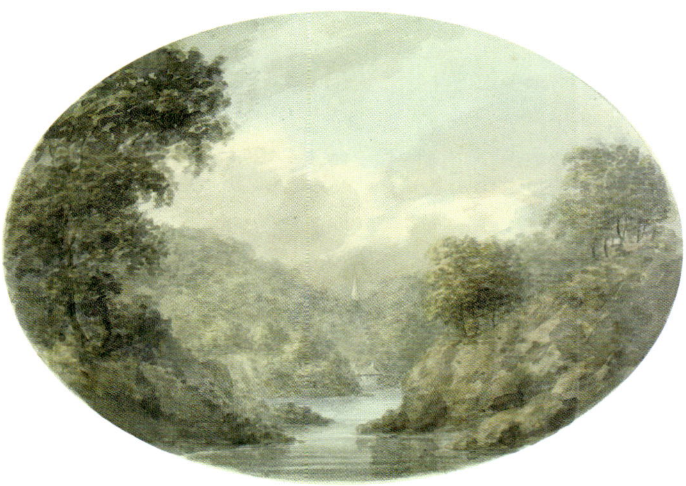

82. JANE MARY and FRANCES DOROTHEA OGLANDER. *On the Wye, Ruardean Spire, 1802* Unsigned. 209x290 mm. (NLW PB 06056)

Jane Mary was the daughter of the Provost of Oriel College, Oxford, and the widow of John Oglander, Warden of New College, Oxford, and she studied drawing with J.B. Malchair and John Glover. Frances Dorothea was her niece. This view is especially interesting because it had been specifically criticized by William Gilpin as not picturesque, because the church spire was in the middle of the view.

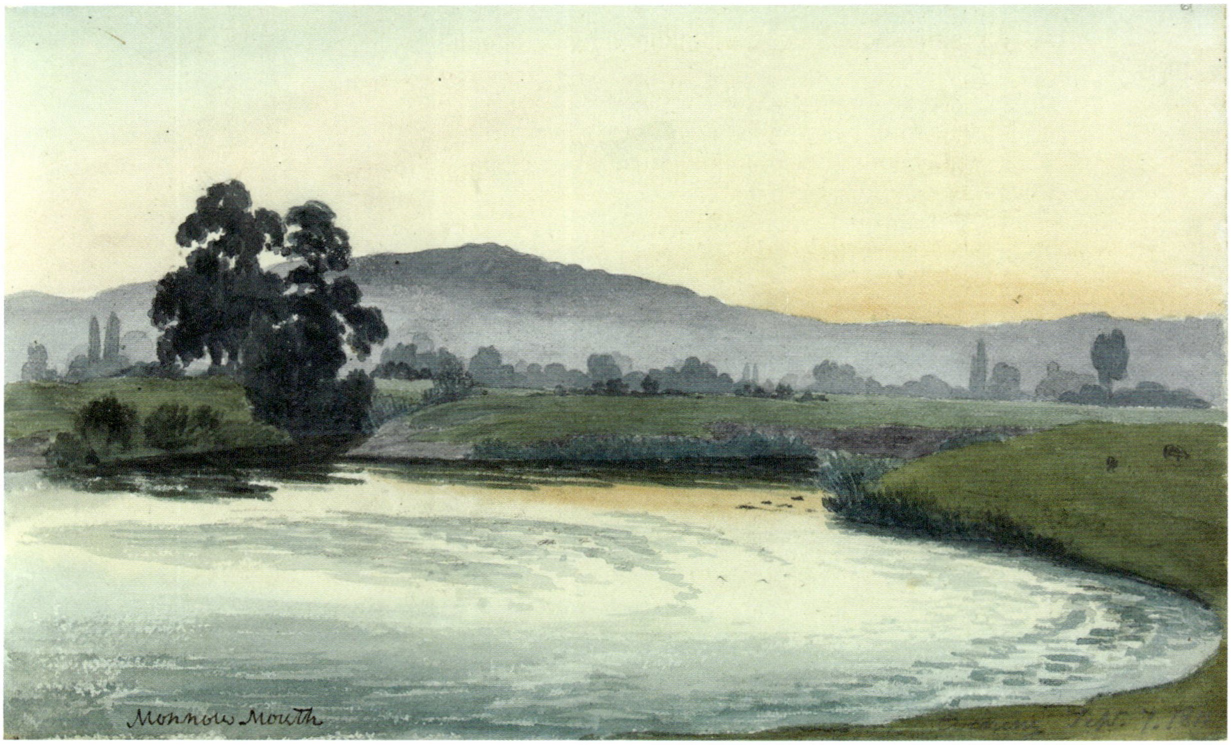

83. THOMAS TUDOR (1785-1855). *Monnow Mouth Sunset*
129x209 mm. (NLW Sketchbook DV 161 PZ 00130)

One of the drawings in this sketchbook is dated 1811. (See no. 40.)

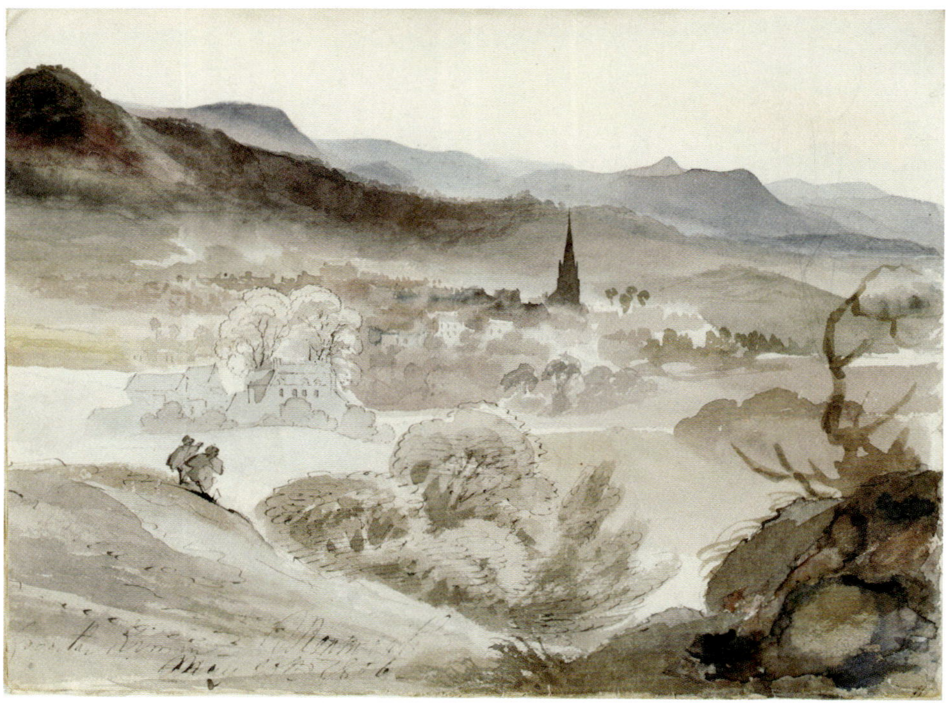

84. JOHN PEARSON (1777-1813). View of Monmouth. The sketchbook is dated 1805. (Victoria and Albert Museum: Given by Mrs E. Sanford, the artist's great-niece, in accordance with the wishes of her aunt, the late Mrs R.C. Foster. 330x260 mm. E1771-1948)

Pearson is thought to have come from Ripon in Yorkshire and to have studied there with Francis Nicholson. This view from the Kymin, looking west over the town, seems to show Troy House on the left.

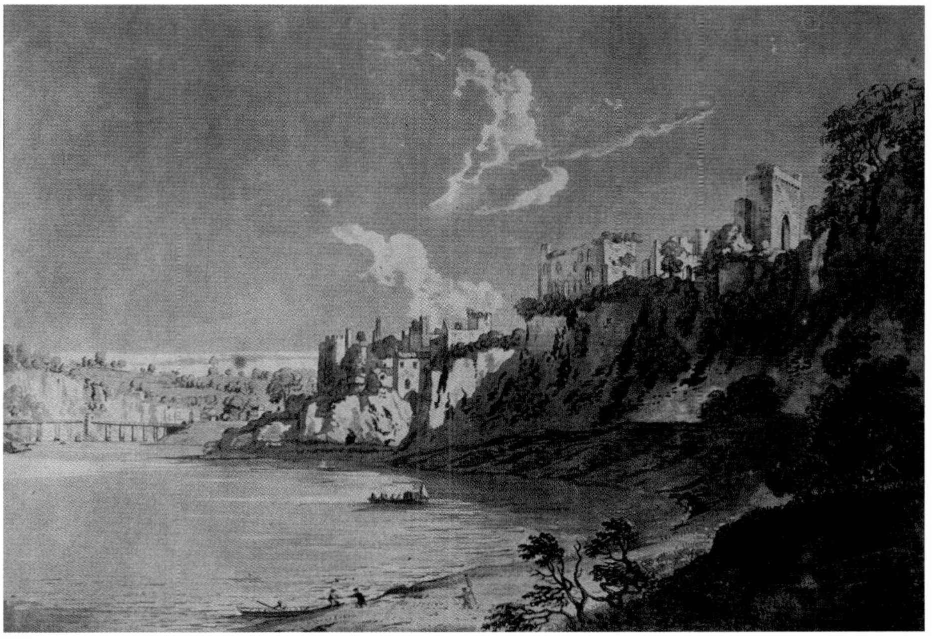

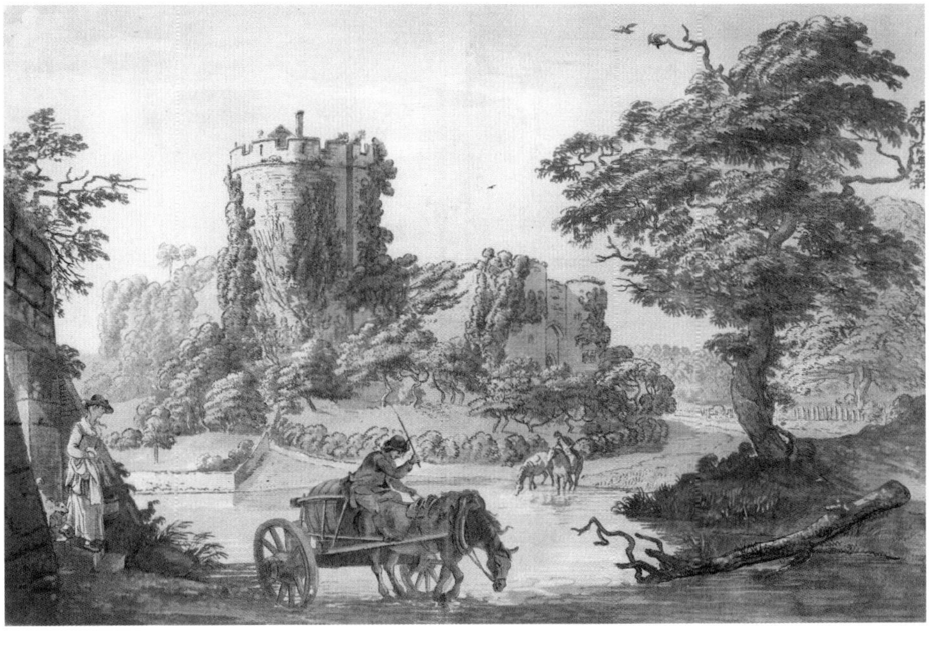

85-86. PAUL SANDBY (1731-1809).

Sandby's first aquatint of Chepstow Castle, based on no. 61, was published in 1775 in his *XII Views of South Wales*. It was much copied. The second is based on no. 70 and was published in *XII Views of Wales* in September 1777. Though not the first artist to use aquatint in Britain, Sandby was the first to use it successfully, having got the secret from Charles Greville and his brother. It is a much better way of reproducing watercolour than engraving or etching, with a far greater ability to convey delicate washes and subtle tones – though engraving was usually involved as well, and all 108 prints in Sandby's *Virtuosi's Museum* (1778) are engraved. Three of them (nos 32, 51 and 65) are further Chepstow views.

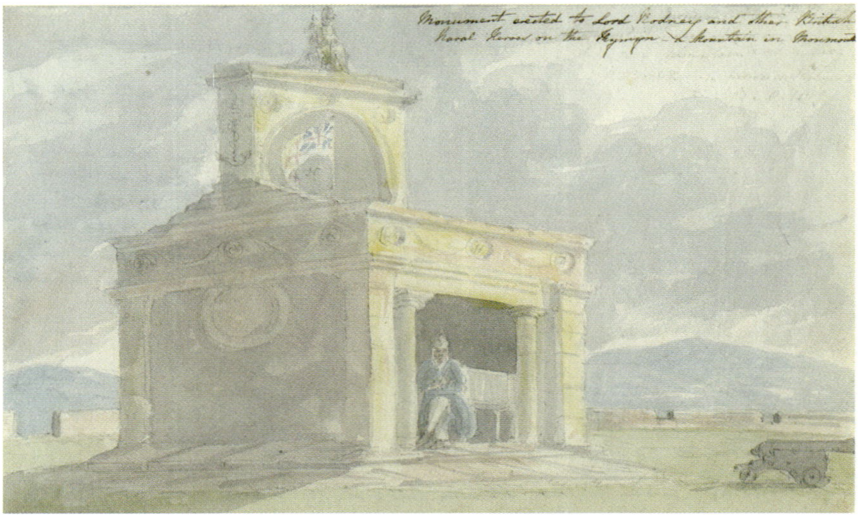

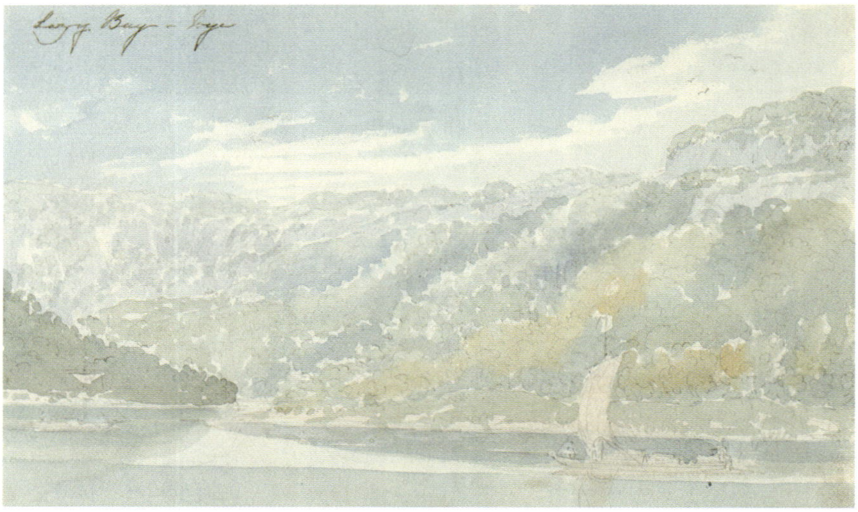

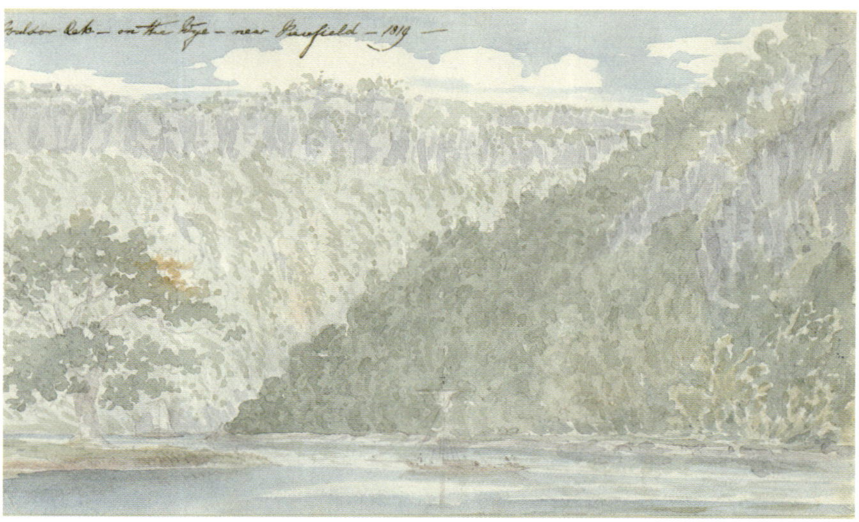

87-89. WILLIAM PAGET (Dates unknown). *Monument erected to Lord Rodney and other British Naval Heroes on the Kymyn – a Mountain in Monmouth.* Unsigned. 145x235 mm; *Lazy Bay – Wye;* and *Waldor (?) Oake on the Wye – near Piercefield – 1819.* All unsigned. 145x232 mm. (Private Collection)

Across the river from Monmouth is a steep hill, covered in cottages, called the Kymin. On the top there was a small circular banqueting pavilion, used by the local gentry as a club for weekly cold collations, and from which there was an excellent view across the county to the Black Mountains. In 1801 a Naval Temple, with a statue of Britannia on top, was erected close by to celebrate British naval victories of the last half century. It was opened by the Duke of Beaufort, whose duchess was the daughter of Admiral Boscawen, and in 1802 Nelson came with Sir William and Lady Hamilton to inspect. There was a painting of the Battle of the Nile which Nelson scrutinized for some time without comment. Is the military-looking figure lolling in the entrance a hero of the Napoleonic wars?

The two river views, perhaps sketched from a moored boat, or from Martridge Meadow at the foot of the Piercefield cliffs, show the view upstream and down from opposite Llancaut and are unusual. Neither 'Lazy Bay' nor a special oak is referred to by any writer yet discovered.

Paget was a clergyman, one of the many who made the Wye tour. Some of his local watercolours are dated 1819.

90. ANON. *A Tour through Monmouthshire and Glamorgan*, illustrated by ROSE and MARIA E. SOTHEBY, with map by JAMES WATHEN. *Chepstow Castle.* 173x240 mm. (NLW MS 6497C)

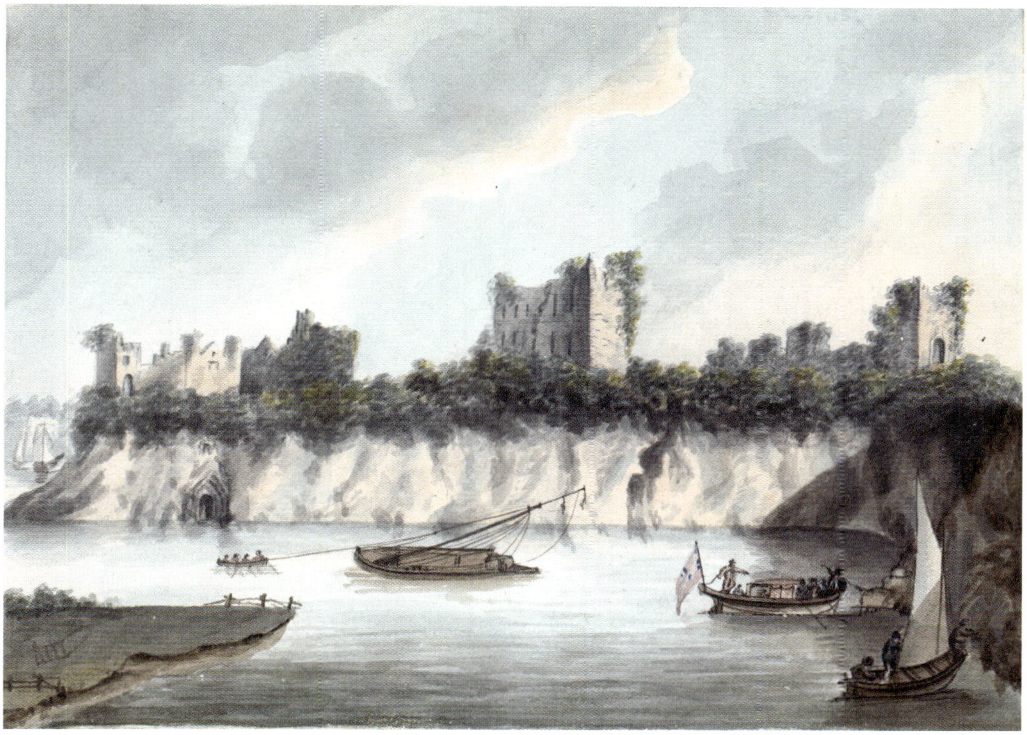

The date of this sketchbook is uncertain. One of the sketches is dated 1809, but there are three partially erased dates at the beginning of the journal, which seem to be 1782, 1783 and 1784. The picture includes a tour boat with a rare sight of a steersman. The map of the river was drawn by James Wathen, which makes the later date more likely for the sketches.

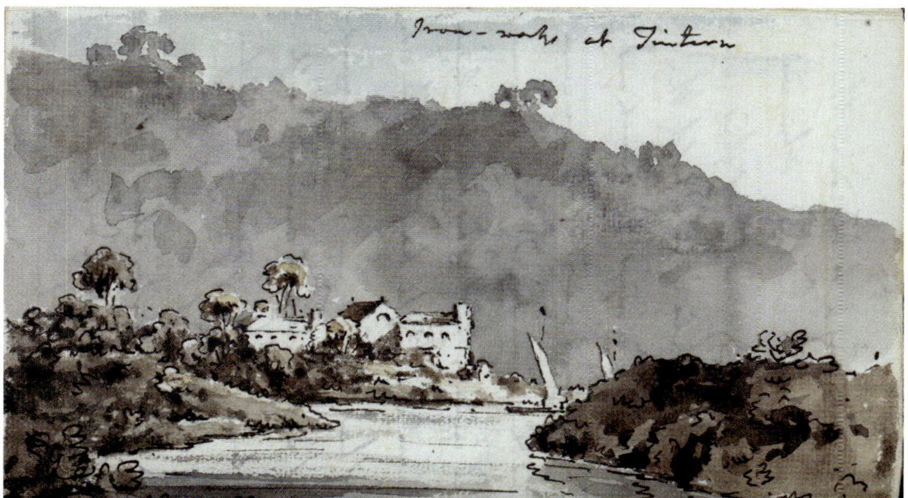

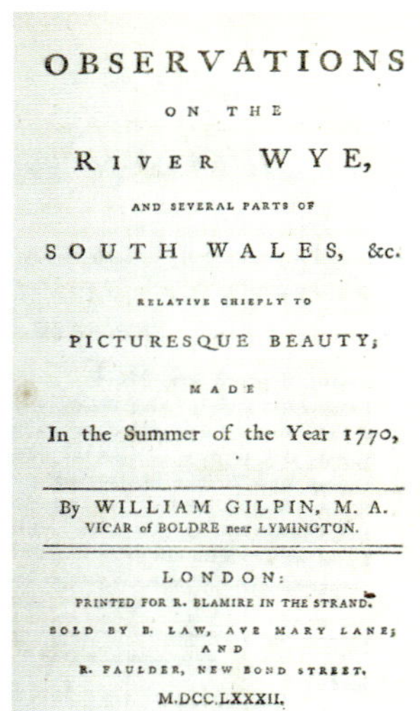

OBSERVATIONS

ON THE

RIVER WYE,

AND SEVERAL PARTS OF

SOUTH WALES, &c.

RELATIVE CHIEFLY TO

PICTURESQUE BEAUTY;

MADE

In the Summer of the Year 1770,

By WILLIAM GILPIN, M. A.
VICAR of BOLDRE near LYMINGTON.

LONDON:
PRINTED FOR R. BLAMIRE IN THE STRAND.
SOLD BY B. LAW, AVE MARY LANE;
AND
R. FAULDER, NEW BOND STREET.
M.DCC.LXXXII.

91-92. WILLIAM GILPIN (1724-1804) Original MS *Observations on the River Wye*, 1770, with drawing of *Ironworks at Tintern*. 115x194 mm. (NLW MS 21630B)

This is a cleaner but still quite rough version of the draft in the Bodleian Library, Oxford, probably made when Gilpin got home. *Observations on the River Wye, and several parts of South Wales, &c. relative chiefly to Picturesque Beauty : made in the summer of 1770*, London, 1782 (though in fact published early in 1783).

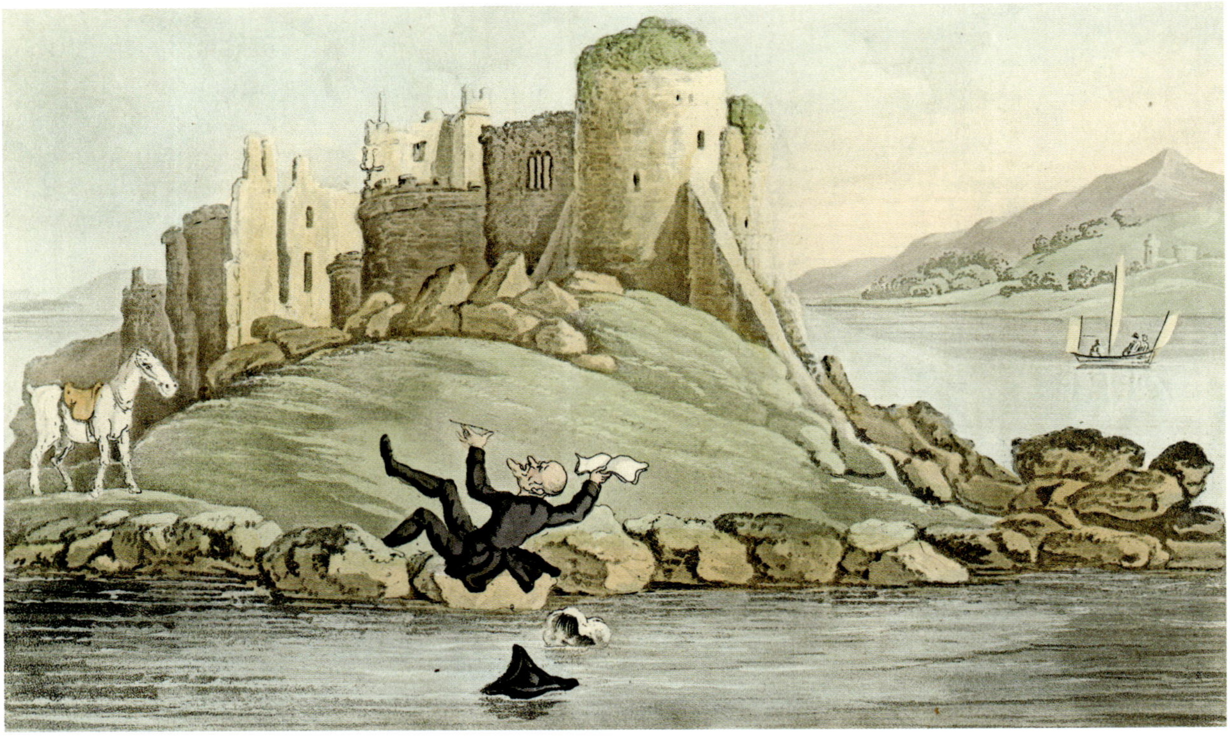

93. THOMAS ROWLANDSON (1757-1827). *Dr Syntax tumbling into the water*

William Combe and Thomas Rowlandson's *The Tour of Doctor Syntax in Search of the Picturesque* (first edition 1809) was an extremely popular parody of Gilpin and his obsession with the picturesque. The castle seems distantly based on Chepstow, which Rowlandson visited in 1797. (See no. 53.)

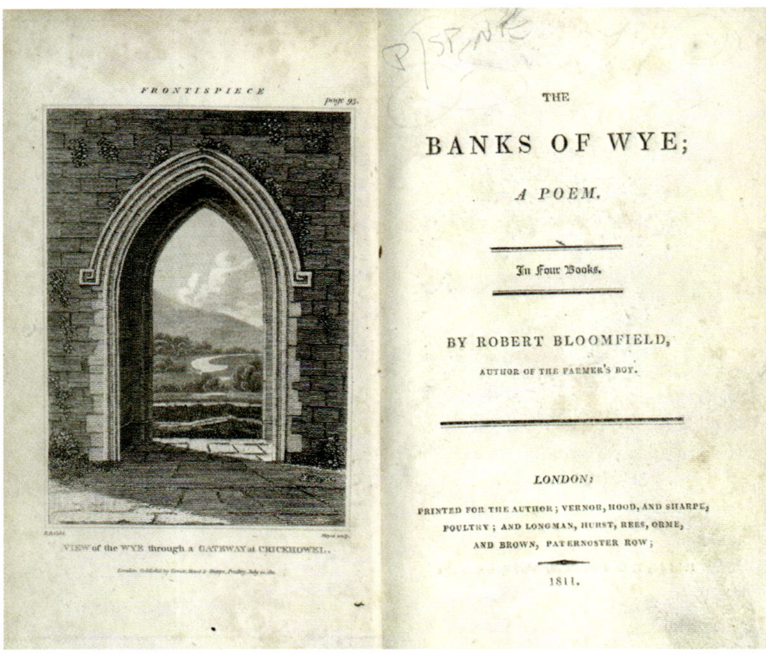

FRONTISPIECE

page 93.

VIEW of the WYE through a GATEWAY at CRICKHOWEL.

THE

BANKS OF WYE;

A POEM.

In Four Books.

BY ROBERT BLOOMFIELD,

AUTHOR OF THE FARMER'S BOY.

LONDON:

PRINTED FOR THE AUTHOR; VERNOR, HOOD, AND SHARPE, POULTRY; AND LONGMAN, HURST, REES, ORME, AND BROWN, PATERNOSTER ROW;

1811.

94. ROBERT BLOOMFIELD (1766-1823). *The Banks of Wye*, London, 1811

Bloomfield became a spectacularly successful poet with *The Farmer's Boy* (1800). In 1807 he and some friends took the Wye Tour, and this poem was the result. Unfortunately his publishers muddled the Wye and the Usk in the frontispiece, Crickhowell being on the latter.

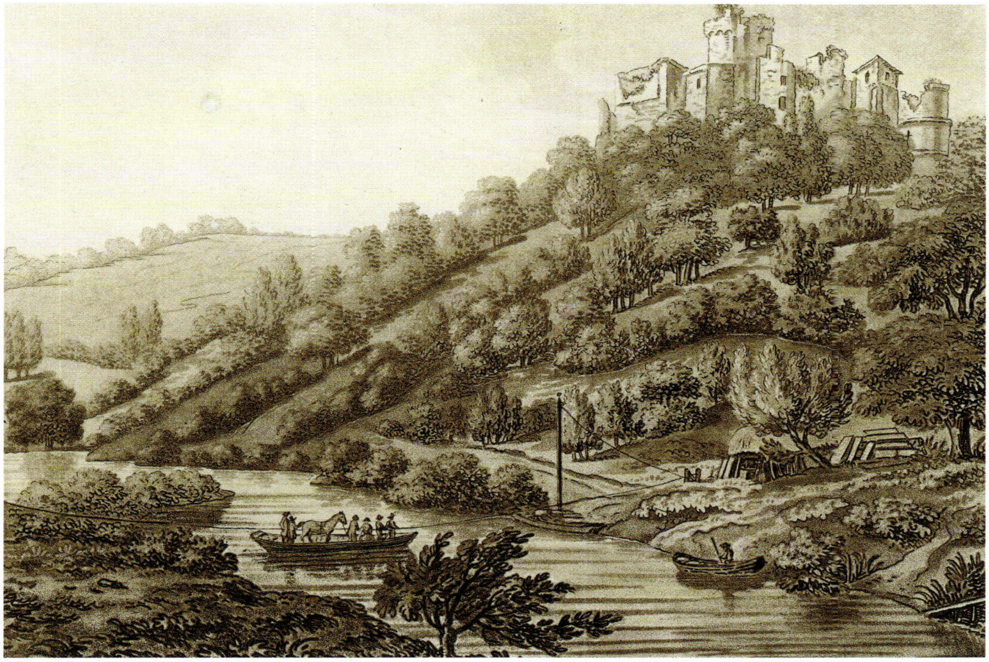

95. SAMUEL IRELAND (d.1800). *Picturesque Views on the River Wye,* London, 1797

Book open at Goodrich Castle, with horse on ferry; Ireland specialized in river scenes and had already published books on the Thames, the Medway, and the Warwickshire Avon, with two forthcoming volumes on the Severn advertised at the back of this one on the Wye.

96. J.T. BARBER (1774-1841).
A Tour throughout South Wales and Monmouthshire, London, 1803

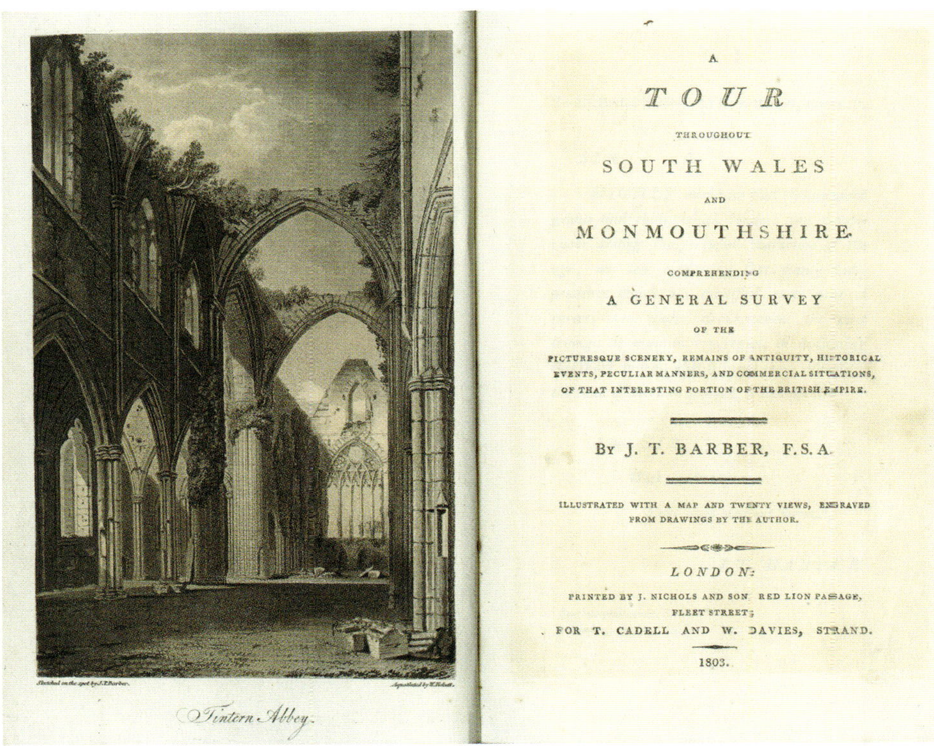

A

TOUR

THROUGHOUT

SOUTH WALES

AND

MONMOUTHSHIRE.

COMPREHENDING

A GENERAL SURVEY

OF THE

PICTURESQUE SCENERY, REMAINS OF ANTIQUITY, HISTORICAL EVENTS, PECULIAR MANNERS, AND COMMERCIAL SITUATIONS, OF THAT INTERESTING PORTION OF THE BRITISH EMPIRE.

BY J. T. BARBER, F.S.A.

ILLUSTRATED WITH A MAP AND TWENTY VIEWS, ENGRAVED FROM DRAWINGS BY THE AUTHOR.

LONDON:

PRINTED BY J. NICHOLS AND SON, RED LION PASSAGE, FLEET STREET; FOR T. CADELL AND W. DAVIES, STRAND.

1803.

Open at title page with Tintern opposite. Barber locked himself in the abbey and 'employed several hours without interruption in sketching the interesting features of the ruin', from which he later created his frontispiece. He exhibited regularly at the RA from 1794 to 1806, the year he turned to insurance and created the flourishing Provident Life Office, adding the County Fire Office in 1807. In 1812, ever more prosperous, he changed his surname to Barber Beaumont. He died at his desk, his artistic ambitions seemingly long forgotten.

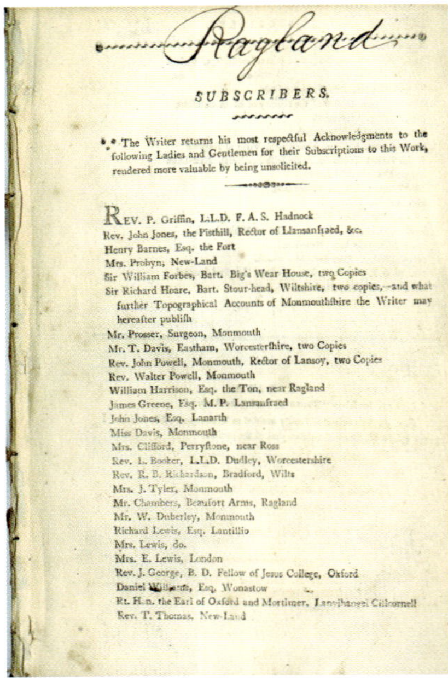

Ragland

SUBSCRIBERS.

*** The Writer returns his most respectful Acknowledgments to the following Ladies and Gentlemen for their Subscriptions to this Work, rendered more valuable by being unsolicited.

REV. P. Griffin, L.L.D. F. A. S. Hadnock
Rev. John Jones, the Pitthill, Rector of Llansanffraed, &c.
Henry Barnes, Esq. the Fort
Mrs. Probyn, New-Land
Sir William Forbes, Bart. Big's Wear House, two Copies
Sir Richard Hoare, Bart. Stour-head, Wiltshire, two copies,—and what further Topographical Accounts of Monmouthshire the Writer may hereafter publish
Mr. Prosser, Surgeon, Monmouth
Mr. T. Davis, Eastham, Worcestershire, two Copies
Rev. John Powell, Monmouth, Rector of Lansoy, two Copies
Rev. Walter Powell, Monmouth
William Harrison, Esq. the Ton, near Ragland
James Greene, Esq. M. P. Lansanfraed
John Jones, Esq. Lanarth
Miss Davis, Monmouth
Mrs. Clifford, Perryftone, near Ross
Rev. L. Booker, L.L.D. Dudley, Worcestershire
Rev. E. B. Richardson, Bradford, Wilts
Mrs. J. Tyler, Monmouth
Mr. Chambers, Beaufort Arms, Ragland
Mr. W. Duberley, Monmouth
Richard Lewis, Esq. Lantillio
Mrs. Lewis, do.
Mrs. E. Lewis, London
Rev. J. George, B. D. Fellow of Jesus College, Oxford
Daniel Williams, Esq. Wonastow
Rt. Hon. the Earl of Oxford and Mortimer, Lanvihangel Cilcornell
Rev. T. Thomas, New-Land

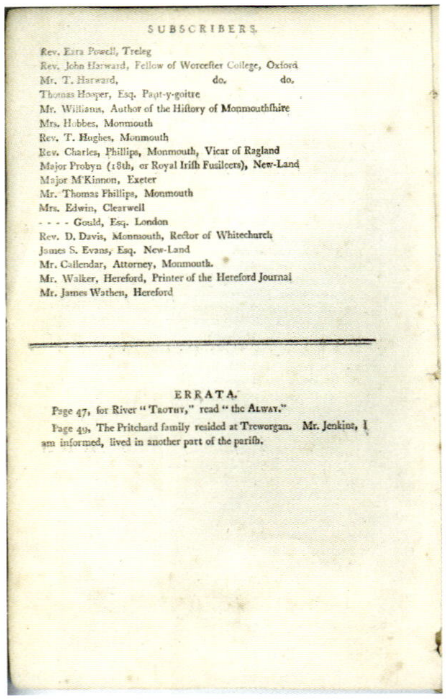

SUBSCRIBERS.

Rev. Ezra Powell, Treleg
Rev. John Harward, Fellow of Worcester College, Oxford
Mr. T. Harward, do. do.
Thomas Hooper, Esq. Pant-y-goitre
Mr. Williams, Author of the History of Monmouthshire
Mrs. Hobbes, Monmouth
Rev. T. Hughes, Monmouth
Rev. Charles Phillips, Monmouth, Vicar of Ragland
Major Probyn (18th, or Royal Irish Fusileers), New-Land
Major M'Kinnon, Exeter
Mr. Thomas Phillips, Monmouth
Mrs. Edwin, Clearwell
- - - - Gould, Esq. London
Rev. D. Davis, Monmouth, Rector of Whitechurch
James S. Evans, Esq. New-Land
Mr. Callendar, Attorney, Monmouth
Mr. Walker, Hereford, Printer of the Hereford Journal
Mr. James Wathen, Hereford

ERRATA.

Page 47, for River "Trothy," read "the Alway."
Page 49, The Pritchard family resided at Treworgan. Mr. Jenkins, I am informed, lived in another part of the parish.

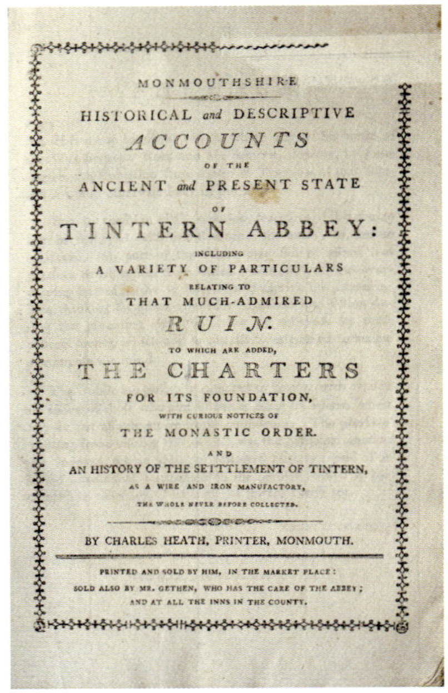

MONMOUTHSHIRE
HISTORICAL and DESCRIPTIVE
ACCOUNTS
OF THE
ANCIENT and PRESENT STATE
OF
TINTERN ABBEY:
INCLUDING
A VARIETY OF PARTICULARS
RELATING TO
THAT MUCH-ADMIRED
RUIN.
TO WHICH ARE ADDED,
THE CHARTERS
FOR ITS FOUNDATION,
WITH CURIOUS NOTICES OF
THE MONASTIC ORDER.
AND
AN HISTORY OF THE SETTLEMENT OF TINTERN,
AS A WIRE AND IRON MANUFACTORY,
THE WHOLE NEVER BEFORE COLLECTED.
BY CHARLES HEATH, PRINTER, MONMOUTH.
PRINTED AND SOLD BY HIM, IN THE MARKET PLACE:
SOLD ALSO BY MR. GETHEN, WHO HAS THE CARE OF THE ABBEY;
AND AT ALL THE INNS IN THE COUNTY.

97-99. CHARLES HEATH (1761-1830).

Heath set up a press in Monmouth in 1791, from which he issued a stream of guide books, frequently revised and reprinted, over the next nearly forty years. He was mayor of Monmouth. An ardent antiquarian, he was given in old age to loquacity.

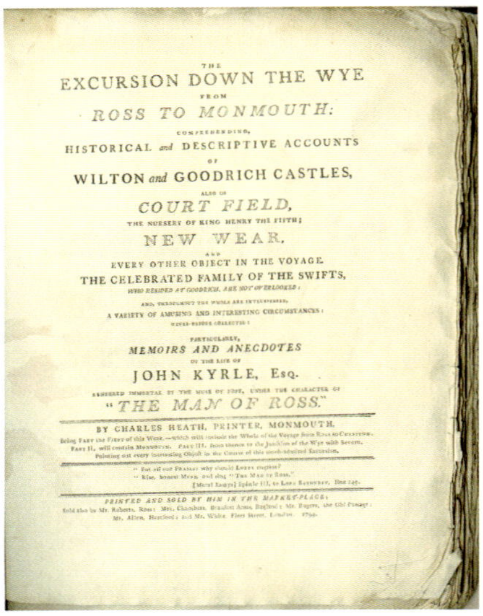

THE
EXCURSION DOWN THE WYE
FROM
ROSS TO MONMOUTH:
COMPREHENDING,
HISTORICAL and DESCRIPTIVE ACCOUNTS
OF
WILTON and GOODRICH CASTLES,
ALSO OF
COURT FIELD,
THE NURSERY OF KING HENRY THE FIFTH;
NEW WEAR,
AND
EVERY OTHER OBJECT IN THE VOYAGE.
THE CELEBRATED FAMILY OF THE SWIFTS,
A VARIETY OF AMUSING AND INTERESTING CIRCUMSTANCES:
PARTICULARLY,
MEMOIRS AND ANECDOTES
OF THE LIFE OF
JOHN KYRLE, Esq.
"THE MAN OF ROSS."
BY CHARLES HEATH, PRINTER, MONMOUTH.
PRINTED AND SOLD BY HIM IN THE MARKET-PLACE:

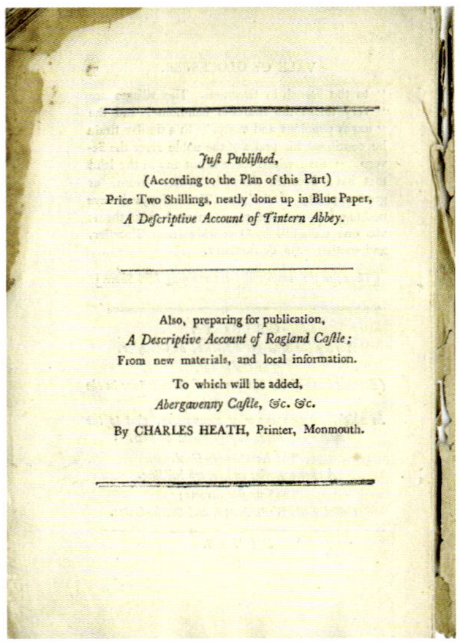

Just Published,
(According to the Plan of this Part)
Price Two Shillings, neatly done up in Blue Paper,
A Descriptive Account of Tintern Abbey.

Also, preparing for publication,
A Descriptive Account of Ragland Castle;
From new materials, and local information.
To which will be added,
Abergavenny Castle, &c. &c.
By CHARLES HEATH, Printer, Monmouth.

97 and **97A** (top left and centre). The subscribers' list from Heath's first guide-book: *Historical and Descriptive Accounts of the Ancient and Present State of Ragland Castle ...* The front page is missing from this copy, but the guide was published in either 1791 or 1792. **98** (above left). *The Excursion down the Wye ...* published in 1799. **98A** (above right). Advertisement from the back of *Monmouthshire/Descriptive Accounts of Persfield and Chepstow including Caerwent, and the Passages ... 1793.* **99** (top right). *Tintern Abbey.* The guide cost two shillings.

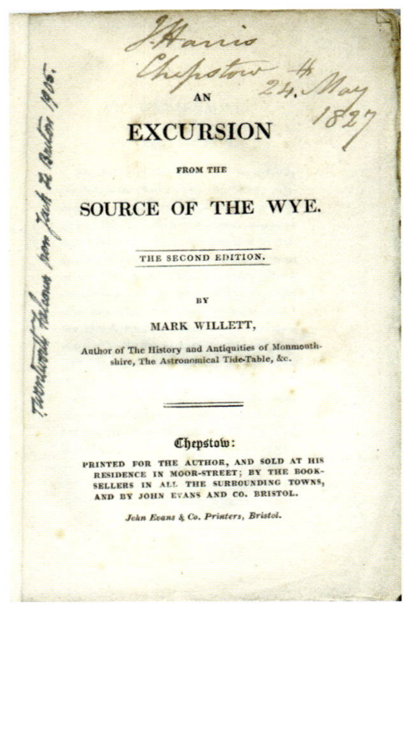

J Harris
Chepstow 24 May 1827

AN
EXCURSION
FROM THE
SOURCE OF THE WYE.
THE SECOND EDITION.
BY
MARK WILLETT,
Author of The History and Antiquities of Monmouthshire, The Astronomical Tide-Table, &c.
Chepstow:
PRINTED FOR THE AUTHOR, AND SOLD AT HIS RESIDENCE IN MOOR-STREET; BY THE BOOKSELLERS IN ALL THE SURROUNDING TOWNS, AND BY JOHN EVANS AND CO. BRISTOL.
John Evans & Co. Printers, Bristol.

100. MARK WILLETT, (fl. 1804-1835). *An Excursion from the Source of the Wye*, Chepstow, nd. (1810). Title page.

Willett's guide cost two shillings.

Additional Colour Plates

As we have not been able to include all the pictures we would have liked in the exhibition, we have added to the catalogue images of some of the most important of these, as well as of some works which are held in Chepstow Museum.

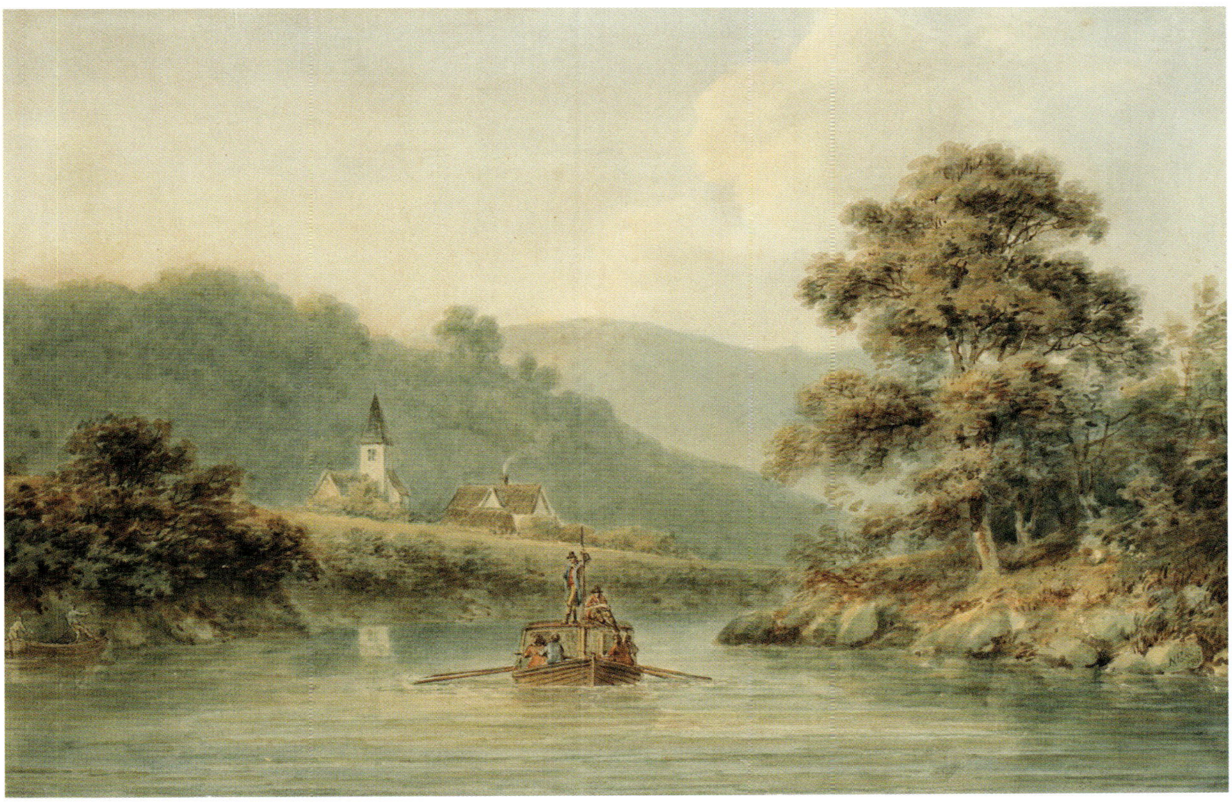

Plate I. Nicholas Pocock (1740-1821). Wye *Tour Boat passing Welsh Newton*
Norfolk Museums & Archaeology Service (Norwich Castle Museum & Art Gallery)

Nicholas Pocock came from a family of mariners in Bristol, and spent much of his early adult life as a sea captain. But his log books were always illustrated with pen and wash drawings, and at the age of 38 he set up as an artist. Bristol is close to Chepstow, and he did several paintings of the Wye valley, among them this picture of an unusually large tour-boat passing Welsh Newton church (not Dixton as has been thought). Tour boats came in many different sizes over the years, but awnings were usually of canvas, and not strong enough to stand or sit on, and there were usually two oarsmen not four. Nonetheless this is the best picture of a tour boat we have.

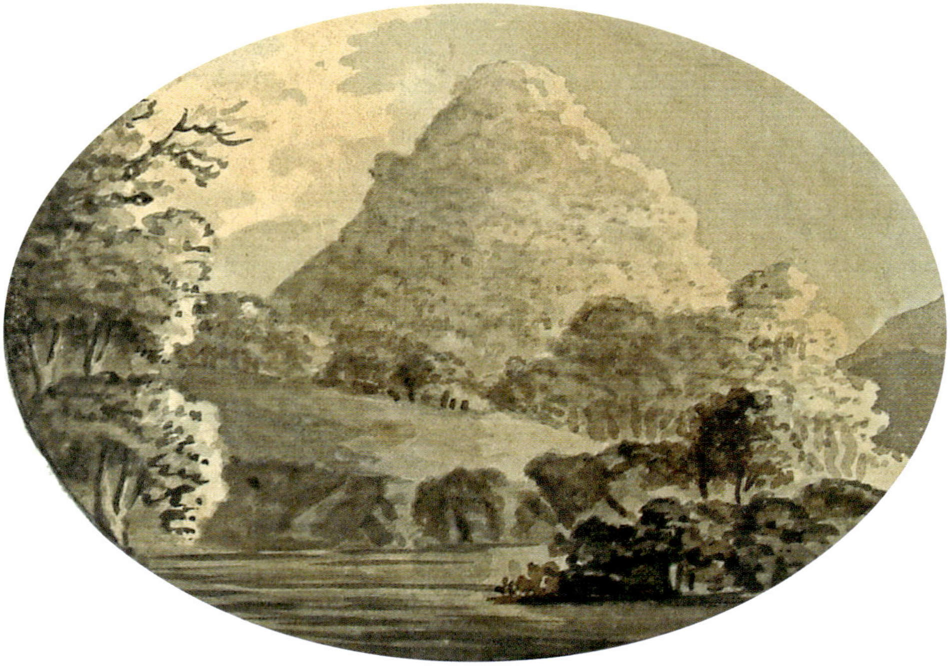

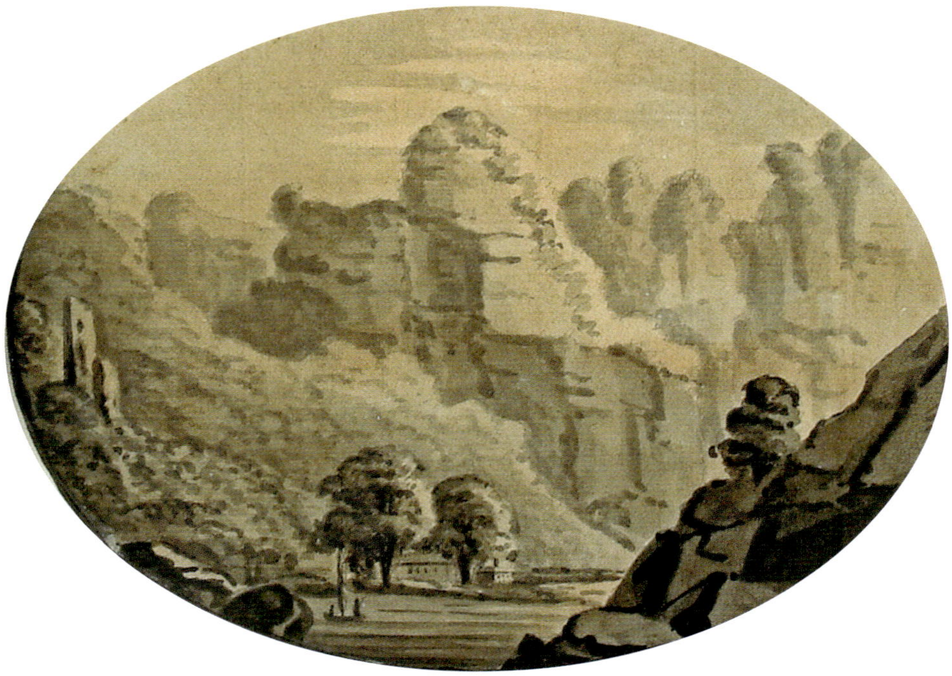

Plates II-III. Anne Cooper. *Rosemary Topping* and *Coldwell Rocks, 1786* (Chepstow Museum, purchased 2007 with grant aid from The Art Fund, MLA/V&A Purchase Grant Fund, and The Beecroft Bequest)

Rosemary Topping was an unusually shaped hill, remarked on by several tourists, but rarely painted. Anne Cooper, whose diary is quoted from several times in the main text, came from Dursley in Gloucestershire. After her death in 1804, Robert Bloomfield came down the Wye with her widower and other friends.

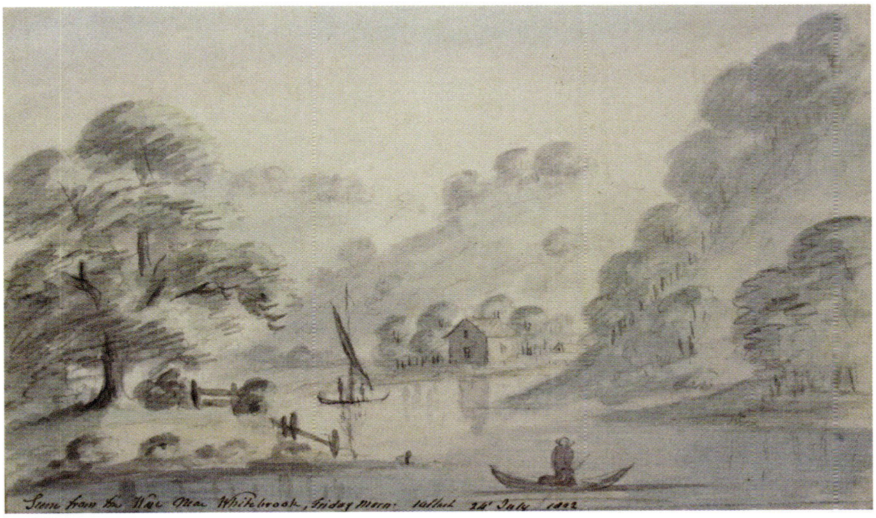

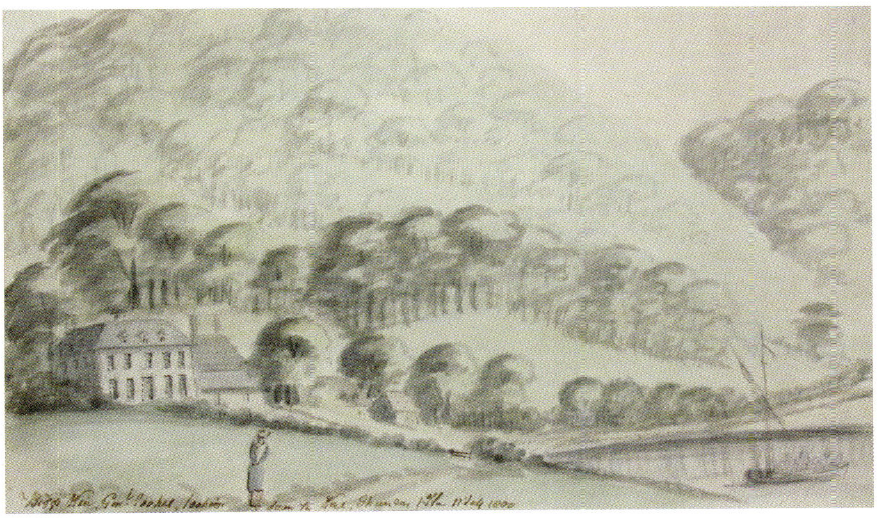

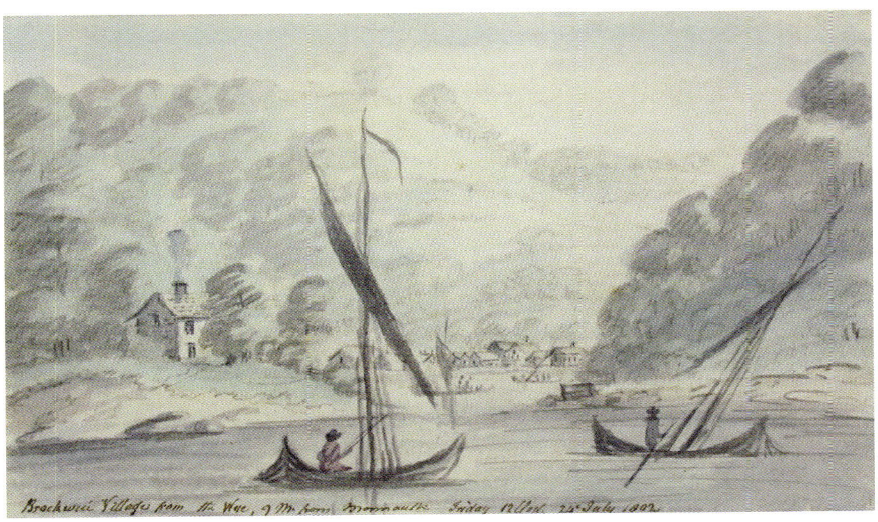

Plates IV-VI. James Wathen. *Scene from the Wye near Whitebrook, Friday morn. 10 clock 24th July 1802; Biggs Weir, Genl. Rookes, looking down the River, Thursday 1 Clock 23 July 1802;* and *'Brockweir Village from the Wye, 9 m from Monmouth Friday 12 Clock 24th July 1802. Whitebrook, Bigsweir* and *Brockweir* (Herefordshire Archive Service)

Wathen painted many ordinary river scenes neglected by better and better known artists. Here he drew the spot where the Whitebrook enters the river from the western side, demonstrating his speed as a draughtsman by going on down to Brockweir to draw that two hours later. There were paper mills on the Whitebrook, but not in this drawing. Further down, on Penyvan hill, high above the river on the Monmouthshire bank, opposite St Briavels and just before Bigsweir, there was a maypole round which Willett called 'daunsing fawns and faunesses' cavorted, though May 1st was rather too early for tourists to join in. Bigsweir House was the seat of the Rooke family, connections of the Admiral who captured Gibraltar in 1704, giving Britain command of the straits. Visiting here in 1775, Francis Grose thought it 'one of the most romantic Situations conceivable'. There was no bridge at Bigsweir till the elegant cast-iron one was erected in 1825-1827. Brockweir was a small but important port seven miles from the sea. See Plate VII.

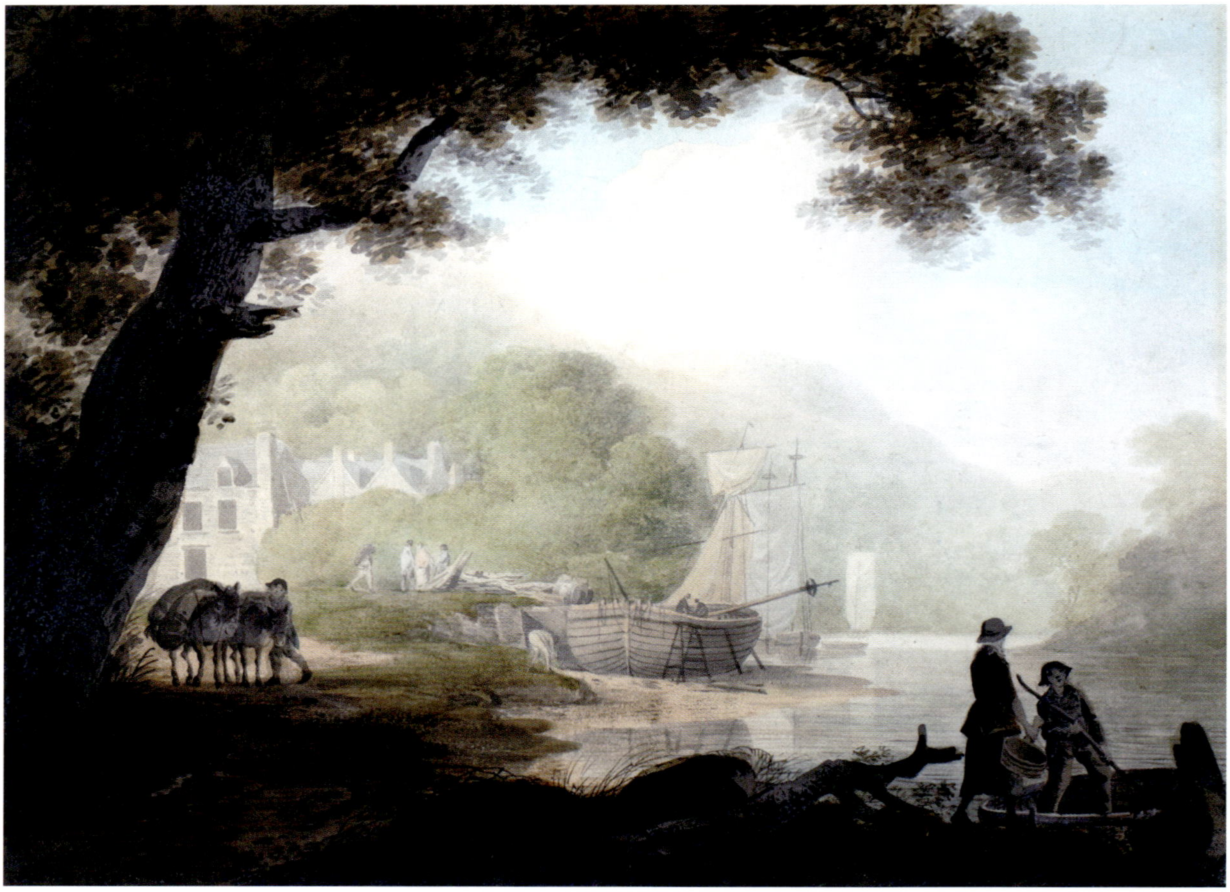

Plate VII. William Payne. *Brockwear Quay on the Wye,* 1792
(Chepstow Museum, purchased 2008 with grant aid from Heritage Lottery Fund 'Collecting Cultures' Scheme and The Beecroft Bequest)

Sea-going vessels were not able to go much further up the river than Brockweir, except on very high water, so they transferred their cargoes here to trows or barges. There was also a dock for shipbuilding and repairing. It was not a stopping point for tourists, perhaps because it was so close to Tintern, the great excitement of their second day. Payne shows a vessel at the quay with its mast lowered (a necessary feature of trows for passing under the bridges at Wilton, Monmouth and Chepstow). Vessels were square-rigged, as the Wye gorge was so deep the wind blew up and down, not across the river. There would be no proper towpath till after 1809, so at the time Payne was visiting horses could not be used to haul the barges, but they could be and were used as pack animals, as in the left of the picture. In the darker foreground detail at the right is what may be the ferry boat which continued to function until a bridge was built here in 1906. The woman with the basket must be going shopping. But Payne is never a strict topographer, and she and the ferryman may just be there to amuse the eye.

The only son of a London hop and coal merchant, Payne showed early talent for drawing and was exhibiting at the Society of Artists of Great Britain at the age of 16, when he was sent to train as a draughtsman at the Board of Ordnance Drawing Room in the Tower. He was employed by the Board mainly at Plymouth until 1790 when he returned to London and exhibiting. Here his very distinctive style, with its easily imitable manner of drawing trees, made him a popular drawing master. He was very prolific, exhibiting widely and often and inventing a pigment known as Payne's Grey. One of his pupils was John Glover.

See Catalogue no. 27.

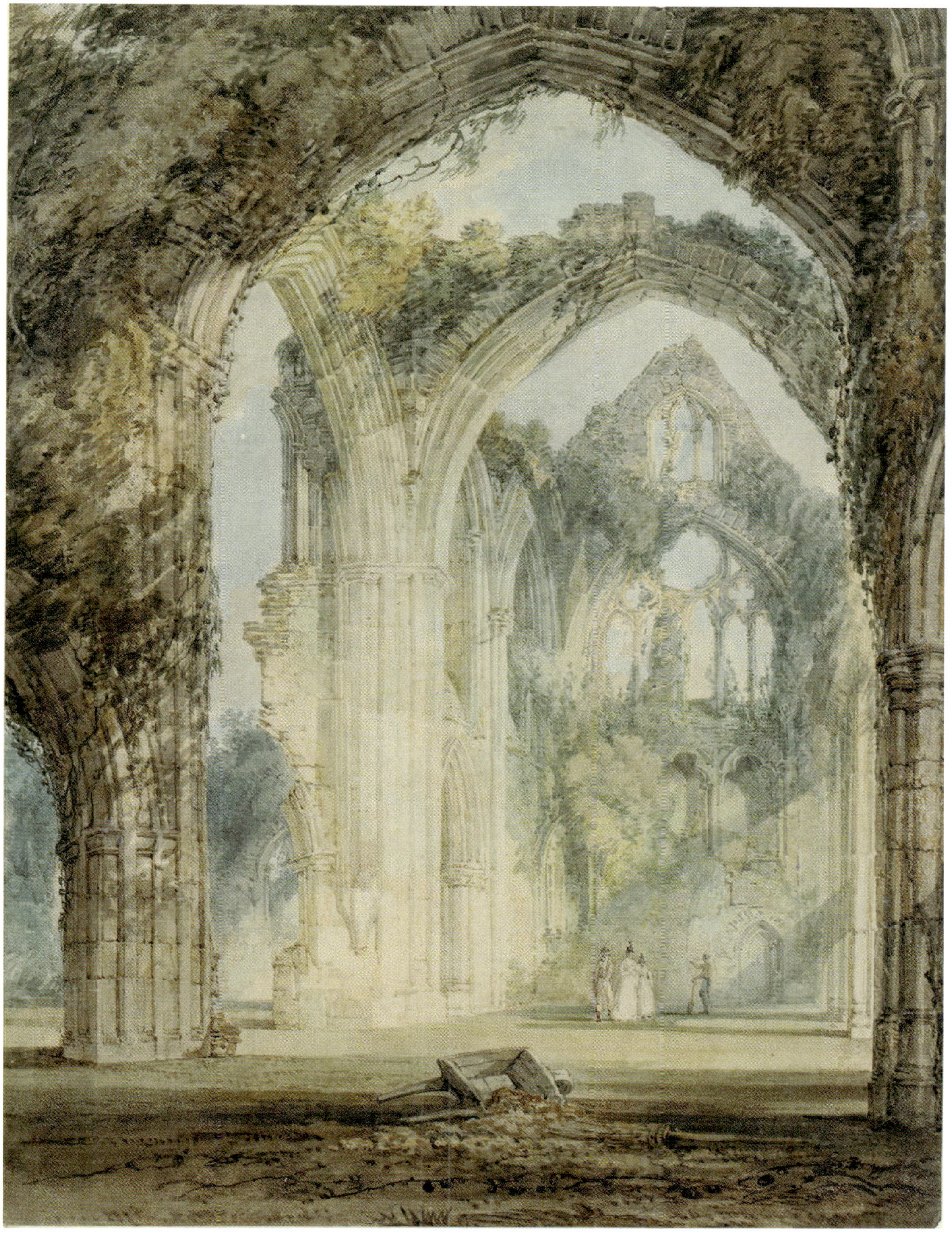

Plate VIII. J.M.W. Turner. *Interior of Tintern Abbey* (British Museum)

Compare Catalogue no. 50.

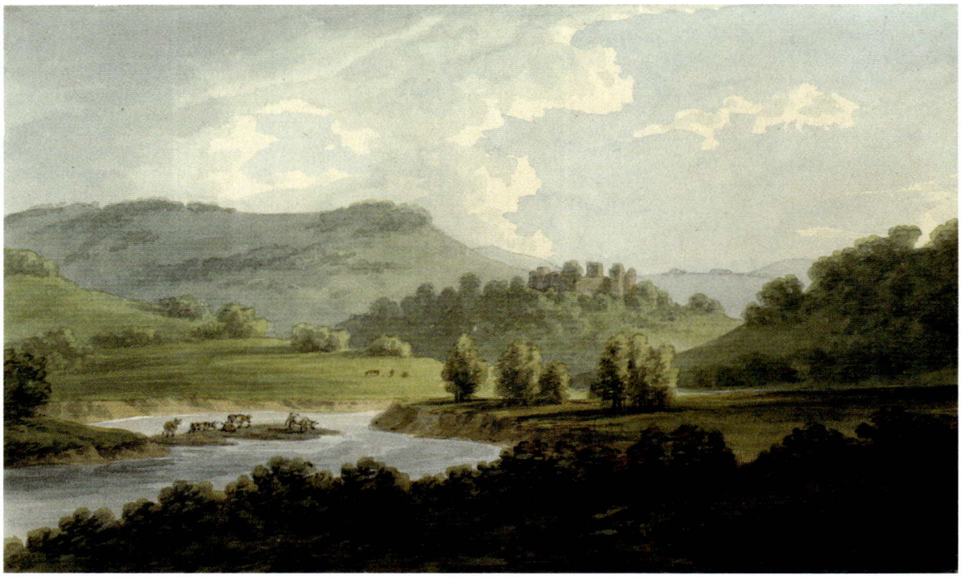

Plate IX. John 'Warwick' Smith. *Goodrich castle* (British Museum)

Compare Catalogue no. 3.

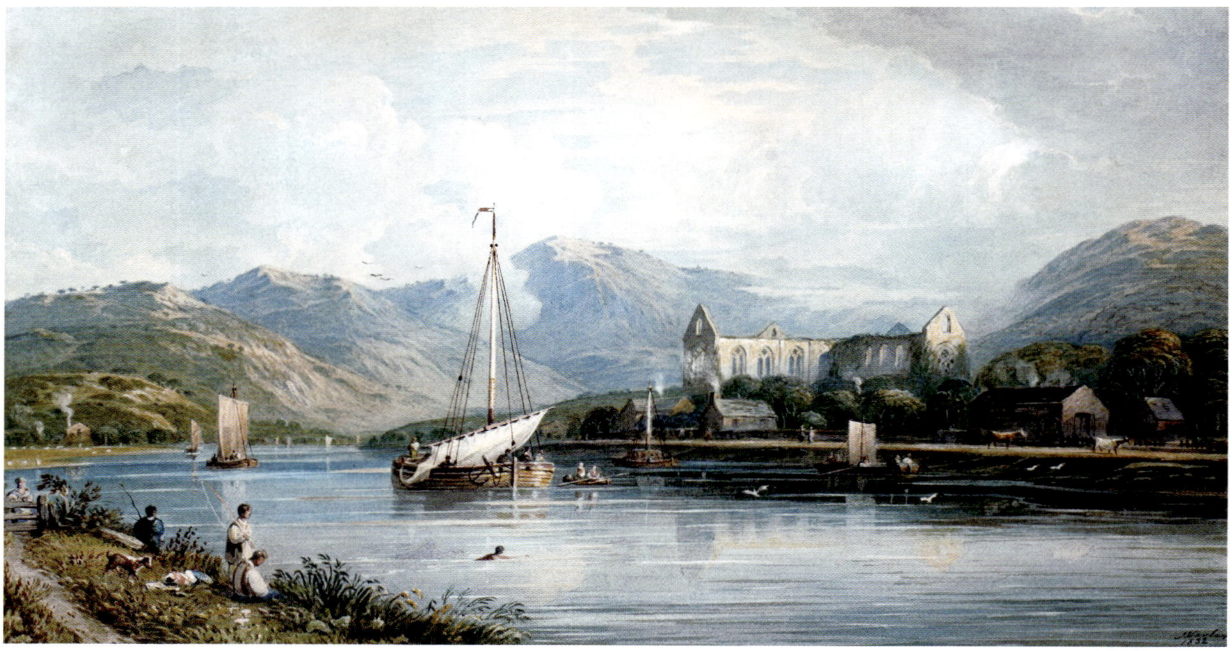

Plate X. John Varley. *Tintern abbey*, 1832
(Chepstow Museum, purchased 2008 with grant aid from Heritage Lottery Fund 'Collecting Cultures' Scheme, the Art Fund and the MLA/V&A Purchase Grant Fund)

This painting of Tintern Abbey, in which the surrounding hills are perhaps more reminiscent of north Wales, would appear from its scale to be an exhibition picture. It is dated 1832, and the following year Varley exhibited a Tintern Abbey (no. 94) and a Chepstow Castle (no. 58) at the Old Watercolour Society. Varley told his many pupils to 'Go to Nature for Everything', and is considered the father figure of plein-air painting in the early nineteenth century. But he increasingly disregarded his own instruction, saying 'Nature wants cooking' as his pictures became more and more idealised, after the old-fashioned manner of Claude. In reality the river was never this clear, and at this height would have been a roaring red torrent, extremely dangerous for bathing. See Catalogue no. 5.

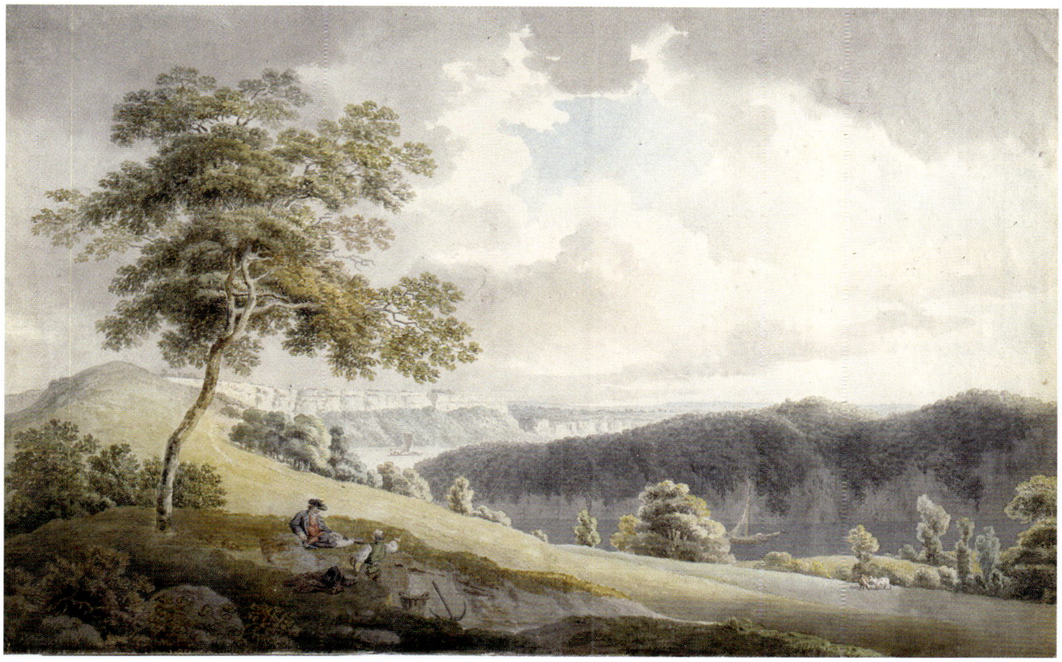

Plate XI. Michael 'Angelo' Rooker. *Chepstow from above Lancaut*
Norfolk Museums & Archaeology Service (Norwich Castle Museum & Art Gallery)

This is another of the Wye landscapes which seem to have interested Rooker as much as the architectural sights. As in this example, he went to places no other artist seems to have thought of. Compare Catalogue no. 21.

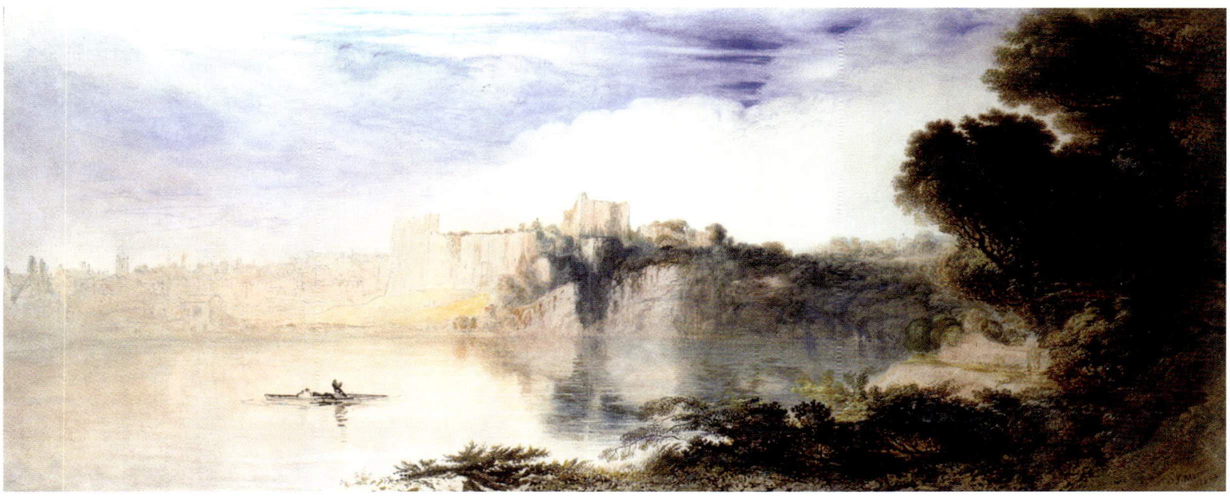

Plate XII. John Martin. *View on the river Wye, Looking towards Chepstow Castle*, 1844
(Chepstow Museum, purchased 2008 with grant aid from Heritage Lottery Fund 'Collecting Cultures' Scheme, the Art Fund and the MLA/V&A Purchase Grant Fund)

This is another of the four known pictures of the lower Wye valley exhibited by John Martin in 1845, 1847 and 1850. (Compare Catalogue no. 72). It takes a very wide view of the castle, and includes as well as a lone boat, the buildings of the Elmdale brickworks among the trees on the right.

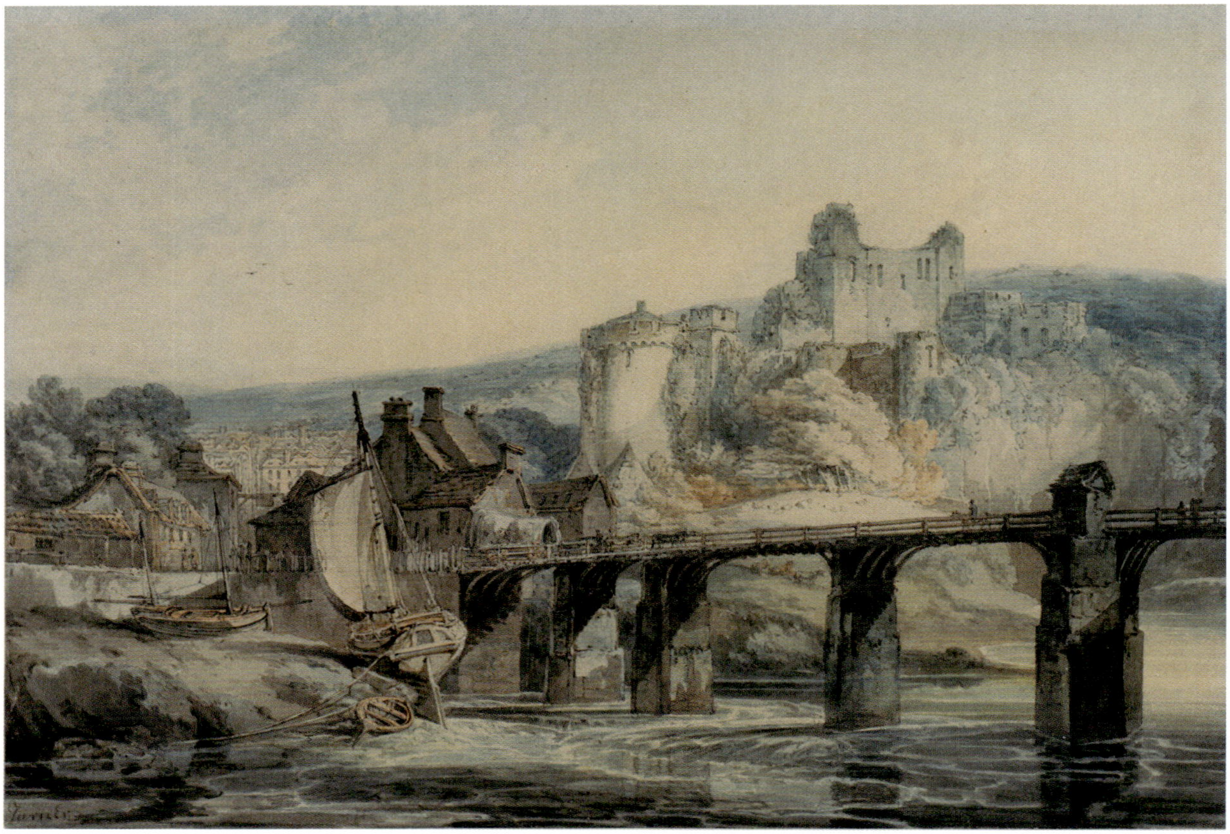

Plate XIII. J.M.W. Turner. *Chepstow castle*, *c*.1793-94
(The Samuel Courtauld Trust, The Courtauld Gallery, London)

Turner prepared his watercolours very carefully (see Catalogue no. 76), and he was as interested in different types of paper and how they responded to watercolour as he was in the colours themselves. The Courtauld picture of Chepstow Castle is, among other things, one of a set of experiments he made in the 1790s exploring the natural translucence of paper. He painted the verso in different washes and when the picture is viewed from the right the blue and brown and grey give extra depth to the image. (These washes were only discovered in 1985 when the old backing was removed.) Watercolours often served as models for the engravings by which so many artists lived, and this one was published in the *Copper-Plate Magazine* in 1794, which included Sandby, Girtin and Hearne among its contributors. This was the second of Turner's works to be made a print, and he produced fourteen more for the magazine.

Although he was still not twenty when he made this sketch, and the blue-grey treatment shows the influence of his teacher, Edward Dayes, he had already left the literalism of his very earliest work behind. The point of view, for instance, seems to be the impossible one of the middle of the river. (The small hut on the bridge marks the point at which responsibility for it was divided between Monmouthshire and Gloucestershire.) The usual dirtiness of the river here is disguised by the reflections of the sky in the swirling surface of the water, and the diagonal of the bridge carries the eye over to the town where another diagonal takes it up and on to the castle whose height Turner has exaggerated while not being too specific about its details. Topography is giving way to art.

Chronology

1743 Valentine Morris inherits Piercefield
1745 John Egerton rector of Ross-on-Wye
1748 Valentine Morris comes of age
1755 First Monmouthshire Turnpike Trust
1756 Bishop Pococke visits Piercefield
The Duke of Beaufort orders the clearing of Tintern Abbey
1757 Edmund Burke, *A Philosophical Enquiry into the Sublime and Beautiful.*
1763 First stage coach from London to Monmouth
1767 Arthur Young visits Piercefield
1769 John Wesley visits Piercefield
1770 Sir Thomas Whately, *Observations on Modern Gardening*
Thomas Gray takes the Wye Tour
William Gilpin takes the Wye Tour, probably with John 'Warwick' Smith as his amanuensis
Modern Universal British Traveller
1772 Francis Grose, *The Antiquities of England and Wales*, vol 1
Valentine Morris leaves Piercefield
1773 *The Antiquarian Repository*
Paul Sandby visits South Wales with Sir Joseph Banks and others
1774 Henry Penruddocke Wyndham tours Wales (*A Tour through Monmouthshire and Wales made in the Months of June and July 1774*, published 1775)
1775 Francis Grose visits the Wye
Paul Sandby, *XII Views in Aquatinta from Drawings Taken on the Spot in South Wales*
1776 Thomas Hearne and William Byrne, *Antiquities of Great Britain*, vol 1
1777 Francis Towne visits the Wye
1778 Richard Joseph Sulivan visits the Wye
Moses Griffith paints the Wye
1780-81 Paul Sandby, *Virtuosi's Museum*
England Displayed
1781 First visit of John Byng, later Lord Torrington
Second edition of Wyndham's *Tour*, illustrated by Samuel Hieronymus Grimm
1783 William Gilpin, *Observations on the River Wye and several parts of South Wales, &c relative chiefly to Picturesque Beauty made In the Summer of the Year 1770*

1784 John 'Warwick' Smith's first Wye watercolours
George Walpoole, *The New British Traveller*
1785 *Pocket Vade-Mecum Through Monmouthshire and a Part of South Wales*
Birth of Thomas Tudor
1786 Reverend Edward Davies, *Chepstow, A Poem in Six Cantos*
1787 John Byng's second visit to the Wye
1788 Stebbings Shaw *Tour of the Wye* published 1789
Michael 'Angelo' Rooker and William Day paint the Wye
1789 French Revolution
1791 Charles Heath sets up his printing business in Monmouth and begins to issue guides
William Payne first paints the Wye
1792 J.M.W. Turner pays first visit to the Wye
First prints of the Wye by Edward Dayes
1793 War with France : European travel restricted
Wordsworth's first Wye visit
1794 Coleridge visits the Wye
Sir George Beaumont and Thomas Hearne visit the Wye
Samuel Ireland visits the Wye: *Picturesque Views on the River Wye* published 1797
James Baker, *A Picturesque Guide through Wales and the Marches*
1796 Thomas Rowlandson tours Wales
David Williams, *History of Monmouthshire*
1797 Duke of Rutland takes the tour
Sir Richard Colt Hoare takes the tour
Richard Warner's first visit
John White Abbott's first Wye visit
1798 Henry Skrine, *Two Successive Tours throughout the whole of Wales*
William Wordsworth, *Lines composed a few miles above Tintern Abbey, on revisiting the banks of the Wye during a tour, July 13, 1798*
William Coxe and Sir Richard Colt Hoare make their first tour of Monmouthshire together, their second the following year.
1800 *Lyrical Ballads*
The Cambrian Directory
J.S. Cotman visits the Wye (and again in 1802)
1801 William Coxe, *An Historical Tour through Monmouthshire*
Joseph Powell visits the Wye
1802 Lord Nelson and Sir William and Lady Hamilton take the Wye Tour
G.W. Manby, *An Historic and Picturesque Guide from Clifton*
1803 J.T. Barber publishes *A Tour throughout South Wales and Monmouthshire*
Joseph Farington, Cornelius Varley, Joshua Cristall and William Havell visit the Wye
1806 Agostino Aglio paints Tintern Abbey
1807 Robert Bloomfield makes the tour; *The Banks of Wye* published 1811
J.P. Malcolm, E*xcursions in Kent, Gloucestershire, Herefordshire, Monmouthshire and Somersetshire*

1808 *The Cambrian Travellers Guide* first edition
William Turner of Oxford visits the Wye
1810 Louis Simond visits the Wye (*Journal of a Tour and Residence in Great Britain by a French Traveller*, 1815)
Mark Willett, *An Excursion from the Source of the Wye*
1814 David Cox moves to Hereford
1815 Battle of Waterloo; end of Napoleonic wars; travel to Europe resumes
1818 Thomas Dudley Fosbroke, *The Wye Tour or Gilpin on the Wye*
1820 Death of George III
1821 New road cut under Wyndcliff from St Arvans to Tintern
1822 First steam packets from Bristol to Chepstow
1823 Joshua Cristall moves to Goodrich
1827 John White Abbott's second visit
John Chessell Buckler paints Goodrich Castle
New road from Tintern to Monmouth along the Wye valley
Moss Cottage opened and paths made up Wyndcliff
1830 Death of George IV
1834 William Collins visits the Wye
1837 Death of William IV; Queen Victoria ascends the throne
1835 Samuel Palmer visits the Wye
1848 William Callow visits the Wye
1850 Chepstow to Swansea railway opened
1851 Gloucester to Chepstow East railway opened
1876 Wye Valley railway opened

Bibliography

<u>Manuscripts</u>

<u>British Library</u>
Add MS 15776. *A Journey from London to Holyhead* by Jeremiah Milles.
Add MS 17398. Francis Grose's *Tours*, 1775.

<u>Chepstow Museum</u>
Anne Cooper, *Journal of a Tour down the Wye*, 1786.

<u>Kidderminster Public Library</u>
The Journal of Edward Knight, 1759-61.

<u>National Library of Wales</u>
MS 1084A *Journal of a Tour in Wales and the Border ... in the summer of 1804*.
MS 1340C Thomas Martyn, *A Tour to South Wales, 1801*.
MS 1497B 1781 GC *A Tour in S Wales*.
MS 2862A 1776 *Journal of a Tour through Wales*.
MS 4419B *Sketch of a pedestrian tour begun September 3 1798* by GN DJJ RP.
MS 4489C *1796. Journal of a Tour from York into Wales*.
MS 5446B 1775 & 1811 Transcript of *Diaries of Tours in South Wales*, Gery-Cullum, Sir Thomas, & Gery, Rev Sir Thomas).
MS 6947C *A Tour through Monmouthshire and Glamorgan* by Rose Sotheby and Maria E. Sotheby.
MS 11492B 1787 *Journal of a Tour from London ... including Monmouthshire*.
MS 11790A 1799 Dr Robertson. *Journal of a Tour through Wales*.
MS 15172D 1780 *A Tour through Gloucestershire & Wales*, John Pridden – *Pridden's Topographical Collections – A Tour in Monmouthshire & S Wales in 1780* by Revd John Pridden MA FSA.
MS 15190C 1790 Shepherd W. & Nicholson F. *A Tour though Wales*.
MS 16133C 1797 *A Tour through Wales Cursory Remarks made in a Tour though different parts of England and Wales in the months of August & September 1797*.
MS 16988C.
MS 19758A 1791 Sophia Ward, *A Tour from London to S Wales & SW England*. ((23 August – 12 October 1791) by Sophia Ward née Watts [info on card inside journal] – daughter of William Watts (barrister) b. Nov 5 1766 d. Sep 17 1861 married John Ward May 22 1789 great-grandmother to F. Hugh Smith).
MS 22340B 1833 *Journals of a tour in N Wales and the area around Clifton, Ross Chepstow & Gloucester*. Thomas Letts.
Cwrtmawr MS 199B 1789 *Diary of a Journey into Wales*.

<u>Private collection</u>
Journal of Jane Blanchard, 1847.

Contemporary Printed Sources

'An Interesting Tour in the County of Monnmouthshire. By A Gentleman, 1808', quoted in Alan Roderick, Travels in Gwent, Newport, 1992, pp.147-8.
'A Tour of the River Wye' in *Welsh Tours* 1798.
James Baker, *A Picturesque Guide through Wales and the Marches*, second edition, Vol I, Worcester, 1795.
J.T. Barber, *A Tour throughout South Wales and Monmouthshire*, London, 1803.
Robert Bloomfield, *The Banks of Wye*, London, 1811; 'Journal of a Tour down the River Wye', in *The Remains of Robert Bloomfield*, London, 1824.
Luke Booker, *The Springs of Plynlimmon : A Poem* (with copious notes), Wolverhampton, 1834.
John Britton, *The Autobiography of John Britton*, London 1851.
Revd Edmund Butcher, *An Excursion from Sidmouth to Chester*, London, 1805.
Edmund Burke, *A Philosophical Enquiry into the Sublime and Beautiful*, London, 1757
William Callow, *An Autobiography*, edited by H.M. Cundall, London, 1908.
The Cambrian Directory, second edition, Salisbury, 1801.
Charles Frederick Cliffe, *The Book of South Wales, the Bristol Channel, Monmouthshire and the Wye*, third edition, London, 1854.
William Cobbett, *Rural Rides*, from 1821.
Edward Collins, *Tintern Abbey; or, The Beauties of Piercefield, a Poem in four books*, Chepstow, nd [1825].
Wilkie Collins, *Memoirs of the Life of William Collins*, 1848.
The Journeys of Sir Richard Colt Hoare, edited by M.W. Thompson, Gloucester, 1983.
William Combe and Thomas Rowlandson, 'The Tour of Doctor Syntax in Search of the Picturesque' in Ackerman's *Poetical Magazine*, 1809.
George Alexander Cooke, *Topographical and Statistical Description of the County of Monmouth*, London, nd [*c*.1810].
Joseph Cottle, *Reminiscences of S.T. Coleridge and R. Southey*, London, 1847.
William Coxe, *An Historical Tour through Monmouthshire*, London, 1801; of which *A Picture of Monmouthshire*, London, 1802, and *A Description of the Town and Neighbourhood of Chepstow*, Chepstow, 1806, are abridgements.
George Cumberland, *Tour in North Wales*, 1784, NLW.
Edward Davies, *Chepstow, a Poem in Six Cantos*, edited by Bryan Woodfield, Chepstow, 1992 (original, Bristol, 1786).
Daniel Defoe, *A Tour Through The Whole Island of Great Britain*, Vol II, Letter III, London, 1724.
P.J. de Loutherbourg, *The Romantic and Picturesque Scenery of England and Wales*, London, 1805.
Charles Dibdin, *Observations on a Tour Through Almost The Whole of England*, 1801.
The Revd J. Evans, and J. Britton, *The Beauties of England and Wales*, Vol XI, Monmouthshire, London, 1810.
The Diary of Joseph Farington, edited by Kenneth Garlick and Angus Macintyre, Vol VI, New Haven, 1979.
Thomas Dudley Fosbroke, *The Wye Tour or Gilpin on the Wye*, Ross, 1818, new enlarged edition, 1822, fourth edition, 1834, new edition, 1837; *Ariconensia*, Ross, 1821.
The Gentlemen's Magazine.
William Gilpin, *An Essay on Prints*, London, 1768;
Observations on the River Wye and several parts of South Wales, &c relative chiefly to Picturesque Beauty made In the Summer of the Year 1770; London, 1782 (though not actually issued till 1783);
Three Essays, London, 1792.
Jacob Green, *Notes of a Traveller during a tour through England, France, and Switzerland in 1828*, New York, 1831.
Charles Greville, *Memoirs*, vol I, London, 1885.
Francis Grose, *The Antiquities of England and Wales*, 1772-6, with two supplementary volumes 1777-1787.
Thomas Hearne, *Antiquities of Great Britain*, London, 1786-1807.
Charles Heath, *Raglan Castle, Chepstow and Piercefield, Tintern Abbey, Excursion down the Wye, Monmouth,* etc., 1791 *et seq*.
Samuel Ireland, *Picturesque Views on the River Wye*, London, 1797.

Leigh's *Guide to Wales & Monmouthshire*, London, 1831.
J.P. Malcolm, *Excursions in Kent, Gloucestershire, Herefordshire, Monmouthshire and Somersetshire*, London, 1807.
G.W. Manby, *An Historic and Picturesque Guide from Clifton*, Bristol, 1802.
William Marshall, *Planting and Rural Ornament being a second edition with large additions of Planting and Ornamental Gardening A Practical Treatise*, Vol I, London, 1796.
William Mason, *The English Garden,* four books, London, 1772-1781.
William Mavor, *The British Tourist; or traveller's companion*, six vols, London, 1798 ; and third edition 1809.
John Nichols, *Literary Anecdotes of the Eighteenth Century*, Vol VIII, London, 1812-16.
George Nicholson, *Cambrian Travellers Guide*, Stourhead, 1808, second edition 1813.
John Ogilby, *Britannia*, London, 1675.
[Armand-Louis-Bon Maudet comte de Penhouet], *Letters describing a Tour through part of South Wales*, London, 1797.
The Penrice Letters 1768-1795, edited by Joanna Martin, South Wales Record Society, Swansea & Cardiff, 1993.
The Penny Magazine, Supplement, July 31 to August 31, 1835.
The Pocket Vade Mecum, 1785.
The Travels through England of Dr. Richard Pococke, edited by James Joel Cartwright, Camden Society, New Series, Vols 42 and 44, 1888-1889.
[Prince Puckler-Muskau] *Tour of England, Ireland and France in the years 1828 and 1829 ... by a German Prince*, Vol II, London, 1832.
The Life of Marmaduke Rawdon of York, Camden Society no 85, London, 1863.
Leitch Ritchie, *The Wye and its Associations, A Picturesque Ramble*, London, 1841.
Thomas Roscoe, *Wanderings and Excursions in South Wales*, London, nd (after 1839).
[Duke of Rutland], *Journal of a Tour through North and South Wales*, London, 1805.
Paul Sandby, *XII Views in Aquatinta from Drawings Taken on the Spot in South Wales*, London 1775; *The Virtuosi's Museum* ... views ... drawn by P. Sandby, Esq, London, 1778-1781.
Stebbings Shaw, 'A Tour to the West of England in 1788', in J. Pinkerton, *Voyages*, Vol II, 1808.
Louis Simond, *Journal of a Tour and Residence in Great Britain during the years 1810 and 1811*, second edition, London, 1817; French edition, Paris, 1817. *An American in Regency England : the Journal of a tour in 1810-11*, edited by Christopher Hibbert, London, 1968.
Caroline Sinclair, *Hill and Valley, or Hours in England and Wales*, New York, 1838.
Henry Skrine, *Two Successive Tours throughout the whole of Wales*, London, 1798.
Dr. S.H. Spiker, *Travels through England, Wales, & Scotland, in the year 1816*, London, 1820.
Richard Joseph Sulivan, *A Tour through parts of England, Scotland, and Wales in 1778 in a series of letters*, second edition, London 1785.
John Taylor, *Tintern Abbey and its Founders*, London, 1869.
W.M. Thackeray, *Cockney Travels*, London, 1842.
W.H. Thomas, *Tinterne and its Vicinity*, London, 1839.
The Torrington Diaries, edited by C. Bruyn Andrews, London, 1934.
Louisa Anne Twamley, *An Autumn Ramble on the Wye*, Birmingham, nd, Preface 1838.
Horace Walpole's Correspondence, edited by W.S. Lewis, Vol 31, Oxford, 1961.
George Walpoole, *The New British Traveller*, London, 1784.
Richard Warner, *A Walk through Wales, in August 1797*, Bath and London, 1798; *A Second Walk through Wales, in August and September 1798,* Bath and London, 1799.
Daniel Carless Webb, *Observations and remarks during four excursions, made to various parts of Great Britain, in the years 1810 and 1811*, London, 1812.
Thomas Whately, *Observations on Modern Gardening*, London, 1770.
Henry Wigstead, *Remarks on a Tour to North and South Wales in the year 1797*, London, 1800.
Mark Willett, *An Excursion from the Source of the Wye*, Chepstow, nd [1810];
The Stranger in Monmouthshire and South Wales, Chepstow, nd [1825], 268-269.
David Williams, *The History of Monmouthshire*, illustrated by Rev John Gardnor, London, 1796.

Henry Penruddocke Wyndham, *A Tour through Monmouthshire and Wales made in the Months of June and July 1774*, Salisbury, 1775; and second edition, 1781.
Arthur Young, *A six weeks tour through the southern counties of England and Wales*, third edition, London, 1772.

Modern Printed Sources

The Agrarian History of England and Wales, general editor Joan Thirsk, Vol 6, Cambridge, 1989.
Richard C. Allen, 'The Administration of Poor Relief' in *Gwent County History*, Vol 3, Cardiff, 2009.
Michael Andrews, *The Search for the Picturesque*, Aldershot, 1989.
C.P. Barbier, *Samuel Rogers and William Gilpin*, London, 1959;
William Gilpin, London, 1983.
Ralph Bigland, 'Historical, Monumental and Genealogical Collections Relative to the County of Gloucester', *Transactions of the Bristol and Gloucestershire Archaeological Society*, Vol 3, 1992, edited by Brian Frith.
John Bonehill and Stephen Daniels (eds), *Paul Sandby; Picturing Britain*, London, 2009.
Rotha M. Clay, *Samuel Hieronymus Grimm*, London, 1941.
P.W. Clayden, *Early Life of Samuel Rogers*, London, 1887.
S.D. Coates, *The Water Powered Industries of the Lower Wye Valley*, Monmouth, 1992.
Samuel Taylor Coleridge, *The Collected Works*, general editor Kathleen Coburn; Associate editor Bart Winer; vol 16, *Poetical Works*, edited by J.C.C. Mays, Princeton 2001.
Patrick Conner, *Michael Angelo Rooker*, V&A London, 1984.
Paul Courtney, 'Towns, Markets and Commerce', in *Gwent County History*, Vol 3, 2009.
Edward Godfrey Cox, *A Reference Guide to the Literature of Travel*, Vol 3, Great Britain, Seattle, 1949.
Beth Darlington, *The Love Letters of William and Mary Wordsworth*, London, 1982.
J.A.H. Evans, 'Nathaniel Wells of Piercefield and St Kitts: From Slave to Sheriff', *The Monmouthshire Antiquary*, Vol XVIII, 2002, 91-106.
Grahame E. Farr, *Chepstow Ships*, Chepstow, 1954.
John H. Farrant, 'The Travels and Travails of Francis Grose, F.S.A' in *The Antiquarians' Journal*, Vol 75, 1995, 360-380.
William Feaver, *The Art of John Martin*, 1975.
Christopher Morris, (ed), *The Illustrated Journeys of Celia Fiennes, c.1682-c.1712*, London, 1982.
H.L.V. Fletcher, *Herefordshire*, London, 1948.
A.D. Fraser Jenkins, 'The Romantic Traveller in Wales', in *Amgueddfa*, 6, Winter 1970.
Edward Gill, *Nelson and the Hamiltons on Tour*, Gloucester, 1987 and 'Lord Nelson's hat and the country printer', *Country Quest*, Winter 1961, 20.
Geoffrey Grigson, *The Shell Country Alphabet*, London, 1966, reissued 2009.
William Hauptman, *John Webber, 1751-1793*, Kunstmuseum Berne and Whitworth Art Gallery, Manchester, 1996.
Louis Hawes, *Presences of Nature*, New Haven, 1982.
Nicholas Herbert, *Road Travel and Transport in Georgian Gloucestershire*, Ross-on-Wye, 2009.
Luke Herrmann, *British Landscape Painting of the Eighteenth century*, London, 1973. *Paul and Thomas Sandby*, London, 1986.
Pat Hughes and Heather Hurley, *The Story of Ross*, Logaston, 1999.
Peter Hughes 'Paul Sandby's Tour of Wales with Joseph Banks'in *Burlington Magazine*, CXVII, 1975.
David Japes, *William Payne, A Plymouth Experience*, Exeter, 1992.
Paul Joyner, *Samuel Hieronymus Grimm : Views in Wales*, NLW, Aberystwyth, 1983; *Thomas Tudor, An artist from Monmouth,* NLW, Aberystwyth, 1996.
Keith Kissack, *Monmouth The Making of a County Town*, Lavenham, 1978 ; *The River Wye*, London, 1978; 'Thomas Tudor, a Monmouth artist', in *Gwent Local History* 53, Autumn 1982.
Professor Knight, *Coleridge and Wordsworth in the West Country*, New York, 1914.
Lowell Libson, *Cornelius Varley, The Art of Observation*, 2005.
R. Lister, *Samuel Palmer, a biography*, London, 1974.
Peter Lord, *The Visual Culture of Wales : Imaging the Nation*, Cardiff, 2000.

Rosalind Lowe, *Sir Samuel Meyrick & Goodrich Court*, Logaston, 2003.
H.L. Mallalieu, *The Dictionary of British Watercolour Artists up to 1920*, second edition, Woodbridge, 1986; *The Norwich School*, London, 1974.
Molly McClain, *Beaufort, The Duke and his Duchess, 1657-1715*, London and New Haven, 2001.
Julian Mitchell, 'Joshua Gosselin in Monmouthshire', *The Monmouthshire Antiquary*, Vol XIX, 2003; 'Francis Grose in Monmouthshire 1775', *The Monmouthshire Antiquary*, Vol XXV-XXVI, 2010; 'A new look at Sir Richard Colt Hoare', *The Burlington Magazine*, forthcoming.
Donald Moore, *Moses Griffith, Artist and Illustrator in the service of Thomas Pennant*, NLW, Aberystwyth, 1979.
Bernard Morris, *George Orleans Delamotte, A South Wales Sketchbook*, Swansea, 2007.
David Morris, *Thomas Hearne and His Landscape*, London, 1989.
Ian Ousby, *The Englishman's England*, Cambridge, 1990.
Liz Pitman, *Pigsties and Paradise : Lady Diarists and the Tour of Wales 1795-1860*, Llanrwst, 2009.
J.R. Poynter, *Society and Pauperism*, London, 1969.
Anne Rainsbury, 'Chepstow Castle as a Picturesque Ruin', in *Chepstow Castle, Its History & Buildings*, edited by Rick Turner & Andy Johnson, Logaston, 2006
Brian Robins, 'An Introduction to the Journals of John Marsh', *The Huntington Library Quarterly* Vol 59 no 1 (1996), 125-144.
Alan Roderick, *Travels in Gwent*, Newport, 1992.
Mark L. Rood, *Wordsworth, The Chronology of the Early Years*, Cambridge, Massachussetts, 1967.
Ronald Russell, *Guide to British Topographical Prints*, Newton Abbot, 1979.
Anne Stott, *Hannah More The First Victorian*, Oxford, 2003.
Eric Shanes, *The Golden Age of Watercolours*, 2001.
Susan Sloman, 'Joshua Cristall's Figure Compositions' in *Watercolours and Drawings*, Vol 3, no 4, Autumn, 1988.
Victor Richard Stockinger, *The Rivers Wye and Lugg Navigation*, Hereford, 1996.
Basil Taylor, *Joshua Cristall*, (V&A catalogue, 1975).
W.D. Templeman, *The Life and Work of William Gilpin*, London, 1939.
John Tisdall, *Joshua Cristall 1768-1847 In Search of Arcadia*, Hereford, 1996
Christopher Titterington and Timothy Wilcox, *William Turner of Oxford*, Oxfordshire County Museum Services, 1984.
William Vaughan, Elizabeth E. Barker and Colin Harrison, *Samuel Palmer 1805-1881 Vision and Landscape*, BM, London, 2005.
Victoria County History, Gloucestershire, edited by N.M. Herbert, Vol V, Oxford, 1996.
Ivor Waters, 'Theatres' in *Chepstow Miscellany*, 1958;
The Unfortunate Valentine Morris, Chepstow, 1964;
Piercefield on the Banks of the Wye, Chepstow, 1975;
'High Tides', in *A Chepstow Notebook*, Chepstow, 1980;
Chepstow Printers and Newspapers, Chepstow, 1981;
Chepstow Packets, Chepstow, 1983;
Chepstow Town Gate, Chepstow, 1985;
The Port of Chepstow, Chepstow, 1989.
John Wesley in Wales, 1739-1790, edited by A.H. Williams, Cardiff, 1971.
David Whitehead and Ron Shoesmith, *James Wathen's Herefordshire 1770-1820*, Logaston, 1994.
Elisabeth Whittle, 'All These Inchanting Scenes' : Piercefield in the Wye Valley', *Garden History*, 24, 1, summer 1996.
Scott Wilcox, *Sun, Wind and Rain, The Art of David Cox*, New Haven, 2008.
Tim Wilcox, *The Triumph of Watercolour*, London, 2005.
Andrew Wilton, *Turner in the British Museum*, London, 1975; *The Life and Work of J.M.W. Turner*, 1979; *Turner in Wales*, Mostyn Art Gallery, Llandudno, 1984; and *The Great Age of British Watercolours, 1750-1880*, 1993.
Robert Woof and Stephen Hebron, *Towards Tintern Abbey,* Grasmere, 1998.
The Letters of William and Dorothy Wordsworth, edited by Alan G. Hill, second edition, Oxford, 1982.
The Love Letters of William and Dorothy Wordsworth, edited by Beth Darlington, London, 1982.

References

1. *Correspondence of Thomas Gray,* edited by Paget Toynbee and Leonard Whibley, Vol 3,Oxford, 1935, p.1142. In the 1808 edition, edited by William Mason, the 'wonders' are 'beauties'.
2. Charles Heath, *The Excursion down the Wye from Ross to Monmouth*, 1803, np, hereafter called *The Excursion.*
3. [Duke of Rutland], *Journey through North and South Wales*, London, 1805, p.34.
4. Charles Heath, *Monmouth*, 1804, np.
5. T.D. Fosbroke, *The Wye Tour, or Gilpin on the Wye*, Ross, 1818, Introduction, p.i.
6. John C. Eisel, 'Life on the River : Some Aspects of the Navigation of the Wye 1770-1855' in *A Herefordshire Miscellany*, (ed) David Whitehead and John Eisel, Hereford, 2000; and V.R. Stockinger, *The Rivers Wye and Lugg Navigation, A Documentary History 1551-1951*, Hereford, 1996, p.187.
7. Robert Bloomfield, *Journal of a Tour down the River Wye*, London, 1824, p.15.
8. P.W. Clayden, *Early Life of Samuel Rogers*, London, 1887, p.182.
9. The book is dated 1782 but was not actually published till early 1783. Hereafter called *Observations*.
10. Christopher Morris (ed), *The Illustrated Journeys of Celia Fiennes, c.1682-c.1712*, London, 1982.
11. Daniel Defoe, *A Tour Through The Whole Island of Great Britain*, London, 1724-26, Vol II, Letter III, p.76.
12. BL Add MSS 15,776.
13. Anthony and Pip Burton, *The Green Bag Travellers*, London, 1978, p.18.
14. Robert Weeks, 'Transport and Communications', in *GCH*, Vol 3, Cardiff, 2009, p.243.
15. The post chaise system was like modern car-hire. You rented a carriage and horses, or if you had your own carriage, just the horses, leaving them at your destination. In 1764 Joseph Tibbs, landlord of the Kings Arms, Mitcheldean, and brother of John Tibbs of the Beaufort Arms, Monmouth, advertised in the *Gloucester Journal* that he had a stall stable for 20 horses, and had 'lately bought four very good Chaise-Horses' and that 'A new neat Post-Chaise, or Charriot, may be had on the Shortest Notice'. Quoted in Nicholas Herbert, *Road Travel and Transport in Georgian Gloucestershire*, Ross on Wye, 2009, p.73.
16. Charles Heath, *Monmouth*, 1804, np.
17. Arthur Young, *A Six Weeks Tour through the southern counties of England and Wales*, London, 1768, p.120.
18. NLW MS 1084A.
19. See Julian Mitchell, 'Francis Grose in Monmouthshire' in *The Monmouthshire Antiquary*, Vol XXV-XXVI, 2009-10.
20. BL Add MS 17, 398, pp.60-61 and 69.
21. Molly McClain, *Beaufort, The Duke and his Duchess, 1657-1715*, London and New Haven, 2001, p.195.
22. Charles Heath, *Tintern*, 1801, np.
23. Essex Record Office, D/DFr F4. All quotations are taken from Liz Pitman, *Pigsties and Paradise : Lady Diarists and the Tour of Wales 1795-1860*, Llanrwst, 2009.
24. Catherine Sinclair, *Hill and Valley*, New York, 1938, p.237.
25. Ian Ousby, *The Englishman's England*, Cambridge, 1990, p.10.
26. BL 792.c.28 (1).
27. Henry Wigstead, *Remarks on a Tour to North and South Wales in the year 1797*, London, 1800, p.69.
28. *The Travels through England of Dr. Richard Pococke*, edited by James Joel Cartwright, Camden Society Part II, New Series, Vol 44, 1889, pp.114-115.
29. *Select Letters ... of William Shenstone* edited by Mr Hull, London, 1778, Vol 1, pp.265-270, and 286-292.
30. P. Bicknell, *Beauty, Horror and Immensity*, Cambridge, 1981, p.1.

31. This did not change till the 1790s, when as one of the consequences of the French Revolution and the wars that followed, the continental art market moved to London. See Philippa Simpson, 'Facing up to the Past : The Old Masters and the British School in Turner's London' in *Turner and the Masters*, edited by David Solkin, Tate Britain, London, 2009, pp.29-39.
32. Esther Moir, *The Discovery of Britain*, London, 1964, p.58.
33. Michael Kitson, *Claude Lorrain : Liber Veritatis*, London, 1978.
34. Prince Puckler-Muskau, as late as 1832, is still interested in this, and praises the Wye for the way the views are framed: 'for pictures require to be bounded or framed'. [Prince Puckler-Muskau] *Tour in England, Ireland and France in the years 1828 and 1829*, Vol II, London, 1832, p.199.
35. I am extremely grateful to Jane Garnett for this observation, derived from personal experiment at Lakes Nemi and Albano.
36. Thomas Whately, *Observations on Modern Gardening*, London, 1770, p.106.
37. 'Delightful' melancholy is a term used by G.W. Manby in *An Historic and Picturesque Guide from Clifton*, Bristol, 1802, p.i. Malcolm Andrews, *The Search for the Picturesque*, Aldershot, 1989, is the best recent account of the convolutions through which picturesque theory went.
38. Quoted in P. Bicknell, *op.cit.* p.33.
39. Rev. M. Tyson to Richard Gough, Dec 12th 1779, in John Nichols, *Literary Anecdotes*, 1812-16, VIII, pp.57-58. The reference is to Thomas Pennant's *A Tour in Wales 1773*, London, 1778.
40. *The Collected Works of Samuel Taylor Coleridge*, general editor Kathleen Coburn, associate editor, Bart Winer, Vol 16, Part I Poetical Works, Princeton, 2001, p.120.
41. He gives this date in the 1826 preface to the eighth edition of *The Excursion*.
42. David Solkin, 'Turner and the Masters : Gleaning to Excel' in *Turner and the Masters*, Tate Britain, London, 2009, p.17.
43. See John Bonehill and Stephen Daniels (eds), *Paul Sandby Picturing Britain*, London, 2009.
44. W.S. Lewis (ed), *Horace Walpole's Correspondence*, Vol 31, Oxford, 1961, p.320. Anne Stott, *Hannah More The First Victorian*, Oxford, 2003, pp.106-107.
45. George Cumberland in *An Attempt to Describe Hafod*, 1796, p.5. The poet was Thomas James Mathias.
46. Michael Clarke, *The Tempting Prospect, A Social history of English Watercolours*, London, 1981, p.14.
47. Martin Hardie, Water-colour Painting in Britain, 1966-68, Vol I, p.18.
48. For a detailed description of his working methods, from preparation of the paper to the finishing touches, see John Bonehill and Sarah Skinner, '"Grand Secrets" : Sandby's Materials and Techniques' in Bonehill and Daniels, *op.cit.*, p.65ff.
49. A.D. Fraser Jenkins, 'The Romantic Traveller in Wales', in *Amgueddfa*, 6, Cardiff, 1970, p.31.
50. David Solkin, *op.cit.*
51. NLW MS 1340C.
52. Heath, *Tintern*, 1801, np.
53. *The Agrarian History of England and Wales*, general editor Joan Thirsk, Vol 6, Cambridge, 1989, pp.97-100 and 700-760 ; J.R. Poynter, *Society and Pauperism*, London, 1969, p.45; Richard C. Allen 'The Administration of Poor Relief' in *GCH*, Vol 3, pp.285-311.
54. William Gilpin, *Observations ... particularly the Mountains, and Lakes of Cumberland and Westmoreland*, third edition, Vol II, p.44.
55. Stebbings Shaw, 'A Tour to the West of England in 1788', in J. Pinkerton, *Voyages*, Vol II, 1808, p.225.
56. Charles Dibdin, *Observations on a Tour Through Almost The Whole of England*, 1801, quoted in Alan Roderick, *Travels in Gwent*, 1992, p.17.
57. Mark Willett, *The Stranger in Monmouthshire and South Wales*, Chepstow, nd [1825], pp.268-269.
58. *John Wesley in Wales, 1739-1790*, edited by A.H. Williams, Cardiff, 1971, pp.82-3.
59. P.J. de Loutherbourg, *The Romantic and Picturesque Scenery of England and Wales*, London, 1805, np.
60. John Harris, *The Artist and the Country House* (revised edn 1985), 95-96 and plates 123-125, where Smith is said to have died in 1719. But Keith Kissack has pointed out that the Monmouth church in the Troy painting is clearly the one rebuilt in the 1730s, not the medieval one sketched by Thomas Dineley in 1684 (*The Account of the Official Progress of His Grace Henry First Duke of Beaufort through Wales in 1684*, [1888], p.ccv). Attribution, therefore, remains doubtful.

61. The plates were collected and published by Robert Sayer in 1774 in three volumes. Ronald Russell, *Guide to British Topographical Prints*, Newton Abbot, 1979, p.29.
62. Francis Grose, *The Antiquities of England And Wales*, London 1772-76 and *Supplement,* London, 1777-87. For a full account of Grose and the publication of his *Antiquities*, see John Farrant, 'The Travels and Travails of Francis Grose, F.S.A.' in *The Antiquarian's Journal*, Vol 75, 1995, pp.360-380. See also, Julian Mitchell, 'Francis Grose in Monmouthshire', *op.cit.*
63. There is a reference to the Chartist Riots of the autumn of that year.
64. For instance those of Sir John Cullum (1775) and Frances Bridger (1776). I owe these references to Liz Pitman.
65. Robert Bloomfield *The Banks of Wye*, London, 1811.
66. J.T. Barber, *A Tour throughout South Wales and Monmouthshire*, London, 1803, p.269.
67. William Hill, quoted by Charles Lane in *The Wye Tour*, Chapter I, (unpublished).
68. Boats did continue to be available, for instance to Mr and Mrs S.C. Hall in 1859, but they spent more than two days on their tour. See their *The Book of South Wales, The Wye and the Coast*, 1861, p.34 fn.
69. Richard Joseph Sulivan, *A Tour through parts of England, Scotland, and Wales in 1778 in a series of letters*, second edition, London, 1785, p.226ff.
70. [Penhouet], *Letters describing a Tour through part of South Wales*, London, 1797.
71. Early editions are undated but he gave this date in the preface to later editions.
72. *The Autobiography of John Britton*, London, 1851, pp.194-5.
73. NLW MS 16133C.
74. Many of these seem to have disappeared, but there is an important collection in the Hereford County Record Office/Herefordshire Archive Service.
75. Whitehead and Shoesmith, *op.cit.*. See also DNB article by David Whitehead.
76. See, Julian Mitchell, 'A New Look at Colt Hoare' in *The Burlington Magazine*, April-May 2010.
77. *A Picture of Monmouthshire*, London, 1802; and *A Description of the Town and Neighbourhood of Chepstow*, Chepstow, 1806.
78. The Revd J. Evans, and J. Britton, *The Beauties of England and Wales*, Vol XI, London, 1810.
79. Grahame E. Farr, *Chepstow Ships*, Chepstow, 1954, pp.14-15; Ivor Waters, 'Chepstow Packets' in *Chepstow Packets*, 1983, p.17ff.
80. Ivor Waters, *Chepstow Printers and Newspapers*, 1981, pp.19-31.
81. Fosbroke, 1834, pp.116-117.
82. Daniel Carless Webb, *Observations and remarks during four excursions, made to various parts of Great Britain, in the years 1810 and 1811*, London, 1812.
83. Louisa Anne Twamley, *An Autumn Ramble on the Wye*, Birmingham, nd, Preface 1838; Leitch Ritchie, *The Wye and its Associations, A Picturesque Ramble*, London, 1841.
84. Charles Frederick Cliffe, *The Book of South Wales, the Bristol Channel, Monmouthshire and the Wye*, third edition, London, 1854, p.355.
85. W.H. Thomas, *Tinterne and its Vicinity*, London, 1839.
86. In *A Collection of Welsh Tours*, third edition, London, 1798, p.49.
87. See *The Poems of Alexander Pope*, Vol III, (ed) F.W. Bateson, London, 1951, p.11, fn to line 250; and Howard Erskine-Hill, *The Social Milieu of Alexander Pope*, New Haven and London, 1975, p.33ff. The latter contains a detailed description of Kyrle's life and good works, and, arguing from descriptions in the poem, Erskine-Hill feels Pope may have seen Ross from a distance, but did not enter the town. There is no evidence either way.
88. Monthly Supplement of *The Penny Magazine* of Henry Brougham's Society for the Diffusion of Useful Knowledge, July 31 to Aug 31, 1835, p.339; repeated word for word in *A brief Account of the Picturesque Scenery of the Banks of the Wye between Ross and Chepstow*, Gloucester, 1836.
89. NLW MS 19758A.
90. Samuel Ireland, *Picturesque Views on the River Wye*, London, 1797; George Nicholson, *The Cambrian Travellers Guide*, Stourhead, 1808, second edition 1813; Leigh's *Guide to Wales & Monmouthshire*, London, 1831.
91. Luke Booker, *The Springs of Plynlimmon*, Wolverhampton, 1834, pp.15 and 76-77.

92. William (later Sir William) Herschel (1738-1822) was a Hanoverian musician and astronomer, who had just discovered the planet Uranus.
93. J.P. Malcolm, *Excursions in Kent, Gloucestershire, Herefordshire, Monmouthshire and Somersetshire*, London, 1807, p.79.
94. Edward Collins, *Tintern Abbey ; or, The Beauties of Piercefield, a Poem in four books*, Chepstow, nd [1825], p.7.
95. Charles Lane, *op.cit.*
96. *The Penrice Letters 1768-1795*, edited by Joanna Martin, p.107, Thomas Mansel Talbot to Michael Hicks Beach, 11th August 1791.
97. Henry Skrine, *Two Successive Tours throughout the whole of Wales*, London, 1798, p.18.
98. NLW MS 1340C.
99. *The Diary of Joseph Farington*, edited by Kenneth Garlick and Angus Macintyre, Vol VI, New Haven, 1979, pp.2127-2132.
100. Charles Lane, *op.cit.*
101. William Mavor, *The British Tourist ; or traveller's companion*, six vols, London, 1798; and third edition 1809, p.168.
102. Charles Lane, *op.cit.*
103. NLW MS 5446B.
104. Louis Simond, *Journal of a Tour and Residence in Great Britain during the years 1810 and 1811*, second edition, Vol I, London, 1817, pp.270-271. See also the introduction by Christopher Hibbert to *Louis Simond, An American in Regency England*, London, 1968.
105. Charles Lane, *op.cit.*
106. William Cobbett, *Rural Rides*, edited by G.D.H. and M. Cole, 1930, p.18ff.
107. Gloucestershire Archives, Mary Anne Hibbert: 'Journal of a tour on the Wye & from Bath to Cheshire July 1823', D1799 F322. All quotations are taken from Liz Pitman, Pigsties and Paradise : Lady Diarists and the Tour of Wales 1795-1860, Llanrwst, 2009.
108. Willett, *Strangers Guide*, fourth edition, Bristol, nd, p.85.
109. Charles Lane, *op.cit.*
110. Charles Greville, *Memoirs*, vol I, 1885, p.219.
111. Journal of Jane Blanchard, 1847. (Jonathan Badham collection).
112. Quoted in David Whitehead and Ron Shoesmith, *James Wathen's Herefordshire 1770-1820*, Logaston, 1994, no pagination.
113. Wigan Archive Services, WLCT: Sarah Haslam: Welsh travel journal 1802, MS969 EHC177. All quotations are taken from Liz Pitman, *Pigsties and Paradise : Lady Diarists and the Tour of Wales 1795-1860*, Llanrwst, 2009. Sarah Anne Haslam married John Wilmot, MP, in 1793, and together they came down the Wye in 1795 and again in 1802. Like other tour diarists, she later copied her journal, either for her own amusement or for family and friends, and there is a copy of the 1802 diary in Cardiff, NMW. The Wigan diary, though, is the original in which she wrote and sketched on the spot, and is, according to Liz Pitman both livelier and fuller.
114. In Norwich Museum, where the boat is wrongly described as passing Dixton. It is in fact passing Welsh Bicknor.
115. William Coxe, *An Historical Tour through Monmouthshire*, London, 1801. The Wye Tour is described in Chapters 35 and 36, pp.340-356.
116. Hampshire Record Office, Margaret Martineau, *Travel diary for 1824*, 83M93/21. All quotations are taken from Liz Pitman, *Pigsties and Paradise : Lady Diarists and the Tour of Wales 1795-1860*, Llanrwst, 2009.
117. Stockinger, 1996, *op.cit,* pp.28 and 195-263.
118. See Robert Woof and Stephen Hebron, *Towards Tintern Abbey*, Grasmere, 1998, p.140.
119. Grose, *Antiquities*, Vol II, 1774, Goodrich castle, Plate II; H.L.V. Fletcher, *Herefordshire*, London, 1948, pp.84 & 133.
120. Edward Collins, *op.cit.*, p.34.
121. A Jacob's ladder was of rope, with wooden steps.
122. For the full story of Goodrich Court, see Rosalind Lowe, *Sir Samuel Meyrick and Goodrich Court*, Logaston, 2003.

123. Professor Knight, *Coleridge and Wordsworth in the West Country*, New York, 1914, pp.168-169.
124. Anne Cooper, *Journal of a Tour down the Wye*, 1786 (Chepstow Museum).
125. The Society for the Recovery of Persons Apparently Drowned, founded by Drs William Hawes and Thomas Cogan in 1774, claimed considerable success and soon became the Royal Humane Society. For an example of local application of their method, see Julian Mitchell, 'Francis Grose in Monmouthshire in 1775', *op.cit.*
126. *Hereford Journal*, July 13th, 1808.
127. NLW MS 4419B, 1798.
128. Anon, *Welsh Tour*, 1798, p.403.
129. NLW MS 2862A, 1776.
130. Anon, *Welsh Tour*, 1798, p.55.
131. Information from John Evans.
132. Clayden, *op.cit*, p.182.
133. Keith Kissack, *Monmouth, the Making of a County Town*, London, 1975, p.243.
134. Of Hadnock, see above.
135. Edward Bright of Maldon (1721-50) was a postboy, then a candle manufacturer and grocer. He was 5'9' tall, 5'6' round the chest and 6'11' round the stomach. He weighed more than 584 pounds and his 'corpulency so overpowered his strength that life was a burthen and his death a deliverance'. I am most grateful to Andrew Helme for this information.
136. They saw *The West Indian*, by Richard Cumberland (1732-1811), which, directed by David Garrick, had been a tremendous success at Drury Lane in 1771; and Isaac Bickerstaff's almost plotless musical comedy *The Padlock*, an even greater hit for Garrick, being performed all over Europe. It owed its success to Charles Dibdin, the composer, who blacked up to played the part of a comic negro slave. *ODNB*. Dibdin visited Monmouth himself, see above, p.19.
137. This was under the mayoralty of Henry Parry. He was mayor in 1778, 1787 and 1798. Bradney, *op.cit.*, Part I, 2.
138. NLW MS 6497C. See Catalogue no. 90 for its undecided date and authorship.
139. Pitman, *op.cit.*, p.74.
140. Keith Kissack, *op.cit.*, pp.241-2.
141. James Parry, *The True Anti-Pamela*, London, 1741, p.273.
142. Quoted in Alan Roderick, *Travels in Gwent*, Newport, 1992, p.51.
143. NLW MS 4489C, 1796.
144. George Alexander Cooke, *Topographical and Statistical Description of the County of Monmouth*, London, nd, [*c.*1810], p.23.
145. Pitman, *op.cit.*, p.55.
146. Geoffrey Grigson, *The Shell Country Alphabet*, London, 2009, p.235.
147. Pitman, *op.cit.*, pp.22-23.
148. These had been copper works till about 1760. Paul Courtney, 'Towns, Markets and Commerce', in *GCH*, Vol 3, 2009, p.264.
149. NLW MS 4419B, 1798.
150. NLW MS 6497C. See Catalogue no. 90.
151. Willett, *Survey*, p.188.
152. A local word for a young salmon on its return from the sea, usually called a grilse.
153. *The Love Letters of William and Mary Wordsworth*, (ed) Beth Darlington, London, 1982, pp.198 and 218; *Letters of William and Dorothy Wordsworth*, Vol 6, second edition, (ed) Alan G. Hill, Oxford, 1982, pp.280 and 548.
154. NLW MS 1084A, 1804.
155. NLW MS 11492B 1787, 40.
156. *The Life of Marmaduke Rawdon of York*, Camden Society no 85, London, 1863, p.181.
157. S.D. Coates, *The Water Powered Industries of the Lower Wye Valley*, Monmouth, 1992, p.10.
158. W.D. Templeman, *The Life and Work of William Gilpin*, London, 1939, pp.147 and 188.
159. *The Journeys of Sir Richard Colt Hoare*, *op.cit.*, pp.83 & 101.

160. NLW MS 1084A.
161. Grose, *Antiquities*, Vol II, Tintern Abbey, Plate II.
162. Jacob Green, *Notes of a Traveller during a tour through England, France, and Switzerland in 1828*, New York, 1831, Vol II, pp.118-120.
163. *The Gentlemen's Magazine*, 1802, pp.300-303; John Taylor, *Tintern Abbey and its Founders*, London, 1869, p.66ff.
164. NLW MS 1084A.
165. *An Interesting Tour in the County of Monnmouthshire. By A Gentleman, 1808*, quoted in Roderick, *op.cit.*, pp.147-148.
166. Brian Robins, 'An Introduction to the Journals of John Marsh', *The Huntington Library Quarterly* Vol 59 no. 1 (1996), pp.125-144.
167. William Makepeace Thackeray, *Cockney Travels (1842)*, in Alan Roderick, *op.cit.*
168. Pitman, *op.cit.*, pp.91-92.
169. Fosbroke, 1834, p.90.
170. Fosbroke, 1818, p.102.
171. Kidderminster Public Library, *The Journal of Edward Knight, 1759-61*.
172. NLW MS 16988C, 324.
173. Peter D.G. Thomas 'Politics and Power, 1702-90', in *GCH*, Vol 3, 2009, pp.137-141.
174. George Cumberland, *Tour in North Wales*, 1784, in NLW, quoted by Elisabeth Whittle in '"All These Inchanting Scenes" : Piercefield in the Wye Valley', *Garden History*, 24, summer 1996, p.1.
175. NLW MS 4489C, 1796.
176. Ivor Waters, *The Unfortunate Valentine Morris*, 1964, and *Piercefield on the Banks of the Wye*, 1975; and J.A.H. Evans, 'Nathaniel Wells of Piercefield and St Kitts : From Slave to Sheriff', in *The Monmouthshire Antiquary*, Vol XVIII (2002), pp.91-106.
177. NLW MS 1497B, *A Tour in Wales 1781* by CG.
178. Dr. S.H. Spiker, *Travels through England, Wales, & Scotland, in the year 1816*, London, 1820, Vol II, pp.82-84.
179. See also Plate XXXII in *The Virtuosi's Museum*, 1778.
180. Ivor Waters, 'High Tides', in *A Chepstow Notebook*, 1980, 194ff.
181. 'Twenty-one miles of cannon would equate to around 4928 tons of iron if they were cast directly from a blast furnace. If an allowance were made for scrap and wastage then it would have been around 5200 tons. If the pipes were of a better quality and cast from iron that had been refined then it would have taken around 7250 tons to make them. And these figures could be on the low side. The lower figure would have taken the total annual output of between 5 and 7 charcoal fuelled blast furnaces while the higher figure would have taken between 7 and 9 and occupied several forges for a year. In other words Torrington could not have seen 21 miles of pipes except in his pipedreams.' Personal communication from John Evans, to whom my special thanks.
182. Heath, *The Excursion*, 1815, p.117.
183. Pitman, *op.cit.,* p.32.
184. NLW MS 2258C.
185. NLW MS 4489C.
186. The Rev. Edmund Butcher, *An Excursion from Sidmouth to Chester*, London, 1805, p.101.
187. Nicholas Herbert, *op.cit*., p.57
188. Ivor Waters, *Chepstow Packets*, pp.17ff.
189. Her mother, grandmother and great-grandmother all lived to be over 100, and she herself died at 90. Anne Rainsbury, 'Chepstow Castle as a Picturesque Ruin', in *Chepstow Castle, Its history & Buildings*, edited by Rick Turner & Andy Johnson, Logaston, 2006, p.246.

Index

(Numbers in italics relate to the page numbers for illustrations in the text, in bold relate to the Catalogue entries and Additional Colour Plates)